BUDDHA'S WARRIORS

BUDDHA'S WARRIORS

The Story of the CIA-Backed Tibetan

Freedom Fighters, the Chinese Invasion, and

the Ultimate Fall of Tibet

MIKEL DUNHAM

Jeremy P. Tarcher/Penguin

a member of Penguin Group (USA) Inc.

New York

JEREMY P. TARCHER/PENGUIN
Published by the Penguin Group
www.penguin.com

Penguin Group (USA) Inc., 375 Hudson Street, New York, New York, 10014, USA •
Penguin Group (Canada), 10 Alcorn Avenue, Toronto, Ontario, Canada M4V 3B2 (a division of Pearson
Penguin Canada Inc.) • Penguin Books Ltd, 80 Strand, London WC2R 0RL, England •
Penguin Ireland, 25 St Stephen's Green, Dublin 2, Ireland (a division of Penguin
Books Ltd) • Penguin Group (Australia), 250 Camberwell Road, Camberwell, Victoria 3124,
Australia (a division of Pearson Australia Group Pty Ltd) • Penguin Books India Pvt Ltd,
11 Community Centre, Panchsheel Park, New Delhi–110 017, India • Penguin Group (NZ),
Cnr Airborne and Rosedale Roads, Albany, Auckland 1310, New Zealand (a division of
Pearson New Zealand Ltd) • Penguin Books (South Africa) (Pty) Ltd, 24 Sturdee Avenue,
Rosebank, Johannesburg 2196, South Africa

Penguin Books Ltd, Registered Offices: 80 Strand, London, WC2R 0RL, England

The publisher and the author have made every attempt to obtain permission from and to credit
the copyright owners and photographers. If any mistakes have been made, however, we
welcome any corrections or other information that readers can provide.

Library of Congress Cataloging-in-Publication Data

Dunham, Mikel, date.
Buddha's warriors : the story of the CIA-backed Tibetan freedom fighters,
the Chinese invasion, and the ultimate fall of Tibet / Mikel Dunham.
p. cm.
Includes bibliographical references and index.
ISBN 1-58542-348-3
1. Tibet (China)—History—1951– 2. Tibet (China)—Politics and government—1951–
I. Title: Story of the CIA-backed Tibetan freedom fighters, the Chinese
invasion, and the ultimate fall of Tibet. II. Title.
DS786.D823   2004   2004055379
951'.505—dc22

Printed in the United States of America
1   3   5   7   9   10   8   6   4   2

This book is printed on acid-free paper. ∞

Book design by Meighan Cavanaugh

Most Tarcher/Penguin books are available at special quantity discounts for bulk purchase for
sales promotions, premiums, fund-raising, and educational needs. Special books or book excerpts
also can be created to fit specific needs. For details, write Penguin Group (USA) Inc.
Special Markets, 375 Hudson Street, New York, NY 10014.

For Adrian, Zachary,
and Margaret

CHINA
(Sinkiang)

JHANG THANG

T I B

PRIOR TO CHINESE

GARTOK

NGARI

U-TS

MUSTANG →

Tsangpo River
(Brahmaputra)

SHIGATSE

SAKYA

POKHARA

NEPAL

LH

⊙ KHATHMANDU

SIKKIM YATUNG
Gangtok
Kalimpong
Darjeeling

INDIA

BH

CONTENTS

Foreword by His Holiness the Dalai Lama   *xi*

Author's Note   *xiii*

Preface: Levity and Lies   *1*

1. LEOPARD CUBS   *13*

2. RAHULA DRAWS HIS BOW   *45*

3. SHOTGUN WEDDING   *81*

4. TREACHEROUS WATERS   *117*

5. BLOODBATH AND THE BODHI TREE   *153*

6. GOMPO TASHI AND THE CIA   *191*

7. TIBETANS FROM THE SKY   213

8. POISON EATERS   249

9. NEW HOPES AND NEW DEVASTATIONS   307

10. LAST STAND   351

Epilogue: Where Is Tibet?   397

Acknowledgments   416

Bibliography   417

Index   424

THE DALAI LAMA

FOREWORD

The Chinese invasion and occupation of Tibet has been one of the great tragedies of this century. More than a million people have died as a result. An ancient culture with its buildings, literature, and artifacts has been attacked and largely destroyed, and the living holders of its traditions have been prevented from passing them on in their homeland.

International awareness of what took place during the past fifty years in the Land of Snows may generally have grown, but what may not be so well known or appreciated is the fact that there was an armed resistance. In Kham, Eastern Tibet, in particular, where people retained the warrior-like qualities of old, groups of men banded together to oppose the Chinese by force. These guerillas, riding on horseback and often equipped with outdated weapons, put up a good fight. They expressed their loyalty and love for Tibet with indomitable courage. And although they were ultimately unsuccessful in preventing the Chinese from overwhelming Tibet, they let the so-called People's Liberation Army know what the majority of Tibetans felt about their presence.

Although I believe that the Tibetan struggle can only be won by a long-term approach and peaceful means, I have always admired these freedom fighters for their unflinching courage and determination. And I am glad that Mikel Dunham has been able to tell these brave men's story in this book, much as they told it to him.

AUTHOR'S NOTE

With few exceptions, the primary sources for my book played an active role in the Tibetan resistance. Most of their interviews were taped in refugee camps in India and Nepal. I have identified my sources by their real names except when I was specifically asked not to, for political reasons. To distinguish primary sources in my narrative, I have quoted their stories in italics. Other firsthand accounts, folded into my narrative but previously published elsewhere, have been italicized for uniformity. The latter have been attributed in the standard manner.

Since the ancient Tibetan lunar calendar was still used at the time of the communist invasion, some of the witnesses' dates may be at variance with Western reckoning. Likewise, names of places and numbers of forces in conflict may be inconsistent with other histories. Nevertheless, I have left these eyewitnesses' accounts intact, except when their reckonings are significantly faulty or unnecessarily confusing to the contemporary reader.

MIKEL DUNHAM
May 20, 2004
Santa Monica,
California

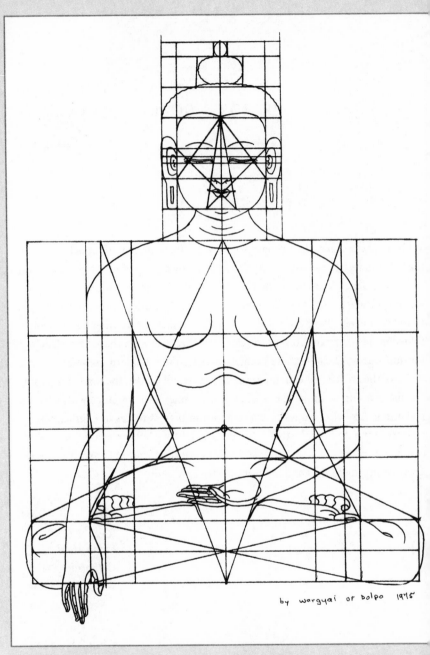

Buffer zone: Artist's grid used to create the proportional boundaries of the Buddha
(Pema Wangyal of Dolpo)

PREFACE

LEVITY AND LIES

Prior to World War II, few countries aroused less interest at the U.S. State Department than Tibet. Tibet was that vast zone of neutrality lodged between the three behemoths of Asia—India, China, and the Soviet Union— a mighty classic buffer zone. Topographically, the boundaries were all but impenetrable. The inhabitants were said to live in willful isolation, jealously keeping their borders sealed off from foreigners. While romantics may have envisioned a Shangri-la, Washington bureaucrats took a pragmatic view: Tibet was a convenient vacuum, a blank space on the map, void of notable geopolitical significance.

Pearl Harbor changed that view. Every inch of Asia was suddenly of the utmost importance. Japanese control of much of the East induced generals to undergo crash courses in Asian geography. Cartographers worked overtime to fill in hitherto generalized charts. Military strategists scrambled to devise all sorts of maneuverability options, which included a study on the practicality of transporting war supplies from India to China through a suddenly interesting Tibet.

Since America had no diplomatic relations with Tibet, whom did one approach to secure permission to travel through its uncharted routes? The Tibetan government was described as an archaic Buddhist theocracy headed by a "god-king" who was a mere six-year-old boy. Did that mean that the State Department would have to strike deals with a little child? Or was someone else really in charge? And, if so, what was the proper protocol? Who had reliable intelligence reports? Were there any?

Forgotten files were dusted off and reassessed.

Old studies pointed toward a political snag:

It appeared that China had a long-standing claim of suzerainty (dominant state controlling the foreign relations of a vassal state, but allowing it internal sovereignty) over Tibet. If that were true, then China controlled Tibet's international affairs while allowing it domestic sovereignty—fancy parlance for a puppet state. If Tibet were a puppet state, why not sidestep the "god-king" and his robed advisors and obtain permission directly from Beijing? Chiang Kai-shek, president of the Republic of China at the time, was something of a wild card. He was a dictator, but he was also Japan's archenemy and therefore an obviously useful ally for the United States. Not only did he oppose the Japanese but he also was battling the communist army of Mao Tse-tung. On both fronts he was "fighting the good fight." Washington contacted him toward the end of 1942.

Chiang Kai-shek's response was reassuring. He claimed he was completely in control of Tibetan affairs; not only would he help the United States fight the Japanese by securing U.S. troops through Tibet, he would gladly deploy Chinese agents *inside* Tibet to ensure safe passage for American personnel. Reassuring news—if Chiang Kai-shek's claims were true.

Conflicting reports on file suggested otherwise: Tibet regarded itself as an independent nation, and there was mounting evidence to support the Tibetan claim.

Britain had faced the same problem in the 1890s when it attempted to establish trade relations with Tibet by bypassing Tibet and negotiating directly with the Chinese. Britain and China signed an agreement in 1893, but when the Tibetan government caught wind of the secret proceedings, its utter rejection of the plan—and China's inability to militarily circumvent Tibet's rejection—convinced the Viceroy of India, Lord Curzon, that China's claim of suzerainty was, in his words, a "constitutional fiction" and "a political affectation."[1]

In fact, all Chinese officials had been unceremoniously booted out of Lhasa, Tibet's capital, years before. How did that jibe with Chiang Kai-shek's claim of suzerainty? To add to the debate, a series of communiqués were arriving in Washington from Lhasa, making it clear that the Tibetan government adamantly opposed Chinese agents infiltrating its southern boundaries. In fact, it rejected *any* kind of Chinese involvement. Americans were welcome, but only if they went through the proper Tibetan channels.

Weeks passed. President Franklin Roosevelt lost patience.

He called in Brigadier General "Wild Bill" Donovan, mastermind of the Office of Strategic Services (OSS, soon to become the CIA), to sort things out. Donovan organized a two-man envoy to go to Lhasa to meet with the *Kashag*, the Dalai Lama's four-to-six-member Cabinet and the apparent ruling body.

The Americans arrived in Lhasa in December 1942. It turned out to be an easy assignment. They found the *Kashag* cooperative and compliant. The Americans negotiated official sanction to transport war supplies through southernmost Tibet. In return, the *Kashag* was granted (so they believed) something long desired: diplomatic relations with a major foreign power. Did this not indicate, once and for all, that the United States had acknowledged Tibet's independence?

In fact, although assurances were made, the American delegation had no real power to make any promises on behalf of the State Department. Nevertheless, in March 1943, Donovan reported back to the President that the mission had been a success and that the *Kashag* would allow troops to travel through southern Tibet. Roosevelt's response was positively jolly:

---

[1]"Letter of Curzon to Lord Hamilton, Secretary of State for India," January 8, 1903, as quoted in Preman Addy, *Tibet on the Imperial Chessboard*, 91.

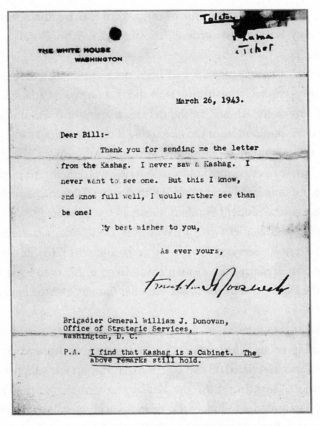

(Collection of Roger E. McCarthy)

Roosevelt's parody on the popular ditty "I never saw a purple cow, I never hope to see one"—the levity and the basic indifference therein—set a precedent that the President could not have foreseen. Sixty years later, even though there is ample documented evidence to prove otherwise, the ensuing string of U.S. presidents—all of whom have waved the flag of human rights—has continued to be impervious to the plight of the Tibetan people. Economic affiliations with China preclude the question of human rights to a large degree. If foreign nationals want to do business in China, they quickly learn that the question of Chinese occupation of Tibet is strictly off-limits.

Tibet is no longer a blank space on an intelligence map. It is universally identified as the Tibetan Autonomous Region of China. How did this transformation occur in the intervening years?

In 1949, Mao Tse-tung, having successfully ousted Chiang Kai-shek's Nationalist regime from Mainland China, turned his attention to Tibet. Ignoring Tibet's claim of independence, the People's Liberation Army invaded from the east "on behalf of the people of Tibet." The Maoists didn't address the fact that Tibet had large reserves of gold, copper, lead, and zinc, millions of acres of virgin timber, and other natural resources coveted by the Chinese. Oil, borax, and uranium would later be discovered as additional natural resources and robustly pursued by the communist occupation.

By 1956, the PLA had, at best, wobbly control over the eastern province of Kham and, to a lesser extent, Amdo and Golok. Only the Central Government in Lhasa, and its bothersome Dalai Lama, remained untouched by Chinese "reform." Chinese land reforms in Eastern Tibet included the catastrophic replanting of barley crops (Tibet's most important agricultural staple) with the Chinese-favored wheat. The crops failed, and approximately 500,000 Tibetans (a conservative estimate) starved to death as a result. It was the first time in recorded history that Tibet had experienced famine. Mao's propaganda machine called the replanting a part of "The Great Leap Forward."

Despite Mao's intitial promise to respect Buddhism, the normal activities of the monasteries of Eastern Tibet were severely curtailed. Later, they would be shut down, or blown to bits. Head lamas, monks, and nuns were publicly humiliated through forced fornication, torture, imprisonment, and execution. The Khampas could take no more. A guerilla war ensued. It didn't begin as an organized rebellion. The Amdoans, the Goloks, and the Khampas simply rose in violent protest—almost simultaneously and without knowledge of each other's activities—against the brutality of the Chinese occupation.

By 1959, the Chinese, in an effort to check the insurrection, inundated Tibet with hundreds of thousands of troops. All the window dressing about Tibetan autonomy was unceremoniously dropped.

The Dalai Lama fled for his life, and scores of thousands of devotees followed him into India. Those left behind faced a bloodbath. As early as 1960, the International Commission of Jurists concluded that there was a *prima facie* case of genocide against the Chinese in Tibet. The Cultural Revolution of the 1960s only exacerbated the ongoing tragedy. Ninety-five percent of the monasteries and temples in Tibet were razed to the ground. All told, *1.2 million deaths* were directly attributed to the Chinese takeover.[2]

In the current era, only China's totalitarian occupation keeps Tibet subdued. Today, mere possession of a photograph of the Dalai Lama is a serious crime there. Chinese preservation of Tibetan culture is sanctioned solely as a Disneyesque facade for the economic perks of tourism. All other policies are dedicated to the eradication of Tibetan identity. The most serious threat facing Tibet's future is Beijing's program of "population transfer." There are now over 7.5 million Chinese in Tibet, compared with a Tibetan population of 6 million. Tibetans are a minority in their own country who, in order to get decent jobs or even qualify for secondary education, must be fluent in Chinese at the expense of learning their native tongue. The draconian days of the Cultural Revolution may be discounted by contemporary Chinese politicos as "ancient history," but the notion of Tibet as an "autonomous region" is, at best, theoretical and, at worst, cynically absurd. There is no autonomy—not even close. There is no freedom. Subtle, insidious forms of oppression and assimilation are still very much at work.

And none are more insidious than Washington's willingness to parrot China's rewriting of Tibetan history.

The Chinese version goes something like this:

Historically, Tibet has been an indivisible part of China. As far back as the seventeenth century, the emperor of China was "uncle" to the Dalai Lama. Tibet paid tributes to the emperors. Tibet was never a separate nation. Bad things may have happened there, but it is a matter for Chinese Internal Affairs. *Besides, if the Tibetans disliked the Chinese so much, why didn't they put up a fight?* Agreements were signed that proved their willingness to be taken under the wing of Mother China. Tibetans love China and all the wonderful things it has brought to their culture. Is it not a little naïve for the idealists of the international community to come to the defense of people who never asked for help nor even tried to defend themselves?

It is my intention to show that not only did Tibetans defend themselves, but that these people had names and faces and individual histories, and that

---

[2]International Commission of Jurists, *The Question of Tibet and the Rule of Law*, 132–33.

their firsthand accounts (which illustrate the extent to which they were willing to defend themselves) belie the contortions the Chinese have gone through in an effort to whitewash their blood-soaked colonialism.

This is not a Shangri-la story.

The Tibetans described in this book, the valiant men who fought the Chinese to their deaths, were not saints.

Buddha's Warriors is the story of Kham, the southeastern section of Tibet, and the northeastern provinces of Amdo and Golok. It is the story of the warrior Buddhists who inhabited these isolated regions. Their ancient reputation for rugged physical bearing and ferocious independence—Marco Polo was the first Westerner to describe their intimidating nature—constituted anything *but* the gentle Tibetan stereotype popularized by modern Western lore. These tribes were feared.

And foreigners weren't the only people to fear the tribes. Fellow Tibetans gave them a very wide berth: Lhasans trespassing through Kham knew that they did so at their own peril. The impenetrable mountain ranges, vertiginous gorges, and savage rivers provided the warriors with the perfect backdrop for ambushes. Strangers ventured through Kham with the same trepidation the American pioneers experienced when broaching hostile Apache territory. Khampas were heavily armed. Khampas were incomparable horsemen, hunters, and trackers. They used these skills to hone the fine art of brigandage and they were proud of it. If they surrounded an intruder's camp in the middle of the night, losing possessions was the least of the intruder's worries. There was no negotiating with Khampas: In any case, the isolation of the region had created a dialect as harsh and dense as the mountain ranges in which the Khampas lurked. In Kham you learned about stealth. In Kham, only the strongest survived.

But to dismiss Khampas (as well as Amdoans and Goloks) as lawless savages is to misunderstand the complex origins of their independent nature. Autonomy was a natural result of Eastern Tibet's wild topography and severe climate—a good thing, given the country's aggressive neighbors: Mongolia to the north and China to the east. Eastern Tibet had always existed with the threat of invasion and the knowledge that Tibet's Central Government could never be relied on for military backup. From time immemorial, Eastern Tibet had been left to fend for itself. Capitalizing on their intimate knowledge of the countryside, the Khampas, Amdoans, and Goloks had adopted guerilla warfare techniques that successfully thwarted any would-be invaders. Even Genghis Khan found diplomacy more efficacious than sheer might: Unable to subjugate the Eastern Tibetans, he begrudingly admired their wild nature and incorporated them into his burgeoning army.

Perhaps that's what Mao Tse-tung hoped to do in the 1950s. If so, he woefully underestimated the Khampas' implacable love for and devotion to Buddhism.

Buddhism provided Khampas with a moral code and sense of oneness with all things Tibetan. Their culture, their written language, their sense of community—all were tied to the introduction of Buddhism 1,200 years before. To be a Khampa was to be a Tibetan Buddhist; it was as simple as that. Analyzing Khampas *without* accounting for their spiritual creed was comparable to making a survey of medieval Italians without addressing the impact of the Catholic Church. Some of the greatest monasteries in Tibet were strewn along the Khampa mountain ranges. Several of the Dalai Lamas had been born in Kham. In fact, although Khampas had no love for Lhasa's Central Government, their allegiance to the Dalai Lama was without parallel. As far back as anyone could remember, the Dalai Lama's personal bodyguards had been—who else?—Khampas.

The Khampa code of conduct while killing an enemy was the same as while picking flowers for Buddha's altar: proceed with unquestioning devotion; prostrate to lamas, but stand up for your rights.

And here was the anomaly:

How could warrior tribes worship Buddha—the ultimate advocate of nonviolence? The available Western literature on Buddhist warriors failed to include a religious context with which I could answer my question. I had seen old photographs of the Khampas: handsome, proud men with fox-fur hats perched at a swaggering angle, rifles carelessly slung across broad shoulders, knives tucked beneath their belts, ever ready to be drawn. Attempting to equate their physical ferocity with their professed spiritual belief only deepened the mystery. Were they an aberration of the Tibetan culture, or was I simply being naïve? And if the latter were true, to what extent did my naïveté play into the Chinese propaganda machine?

. . .

THE INCEPTION OF THIS BOOK TOOK PLACE IN 1995 ON A BLUSTERY late-fall evening in a wood cabin in the Catskill Mountains. I was spending a few days with my Tibetan lama, who was born in Kham. We were poring over last-minute details of the murals I was to paint in his newly constructed temple in India. Having agreed on the precise placement of the various deities to be included in the pantheon, my lama turned his attention to the minutia of background rivers, mountainscapes, and various flora and fauna that would reflect Buddhist scripture, but also, I began to realize, the Khampa terrain. Prior to his escape from the Chinese in 1960, he had accumulated an encyclopedic knowledge of the native wildlife. We crouched around a potbelly stove, stoking wood in an effort to stave off the wind that whistled through the poorly constructed cabin. He described the Khampa ponies to me, a description which, at some point, segued into the men who had ridden those compact steeds—the Khampa warriors. There was newfound animation in his voice, a heightened glimmer to his eyes, and unabashed pride as he recounted various exploits of his much-feared countrymen. He told me of his boyhood homemade bow and arrows, the games he played with other children, and the exuberance they experienced in the make-believe world of Khampa heroics.

His self-deprecating amusement was as contagious as it was bewildering. Here was a devout lama who kept a diary in which he noted every insect— the date, time, and location—that he had inadvertently killed during his lifetime. How did his exemplary nonviolent mindfulness tally with his undiminished appreciation of the warriors so famous from his province? I confessed that I wanted to know more, that the Khampa, Amdoan, and Golok warriors represented to me a mysterious silence in the Western proliferation of Tibetan book titles, and that I was determined to address that silence. How could I gain access to the Khampas' story? Could the lama point me in the right direction, and would he give me his blessing for such an enterprise?

"Why not?" he answered. "I am not political, but the Khampa resistance to China's occupation of my country is a matter of history. Their story has a right to be told." With the help of his assistant, he agreed to introduce me to a member of the Tibetan Diaspora living in New York City. "Before you go," my lama added, "you should understand that this man's views may be shocking to you. His uncle was Gompo Tashi, the leader of the resistance, so he knows or knew everyone who was part of the story."

Two weeks later, the assistant and I were sitting in this Khampa's Lower East Side apartment, recording my first interview. The lama had been right. I was shocked. Almost immediately, Kalsang plunged into the topic of the CIA's secret training of the Khampas, the ruthless savagery with which the Khampas had faced the Chinese, and, most surprising, his guarded criticism of the role the Dalai Lama had taken since setting up his Goverment-in-Exile in Dharamsala, India.

I was in a new world and, for me, there was no turning back. I spent the next five years going back and forth from America to India and Nepal, scouring the Tibetan refugee camps, using one contact to create the next, assembling hundreds of hours of taped interviews in an effort to talk to every Khampa warrior who wanted to tell his story. Books were being published about the Khampas and the CIA involvement, but none of them allowed the combatants to tell the story in their own words—stories narrated, first and foremost, by Buddhists. These men could not be dismissed as a few aberrant Tibetans. Whole monasteries, I would learn, armed themselves and went to war.

The Buddhist warriors I met were now old men. Each time I returned to a Khampa enclave, someone else I had previously interviewed had passed away. My sense of urgency to record firsthand accounts only increased.

Along the way, I made many fortuitous connections. Through a maven of New Delhi society, I gained access to retired General S. S. Uban, the dashing turbaned officer who had trained Khampas for the Indian government after China invaded India in 1962. I befriended Athar Norbu, one of the first six Khampas to be trained by the CIA.

And most important, I befriended the CIA officer who created the Tibetan Task Force back in the 1950s and who trained the first Tibetans on Saipan and organized their training program. He became to me mentor, muse, contact for interviewing other CIA members of the Tibetan team, and, throughout, disciplinarian for getting the facts right. Together, Roger McCarthy and

I interviewed the Dalai Lama in Dharamsala. To watch His Holiness give Roger a prolonged bear-hug, thanking him for his invaluable work on behalf of the Tibetan nation, was to understand the heart connection that bypasses any notions of good guy and bad guy, of past and future, of war and peace.

So who were these brave men credited with implementing the Dalai Lama's successful escape? Who were these lion-hearts the CIA schooled? Who were these deeply saddened, aging, and, for the most part, penniless refugees still waiting to return to their homes in Tibet? What happens to the natives when a foreign country invades and occupies their terroritories? What happens to the people's hearts when their future is dictated by a foreign power?

It is the Buddhist warriors' words, not mine, that, I am hopeful, will answer these questions.

May their lives—many of which have ended since I began this project—continue in these pages.

Gesar, the legendary warrior of Tibet *(Jamyang of Amdo)*

1

Leopard Cubs

The year was 1947, though not in the small mountainous kingdom of Derge.[1] The Khampas reckoned time by the ancient Tibetan lunar calendar. Their system indicated that the year was 2074. To the Western eye, both dates would have seemed irrelevant. Derge was medieval.

The isolation of this time-warped kingdom was almost inviolate. Transportation was of the two- or four-legged variety. To get to Derge, one needed good balance, sturdy calves, a sixth sense for bandits, and immunity from vertigo. From the east, traders were compelled to traverse nine bridges crossing nine streams dwarfed by nine gorges encased by vertical cliffs of such height that direct sunlight was the exception, not the rule. The western approach was equally arduous. Rivers and mountain ranges, running north and south, blocked the way. Just west of the main town of the kingdom,[2] one of the great

---

[1]Rhymes with the Russian name Sergei. Derge was one of the many tribal kingdoms in Kham, the large southeastern section of Tibet.
[2]Derge Droncher—literally, "the City of Derge."

rivers of Asia, the Drichu,[3] coursed in savage twists and turns like a wrathful snake deity.

The town itself was nestled in a diminutive valley embraced by palisades. Above the foaming river, its tiers of homes and shops rose through a warren-like system of narrow streets and passageways—always moving upward—up toward the vast, thousand-monk monastery that reigned at the apex like a top-heavy crown.

This is not to imply that Derge's religious center was above the mortal fray. Everyone was intricately connected to everyone else. Lamas, peasants, artisans, merchants, beggars, and nobility all lived within close proximity of one another. Humble or rich, lay or monastic, buildings were constructed with the same hodgepodge of stone, adobe, and wood. A man's position in life was judged by the breadth and height of his home, not the architectural niceties. There was also an observable equality in what the inhabitants *didn't* have: Derge was pre-telephone, pre-electric, pre-plumbing, and pre-industrial. Rudimentary pulleys were the cutting edge of technology. Money existed, but commerce was still fairly barter-dependent. Most of the goods and clothing were handmade. Home security systems took the form of black mastiffs chained by the door.

The average home was two stories high. The ground floor of tamped dirt served as a shelter for animals and a storage space for grain and fodder. The second floor, reached by scaling a primitive ladder (usually nothing more than a serrated tree-trunk), served as living quarters. Up there, the floor space was divided into a poorly ventilated kitchen, sparsely furnished bedrooms, and an altar room.[4] Indoor bathrooms (and the accompanying twentieth-century notion of hygiene) were nonexistent. Windows were small openings covered with translucent paper. Glass panes, even among the rich, were more rare than diamonds.

The homes of merchants and nobles were often three-story, three-wing affairs, with a fourth wall added to create a large central courtyard. Nothing

---

[3]Yangtze, in Chinese.
[4]The altar room was where Tibetans exhibited their remarkable decorative skills. Excess income would be spent on religious statues, paintings, silk brocade, silver ritual bowls, etc. But unlike American "living rooms," which double as showcases of refinery, Tibetan altar rooms were used on a daily basis.

terribly fancy, although the adjunct of wooden balconies signaled a certain amount of telltale affluence. The real tip-off was found in the interiors. Thick, handsome carpets cushioned the plank floors. Couches were softened by silk. Low-lying tables were intricately carved, brightly painted. Walls glistened with silk brocade and other amenities acquired during pilgrimages to Lhasa or purchased from caravans originating in China, India, or Mongolia.[5]

The flat rooftops of domestic architecture provided additional living space. Rooftops offered the perfect counterbalance to dark, smoky interiors. They boasted sun, fresh air, and the soothing effect of a host of multicolored prayer flags snapping in the breeze. Rooftops were where Tibetans dried and winnowed grain, stored firewood, burned incense to placate the local mountain deities, braided hair, darned clothes, prepared food, and drank strong tea. They were extended social arenas as well: When neighbors were taking the air, they could relay tidbits of juicy gossip, fend off jibes, or exchange belly laughs from aerie to aerie.

THE PRINCE OF DERGE STROLLED THE PERIMETERS OF HIS ROOF-top. From his vantage point, with one spin on his toe, he could survey the entire town.

His name was Donyo Jagotsang. He was ten years old. He was strong. He was bright. He had a very clear notion of the extent to which the name Jagotsang afforded him a life of privilege:

The Jagotsangs were one of the wealthiest families in Derge. We had a huge estate, lots of animals—cattle, mules, beautiful horses, yaks—and many servants. My father's name was Dorje Jagotsang—one of the most powerful men in the region. He was a Minister of the King of Derge. My father was also chieftain of his own tribe, which consisted of four or five thousand families. He was directly responsible for their well-being, so you can imagine how busy he was. Everyone looked up to him. When less fortunate people had problems, they came to him for help. He had so many responsibilities: protecting his vast tracts of land, keeping his tribe at peace, administering to the King's wishes . . .

---

[5]Lowell Thomas Jr., *The Silent War in Tibet,* 54–55.

I, on the other hand, was completely carefree. Derge had no schools in those days. And since none of my siblings (two brothers and seven sisters) were sent to the monastery, we just played around most of the time. The richer families of Derge hired tutors to come to the house to teach reading and writing: That's how I received my education. Other than that, we children were pretty much free to do what we wished. We were never lonely. We weren't isolated from the rest of the population or anything like that.[6]

In fact, social hierarchy was sublimated by a number of factors. When the harvest was in, peasants and nobles joined together to feast, to drink the mild *chang* (barley beer), and to watch a program of theatricals of dancing which the noble arranged to take place in his courtyard. When a nobleman took his family on a picnic—a favorite summer pastime of Tibetans—the servants went along, not merely to serve, but to participate in archery contests, races, games, and singing. Servants' children often studied with the landlord's children's tutor. Religion made another strong bond between classes. Owner and peasant alike sang the same songs of the ancient saints: the protective gods of either might save the estate in time of trouble. The monastery to which the nobleman sent his son also accepted sons from tenant families.

Even the selection process of the Dalai Lama, a living god, was not dependent upon class distinction. The current Dalai Lama had been born of a non-noble family up in the farthest reaches of Amdo. Society *was* feudal. Separate classes *did* exist. But the Buddhist system—from top to bottom—often blurred the social lines. It was a system of implied equality, a deeply spiritual and individualistic system that, with an authoritative pacifism unique in the world, insisted all life was sacred—from lowly insects to magnificent snow-lions. It was a system that had provided Tibetans stability (and an equal shot at life in the next reincarnation) for more centuries than anyone could remember.

Donyo Jagotsang, the boy prince, understood all of this.

He also understood that the system in Kham sometimes broke down.

When he became a man, in addition to inheriting the positions of landlord, chieftain, and administrator, he would also become—sooner or later—a warrior.

---

[6]Donyo Jagotsang, interview with the author.

Tribes fought other tribes in Kham. That, too, was a way of life. Home-spun justice tended to be harsh and quick. When disputes over land and property erupted into violence, there was no outside authority that had the wherewithal (or inclination) to intervene. The Central Government in Lhasa—so distant, so far to the west—was useless in times of intertribal war. Besides, Lhasa's military power in Eastern Tibet didn't amount to more than a token army of poorly paid soldiers. They weren't warriors.

*And not that it was any of Lhasa's business what Khampas did. My father taught me that the Khampa tribes east of the Drichu River hadn't paid taxes to Lhasa for many decades. You see, we were situated in the buffer zone between Lhasa-ruled Tibet and the China border. The Central Administration in Lhasa exercised no real authority over our section of Tibet. Mind you, there was no question of Khampas being Tibetan. On every level, in every conceivable way—the language we spoke, the religion we worshiped, the customs we observed—we were Tibetans, always had been, always would be. But our isolation: The Chinese had tried to use this to their advantage. And it didn't matter who ruled in Beijing—they were always crossing Tibetan soil, trying to exercise control over Khampa land. So you see, we Khampas had always been on our own—particularly in times of trouble. We had no choice but to fight for and protect what was ours. That's what **made** us Khampas. The Chinese had always been close by, breath-ing down our backs. But there was a limit to how much outside interference—east or west—we would tolerate. Beyond a certain limit, there was sure to be trouble.*[7]

Indeed, the atmosphere in Derge might be likened to that of the "Wild West" of nineteenth-century America. Khampas were famous and feared for their reputation as warriors, for their stoicism and fortitude, and for their physical stature (they towered over Central Tibetans). Adding to this mystique was the preponderance of personal weaponry among the Khampas. Every self-respecting male owned at least one silver-embellished pistol or rifle—even if it was nothing more than a flintlock. The poorest of beggars carried a sword or oversized knife hitched at his waist, and he knew how to use it.

For all of their ruggedness, Khampas were a handsome lot. Prominent cheekbones, chiseled noses, strong jaws, and eyes sizzling beneath fox-fur

---

[7]Donyo Jagotsang, interview with the author.

hats—they rode high in the saddle. Style was a natural extension of deportment: They were especially fond of wearing one dangling silver-and-turquoise earring—the bigger the stone, the better. It helped prevent being reborn as a donkey.

But vanity was tempered by Buddhist upbringing. Swagger could soften into self-effacement at a moment's notice. Behind the proud profiles was a collective humility before the feet of Buddhist statuary. Prostration before Buddha was as natural as keeping one's hand on the hilt of one's sword. Khampas also had a propensity for lightheartedness. They loved a good joke on themselves and, as if to back this up, there was a popular legend that a monkey had sired the first Tibetans.

But when dealing with Khampas, it was best to remember that there was also something of the leopard in them. A pacified leopard is still a leopard. The smile faded when it came to protecting what was theirs. Khampas were powerfully built. Khampas were equestrians without equal. Khampas were deadeye marksmen.

The people who would have caged the Khampas were represented in Derge by a small contingent. Their delegates could be seen from the Prince of Derge's rooftop. Right down toward the Drichu—among the shadows and mire of a willow grove—was the Chinese quarter.

A few lean-to shops, a few drab huts for carpenters, a squat building housing the self-styled "magistrate" who represented the *Kuomintang*.[8] The Nationalist Chinese presence was something of a joke to Khampas. In sharp contrast to the rest of sun-drenched Derge, the Chinese quarter was a lowly mudhole. If you didn't know how covetous and crooked and godless they really were—that's how the Prince's father spoke of them—you could almost feel sorry for them.

Donyo had seen his father pay lip service to the "magistrate" and the occasional small units of Nationalist Chinese soldiers that straggled through eastern Kham like a pack of scavenger dogs.

Sometimes my father would even help them transport goods through the mountains. But we had no respect for them. They were rude, poorly dressed, not

---

[8]Also known as the KMT, the Nationalist Chinese Party of Chiang Kai-shek.

very organized, easy to bribe. You see, the Kuomintang had a reputation of total corruption. The Chinese who were sent to Tibet were the dregs of society. I was even told—though I never personally saw it—that the Chinese smoked opium. We thought that sort of thing was very, very bad. Khampas endured the Kuomintang, which was minimal, but we didn't really fear them.[9]

Besides, who knew how much longer the Nationalists would be around? There were rumors that another group of Chinese, the communists, were fighting the Nationalists in Mainland China, and it was said that the "Reds" were getting the upper hand.

Over the centuries, the Chinese had come to represent a recurring nuisance. From decade to decade, the Chinese might wear different political hats, but they all shared an obsession with colonialism. An age-old idea called the "Celestial Empire" was what fed their sense of superiority over the "barbarian" Tibetans.

Staring down from his ancestral rooftop, the Prince of Derge adjudged the Chinese to be the barbarians—out of their element, humorless, and profane. He didn't need an adult to point out their shortcomings.

I remember how shocked I was when I watched the way the Chinese treated their horses. They were so cruel to animals—unthinkable in Tibetan society. Their presence was not frightening but it was ugly—something we tried to ignore. My father always said, "Best not to scratch at a rash."[10]

The Prince of Derge knew that there was a world that extended beyond China and India. He had heard that there was a place called America—a very powerful country somewhere in the vicinity of Europe (wherever *that* was). He had even heard that there was an invention called an airplane.

So many things to dream of! A boy on a rooftop could fantasize a thousand different adversities over which, as a man, he could prevail and thereby prove his courage. But there were some things—even for a boy as bright and imaginative as Donyo Jagotsang—that were beyond his wildest nightmares.

A carefree Khampa prince was about to step over the ledge of medieval Tibet and into the abyss of twentieth-century warfare.

---

[9] Donyo Jagotsang, interview with the author.
[10] Ibid.

. . .

SEVEN DAYS NORTHWEST OF DERGE, IN THE SOUTHERNMOST PART of Amdo, a caravan of pack animals hauling a tea consignment (and trailed by two traveling minstrels) approached the bustling town of Jyekundo.

A Westerner would have found the altitude disorienting. Although Jyekundo was situated at thirteen thousand feet, it lacked the accompanying mountains usually associated with high places. In fact, Jyekundo was at the gateway of the famous grasslands that stretched northward up through Golok, Amdo, and all the way into Mongolia.

The swooping treeless valley surrounding the town was so wide in scope that even the multitude of yaks, sheep, and black nomads' tents peppering the tawny basin seemed diminutive by comparison—a vast backdrop further magnified by a sky of unbroken blue. In Jyekundo, one's head was in the heavens.

Jyekundo, of course, had its monastery; a large one at that—though, unlike Derge's, this pile failed to visually dominate. The true heart of the town was its main thoroughfare; straight and wide, right through the center of town and lined with all sorts of shops and inns catering to Jyekundo's thriving export-import business.

In the mid–twentieth century, Jyekundo was one of the most important trading centers in Eastern Tibet—China to the east, Amdo and Mongolia to the north, Kham and India to the south, Lhasa to the west—all the main arteries converged at its junction. There were times during the year when its pace was as slow as the most remote village's. But when the weather was suitable for extended trips, it became a heady fusion of far-flung merchants and the accompanying news of outside events. Traders filled the inns, sometimes for weeks on end until the weather was right, or until there were enough small caravans to create one huge convoy. Bandits were a common threat in the remote areas; "safety in numbers" was a rule strictly adhered to—especially where valuable consignments were concerned. At times, the range of goods was astonishing: tea from China, cigarettes from India, expensive fabric from Lhasa, metals and semi-precious jewels including *zi*,[11] dark blue

---

[11]Oblong agate stones with a veinlike pattern of concentric circles that form "eyes"; highly prized by Tibetans, they are sometimes referred to as "Tibetan pearls."

Bengali cloth coveted by the Chinese, and huge chests of silver dollars—
the only currency that really mattered in 1947 Kham. Adding to the general mix of excitement and confusion were the nomads who funneled into
town with their ponies, untanned hides, raw wool, fur, musk, yak tails,[12] as
well as more practical supplies that catered to a journeyman's immediate
needs.

Naturally, with so much bounty spilling into the street, you made sure you
had protection—if you intended to keep your possessions. And it was not
difficult to find an armed Khampa for hire.

Up the main road, into this hive of wheeling and dealing, came the newly
arrived tea caravan. It paused at the first bunch of stalls while the leader went
in search of lodging. The minstrels, who had been tagging along for safety,
bid good-bye to their protectors and followed the path that ascended to the
monastery.

Standing at the front gates of the monastery was a teenage boy by the
name of Drawupon. He had just finished his studies for the day and was rel-
ishing the sunny view after so many hours in the darkened lamasery.

Drawupon was a striking-looking youth. He was already six feet tall. His
face was boyish, but his broad shoulders and strong limbs bespoke of
impending manhood. His mother complained that she couldn't keep him in
chubas[13] and, in fact, the *chuba* he wore was a new one, with enough extra
material to accommodate his irrepressible growth.

*Chubas were, basically, nothing more than oversized robes. We Khampas
lived and slept in them. Sometimes they were made of heavy wool; sometimes
they were made of sheepskins with the wool on the inside. They had sleeves that
hung down to your knees. This protected your hands up in the high passes and
during the cold months. What you did was, you hiked up the robe at the waist
and secured the excess material with a belt so that there was a big pouch for
holding things. This pouch was called an* ampa. *In the ampa you carried everything you needed: a needle, thread, thimble, a sharp utensil made out of horn to
untie knots, flint stone for starting fires, a small knife and bowl for eating. It was*

---

[12]Throughout Central Asia—all the way to the tip of southern India—yak tails were flaunted as
unsurpassed flywhisks.
[13]The national dress of Tibetans.

a practical system. If you suddenly had to break camp, all you had to do was strap on your belt and mount your horse. Practical . . . but the leather belts were also beautiful. They were dyed red and black (like our boots) and crafted so that no two belts were alike. Sometimes they were embellished with silver and gold. Inside the belt, we thrust a medium-size knife and a sword for enemies. I suppose a man's reputation, to some extent, was determined by the quality of his chuba. In those days, it was popular to have a ten-inch border of leopard trim attached to the hem and neckline.[14]

Drawupon half-ran down the stone steps dropping into town. His plan was to speak to his father, providing he wasn't too busy. A young lama in the monastery had mentioned that his uncle was about to sell a pony Drawupon had had his eyes on for months.

We would spend a great deal of money for a really fine pony. The richer the man, the finer the horse. The quality of a Khampa's saddle and saddle blanket were equally important. The saddles could be quite expensive—especially if they were ornamented with silver and gold. You could tell what kind of man you were looking at by the horse he rode, so we took really good care of our rides. They were always well fed and well groomed. They had waterproof wool covers to protect their bodies during cold weather. If they suffered, we suffered, do you see?[15]

Drawupon's descent into town (and his hopes for a prized pony) stopped short the moment he set eyes on two men coming up the path. It was their distinctive hats, rather than the men themselves, that riveted the boy's attention: They were conical in shape, maroon in color, and their pointy tops flopped from side to side under the additional weight of cream-colored tassels. Drawupon greeted the minstrels, inquired where they were from, asked if the monastery had invited them to perform and, most important, if it would be a performance of *The Warrior Song of King Gesar.*

The minstrels answered yes, and Drawupon smiled in anticipation. A huge crowd would attend. What Khampa could resist the heroics of King Gesar, the original Khampa warrior? A bonfire would be lit at twilight. Towns-people, nomads, and visitors alike would congregate for a feast,[16] then, as the

---

[14]Drawupon, interview with the author.
[15]Ibid.
[16]Since most Tibetans had no currency, the price of admission was understood to be offerings of food.

performance drew near, they would vie for room around the flickering arena. Each hero in the epic had a different tune with which to sing his own praises. Sometimes the crowd would sing along. And so, soothed by the crackling of the bonfire and an overhead blanket of blazing stars, the audience would listen into the wee hours to the harrowing adventures—and romances—of their legendary Superman.

Legendary but—unlike Western comic-book heroes—not imaginary.

King Gesar had been real flesh and blood; a mortal who, in the eleventh century, had traversed most of Asia, waged and won eighteen wars—not for personal glory, but to protect the teachings of Buddha. The King had fought demons. He had talked to gods. And there was really nothing terribly remarkable in this, if you saw his magical powers in the proper context: King Gesar had been none other than an incarnation of Guru Rinpoche.[17] Guru Rinpoche was the enlightened being from Udiyana[18] who had subdued the aboriginal Bon-pa[19] demons and established Buddhism as the national religion of Tibet in the eighth century A.D. And as everyone knew, Guru Rinpoche was an incarnation of Buddha—the "Second Buddha." Like His Holiness the Dalai Lama, King Gesar and Guru Rinpoche were gods in men's bodies.

In those days, attending a minstrel show was a major event. King Gesar was so loved—even the Chinese loved him and tried to bend the stories so that they could claim that he was Chinese. This was all nonsense, of course. It was well known that Gesar of Ling was a local hero. His kingdom, the kingdom of Ling, was a mere five-day ride from Jyekundo! There's still a village there called Lingtsong. It's just off the road going down toward Derge. The people of Lingtsong say they are the direct descendants of the son of Gesar. But I doubt that there is a village in Kham that doesn't claim some sort of lineage to the Gesar family.

There's an old saying in Tibet: A sword is worthless without a handle. In Tibet, a man's reputation is meaningless without lineage to back it up. Highborn or lowborn, you could say that Gesar was in every Khampa's blood. His heroics made us Khampa boys want to be equally brave when we grew up. He set the example of what a Khampa warrior should be.

---

[17]Also known as Padmasambhava.
[18]An ancient kingdom thought to be located in present-day Pakistan, perhaps in the Swat valley.
[19]Bon was the indigenous animistic religion widely practiced prior to the introduction of Buddhism.

In wartime, Khampas always remembered our Buddhist beliefs and prac-
tices. Every morning, we would offer prayers to our personal deities. Before we
went into battle—if there was time—we would call a monk to us who would
offer special prayers to special deities, as well as to our local mountain deities.
We would burn incense and make offerings of flowers. If the enemy was bearing
down on us and there was not time, we simply said our prayers to ourselves
while charging into battle. We never fought anywhere without wearing our
malas[20] and our guas,[21] that protected us from the bullets and arrows of ene-
mies, if your faith was really strong. (If your faith faltered, the amulets would be
of no protection.)

After victorious battles, we would offer a group puja[22]—again, if we had the
time. If we didn't, we would offer private thanks to the deities. Just like King
Gesar on the battlefield.[23]

Drawupon turned down the main thoroughfare. The need to inform his
father of the pony for sale *and* the impending minstrel show—double
urgency!—lent his long stride fresh purpose.

However . . .

The crowd loosely assembled around his father's office did not bode well
for a sudden intrusion. Besides the usual clutch of old men squatting at the
side of the doorway—subsumed in politics, no doubt—there were a half-
dozen tethered mules encumbered with hides, and several nomads shuffling
in front of the curtained doorway. From inside, Drawupon could hear voices
entreating his father to reconsider some matter of apparent importance.

Officially, Jyekundo was under the jurisdiction of the Nangchen king. Drawupon's father, Jigme Tsering, was the District Administrator of Jyekundo and,
as such, the overseer of most of the problems that arose in the area. He was
wealthy and very influential.

One of his father's servants backed his way through the curtain with a tray
of empty teacups. Though the prospects were dim, Drawupon stopped him
in order to assess how busy his father really was. The servant shook his head
dubiously. The day had been a crazy one: a merchant just returning from the

---

[20]Buddhist rosary of 108 beads.
[21]A silver box containing lama-blessed amulets and prayers that hangs around a warrior's neck.
[22]A general term that indicates any kind of religious ceremony in Tibet.
[23]Drawupon, interview with the author.

east had occupied his father's morning with news of Mao Tse-tung's continuous victories in China. And now he was trying to pacify several nomads
who were squabbling about grazing rights—a matter muddied by some sort
of foiled attempt (from the local representative of the *Kuomintang*) to take an
active role in the dispute. *Kuomintang* interference always doubled his
father's work and put him in a foul mood.

The teenager weighed the pros and cons. He would have been welcome
inside—as a family observer. But to interrupt the proceedings in order to
broach a personal matter would have been disrespectful and juvenile. On the
other hand, he was still tempted to go inside. As the oldest son (his younger
brother was a monk up at the lamasery), Drawupon knew that one day he
would inherit his father's position. He enjoyed the role of understudy. He
spent a lot of time observing how his father *listened* to tribal complaints, politics, and caravan-related enterprises.

But not today. How could he hold his tongue? No, he would come back in
an hour. Without any real destination in mind, he drifted toward the south
of town.

He passed a stall-keeper who boasted a newly arrived shipment of tea
from Ya-an. Noticing the five-pound tea brick on the peddler's table, Drawupon reached over and extracted a leaf fragment for closer examination.
His nose went into what a Western wine expert might call the connois-
seur mode: he wafted the leaf to encourage the release of aromatic atoms—
strong, mature, and fermented to perfection. The color was deeply brown,
rich as a sable pelt. No twigs in the brick. Of the five standard teas traded in
Tibet, this was *gomang chupa,* the best quality, the only kind served in his
family's home.

He passed by the Chinese merchant's place. Through the open door, he
could see the scrawny man, dozing with a slender clay pipe resting in the
crook of his arm.

*Really, before the communist invasion, there was relative peace with Nation-
alist Chinese. For one thing, their numbers were insignificant. I watched my
father in many dealings with them—many of them smoked opium and were
useless. The guys with official positions sometimes had to be bribed but, other
than that, they didn't bother us that much. Commercially, they were significant.
Jyekundo was the distribution center for Chinese trade and was the only town in*

the area where Chinese were allowed to reside. They bought our musk, our yak and sheep skins, and our gold dust. And we really couldn't do without their tea. Tibetans were—are—addicted to Chinese tea.

From time to time, of course, there would be skirmishes between local tribes and the Kuomintang. *Occasionally, our guys would raid the Chinese arsenals, things like that. We loved helping ourselves to their guns and ammunition! I guess you could say that we chose to be careful around them but we didn't really fear them.*[24]

Drawnupon passed two urchins whose parents worked in his family's household. They were plucking lice from each other's heads, but upon seeing him, they jumped up with a news scoop: *King Gesar* was going to be sung the following night! Drawupon feigned surprise for their benefit and walked on.

He passed a nomad woman and her handsome daughter who, together, always peddled sour yak milk next to the silversmith's establishment.

Having been lost in thought for several minutes, he was surprised when, looking up, he discovered himself in open countryside. Twenty yards to the south flowed the Drichu River on its way to Derge and beyond. In the shallows, several men were panning for gold dust.

You could usually find a grain or two if you were patient. Gold wasn't mined in Tibet, of course. All mining was prohibited. To rob the earth of its belongings was considered evil but it was OK to take it from the water since the water had taken it from the earth.[25]

Drawupon looked to the right, where an unmarked trail meandered toward the west. One day he would take that road. The insignificant-looking path was the main route to Lhasa, the holiest and grandest city in Tibet. Drawupon's father had told him, though it was difficult to believe, that tens of thousands of people lived in Lhasa. Of course it was the home of His Holiness the Dalai Lama, the incarnation of Chenrezig.[26] Some day Drawupon

---

[24]Drawupon, interview with the author.

[25]Ibid.

[26]Tibetan for the Sanskrit *Avelokiteshvara,* which can be transcribed as "looking constantly at all sentient beings with great love and compassion and without blinking." Chenrezig is the patron deity of Tibet—the Bodhisattva of Compassion—and, on earth, takes the mortal form of the successive Dalai Lamas. The appellation "god-king," in reference to the Dalai Lama, is a Western construct and not used by Tibetans.

would make the pilgrimage to Lhasa and gaze up at the Potala Palace with his own eyes—a dream he shared with all Tibetans.

My father told me that the communists had no respect for religion. It was said that everywhere they went, they targeted the religious centers as "enemies of the people." Well, this didn't make any sense to us. Didn't Mao Tse-tung understand that it was the Tibetan people who, with all their hearts, supported and maintained the monasteries? The communist idea was really unthinkable. To take away Buddhism was to take away Tibet. After all, one-fourth of the male population was monks. Even the Kuomintang understood this and kept their hands out of religious matters.[27]

Perhaps the rumors were false. Many Tibetans took this side of the argument. Maybe it was the *Kuomintang* (losing ground against the communist upswell) who spread lies about the "Reds" in order to demonize them and thus curry favor with Tibetans. It wouldn't be the first time the Nationalists had lied.

Surely this military genius, this Mao Tse-tung, couldn't be *that* dense when it came to the benefits that "the people" derived from Buddhism and its monasteries. Even if he wasn't spiritually inclined, could he not see the practical applications? If people were sick or dying, it was a monastery-trained doctor who treated them. If a person was literate, it was, with few exceptions, because he or she had studied at a monastery. All the arts were learned at monasteries. All books were printed and all libraries were housed in the monasteries. If a man fell on hard times, it was the monasteries that provided him with economic relief. Who did the merchants acknowledge as having the greatest purchasing power in Tibet? The monasteries. Who brought the people of a region together for festivals, thereby giving Tibetans a sense of unity? The monasteries. Who determined the most auspicious day for a farmer to sow his spring crops, or a nomad to take his herds to the highlands? The robed astrologers. Who determined a newborn's name? The lamas.

Even the *pace* of a community was syncopated not by Western clocks but by the occasional blaring of deep-throated horns drifting down from the *gompa.*[28] The concept of a year may have been grounded in the passing of

---

[27]Drawupon, interview with the author.
[28]Tibetan for "monastery."

seasons, but it was the lamas' religious rites and Buddhist holidays that gave the year its cadence.

Surely the rumors about the communists were wrong. Drawupon remembered one of his father's favorite adages: *"A new tunnel still goes through an old hill."*

The sun was setting toward Lhasa. Now, perhaps, he could empty his father's mind of Mao Tse-tung and talk about that pony. And tomorrow night—the minstrels at the monastery.

Life was all promise as he headed back into Jyekundo. Even the saddest of passages from *The Warrior Song of King Gesar* could be sung with innocent relish:

Men and women,
Scattered from homeland, family, friends,
Wander desolate and uncertain . . .
If goodness and bravery still dwell in this world
As other than a flickering shadow on the edge of sleep,
If wisdom and harmony still dwell in this world
As other than a dream lost in an unopened book,
They are hidden in our heartbeat.[29]

JOWO ZEGYAL WAS A SACRED DESTINATION, ONE OF THE FIVE GREAT mountains—power places associated with Guru Rinpoche.

It was a hard five-day trek by foot, though, as the eagle flew, Jowo Zegyal was just a day's journey south-southwest of Jyekundo—over a mountain range, toward and slightly north of Riwoche. Once you approached the general vicinity—between the Gyalmo Ngulchu (Queen of the Silver Water River) and Dza-chu (Moon River)—you couldn't miss it. Jowo Zegyal[30] towered over the Khampa countryside in kingly fashion.

Even by Tibetan standards, the mountain was remote. It served as guard for the District of Dhoshul. It was a hidden land, sparsely populated (settlements consisting of more than five families were "large villages"), and the

---

[29]From the translation by Douglas J. Penick.
[30]Literally, "King of the Big."

king also served as the abbot of the main monastery. The Chinese population was and always had been zero.

Gochen was a village in the Dhoshul District. It was a small enclave surrounded by naked birch trees, an outcropping of multicolored marble and, at the lower end, a boulder-choked river. It was midwinter, 1947. A group of young boys were playing next to the frozen stream.

Ice slicks that had adhered to the boulders were used by the boys as glittering slides. The boys had created individual (and very competitive) sleds by flattening out huge patties of yak dung, shaping them to exacting personal needs, pouring water over the sculptures, which then froze solid, and polishing the bottom sides until they were as smooth as silk. Finally, the sleds were ready. The kids held contests to see who could slide over the undulating ice the fastest and furthest.

A six-year-old held up his sled in triumph. His nickname was Cyclone.[31] To his parents' exasperation, their son had come by the moniker all too honestly. Sometimes his boundless energy, curiosity, and fearlessness combined with harrowing results. On more than one occasion, search parties had scrambled up remote inclines, frantically calling out the boy's name. At the age of four, he had followed a herd of mountain goats up to a death-defying cliff. Another time, while he was atop a crag overlooking a rushing river, his imagination convinced him that his mother had stretched a voluminous scarf all the way down to the stream. It seemed like an invitation to roll down the slope as fast as he could—an offer he accepted, while his paternal grandfather looked up in horror. Yet another time, while no one was watching, he grabbed a visitor's rifle and pulled the trigger; the resultant explosion and the sobering realization that he was in big trouble caused him to head for the hills, which ended in yet another search party. Parental punishment was immediate and stinging, but Cyclone's natural exuberance remained unchecked.

I can remember feeling so lucky to have been born so close to Jowo Zegyal. Guru Rinpoche had actually been there, meditating in the mountainside caves and blessing the area with his presence. Jowo Zegyal was also a secret place of Chenrezig and there were three famous dharmapalas[32] who lived up in the

---

[31]Gudu Lungstub, in Tibetan.
[32]Fierce tantric protector deities.

mountains. It was a very powerful spot. And filled with natural beauty. Winter or summer, the mountain peaks were always white and shining with snow. There was also a lake at the base, that was very special. Its sacred water was white—almost like milk. The mineral beach around the lake looked like crystal sugar, and when you put it in your mouth, it melted. Many waterfalls tumbled down toward it. In the warmer months, its shoreline was surrounded by a variety of wildflowers and herbs with natural healing powers, some of which, we were told, couldn't be found anywhere else in Tibet. Everything from this mountain, including the stones and sand, was used for medicine.[33]

Cyclone and his friends used this magnificent setting as the backdrop for their equally dramatic games, which found their inspiration in the legend of King Gesar.

We all played with bows and arrows and with sticks and stones. Those were our toys. The folk tales about King Gesar of Ling were very popular among us children. We organized Gesarlike dramas, divided into two sides—Gesar's army and Gesar's enemies. Sometimes we used real arrows. At the time, we didn't care, and luckily no one ever got hurt. When the adults would see us using real arrows, they would stop us and tell us not to play that way. But when they left, we went back to the real arrows.

I remember one time when I got myself into a lot of trouble by imagining myself to be King Gesar. We were staying with my father's family in the summer camp at the higher altitudes. We had taken the animals there for grazing. The people of Dhoshul District were seminomadic. In the summertime, the entire village would move to the high meadows with the herds and we all lived in big yak-hair tents. The summer meadows were not owned by the semi-nomads. The King owned them, so everyone could go wherever they liked. It was so beautiful up there. There were many edible fruits and wild vegetables and mushrooms. You put a little butter and salt inside the mushrooms and cooked them over the fire . . . delicious! There were also a lot of wild herbs up there and, when the animals ate them, their milk took on the aroma of the herbs. The doctors used to say that this "herb milk" contained important healing energy.

---

[33]Unpublished autobiography by Cyclone (real name withheld by request).

Anyway, it was great fun to set up and to live in the tents. They were water-proof and could keep out even the hardest rain. They were large. They could easily house a family of five or six.[34]

But back to King Gesar.

I remember a guest came up to our camp. He arrived on horseback. As was the custom, he went inside the tent to have tea and visit with my family. His horse was tied to a stake outside. I wanted to ride that horse. While everyone was inside the tent, I untied the reins of the visitor's horse and jumped on. The whip was tucked into the saddle so I pulled it out and whipped the horse's bottom and he took off galloping. I thought, "Now I am King Gesar of Ling!" Then I shouted, "Victory to the Positives!" I can still see everyone running out of the tent. I guess it was then that I came to my senses and realized that I didn't have control of the horse. I panicked. I was just about to jump when I heard my mother yelling to me to "grab the reins, grab the reins!" I obeyed and the horse slowed down. I was OK. My mother, on the other hand, was very angry. She beat me really hard and made me promise that I would never do that again.[35]

Cyclone's intellect was as daunting as his imagination. It was obvious he was gifted. His father taught him to read at the age of four. The boy took the challenge seriously and, characteristically, without restraint.

Aba[36] *would wake me early in the morning. Khampas didn't have alarm clocks, but when there was enough light to see the lines on the palms of your hands, it was time to get up. According to the Buddhist point of view, the early morning is the time of greatest wisdom.*

It was not enough to learn how to read. Aba wanted me to be able to read rapidly without any errors. By age six, I was a very good reader, and my family seemed to appreciate my effort. And about that time, Aba and my grandfather

---

[34]Ibid. Cyclone also describes the interior: "There were partitions—sometimes made of yak hair, sometimes woven out of tree branches—that divided the space into four rooms. The first room was where you entered: That's where we sat and visited and ate our meals. There was a fireplace made of clay and stone and it was big enough to hold several pots. A hole in the top of the tent let the smoke out—most of it. Then there was a room to store all the dairy products: milk, yogurt, cheese and butter. Then there was a room for sleeping. And at the far end was an area we set aside for the shrine. The floor was mostly dirt, but we lay down carpets in some of the areas."

[35]Ibid., in conjunction with interview with Cyclone.

[36]Tibetan for "father."

began to teach me how to perform various Buddhist rituals. I had to memorize many things: various chants, the order of events in ceremonies, different mudras,[37] how to display bowls and statues and yak-butter lamps in the shrine room . . .

I remember my paternal grandfather's personal shrine room quite well. It was a special place for me. He had a big statue of Guru Rinpoche on his altar, and I believed that this really was Guru Rinpoche. When I sat in front of the statue, I could sense that he was actually looking at me. I would sit in front of him and chant the Vajra Guru Mantra. *I would always bring flowers or something to offer to him. The statue even opened his mouth and talked to me, although I no longer remember his words.[38]*

Cyclone's predisposition for all things mystical was inherited from both parents. His mother's family were descendants of one of the most famous mountain deities in Kham, called Amyemachin. Among the locals, her family was renowned for having produced great warriors, scholars, orators, and dharma[39] practitioners. Cyclone's father's family, the Pangs, was even more famous, and acknowledged in many Buddhist histories.[40]

Given their heritage, Cyclone's parents had always hoped that their reckless son might prove to be a beneficial leader of the dharma. On the spring morning of his birth, in 1941, countless *phorogs* gathered around the house. *Phorogs* were vegetarian fowl, bigger than doves, which usually kept to very high altitudes. When they descended to the boy's birthplace and trilled in unison, the family took it as a very auspicious sign: the singing sounded exactly like a Buddhist chant.

But the six-year-old's mind was far away from such aspirations as he held his yak-dung sled above his head. His playmates weren't paying attention to him.

They pointed excitedly at a slow-flying swirl of vultures that were cold-eyeing something just beyond the village. In an instant, the boys took off in a whooping and squealing chase.

---

[37]Sanskrit for "seal" or "sign"; in Buddhist usage, a symbolic gesture of the hand used in ceremonies and yogic exercises.

[38]Cyclone, interview with the author.

[39]Sanskrit for "law" or "truth." In Buddhist usage, "dharma" is synonymous for the religion founded by Buddha Shakyamuni and, more specifically, refers to the Buddhist laws and teachings that govern the existence of all sentient beings.

[40]Cyclone, interview with the author.

As Buddhists, my family didn't kill animals. Meat was therefore not a normal part of our diet. But if a predator killed a deer or wild goat, and vultures gave the location away, the villagers would drop whatever they were doing and run to try to retrieve the dead animal before it was eaten. Whoever found or got to the animal first got to keep the skin for himself. But it was understood that the meat would be shared among all the villagers.[41]

Life was a series of carefree adventures. But Cyclone had recently been troubled by a whispered conversation he had overheard his parents having: The State Oracle had recently prophesied that terrible things were brewing in the East, and that by the Year of the Iron Tiger (1950), Tibet would face challenges it had never seen before.

Mao Tse-tung would have agreed with the Oracle.

LITHANG WAS A TWO-WEEK JOURNEY FROM JOWO ZEGYAL IN A southeasterly direction. The trip would have been fraught with ubiquitous suspension bridges spanning gut-wrenching torrents, bandits, high mountain passes, and predators such as wolves, leopards, and, perhaps, even the elusive *de-mong*.[42] You would have needed to *look* like a Tibetan, because you were entering one of the most xenophobic, contentious, and hotly disputed border areas of Kham. The Chinese state of Szechwan was nearby, and they had always—as far back as anyone cared to remember—tried to claim Lithang as their own.

Of course, had you been a sky-walker, you could have circumvented the attendant dangers by compressing a two-week journey into a couple of hours. Hollywood lore has it that the character of Luke Skywalker, the hero of the Star Wars trilogy, was inspired, at least in name, by the famed sky-walkers of Tibet. *Loung-gompas* (sky-walkers or sky-dancers) were ascetics who, through intense tantric training, could attain supernatural speed and lightness of body. If a nomad saw a *loung-gompa* about to overtake him, he knew to give the mystic as wide a berth as possible. This was not a demonstration

---

[41]Ibid.

[42]Tibetan bear with shaggy, dark yellow fur; was reputed to spontaneously defecate when confronted by a human.

of ambulance-outranks-automobile etiquette—although there was an implied deference to spiritual superiority. But beyond that, real fear accompanied such encounters. One should avoid eye contact and, above all, one should do nothing to stop the holy man. To distract a sky-walker or awaken him from his deep meditative trance might prove to be a fatal shock to his elevated state. An enlightened being dying at your feet? No nomad wanted the responsibility of an adept's death woven into the fabric of his *las*.[43]

In any case, if you weren't a *loung-gompa* and you managed to somehow get to the Lithang District in one piece, you would have found yourself closer to the Burmese border than to Jowo Zegyal.

Running southwest through the district was the powerful Lithang River. It bullied its way through an expansive valley so wide that a Khampa on horseback would spend a day traversing it. Fair-weather clouds scudded overhead and cast shadows across high grass bent by the wind. It was outstanding grazing land populated with huge herds of *dzo*,[44] yaks, cattle, and sheep.[45] One glance at this lush panorama—with its jagged necklace of distant mountains—would inform the outsider that Lithang was a rural paradigm of self-sufficiency. Little wonder the Chinese had always coveted it.

The few necessities natives couldn't glean from the land were bartered for in the thriving town of Lithang that gathered itself, like an apron donned as an afterthought, around the base of the district's central monastery. The lamasery was a city unto itself. Over five thousand monks lived within the multiterraced walls. A merchant's dream: there was buying power inside

---

[43]Tibetan for the Sanskrit "karma," literally, "action" or "deed." Western culture has tended to blur its actual meaning. *Karma* refers to the accumulated deeds performed by an individual during his successive reincarnations, which, according to their positive or negative value, lead the being either in the direction of samsara or nirvana. Samsara embodies the idea of the endless cycle of birth-death-rebirth and the suffering that is inherent in such an existence. (Imagine Buddhists' puzzlement, several years ago, when they were introduced to a Western ad-blitz for a perfume called "Samsara." Why would any woman pay money to dab the scent of suffering behind her ear?) Nirvana is not a place. Unlike the Judeo-Christian notion of heaven, nirvana is a condition resulting from extraordinarily positive karma. Nirvana is the end of the endless cycle of suffering, the eternal, blissful state of nothingness.

[44]Offspring of the male yak and the common cow, which provide an excellent source of milk as well as transport.

[45]Dairy products were the lifeblood of the seminomadic economy, although Lithang's relatively low altitude (ten thousand feet above sea level) also supported bountiful crops of barley and wheat and, to a lesser extent, potatoes, turnips, radishes, and peas.

those walls. It was no accident that
the seasonal trade fairs were held at
the main entrance of the religious
compound.

The spring fair of 1947 was into
its fifth day. Hundreds of lamas and
laymen (and a smattering of Chinese)
scoured the wares displayed on carpets
outside the monastery's perimeter.
Cobblers and carpenters, leathersmiths
and tailors, potters with their earthen-
ware jars glazed green, salt salesmen,
cloth salesmen, horse traders, all
hawked their goods with a noisy zest—
now tempered with courtesy, now leav-
ened with bawdy jokes.

Athar *(Collection of Athar Lithang)*

Milling about a potter's stand was a sixteen-year-old novice monk by the
name of Athar. His countenance was gentle and unassuming. He was not
particularly tall but—if you studied him closely—there was compactness
beneath his robe, a muscular density that quietly announced itself. (Fifty
years later, the man who organized the CIA's Tibetan program would
remember him as being "built like a fireplug."[46]) His mother, who lived in the
nearby village of Chumba, had asked him to get her a couple of medium-size
storage jars; in lieu of money, the sack of grain slung over his shoulder was to
be used for bartering with the potter.

His father died when he was three, and all of his brothers, like him, became novice monks at the Lithang Monastery. It was the largest monastery in
Kham. It had 113 branches (each housing about three hundred monks)
around the countryside. It was, on all levels, the center of Khampa life: religion, education, culture, politics, commerce—it was completely supported
by the villagers and nomads of the district. When someone died, his or her
belongings were usually donated to the monastery. There were five libraries

---

[46]Roger E. McCarthy, interview with the author.

housing ancient texts. Books were very important. The monastery had its own printing press, and many books published in Tibet came from its woodblocks, kept carefully wrapped in huge storehouses. The biggest statue of Buddha in Tibet was in Lithang monastery. It was called "*Lha Chen Thopa*," "Big Buddha." It was made of copper and gold, and the locals believed the upper half had been self-created.

Even though Lithang had always been a political powder keg, my family wasn't involved in Khampa fighting prior to the communist takeover. My brothers and I were busy at the monastery . . . but my mother always kept us up to date about Khampa activities.[47]

Like so many other Khampa districts, Lithang worked under a time-honored system whereby the head chieftain held a hereditary title and official seal of leadership. On paper, the *Kuomintang* had circumvented this system by incorporating Lithang into a new Chinese province called Sikang. The reality was different: Lithang and the surrounding tribal kingdoms formed a militant stronghold of warlords whose rule was unassailable. Their power was a serious threat to the *Kuomintang*, because it served as an unwelcome reminder of how bogus the *Kuomintang* "control" really was. The charade had been going on for decades. In 1933, for instance, when the southernmost Khampa village of Lichiang (Likiang) was inundated by the *Kuomintang*, a Lithang chieftain hastily assembled a contingent of five thousand warriors and paid a surprise visit to the besieged border-town to the south. They made quick and bloody work of the *Kuomintang* effrontery. The Khampas sacked the would-be Chinese colonists, then immediately returned home.

That was the way it was: The Chinese had audacity, but the Khampa lords had power.

In those days, it was a standoff. Sometimes, the Khampas would go on the offensive. Occasionally, we would raid the Chinese garrisons, kill a few guards in the middle of the night, and steal their weapons—things like that. We were sneaky. The Kuomintang could never prove who had raided their stockpiles, which were, by the way, supplied by the Americans. All of those big crates of artillery and ammunition had "Made in the USA" stamped on them.[48]

---

[47]Athar, interview with the author, 1997.
[48]Ibid.

Shifting the sack of grain to his other shoulder, Athar squatted on his haunches and amicably began to barter for his mother's pots. He had no idea at the time to what extent he would become acquainted with the "USA" imprint.

Several stalls away, another boy of fifteen wandered through the crowd. Now and then he stood on tiptoe, brought his hand up to his forehead, visor-like, and swiveled back and forth in search of his brother or, better yet, his uncle.

The boy's name was Kalsang. He, like Athar, was a novice monk—though the wool of his robe was of a far finer quality than Athar's. Kalsang's family name was Gyatotsang. In Lithang, no name carried more weight or prestige.

His uncle, the head of the Andrugtsang clan, was one of the richest merchants in Tibet. At forty-two, Gompo Tashi Andrugtsang was in his prime: broad of shoulder, erect in bearing, sophisticated beyond the imagination of most Khampas, Gompo Tashi spent every winter on trading expeditions that took him all over Tibet, Nepal, and India. He would trade in any commodity, although the bulk of his income came from wool, tea, silver, musk, and deer horn. The family had impeccable connections with the richest Lhasans, government officials, and the abbot of Drepung, one of the three great monasteries of the capital. He was a devout Buddhist: He had made pilgrimages to the Indian holy sites of Amritsar, Benares, Sarnath, BodhGaya, and Nalanda, as well as the major holy places in Tibet. Each year he contributed to the maintenance of important monasteries, donating lumps of money that were, in themselves, small fortunes.

In keeping with his reputation, Gompo Tashi took great care in his personal appearance. His *chuba* was of the finest cut. His meticulously parted moustache—the wings of an eagle pumping downward—was preened to the last errant feather. But his masculinity precluded foppishness. He was a fierce Khampa patriot. No family was more firmly aligned with the notion of Khampa independence.

And that was precisely why Kalsang felt such an urgency to locate his uncle. He had heard from his brother that Gompo Tashi had just returned with a huge shipment of rifles and handguns.

My father killed so many Chinese! He had over two hundred rifles. He and his men fought all up and down the disputed Sino-Tibetan border and, in those

General Gompo Tashi—Commander of the *Chushi-Gandruk. (Collection of Kalsang Gyatotsang)*

days, when you overtook the enemy, you killed them. No prisoners. Chinese were beheaded. It was rough back then.

I grew up surrounded by warriors and warrior's tales. It was always the same: The Chinese would come in and the Khampas would push them back. "We are Tibetan," we would tell them. "You are not Tibetan. Don't come to our place." But they never stopped for long—different places, different years, like an illness that never completely goes away. It didn't matter if they infiltrated Lithang, Ba, Mili, Jetang, Markham— wherever. Sooner of later, we had no choice but to fight and protect what was ours.

We couldn't count on Lhasa for help. The Tibetan officials were very stupid, you know. Why didn't they send us their army so that we could push the Chinese back and keep them back? It would have been easy back then. It's true that the Central Government didn't have much of an army back then but, even so, it would have been enough to tilt the balance. We got nothing from them. In the past, we had paid taxes to the Central Government, but what did they do for Khampas in return? They never helped protect our border with China. Khampas, Goloks, Amdos—all of us in Eastern Tibet had to fend for ourselves. It was always like that, that's what you have to understand.

I'll give you an example. About the time of my birth, 1932, when my father was eighteen, the most powerful leader of the Khampas, Butsa Pugen, agreed to talk with the Chinese. It was held at a place called Karpo-Satok, high in the mountains. My father attended that meeting: the Chinese on one side and the Khampas on the other. A thirteen-point agreement was signed and, for a while, there was something like a truce. No big battles, anyway. But the Chinese eventually broke it and we went back to the old way.

A year later, my father was given an interesting pamphlet written in Tibetan. I think the Mongolian and Tibetan Affairs Commission printed it. This pam-

phlet warned what would happen if the communists—who were just gaining influence—ever took over Tibet. First, it said, the communists would act like our friends but later they would torture and kill us and take away our religion. The pamphlet also offered bounties for any communists who were killed: top leaders would bring twenty thousand Chinese dollars if they were alive, ten thousand if they were killed; common communist soldiers would bring in fifty dollars. The author of that book was Chiang Kai-shek, leader of the Kuomintang.

Looking back, though, the years before the communist invasion were relatively peaceful. Chiang Kai-shek's soldiers were kind of pathetic, really. They never got that much support from Beijing. They had few horses and they weren't real horsemen anyway. They were just a bunch of underfed and underequipped infantry. A lot of them smoked opium and you could tell that they didn't really want to fight Tibetans. They didn't even want to be in Tibet! It was not difficult to pay them off. That was our usual method, if it seemed to be the easiest solution. Remember, they had no personal reason to be there. They were just paid to be there. Many of them deserted the army at the first opportunity and slipped quietly back to their native provinces.

Then World War II came along, which had one important impact on Khampa society:

We had never been without guns, but it wasn't until World War II that we had access to first-rate weapons. My uncle, Gompo Tashi, and some of his associates, would purchase them from Burma, Laos, India—we had English and American guns—we even got Russian guns sometimes, from Mongolian traders. As for the exact details of World War II, we were very ignorant. I don't think I was aware of the existence of Germany until after the war. I couldn't even imagine it. I had never seen a world map.

I had heard of Japan, of course, and I remember quite distinctly when the war was over. I was at my uncle's house. An old Khampa hero named Shak Gyatso came running into the house. He announced to Gompo Tashi that the Americans had dropped the biggest bomb ever made on Japan and that everyone was so afraid of the bomb that the war had been ended right then and there.

One more thing about Shak Gyatso: Several years after the Kuomintang fell, after the communists invaded Kham, they conducted a special manhunt for Shak Gyatso who, by that time, was an old man. He was hiding from them in a monastery. The Chinese found him, dragged him out of the temple, chained *him, put him on display in the center of town, forced all the townspeople to attend the event, forced the people to berate their own hero, forced them to watch him being tortured and, finally, murdered.*

And the worst thing about it was that that sort of atrocity became a common event. Well, looking back, it's not as if we hadn't been warned. Back in the thirties, the Thirteenth Dalai Lama had prophesied that the country might collapse in the near future:[49]

"Unless we can guard our own country, it will now happen that the Dalai and Panchen Lamas, the Father and the Son, and all the revered holders of the Faith, will disappear and become nameless. Monks and their monasteries will be destroyed. The rule of law will be weakened. The lands and property of government officials will be seized. They themselves will be forced to serve their enemies or wander the country like beggars. All beings will be sunk in great hardship and overpowering fear; the days and nights will drag on slowly in suffering."[50]

Kalsang pushed his way through the crowd—past Athar crouching down by and negotiating with a potter—until he spied, then caught up with his brother, Wangdu. They held hands for an instant in silent greeting. Not a handshake, just a quiet moment of touching. The loyalty reflected in that gesture spoke volumes about the quiet depths of Tibetan brotherhood—strength they would need in the upcoming years.

They seemed to read each other's thoughts. Without a word, they parted in separate directions: a race to see who could find their famous uncle first. Gompo Tashi, the world traveler. Gompo Tashi, the man who could face down the Chinese. Gompo Tashi, owner of a bristling cache of shiny new weapons.

I knew Kalsang and Wangdu. Athar said. *Everyone knew them, of course. They were the nephews of Gompo Tashi. Especially Wangdu was in people's minds that year. He would have been about seventeen and had recently killed the bodyguard of the King of Milling . . . I can't remember why, but even from childhood, Wangdu was known as violent and unpredictable. Anyway, Wangdu got a pardon from the King, no doubt due to his family connections. I remember*

---

[49]Kalsang Gyatotsang, interview with the author.
[50]The Thirteenth Dalai Lama, August 1932.

how impressed I was by Wangdu. He
was already a young man with a rich,
powerful uncle and a tough reputation,
while I was still a boy from a poor village outside of Lithang and no reputation, and I never dreamed that one day
Wangdu and I would be side by side,
learning how to blow up bridges together
on a faraway island.

There was something I remember
about that fair—the day I bought the
pots for my mother. As I was walking
back to Chumba, I saw Gompo Tashi's
caravan. It was a long train of mules.
Lots of big guards around. They told
me to keep moving. It was a big deal
when Gompo Tashi returned from one
of his trips.

Wangdu. Taken in Darjeeling a few years
before he became commander of the Mustang
resistance. (Collection of Kalsang Gyatotsang)

Anyway, I was just outside of Lithang—I heard the monks up on the rooftop
of the monastery, blowing their conch shells. According to Buddhist tradition,
the sound of the conch shells is the sound of the never-ending victory of dharma
over ignorance. But I remember stopping and looking back up at Lithang and I
saw quite a few vultures circling in the sky and, I don't know, I just started thinking about all the thousands of priceless books and statues up on the hill and . . .
well, the conch shells just sounded kind of sorrowful all of a sudden. It seemed
like an omen of some kind. And that memory came back to me in 1956 when I
heard that three thousand townspeople had crowded into the monastery complex for protection from the communist army that had laid siege. One of my
brothers who survived the massacre described how the Chinese Air Force came
circling in with a fleet of Russian bombers. They circled several times before they
let loose their load. He said the most frightening part was not the actual explosions. He said what really scared him was the high-pitched whine of the bombs
as they dropped down through the sky. I don't know . . . for some reason, the
bombs coming from the sky reminded me of the sound of the conch shells and the
circling of the vultures and that day when I had that strange feeling in my gut.

It's strange how the mind works. Sometimes I think I actually foresaw Lithang lying in rubble.

In Tibet, we call that having the dream before you sleep. Sometimes I think we all did—had the dream before we slept. We all knew about the previous Dalai Lama's warning. He said that in the near future, Tibet would be attacked from without and within. Everyone knew he was talking about the Chinese . . . and "within" could only mean, you understand, Tibetan traitors and collaborators with the communists.[51]

---

[51]Athar, interview with the author.

Rahula *(Jamyang of Amdo)*

2

RAHULA DRAWS
HIS BOW

In 1949, Rahula paid a visit of horror across the Tibetan sky. Rahula ruled the heavens—a bulging, menacing, wrathful deity.

The bottom half of Rahula's body is a serpent's tail—fat, spotted, repulsive. Around his fat waist is a belt of human heads. Spread across his belly is the war face of a three-eyed monster. On his breasts are two more eyes. He has four arms, short but very strong. Each forearm has an eye staring into space. His upper body drips with bone ornaments and writhing sea snakes. One of his hands waves a monster-headed banner. One hand clinches a lasso-snake. The other two fists take aim with a bow and arrow. Rahula sees all. He has nine terrifying heads—three stacked upon three stacked upon three. His hair is on fire. And all about Rahula are raging flames and poisonous gray smoke. The lamas from my district talked about black magic associated with Rahula. They said there were sorcerers who could use Rahula's power for the evil of man, causing people to die of strokes and epilepsy—all sorts of bad things.[1]

---

[1]Pema Wangyal of Dolpo, interview with the author.

Night after night, Rahula's phosphorescent tail slowly streamed through the Tibetan heaven. Gompo Tashi, the rich merchant, and his nephews Kalsang and Wangdu witnessed the dire spectacle from the windswept plains of Lithang. The Prince of Derge witnessed Rahula from the rooftop of his father's house. Drawupon saw Rahula above the shores of the Drichu River in Jyekundo. Cyclone, holding his father's hand at the base of Jowo Zegyal, was told that the signs were ominous. The four members of the *Kashag*, the Dalai Lama's cabinet in Lhasa, argued about the source of Rahula's anger. The last time Rahula had made such a violent show had been decades before, coinciding with the fall of the Manchu Dynasty and the onset of Chiang Kaishek's *Kuomintang*.

What Westerners saw blazing across the sky in 1949 was a comet. For those informed by empirical science, emanations in the sky were not to be feared. They were either quaint ("The Man in the Moon"), metaphorically religious ("Star of Bethlehem"), or kooky ("flying saucers"). Of course everyone could and did envision the reality of an Iron Curtain, brought to their attention by the great rationalist Winston Churchill—a pragmatic image that Tibetans, in particular, would have found impossible to grasp.

An iron curtain? Was any boundary that clear-cut? For over twelve hundred years, the boundaries between Tibet and China had billowed to and fro—like a silk curtain—all the way back to the eighth century A.D., when Tibet's great warrior Buddhist king Trhisong Detsen conquered most of Central Asia. From Afghanistan, northern Pakistan, Nepal, and India, to the Chinese provinces of Sichuan and Gansu, King Trhisong Detsen's expansionism seemed boundless. For a brief period, his troops even occupied the Chinese capital at that time, present-day Xi-an.

China censored any mention of Tibet's past glory. It didn't fit in with their version of history and was stricken from all textbooks. Over the centuries, the Chinese had managed to install a handful of "official representatives" in Lhasa, but that was the extent of their influence. Regardless, in the interim, the Tibetans and the Chinese had basically evolved in opposite directions. What Chinese valued was the notion of "empire." What Tibetans valued— topographically, historically, politically, religiously, and culturally—was isolation. All the Tibetans required of the Chinese was to leave them alone.

1949, Western time.

The currently disputed Tibetan-Chinese border roughly followed the course of the upper Drichu (Yangtze) River, with the Chinese claiming control of the eastern side of the river. Tibetans lacked any kind of diplomacy based on cartography. And they certainly didn't understand the international significance of Western legalese such as de jure or de facto. But young men like Kalsang of Lithang did pride themselves on having common sense:

Try going to Kanze or Derge, both east of the Drichu—try buying a pony with Chinese money—see how far that got you in "Chinese territory"! Send into Golok a puffed-up Chinese official or, better yet, send him as far north as the Kumbum monastery, where the Fourteenth Dalai hailed from—get those people to describe themselves as part of the Motherland! It boiled down to this: The Chinese had always wanted to legitimize their claim to Tibet but it had never been more than an idea—an idea the Chinese had never been able to put into practice.[2]

But still, here was Rahula screaming through the night, exacerbating an already apprehensive Tibetan nation. Chiang Kai-shek was one thing. Mao Tse-tung was another: Victory after victory proved the communists had Chiang Kai-shek on the run.

There would be other rumblings from other gods. Unprecedented hailstorms were reported across the nation. Crops were devastated, particularly in Central Tibet. A major earthquake in the Lithang District—the impact was felt all the way down to Calcutta—would claim more that 1,500 Tibetan lives, altering the course of rivers, changing mountains into gorges, gorges into mountains, erasing all the ancient mule trails and suffusing the southern sections of Kham with the sickening scent of sulfur. The Lithang merchant Kunga Samten Dewatshang (who would later play a significant role in Gompo Tashi's guerilla army) felt the rumbling while in Lhasa on pilgrimage with his mother. Two of his sisters who had remained in Lithang were killed in the disaster. *Prayers were offered in all the monasteries for the well-being of the dead,* he recalled.[3] But given the context of communist ascendancy in the East, a prayer for Tibet, in general, was also on the lips of the mourners.

---

[2]Kalsang Gyatotsang, interview with the author.
[3]Kunga Samten Dewatshang, *Flight at the Cuckoo's Behest*, 34.

Surely Rahula and all the other wrathful deities were taking aim at the godless communists who were intent on destroying Buddhism.

The progressive Thirteenth Dalai Lama had predicted such catastrophes:

> In particular, we must guard ourselves against the barbaric red communists, who carry terror and destruction with them wherever they go. They are the worst of the worst. Already they have consumed much of Mongolia, where they have . . . robbed and destroyed the monasteries, forcing the monks to join their armies, or else killing them outright . . . It will not be long before we find the red onslaught at our own front door.[4]

In 1912, at the instigation of Sir Charles Bell, the Thirteenth Dalai Lama sent four Lhasan youths to England to study for four years. Eleven years later, the Thirteenth Dalai Lama created an English school in Gyantse. Inventions from the West, such as movie projectors and automobiles, were transported over the Himalaya. A small hydroelectric plant was erected, as well as a telegraph line from Lhasa to Gyantse. Most important, the British substantially increased the sales of military arms and equipment to Tibet and helped introduce contemporary military training to a fledgling army suddenly reevaluated: In the 1910s and 1920s, the Thirteenth Dalai Lama understood that Tibet's isolation, enjoyed for so many centuries, could no longer be sustained in the twentieth century without military might to back it up. This was a new era—an international era. The rules had changed.

The Buddhist hierarchy, represented by the three great monasteries of Lhasa—Drepung, Sera, and Ganden—was very upset by all these changes to the status quo. Strengthening the secular army was unthinkable, if not blasphemous; they objected on the grounds that Buddhist principles were incompatible with the violence implied by a "new army."

A closer look at their outrage, however, reveals a secular underpinning. For one thing, the monasteries would be expected to pay taxes to support this

---

[4]Thirteenth Dalai Lama, "The Last Political Testament," trans. Glenn H. Mullin, in *Lungta*, no. 7, August 1933, 9.

modern army. For another, the new army threatened to rival the monastery's power, which included their own corps of fighting monks who served as their private police force.

In the end, the monastic pressure against progressive measures became too much for the Thirteenth Dalai Lama. By 1924, he dropped his support of a modernized army. Tibet would pay dearly. After the death of the Thirteenth, true to his prediction, political stability in Lhasa rapidly declined.

The succession of Dalai Lamas, based on the principle of reincarnation, inevitably created a vacuum of power. Baby boys—even baby Dalai Lamas—could not lead nations. Until they reached majority, Regents stepped up to take over the running of the country. It was a traditional requisite that the chosen Regent was also a recognized reincarnated lama—almost always hailing from one of the rival Lhasan monasteries. In other words, they brought with them a personal political agenda.

For seven years after the Thirteenth Dalai Lama's death, Reting Rinpoche, the appointed Regent, allowed the military to decline, while lining his pockets at the expense of the Tibetan economic surpluses. During his reign, for instance, his *labrang*[5] grew into one of the three largest trading companies in Tibet. Loved by many, despised by others, he was eventually forced to resign—technically because of his (some insisted) pansexual disregard for his vows of celibacy. Taktra Rinpoche, another high-ranking incarnate, took Reting Rinpoche's place—bringing with him his own power base. Six years later, Reting Rinpoche tried unsuccessfully to regain the Regency by attempting to have Taktra assassinated and, through the machinations of his inner circle, by creating a popular revolt. His coup was unsuccessful, but lines had been drawn. Monasteries chose opposing sides—Reting versus Taktra—culminating in an internecine monastic war. Monks murdered monks, para-

---

[5]Incarnate lamas inherited all the property and wealth of their predecessors. In essence, a *labrang* was a corporation of an incarnate lama's line of incarnations. Any wealth that the lama accumulated during his lifetime automatically became part of the *labrang*. In Reting's case, his corporation became alarmingly powerful and his trading company grew to rival the Pandatsang and Sandutsang families' commercial empires. H. E. Richardson, the British delegate in Lhasa, witnessed this, regarded Reting as hopelessly venal, and wrote that "the Regent is governed by self-interest." IOR, L/PS/12/4165, report of the British Mission in Lhasa for the year from October 1938 to September 1939.

lyzing the government, depleting morale and, in general, creating a divisiveness that the boy Fourteenth Dalai Lama could barely comprehend, let alone prevent.

Reting Rinpoche was eventually imprisoned in the basement of the Potala, where he died—many say, by poison.

And now Rahula was flying through the sky with his poisoned arrow drawn at a Lhasan government whose energies had been drained by civil conflict at the very moment when it most needed unity.

Down the echoing corridors of the Potala a new whispering could be heard. Instead of fighting among themselves, they should be concentrating on getting international acceptance of Tibet as an independent nation. Maybe that was Rahula's warning.

THE *KASHAG* DID ONE THING RIGHT DURING THE SUMMER OF 1949. News came from the east that Chiang Kai-shek's army was retreating to Formosa,[6] with the idea of setting up an exile government there. Mao's PLA (People's Liberation Army) was routing the last of the *Kuomintang* very quickly.

The *Kashag* summoned the head of the Chinese Mission in Lhasa—a delegate with virtually no power—and told him he had two weeks to evacuate all Chinese officials (most of them suspected to be spies either for Chiang Kai-shek or Mao Tse-tung) out of Tibet. The Tibetan Army took the added precaution of dismounting the mission's wireless antenna so that Mainland Chinese—whoever was in control there—would be caught off-guard, which, when the banished Chinese showed up in Beijing, indeed they were. This was on the eighth of July. Two weeks later, Tibet was free of any kind of official presence of China, reverting it to the status it had enjoyed during the Thirteenth Dalai Lama's reign.

Three months later, the communists proclaimed from Beijing that they were in control of the country. On October 1, 1949, Mao Tse-tung announced over the radio that, from here on out, his "liberated" nation would be recognized as the People's Republic of China.

---

[6]Present-day Taiwan.

· · ·

INDIA, ENGLAND, AND AMERICA WERE SHOCKED BY THE RAPIDITY of Mao Tse-tung's ascendancy, and were in a quandary as to how best proceed with this startling news.

Before the world could catch its breath, however, the communists broadcast their intention of sending the PLA into Tibet in order to "liberate them from the imperialists."

Imperialists?

The *Kashag* responded that that wouldn't be necessary, since there were no imperialists in Tibet.

Who, they asked one another, were these "imperialists" that populated and endangered their country?

Here's the list: Robert Ford and Reginald Fox, British radio operators employed by the Tibetan government; Hugh Richardson, British representative at the Indian Mission; Heinrich Harrer and Peter Aufshnaiter, Austrian mountaineers who had escaped from British internment camps in India; Nedbailof, a White Russian hired to work with Aufshnaiter on a hydroelectric project; and Geoffrey Bull, an English missionary.[7] (Fox departed before the Chinese invasion; Richardson returned to India; Harrer and Aufshnaiter escaped to India; and the Chinese captured Ford and Bull.) Also, for a short time in the summer of 1950, American Frank Bessac was in Tibet.[8]

Eight people? Could one country cook up a phony threat, invade another country and just get away with it? Was that the sort of thing that went on in the world outside Tibet?

It can be argued that the communists were disingenuous in their claim of an imperialistic presence in Tibet. But this would ignore the chauvinistic—if not paranoid—strain within the Han self-image, which the communist party readily adopted: it was the ancient duty of the Han to reintegrate and protect all

---

[7]Warren W. Smith Jr., *Tibetan Nation: A History of Tibetan Nationalism and Sino-Tibetan Relations*, 278.
[8]Thomas Laird recently published a book, *Into Tibet: The CIA's First Atomic Spy and His Secret Expedition to Lhasa*, in which he asserts that Frank Bessac was working in Tibet as a CIA contract agent in 1950. But Bessac, in his interview with Laird, flatly denies the allegation, nor does the book back up the declaration with any hard evidence. A CIA source characterized Laird's work as "sensational, paranoid and highly imaginative fiction."

regions that had ever been associated with the "Motherland." The idea of politicized Motherhood, and the Chinese belief in this tenet, informed nearly all of its foreign policy. What child wishes to be separated from its mother? For Tibet to see itself as happily independent of its mother was simply inconceivable to the Chinese, Mao Tse-tung included. Outside influence could be the only explanation. Foreign influence was and always had been a poisonous vapor ever attempting to infiltrate. Empires and dynasties might come and go, but to eliminate foreign influence from the Motherland was eternally righteous.

According to historian Melvyn Goldstein, "The Chinese considered it not to be coincidental that the Thirteenth Dalai Lama had expelled all Chinese from Tibet and severed relations with China in 1913 just after he had spent two years in India and developed a close friendship with the British diplomat Sir Charles Bell. The Chinese saw British policy as an attempt either to eliminate or to reduce to token status all Chinese influence in Tibet and saw the elimination of British 'imperialism' (i.e., influence) as critical to the restoration of what they considered to be China's traditional hegemony over Tibet."[9]

The communists may have been godless, but Chou En-lai (Mao's second-in-command) confided to the Indian ambassador in China that the "liberation" of Tibet was, for the Reds, a "sacred duty."[10]

IN THE MEANTIME, INDIA, GREAT BRITAIN, AND THE UNITED STATES scratched their collective heads. Polemics aside, it seemed highly unlikely that the communists could act on their "freeing of Tibet" any time soon. The sheer logistics of invading a 1,200-mile border running through precipitous mountain ranges seemed beyond the PLA's present ability. First and foremost, there were no existing roads over which the PLA could invade Tibet. And was not war-torn China rife with domestic crises that would preclude the possibility of, at least for the present, military expansion? In the fall of 1949, a British Foreign Office memorandum to the Indian government stated, "Tibet's best chance lies in the hope that the Chinese Communists will

[9]Melvyn Goldstein, *A History of Modern Tibet, 1913–1951*, 623.
[10]K. M. Panikkar, *In Two Chinas, Memoirs of a Diplomat*, 144.

have other matters to occupy their energies for the time being and that they may be deterred from interfering by difficulties involved . . ."[11]

Like the communist Chinese government, India's government was brand-new and had its own domestic problems.

The subcontinent had become independent from Great Britain only two years before. Relations between India and Tibet were, at best, strained. The personal ambitions of Jawaharlal Nehru, India's first Indian Prime Minister, were at loggerheads with Tibet's notion of independence. Tibet didn't fit into Nehru's plans at all. He was preoccupied with a grand vision of a new post-colonial Asia in which he would play a pivotal role. Asia would be a peaceful, self-reliant, pan-Asian brotherhood bound by the mutual outrage of past foreign occupation. China, the most populous nation in the world, was a critical member of Nehru's dream fraternity. Anything that might hinder that relationship—such as Tibet claiming independence—would have to be unceremoniously muffled.

But Chairman Mao did not share Nehru's pan-Asian dream, nor did he regard Nehru as his equal. There would be no real brotherhood. Yet Nehru bent over backward to appease Mao, and no one on earth was more agreeably poised to exploit another man's subservience than Mao. Not only did he see Nehru in these terms—he counted on it.

And Nehru's naïveté went further in sealing the fate of the Tibetans. In general, Nehru protested against all nations who proposed to confront, or in any way challenge, the Chinese. In particular, Nehru, as will be seen, discouraged the United States from considering open diplomatic assistance to Tibet.

Nevertheless, America was becoming *more* interested in the Tibetan question. Now that Mao was at the helm of a communist regime, the Tibetans might be used as an anti-communist force in Asia. The State Department decided to put out feelers. It requested Loy Henderson, the American ambassador in India, to ask Nehru what he thought about the United States sending a mission to Tibet. According to Henderson, Nehru immediately objected. "It would do more harm than good . . ." was the Prime Minister's reply.[12]

---

[11]FO 371-76314.
[12]USFR, 793B.02/1-2050, report of discussion with K. P. S. Menon, cited in a telegram from Loy Henderson to the U.S. Secretary of State, dated January 20, 1950.

.   .   .

WHATEVER RAHULA'S CELESTIAL MESSAGE MAY HAVE BEEN, MAO saw his personal stars in positive alignment. His army was in great shape. The *Kuomintang* was exiled on an island, licking its wounds. Nehru was a pushover. Lhasa was controlled by a gaggle of superstitious bumbling old men. Their "leader" was barely potty-trained. Tibet's army—if you could call it that— was at most ten thousand troops with nineteenth-century weapons. If Mao wanted to occupy Tibet, who was to stop him?

MARCH 1950: THE PLA, WHICH HAD BEEN BUILDING UP TROOPS along the Tibetan border for months now, crossed into Kham.

Its first stop was the trading center of Dartsendo.[13]

For the last century, Dartsendo had been the clearinghouse for Chinese tea exported in great quantities to Tibet. Dartsendo was a town vibrant with a very mixed population. The architecture was dominated by a drab, utilitarian Chinese style, but many of the buildings still retained the flat roofs indicative of a Tibetan population. It was impossible to walk down the narrow streets without seeing lamas in their claret-colored robes, absentmindedly muttering mantras while examining wares displayed in shops. There were eight Tibetan monasteries nestled above the dramatic gorge, and the fiercely roiling Darchu River, which cut through the heart of the town. The roar of the cascading water dominated all sound. Mountains on both sides squeezed inward, and the town was necessarily narrow and cramped. Bridges spanned the Darchu at several points to serve the constantly floating population that, at any time, was around ten thousand people—a metropolis, by Tibetan standards.

Everyone had something to peddle to the Tibetan caravans moving through Dartsendo. The Tibetan craftsmen made their famous black-and-red boots with upturned toes, and all sorts of other leather products, including highly prized saddles, bridles, and harnesses studded with silver. Vividly colored saddle blankets and enormous Tibetan daggers were also on display, as

---

[13]Also known as "Tatsienlu," but renamed "Kanding" by the Chinese.

well as Buddhist statuary, bells, bowls, scepters, thankgha paintings, and a host of other items used in meditative practice. And everywhere, grown men were holding hands.[14]

Into this mix of cultures and crowded streets entered the PLA. No one objected. For many decades, the Chinese had controlled this trading center. Traffic in Dartsendo meant sales, not a military occupation. Whatever Mao's troops were doing, they hadn't come to stir up trouble. Nor did most of the troops stay for very long. They were heading north—just passing through.

The PLA marches through the main street of Dartsendo. *(Collection of George N. Patterson)*

By the middle of April, over thirty thousand troops had gone through town. They were an advance unit of Mao's Eighteenth Army. Mao's immediate goal (and the reason why the locals weren't unduly alarmed) was to build a serviceable road north to Kanze—the next big trading center north—while getting Chinese troops acquainted with the rigors of Tibetan topography. According to author Lowell Thomas Jr., "More than 10,000 [Tibetan] laborers were working day and night to improve the roads. Bridge steel was being moved in barges up-river from Shanghai. Special troops were being acclimatized by months-long training periods at high altitudes where they also learned to subsist on *tsampa*, the barley-flour staple of Tibet."[15]

The amassing of troops included long columns of American- and Russian-built trucks.

---

[14]William Woodville Rockhill, *Land of the Lamas*, 252. Tibetans made use of a sign language concealed by the very long sleeves of their *chubas*. The buyer and seller would grasp each other's hand and communicate by secret finger count. Rockhill concludes: "And so, with many knowing winks, shakes of the head, and remarks to bystanders, the trade goes on till finally they come to an agreement."
[15]Lowell Thomas Jr., *The Silent War in Tibet*, 80.

By August 1950, a motorable road from Dartsendo to Kanze was completed—a remarkable feat, given the difficult terrain. The Tibetans, whose trade would be boosted by the road, were more appreciative than apprehensive.

The PLA's next stop was Kanze, a major commercial hub with none of the claustrophobic feeling of Dartsendo.

The town overlooked a vast and fertile plain dotted with subsidiary villages and monasteries—the largest of which housed over a thousand monks. It was a picturesque place decorated with long *mani* walls,[16] one length of a football field and eight feet tall. The town itself was made up of a warren of alleys and staircases that worked their way up to the vast monastery, which offered a bird's-eye view of the most important center in the Nyarong District—an exceptionally affluent precinct, highly populated and long familiar with Chinese infiltration. The Chinese who lived there, some for several generations—there were over two hundred at the time—were mostly traders. But they also owned the mule-operated gristmills that ground the local wheat. As for Tibetan trade, locals dealt mostly in musk, yak hides, wool, furs, and gold dust. There was even some intermarriage between the two peoples. The Kanze men distinguished themselves with their long black flowing hair ornamented with oversized agate stones. As for the women, everyone agreed that they were some of the most beautiful in Tibet.

Aten, a native of Kanze and a highly successful opium dealer to the Nationalist Chinese, witnessed the entrance of the first communist divisions. (It should be noted that, in 1949, selling drugs carried none of the stigma attached by the twenty-first century. Since the only drug peddled in Kanze was opium, and Aten's only clients were Chinese, and since the drug seemed to have a soporific effect on these foreigners, Tibetans of that time condoned Aten's contribution to local society.)

To us Tibetans it made no difference. Chinese armies of many regimes had come and gone through our land. All of them had been brutal and tyrannical, yet thankfully indifferent, inefficient, and corrupt. Of course, we expected some changes in the beginning, but then the Reds would settle down, reveal their all too human weaknesses, and leave us Tibetans alone. They were Chinese after all.

---

[16]Walls built by the community; each rock had carved, or painted on its surface, the mantra "*Om Mani Padme Hung*," thus the name *mani*. "*Om Mani Padme Hung*" means "Hail to the Jewel in the Lotus," a reference to the patron saint of Tibet, Chenrezig. (See chapter 3.)

The first Red soldiers entered Kanze on the night of the second moon in 1950. . . . I was not too impressed. Most of the soldiers were dressed in shabby rags and armed with a motley collection of fire-arms, which despite their diverse origins were relatively modern. Yet what the Communist Army lacked in quality, they seemed to make up for in size. For a week the long columns never ended. I soon discovered the errors of my initial assessment. The Red soldiers were extremely well disciplined. They were the first Chinese soldiers I had ever seen, that did not loot and bully the populace. Instead, the soldiers were courteous to the extreme, and even went out of their way to help the local people with their harvests and other chores. It was a pleasant novelty.[17]

The communists established their Kanze headquarters in an ancient Tibetan fortress called the Castle of the Female Dragon. Aten was summoned to the castle, along with other chieftains and local dignitaries from the Nyarong District to meet the new Chinese military governor.

On this first meeting, he did not talk too much about Marxist theories. Instead he told us what we knew too well, that the "Nationalist Bandit Regime" was rotten, parasitical and finished forever. He repeatedly stressed that the only thing the Communist government wanted was to better the conditions of the ordinary man and remove the vices of the past. He made it clear it was now the rule of the people themselves and that we the local leaders were to play the most important role in the regeneration of our society. We dutifully nodded our heads and murmured our assents.[18]

JYEKUNDO, DRAWUPON'S HOMETOWN, WAS ALSO BEING INTRO-duced to the "new" Chinese, only this time the PLA established a large base below town:

At first, the PLA worked hard to promote good feelings among the tribes of Jyekundo. They did everything in their power to give the impression that they were not interested in taking over our district. Since my father was District Administrator, I naturally met all of their leaders. Initially, they were so respect-

---

[17]Jamyang Norbu, *Horseman in the Snow,* 68–69.
[18]Ibid.

1950: Khampas have their first taste of communist indoctrination. *(Collection of Robert Ford)*

ful of my father . . . they publicly supported the monasteries and assured my father that he would retain his position of power.

The few Chinese residents in Jyekundo were mostly trading agents of the Dartsendo tea companies. Although they had paid homage to the Kuomintang, *they quickly switched their allegiance to the communists, who seemed to accept them, no questions asked. We all profited from the influx of army personnel— they bought everything we had, and at fair prices, too. And they were very respectful of our women, which made us feel less wary of their presence.*[19]

Historically, the position of women in Tibet was unique among Asian countries. They could own property and were very often the boss of domestic issues. Women kept most of the Tibetan shops. There was no separation

---

[19]Drawupon, interview with the author.

of boys and girls in childhood. Being brought up with males, girls played rough and learned the value of being physically strong. Buddhism also played an elevating role in the position of women. Buddha had allowed women (against the protestations of many of his followers) to be admitted into the religious order. And, perhaps most significant, women were known to have held control over entire principalities—particularly if a chief died young and his widow showed the necessary vigor and intelligence to take up the reins of power. Polygamy and polyandry were accepted customs, and Robert Ford explains the practicality therein: "Polygamy was obvious, for a quarter of the males were monks. Polyandry was usually a matter of keeping a family estate in one piece. A woman could be required to marry all her husband's younger brothers. No complications about paternity arose from such unions, as the offspring were the legal children of the first husband, his brothers being only uncles. It was for reasons of inheritance, too, that in polygamous unions the wives were often sisters."[20]

It followed that, unless one were a nun, it was unconventional for a woman to be celibate. Still, a great deal of decorum was observed between the sexes. Women's apparel completely concealed their figures and was much less provocative than in Western cultures. Public displays of affection were admonished. And a foreign army in their backyard put women in an even more reserved disposition.

Drawupon continues:

Even my aunt said that the communists were different than the other Chinese who had come through Jyekundo. She said she felt completely safe around them.

I remember watching Chinese soldiers go down to the river to help the village people pan for gold—standing in the shallows alongside our men and women, laughing in a friendly way. Completely peaceful. People wanted to believe that the Chinese respected us and weren't in Tibet to harm us or take away our way of life.

My father didn't trust them, though. Not even from the first. He made nice to them but he didn't trust them for a second. He told me to keep my ears open and my mouth shut. It was the number of PLA troops that bothered my father— always getting bigger and bigger. Why were so many troops necessary to "help"

---

[20]Robert Ford, *Captured in Tibet*, 70.

us? he would ask me, like he was thinking out loud. And the way they bowed to the lamas—that really turned my father's stomach. It's fake, he told me, don't believe them.[21]

The communists had good reason to adopt a policy of appeasement. This was not Mainland China, where the downtrodden could easily be induced to "cast away their chains." Besides, the *Kuomintang* had done a good job of educating Eastern Tibetans of the antireligious ideology of the Reds. Mao knew he had his work cut out for him. So the PLA marched into the border towns with great smiling faces and gifts for the lamas.

ONE DAY IN JUNE 1950, THE PLA SMILE DROPPED FOR A MOMENT. Halfway between Jyekundo and Kanze, right off the caravan trade route, was a small but strategically located Tibetan military outpost called Dengko. The PLA picked up radio signals coming from the little town. This alarmed the Chinese. At that time, the number of radios in Tibetan hands was less than ten.[22] The Chinese didn't know that, but even if they did, it would have been ten radios too many. Tibet's lack of communication within the country and without was one of Mao's greatest assets.

The Chinese sent a probe of several hundred troops into the outpost. They knew they might draw fire, but it was worth the risk. Indeed, perhaps forcing resistance out into the open was the point of their maneuver. They may very well have been testing the waters to see what kind of military power really awaited them. The probe crossed the Drichu and, without much resistance, seized the transmitter and a radio operator, and took over the town.

Tibetans were killed, however. Retribution was inevitable. Two weeks later, a wealthy Khampa by the name of Muja Dapon, one of the early heroes of the Tibetan resistance, led a group of eight hundred locals—including three hundred armed monks—back to Dengko and attacked with a fury. It caught the PLA off guard. Muja Dapon gave orders to take no prisoners. His men slaughtered to a man the six hundred Chinese troops.

---

[21]Drawupon, interview with the author.
[22]Robert Ford, *Capture in Tibet*, 44.

Curiously, the Chinese did not respond, nor did the Tibetans stop to wonder why. The Tibetans simply gloated about having cowered their newest enemy: It was a tremendous morale booster, teaching these newfangled communists a lesson.

To Mao and his generals, PLA troops were easily expendable. In truth, the Chinese had attained precisely what they were after: a Tibetan radio operator who would provide them with crucial intelligence, and precise knowledge of how much manpower would be required to take over the town permanently—when the time was right. In the meantime, let the locals think they had the upper hand. It was all part of the generals' plan.

NO ONE IN THE WEST KNEW ANYTHING ABOUT CHINA'S PRELIMI-nary strike in Tibet and, in any case, they had more important things to worry about.

On June 25, 1950, North Korean forces crossed the 38th parallel. That would divert the world's attention for the next several years, precluding any great interest in Chinese military buildup along the Tibetan border. Indirectly, however, the Tibetans were helped by the Korean conflict. The Korean War forced Americans, in particular, to fine-tune their foreign policy on the spread of communism: From that point on, communism would have to be contained *wherever* it might appear. Eisenhower's State Department resolved to keep at least one eye trained on the Tibetan situation—even if the intelligence wasn't that reliable.

Ironically, as limited as the intelligence was, Washington had a better sense of what was going on in Eastern Tibet than most Tibetans. This was no more evident than in the town of Riwoche (rhymes with *repoussé*)—a one-day pony ride east of Cyclone's hometown, Gochen.

Riwoche was situated on the Upper Dzachu River, a three-day ride west of Derge and a two-day ride south of Dengko. It was well kept and prosperous, with a population of five hundred. Riwoche's monastery was one of the largest in Kham—over two thousand monks lived in the surrounding compound just north of town.

For the Chinese army, however, Riwoche was strategically important. It was on the major trade route connecting central Kham to Lhasa. If the communist army could secure Riwoche, the surrounding Khampa districts would be robbed of an escape route west to the nation's capital.

No one in Riwoche had any idea their village was so desirous from a military standpoint. Cyclone, for instance, who was by this time a novice monk living at the large monastery, remembers nothing about the threat of an attack:

We heard stories about the communists but it all seemed very very far away. I was far more interested in studying with my lamas and making my parents proud of me. For me, the world was about Guru Rinpoche and Buddha's Twelve Interdependent Coordinations and the beautiful mountain pastures of summer.[23]

The communists had no intention of taking the town just yet but, like Dengko and all the other negligible barriers in their way, all of Kham would be theirs by winter.

IN THE MEANTIME, WITHOUT THE INTRUSION OF THE INTERNAtional press hampering their progress, and without faraway Lhasa having any kind of firm understanding of the situation to the east, the PLA troops just kept flowing into Tibet. Not only did they move in from the north and south, but they also penetrated west from Dartsendo—in a straight line toward Lithang—home of Athar, Wangdu, Kalsang, and Gompo Tashi.

Athar remembers that summer—both before and after the PLA arrived:

It never took much effort to talk Khampas into pitching a tent and having a picnic, but the Midsummer Festival was looked forward to and attended by everyone in Lithang.

The high lamas from the monastery occupied the biggest tent, and many ceremonies were held inside it. But every family had a tent pitched on the meadow that sloped below Lithang Monastery. The rich families had white tents; the poorest families had black yak-hair tents . . . it didn't matter. Nomads, monks, rich, poor—everyone mixed with everyone else on these occasions. When I walked down the rows between tents, people would come out and invite me

---

[23]Cyclone, interview with the author.

inside to have tea and cakes—even if they didn't know me. It was like that back then. Hospitality was very important.

Many beautiful girls. Dances out on the open plain. There were song contests between the young men and women. The songs could be very bawdy and everyone laughed. There were horse parades, each young buck trying to outdo the other by decorating themselves and their horses with silver and bright-colored decorations and rich furs. There were lots of horse races and trick-riding contests. My favorite was a full gallop contest where each young guy had to swing low on his pony and grab khatas off the ground. The evenings were warm. We drank lots of chang. We flirted with the girls. There were giant piles of juniper set on fire. This was the best time of the year for a young man. The celebrations lasted for weeks.

The PLA came halfway through the celebrations.

There must have been five hundred of them on the first day. Sobering, I can tell you, to see them march over the rise. But after the first shock, things settled down a bit. For one thing, they were very careful to keep their distance. They set up camp some distance from all of our tents and only a few of them walked over to the tent city. They knew what was and was not appropriate in Tibet.

The first place they approached was the high lamas' big tent. They paid their respect with khatas and money and many blocks of tea bound in rawhide— the highest quality tea—all of this was given to the high lamas. Their generosity was met with appreciation. Everyone relaxed. The festival continued as usual, the troops gradually joined the celebrations, but they didn't get drunk or rowdy They were very respectful. And they gave silver dollars freely! It was our first taste of communism, and it was a big improvement over the Nationalist Chinese. The communists only wanted to be nice to us, they kept saying. We were their brothers.

One of their initial tactics that worked especially well that summer was to supply the locals—rich and poor—with modern medicine. They set up a Chinese medical unit outside of town and no one was turned away. They didn't wear us down with propaganda—not like they would later. They told us, "We are coming to your country to develop it, that is all. After a couple of years, we will go back to China." They gave so many big presents to the monasteries that year! But they also spent a lot of time winning over the poorest people and the *laziest good-for-nothings. They told them, "You get to be free and all of you poor people will be the leaders in your country." They gave them food, clothes, silver coins, everything you can imagine. They were very clever. All of their smiles and gifts put us to sleep, like King Gesar.*[24]

In Tibetan lore, the black-necked crane is held dear as supernatural. Depictions of these magnificent aviators—said to migrate over the tallest peaks of the Himalaya—are often featured in the murals of temple walls. The bird also figures in the tale of King Gesar, the warrior king, as told by Cyclone:

It came to pass that a beautiful queen in a faraway land seduced King Gesar. Her magic induced a state of forgetfulness in Gesar so that she could keep him her unwitting and pacified paramour. Nine years passed. Gesar's kingdom had fallen into evil hands. His noble followers, however, had never given up trying to find him. Finally, they employed the skill of a black-necked crane. They fed it a magic potion and sent it in search of their beloved king. After flying far and wide, the bird spotted Gesar sleeping in the foreign queen's courtyard. He was flat on his back with his mouth wide open. The crane swooped down and shat in Gesar's mouth, King Gesar swallowed the potion, and was thereby cured of the queen-induced amnesia.[25]

A black-necked crane flying over 1950 Tibet could have seen what the mapless Tibetans could not: Jyekundo, Kanze, Dengko, Derge, Lithang filled with the newly arrived PLA, who were silently, peacefully carrying out a classic outflanking movement—giant talons poised and ready to snap shut.

The PLA's ultimate and most important target was Chamdo, Kham's capital. Chamdo served as Lhasa's main garrison and Army Headquarters for Eastern Tibet. For such an important town, Chamdo didn't look like much. It was downright ugly. A rarity in Kham, its environs had been deforested, with all the resultant signs of despondence and erosion. Cocked at an incline, it was surrounded on three sides by two major waterways—the Gnomchu River to its west and the Dzachu River to its east—and the frothy confluence at the lower edge of town marked the headwaters of the Mekong River.

---

[24]Athar, interview with the author.
[25]Cyclone, conversation with the author.

Crowding this little wedge of land were five thousand inhabitants, two thousand of whom were monks residing on top of the northern prospect. Added to the local population was a sizable number of Lhasan officials, their wives and families. They were there to oversee the presence of three hundred troops from Lhasa.

A continual presence of Lhasan troops was also an unusual feature for a Khampa town. Since 1917, the Chamdoans (as opposed to most of the Eastern Tibetan natives) had paid taxes to Lhasa's Central Government, which, in turn, paid for the troops stationed there. And because the Khampas paid for the protection, politically, Lhasa could not afford to let the Chamdo people down. To do so was to risk losing the allegiance of the entire Khampa region, the most populated area in Tibet.

Yet from a strategic standpoint, it was a useless location to set up an Army Headquarters. Apart from doors at the bridges, Chamdo was basically indefensible. Even worse, if the communists outflanked Chamdo from the northeast by taking Riwoche—a far better site to have set up defenses in the first place—the Tibetan Army would be cut off from its lifeline to Lhasa.

No one was more aware of Chamdo's shortcomings than the Governor of Kham, a Lhasan aristocrat by the name of Lhalu Shape.

Lhalu was just completing his three-year term of duty in Chamdo. He had proven to be an able administrator and had done what he could—given the vulnerability of Chamdo—to shore up its defenses in light of reports coming in from the east of the influx of Chinese troops. He had also recruited and trained local men to augment his Lhasan troops. Should Chamdo be attacked by the PLA, Lhalu was determined to fight to the end. Unlike many of the deeply conservative Lhasan aristocrats who argued for good relations with the Chinese at all costs, Lhalu clearly saw the communists as the enemy. He also knew that if he failed in his defense of Chamdo, the *Kashag* could and probably would come down on him very hard—just as they had punished his father years before.

It was Lhalu Shape's father, Lungshar, who, along with his wife, had escorted four boys to England during the Thirteenth Dalai Lama's brief flirtation with modernization. (Lhalu was fond of saying that he was the only man in Tibet who had been conceived in England.) When Lungshar and his pregnant wife returned to Tibet, he was convinced that Tibet must be radically reformed, both militarily and politically. The most unpopular of his reforms were the confiscation of aristocratic estates (which lacked proper documentation) and a dramatic raising of taxes on abbots and other monastics who enjoyed great wealth. For several years, his innovations seemed to be taking root. Eventually, however, Lungshar's progressive ideas backfired on him. At the insistence of the Head Abbots of the three main monasteries, the *Kashag* held a special tribunal of cooked-up charges and found Lungshar guilty of undermining the government. In an attempt to alert other officials to think twice before advocating reform, the *Kashag* confiscated Lungshar's estates and blinded him—a punishment that hadn't been used in Lhasa for decades.[26]

The official method of blinding was to place yak knucklebones against the victim's temples. Leather thongs were wrapped around Lungshar's head with a stick on top. The *ragyaba*—the men who performed the mutilation—then slowly turned the stick, which tightened the thongs, which pushed in the knucklebones until the eyeballs popped out. Unfortunately for Lungshar, the *ragyaba* bungled the procedure. Only one eyeball popped out. A knife was produced and the *ragyaba* scooped out the other eyeball with the sharp tip of the blade.[27]

Lhalu Shape was a young teenager when his father was blinded for his progressive politics. Though he seldom mentioned the horrible event, the lesson of treading carefully when it came to the policies of the Central Government could hardly have been lost on him.

As Governor of Kham, Lhalu seemed resigned to the fact that the Central Government's reactionary policies were catching up with it, and that it was only a matter of time before the PLA stormed Chamdo. But Lhalu was a patriot, and his plan of defense made the best of a futile situation: He would hold Chamdo as long as possible, and when it was overcome, he would order the troops to fall back to the more defensible mountain passes just west of Riwoche.

Then something truly astounding happened at the end of August. Lhalu's three-year term of governorship was technically over, so in spite of the fact

---

[26]Melvyn Goldstein, *History of Modern Tibet, 1913–1951*, 162–63.
[27]Ibid.

that the Chinese almost certainly would
attack before winter—Lhasa called Lhalu
Shape back to the capital, to be replaced by
a new Governor.

The timing was bad, but the aristocrat
selected by the *Kashag* to replace Lhalu
would prove to be an even greater
calamity.

Ngabo Jigme Norbu, the new Governor, was tall, elegant, and outwardly
benign. He was not a military man, however, and few were reassured when he
boasted that defending Chamdo was his
number-one priority. Besides, Ngabo had
been Governor of Kham once before,
without winning Chamdoan hearts. He
was formal in the extreme—something
that did not sit well with the rugged spon-
taneity of the Khampas.

Now that he was back, instead of digging into the business at hand, he squan-
dered all of September throwing and
attending reception parties.

Ngabo Jigme Norbu *(Office of Information and International Relations,
Dharamsala)*

Ngabo's lineage was also worrisome to
the locals: Although his mother hailed from one of the preeminent families
of Tibet, she was a nun, and Ngabo was a bastard. In ordinary circumstances,
this might not have been held up to too much scrutiny, but when national
security was concerned, the circumstances of Ngabo's birth flew in the face of
a well-known proverb: "When the throne of Tibet is guarded by a person of
lower birth, then Tibet will be invaded by China."[28]

Robert Ford gives the best firsthand account of Ngabo's actions during
that fatal autumn. Ford held the dubious distinction of being one of the eight
"imperialists" residing in Tibet at the time. He had come to Tibet in 1948,

[28]Shakya, *The Dragon in the Land of Snows*, 15.

hired by the Central Government to build and operate Radio Lhasa. Once the station was up and running, he had been transferred to operate a radio in Chamdo so that Lhasa could be kept informed of events on the eastern front. Previously, communication between Lhasa and Chamdo had been conducted on horseback—a sixty-day ride. Even the *Kashag* had to admit that a radio was one instance in which modernization was a good thing, although what they were really prepared to do to defend Eastern Tibet remained unclear. Historically, the Khampas, Amdoans, and Goloks fended for themselves. The Lhasan leaders' main priority had and always would be to protect their own estates, most of which were situated in Central Tibet.

It wasn't long before Ford began to question Ngabo's sense of duty. Ford stood by in disbelief, for instance, when Ngabo, in late September, had many of Lhalu Shape's defensive measures torn down. These, Ngabo calmly explained, would be considered provocative by Chinese forces. Why should Ngabo care *what* the Chinese thought, Ford wanted to ask. Ford held his tongue but, from then on, he feared Ngabo had no intention of defending Chamdo, should it come to that.

And it would.

ON OCTOBER 7, 1950, CHINA ATTACKED EASTERN TIBET.

Simultaneously, from three directions, forty thousand PLA troops thundered west. In the south, they moved north and west from Lithang. In the north, they charged up and over the western banks of the Drichu River. Their plan was simple: overwhelm any Tibetan resistance by sheer number and speed. Their main target: Chamdo, just as Lhalu had predicted. Secondary target: Riwoche, which would prevent Tibetan troops from capitulating to Lhasa.

Riveted by the unfolding Korean conflict, the rest of the world took little or no notice.

The Chinese, who had already secured the towns of Jyekundo, Derge, Kanze, and Lithang in the name of improving local living standards, now plowed over other Tibetan strongholds—if you could call them that. The Central Tibetan Army troops stationed in Kham numbered in the mere hundreds.

Only Dengko remained firmly in the hands of Tibetan soldiers, mostly

Khampas led by the hero Muja Dapon, who had routed the PLA probe ear-lier in June. In fact, Muja Dapon was able to push the Chinese back across the Drichu, inflicting heavy losses in the process.

Incredibly, the news of the PLA invasion did not reach Ngabo until five days *after* the fact, because a new radio had never been installed after the PLA had initially captured Dengko, although Ngabo had an extra radio in Chamdo and could have sent it to the eastern frontier had he been so disposed. When the news of the invasion did arrive in Chamdo, Ngabo put the river town on alert. Ford rushed down from his radio outpost, which was at the top of the hill next to the monastery, to consult with Ngabo. He knew that Ngabo was hoarding an extra radio and very much wanted it to be rushed north to Riwoche. Ford knew it was crucial that Chamdo be kept advised of news coming in from that junction. Ngabo, composed as ever, refused. Ford recounts the moment in his book *Captured in Tibet*:

Ngabo asked Ford:

"'You are afraid we shall be cut off in Chamdo?'

"'It seems possible that the Chinese will try to cut the Lhasa route.'

"Ngabo nodded.

"'I know the possibility. That is why Riwoche has been reinforced. It is now very strongly held, and there is no sign of activity in that area. I want to keep the spare radio station here in case anything should go wrong with the other one . . . Do not worry . . . We shall win. The gods are on our side.'"

"If they were not it could hardly be for lack of being asked. By the time I returned to the radio station a thin plume of smoke was already rising from the incense-burner on the roof of the monastery, and spiritual activity was being intensified everywhere. People left their work to go round the Holy Walk, turn-ing prayer wheels and counting beads . . . I saw about twenty monks carrying brushwood down the hill. It was unusual to see them carrying anything heavi-er than a rosary, but they had not far to go. A clearing had been made by the river, and here the monks piled up the brushwood in the shape of a pyramid.

"Then the procession came down from the monastery, and I heard the first shots fired since the war began. There were about a hundred monks, including the abbot, in the procession. They came down chanting, while a monk band in the procession played independently: wailing clarinets, clashing cymbals, and booming drums, and the piercing high notes of the conch shells, which were believed to be especially effective in scaring off the devils. Every now and then Khambas flanking the procession drowned the other noises by firing their rifles.

"They were old muzzle-loaders, such as I had seen in the Imperial War Museum. When they were fired[,] flames and smoke shot out of the muzzles, and the recoil spun the Khambas round like prayer-wheels. They made a deep booming sound, which echoed round the mountains for several seconds.

"The procession reached the bottom of the hill. Some of the monks were burning incense, and others carried fearsome-looking images made of coloured butter. These were the devils. They walked to the open space by the river, and already a crowd had come to watch. . . . There was a brief silence as the abbot invoked the gods, and then the bonfire was lighted: more chanting, more music, more gunfire—and then the whole lot together, with every one shouting and yelling at the tops of their voices, as the images were thrown on the burning wood. The noise was deafening as the flames leapt up and burnt the cast-out devils."[29]

Ford made a reconnaissance of what Ngabo's troops were doing. There were about three hundred of them—no more—available for the defense of Chamdo. The troops separated into several groups, some guarding the bridges and some manning Bren guns behind stone barricades at the top of the town. Then news came in that the village of Rangsum (to the north) and Bathang and Markham Gartok (to the south) had been lost. Ford remembers:

"There was now nearly a panic. Lhasa officials and rich Khambas began to send their valuables up to the monastery, and hired ponies and yaks came in from the surrounding villages" in preparation for an evacuation.[30] The shortage of transportation soon became apparent—yet another example of the travesty created by Ngabo's cavalier attitude. Although he had horses enough for his personal escape, he had failed to make transportation available for his underlings, his troops, and his troops' families, who had moved to Chamdo along with their men.

Ngabo had done one thing: He had radioed the *Kashag* about the invasion. Three times, in fact. But there was no immediate response from Lhasa.

---

[29]Robert Ford, *Captured in Tibet*, 110.
[30]Ibid.

It happened that there was a five-day picnic going on in Lhasa, which all the senior officials were attending. Apparently—astoundingly—a communist invasion of Eastern Tibet couldn't dampen the festivities. The *Kashag* did not respond to Ngabo's coded message.

Perhaps even more astounding, Lhasa made no mention of the invasion in any of its radio communications to India or to other radio posts in Tibet, presumably because the *Kashag* was more concerned about avoiding a Tibetan panic than alerting the international community of its plight. Given the Tibetan Government's centuries-old isolation from the rest of the world, it could be argued that they retreated into a kind of group denial: As long as the communists didn't extend their invasion into Central Tibet, why should the aristocratic and monastic leaders be overly concerned about their brothers in Eastern Tibet? But it can also be argued that it was more a matter of cowardice: While ardently wanting help from the outside world, the *Kashag* was even more afraid that, if the Chinese found out Lhasa was seeking outside help, Mao might use it as an excuse to rush in and crush the Lhasan Central Government. One way or another, Lhasan self-interest was a major component to the silence.

Meanwhile, there was a small Tibetan delegation in India at that time, putting out feelers to Britain, America, and India as to what support they might expect from the international community should the PLA invade Tibet. When Indian reporters asked the group about rumors of a communist invasion having already taken place in Eastern Tibet, the Tibetan dignitaries flatly denied it. Given the *Kashag*'s unfathomably myopic preoccupation with their picnic holiday, it seems likely that the Tibetans in India had simply not been informed, in spite of their reason for being in India.

In effect, by remaining silent, the Tibet government had given the PLA carte blanche to proceed with the invasion. The communists had every right to feel confident that there would be no international consequences.

Ford later wrote that the inertia "of the Lhasa Government would have been easier to understand if it had intended to offer only a token resistance to the Chinese and then sue for peace, but it was not doing anything of the kind. The resistance was real, and Tibet's subsequent appeal to the United Nations showed that there was never any question of surrender. I could only think it was a matter of habit. The Lhasa Government was so used to the policy of saying nothing that might offend or provoke the Chinese that it kept it on after provocation had become irrelevant. *It was still trying to avert a war that had already broken out.*"[31]

In the meantime, the silence from Lhasa eroded Ngabo's composure. Frantic, he sent a final message to the *Kashag*:

CHAMDO TO LHASA: Look we have sent three urgent messages and haven't received a single reply. What is going on? As far as we are concerned we see ourselves as virtually caught and every second is important to us. If you don't give us a reply we don't know what to do.

LHASA TO CHAMDO: Right now it is the period of the Kashag's picnic and they are all participating in this. Your telegrams are being decoded and then we will send you a reply.

CHAMDO TO LHASA: Shit on their picnic! Though we are blocked here, and the nation is threatened and every minute may make a difference to our fate, you talk about that shit picnic.[32]

Did Ngabo finally regret not having sent the wireless to Riwoche? Certainly, he was left in the dark as to the situation to the north—his only escape route. His meager intelligence was this: from the east, the PLA were one day away from Chamdo, from the north, Riwoche had not yet been overrun. Getting to Riwoche before the PLA was his only chance. Ngabo unraveled. He radioed the *Kashag* for permission to vacate Chamdo and leave the locals to whatever fate awaited them.

This time, the *Kashag* replied almost immediately:

Permission denied—stay and fight.

MEANWHILE, FROM THE ROOFTOP OF RIWOCHE MONASTERY, Cyclone watched the PLA funnel down the valley. He and his fellow monks had never seen Chinese soldiers before. The troops all wore khaki uniforms

---

[31]Ibid., 115. Author's italics.
[32]Maya, former lay official under Ngabo in Chamdo, from an interview conducted in India by Melvyn Goldstein, *A History of Modern Tibet, 1913–1951*, 690.

and marched in tight
formation, their steps
crisp and in unison.
There were bright red
stars on their odd-
looking hats. Their ri-
fles were different from
the arms used by
Khampas. They looked
determined but not un-
friendly.

We were so surprised.
They were just suddenly
there. There was some
resistance for an hour or
two—minor skirmishes
that were quickly won by
the Chinese. I remember
one old Khampa who

1950: The PLA moving south from Riwoche along the
Dzachu River toward Chamdo. *(Collection of the author)*

refused to give up: When he was captured, he was executed on the spot. But that
was about all. There were so few Tibetan soldiers supplied by the Central Gov-
ernment stationed in Riwoche. What could they have done against the thou-
sands of PLA? So there was no battle at Riwoche or anything like that. They
didn't bother the monastery. In fact, most of them didn't stay in Riwoche at all.
We didn't know where they were going or what their plans were. They just came
in like a swarm of locusts from the north, then moved on—south toward
Chamdo.[33]

Because Ngabo hadn't sent a radio to Riwoche, he was ignorant of the latest developments to the north. Any news he would receive from now on
would be by courier, at least a day old by the time it arrived. Still, he placated
the Chamdoans by promising them that, should the communists get as far as
Chamdo, he would fight until the end.

---

[33]Cyclone, interview with the author.

In fact, he was planning to sneak away in the middle of that very night, before the communists got any closer—in spite of what the *Kashag* had ordered him to do.

Author John Avedon describes what happened next. While the rest of Chamdo was sleeping, Ngabo "packed his belongings, took off the long gold and turquoise pendant earring hanging from his left ear [indicative of his high Lhasan office], changed his yellow silk robes for the plain gray serge of a junior official and decamped in the middle of the night. With the discovery, soon after dawn on October 17, that the Governor had fled, Chamdo erupted in panic. Ngabo had neglected to secure transport from nearby villages so that his troops could undertake an orderly retreat. He had, therefore, simply abandoned them, not even bothering to divvy out the existing animals with his own bodyguard. His sole order, issued to one of the garrison's two colonels, was to destroy the ammunition dump—shells and cartridges of inestimable value to the Khampas, who were compelled to remain and defend their homes. As a result, while great explosions rent the air and officials from Lhasa, their army and families fled the city on foot, Khampa tribesmen went on a rampage, looting and rioting, in a vain search for someone upon whom to vent their rage at betrayal."[34]

Ford, too, as a Lhasa employee, was suddenly in danger of being singled out by the infuriated Khampas. In great peril, he managed to follow Ngabo's escape route. He caught up with Ngabo and his entourage some eight hours later to the west, in the village of Lamda. Along the way, he passed by many of the troops whom Ngabo had betrayed. None of them had horses. According to Ford, ". . . some were accompanied by their wives and children. A few had yaks piled high with pots and pans and other household goods. Some of the women had babies strapped on their backs. . . . They looked tired and dispirited, but they had not entirely disintegrated as a force. N.C.O.s [noncommissioned officers] kept them together as far as possible, and some were even carrying Bren guns. They were not all from the Chamdo garrison: some belonged to Ngabo's bodyguard—he had not even provided transport for them."[35]

---

[34]John F. Avedon, *In Exile from the Land of Snows*, 32.
[35]Ford, *Captured in Tibet*, 127.

When Ford overtook Ngabo at a resting spot, he hardly recognized the governor, especially in his junior official disguise:

". . . he looked frightened and miserable. But he still sat on a higher cushion than anyone else, and we had to go through the formality of paying our respects . . .

"'Have you brought the radio?' he asked.

"I fought down a sudden upsurge of anger.

"'No, Your Excellency,' I said. 'The transport you ordered for it did not arrive.'"[36]

If Ngabo recognized the sarcasm in Ford's voice, he had no observable reaction.

Ngabo's immediate concern was keeping ahead of the Chinese—wherever they were—no one in his group had a clue. Just as they readied to resume their retreat up over the high mountain pass of Lamda, a messenger bolted in with a letter. Ngabo's hands trembled as he read the bad news: the Chinese were just outside of Riwoche—news that was a day old.

The letter fell from his hands and he ordered the group to mount.

Ford calculated that they could still get to the all-important junction of Lho Dzong (a few miles west-southwest of Lamda) before the PLA arrived.

But just as the group started the ascent to the Lamda pass, another messenger arrived with the news that Riwoche had now fallen. This meant they would not escape to Lhasa without a fight.

Yet another runner from the north caught up with Ngabo. If the Governor of Kham had maintained any resemblance of composure, it was now completely lost. The courier informed him that the Chinese had a group of Khampas with them serving as guides. He had heard before that the PLA had recruited Khampas who felt no love for Central Government officials. Probably these Khampa guides had not yet heard of Ngabo's betrayal of the Chamdo people but, when they did, and if they caught Ngabo, he was unlikely to be taken prisoner—that was not the Khampa way.

The climb to the pass—a four-thousand-foot ascent—now became an act of survival. The sun was rapidly setting. Ngabo, Ford, and company arrived

---

[36]Ibid.

at the peak at ten o'clock that night. Their exhaustion was exacerbated by the lack of oxygen and the freezing winds. The descent was equally dangerous. The trail was vertiginously steep, narrow, and slippery.

Halfway down the peak, they unexpectedly met a large contingent of heavily armed Lhasan soldiers coming uphill. (Apparently, Lhasa had dispatched reinforcements for Chamdo several weeks before.) This changed the odds dramatically, at least in Ford's estimation. Even if Ngabo's group were now intercepted by PLA troops pushing down from the north, the Chinese contingent would only be an advanced patrol. With the additional gun and manpower of the fresh Lhasan troops, Ngabo's group fleeing west now had a good chance of fighting their way through to the open road to Lhasa.

Astoundingly, Ngabo trumped his previous acts of cowardice by ordering the fresh troops to ditch their weapons—just throw them over the cliff. His reasoning was that, should the PLA catch up with them, they would regard these additional troops as proof that the Tibetans wanted to engage in battle. Ngabo's rationale was so convoluted and bewildering that the Lhasan troops didn't know how to respond. One thing was certain: They could not disobey his orders. In a kind of dazed compliance, the men tossed their weapons— the very means with which they could have ensured a successful escape—into the abyss.

Yet another messenger rode in from a yak trail: The junction of Lho Dzong had now been cut off by a small group of advanced soldiers—not many, but they were definitely there. Ngabo wanted to know only one thing: Were the advance forces Chinese or Khampas?

The answer was: Khampas employed by the PLA.

Ford could almost see the chill go down Ngabo's back. Ngabo whispered to his secretaries, then turned around and announced his plan of action: Instead of continuing down the mountain and fighting the Khampas, he was going to seek refuge in a nearby monastery, which, he hoped, would keep him safe from the wrath of the wild warriors.

Ford couldn't believe Ngabo's cowardice. The group still had the entire garrison of Chamdo (Tibetan soldiers from Lhasa) by their side—not to mention the newly arrived troops from Lhasa. They could *still* fight their way through.

Ford remembers approaching Ngabo and making an appeal:

"'Your Excellency, is there not still a chance of escape? Their force may be very small.'

"He looked at me coldly.

"'You have my permission to do what you like. Escape if you can. The other officials will come with me.'"[37]

Realistically, there was no way that Robert Ford, a British national, could escape Tibet on his own. Ngabo knew that just as he knew that Ford would, out of necessity, follow the entourage wherever they went.

A few hours later they reached the monastery in question. It overlooked a breathtaking downward sweep of valleys. Just as the demoralized troops began setting up camp, in rode Muja Dapon. He had put up a courageous fight in Dengko but was finally overwhelmed by PLA troops, and forced to retreat. There were seventy men with Muja Dapon and another four hundred close behind. Muja Dapon was everything Ngabo was not. He was a brawny figure with a broad bloodstained sword and a Mauser pistol tucked in his belt. When Muja Dapon heard of Ngabo's retreat, he told Ford he had no intention of just waiting for the Chinese to come and run them down. He claimed that his troops, by themselves, could easily break through to Lho Dzong. A few renegade Khampas didn't scare him and he, like Ford, was certain that the Chinese had not had time to reach the cut-off road in any significant strength. He would persuade Ngabo to fight through the negligible enemy line.

A confident Muja Dapon strode into the monastery where Ngabo was hiding. One hour later, an entirely different Muja Dapon emerged from the door: Sullen and crestfallen, Muja Dapon ordered his men to make camp. Ngabo had ordered Muja Dapon to surrender to the PLA, once they arrived, with the rest of Ngabo's troops.

Muja Dapon's men followed his orders. Monks came out to help. Soldiers gathered firewood. Horses were fed. Yaks and mules were relieved of their heavy loads. The sun reached the apex of the sky, then descended westward, toward Lhasa. Babies cried for their mothers' breasts. The men monitored the slope below them, awaiting the arrival of the enemy.

---

[37]Ibid., 132.

And then, out of this bucolic setting—with a Tibetan sky that exploded into a paradisiacal sunset—one of the most surreal events ever recorded in military history took place.

Obeying Ngabo's orders, without any resistance, the Tibetans watched a much smaller contingent of Chinese soldiers surround the hill. The Chinese set up light mountain artillery and aimed it at the campground. The Tibetans did nothing. And when everything was in place, the PLA simply walked into the enemy camp—into an armed force twenty times their number. There was a bit of shuffling, of course—women herded the children, men clenched their jaws, but no one went for their weapons.

The Chinese had Khampa translators with them. They told the Tibetans they wouldn't be harmed. Where was Ngabo? they asked. The Tibetans stared hard at the ground. The Chinese officers whispered to each other and then shouldered their way into the monastery.

When Ngabo came out, he looked less frightened than he had been since leaving Chamdo. He was back to his old collected self. At his insistence, the troops handed over their guns to the enemy and then they bedded down for the night under a clear sky.

The next morning, more Chinese troops came in from the Chamdo trail. This contingent brought a newsreel camera with them. While the equipment was set up, the Tibetan troops were given back their weapons; then lined up and, with the camera running, laid down their rifles for the second time. They were ordered to sit. They sat. They were given cigarettes. They were told to smile. They smiled. "The Chinese," Ford remembers, "then turned the camera on me, standing between two soldiers armed with tommy-guns. Other films showed the monks welcoming the Chinese and Ngabo signing the surrender of all forces in Kham.

"Then one of the Chinese addressed the Tibetan troops . . . 'We bring you peace,' he said, and that caused much surprise. 'We have come to liberate you from the foreign devils. The Chinese and Tibetans are brothers. . . . We have been separated by the foreigners, who have sat on your necks and kept you apart from the motherland. You can tell these foreigners by their long noses and round blue eyes and light skins.' He looked significantly at me. 'The People's Liberation Army has come to throw them out and set you free.'

"He paused, and there was a buzz of conversation among the Tibetans. They were completely bewildered, for I was the only foreign devil most of them had ever seen. They could not imagine where all the other foreigners were that needed such a large army to turn them out."[38]

Rahula was gone from the sky, but the arrow drawn in his bow had been released, landing squarely in front of a rolling camera.

The first conflict between Tibetans and the PLA was over.

The war had lasted eleven days.

ACCUSED OF BEING A BRITISH SPY, OF PROMULGATING ANTI-communist propaganda, and of being a murderer, Ford was thrown into a Chinese prison for five years.

Meanwhile, Cyclone continued to memorize Buddhist texts while PLA troops slowly upgraded Riwoche into a first-rate army outpost.

Drawupon, Athar, the Prince of Derge, and the brothers Wangdu and Kalsang adapted to the influx of Chinese troops as best they could. They brushed their ponies, oiled their saddles, and sharpened their swords.

Ngabo was escorted back to Chamdo, where he became the communists' greatest Tibetan collaborator.

Gompo Tashi, who had been with one of his trade caravans during the brief war, didn't learn of the disaster until he returned to Lhasa. Shocked by the information, he organized a caravan of fresh yaks and headed it in the direction of India. The Indian black market had lots of arms and ammunition for sale, and Gompo Tashi was in the mood for buying.

The rest of the world—satisfied by the accounts given in Chinese newsreels—returned to more important events unfolding in Korea.

---

[38]Ibid.

Chenrezig (Avelokiteshvara), of whom the Dalai Lama is an emanation *(Jamyang of Amdo)*

3

SHOTGUN WEDDING

He was born very far away from Lhasa, in the northeastern section of Tibet called Amdo. He left Amdo when he was barely more than a toddler. How much did he really remember of that distant home? Since he was a young child, time enjoyed with his family was sporadic. He was cut off. Except for his next-older brother, he had no relationship with his peers. He had spent his brief life in the company of grown men—the most powerful men in the land. They prostrated themselves before him. The crowds, four hundred feet below his aerie, sobbed at the sight of his golden palanquin. They dared not look into his eyes.

He was the Fourteenth Dalai Lama, an emanation of Chenrezig, the Bodhisattva of Compassion, and he was sixteen years old.

He inherited Tibet from himself, from the thirteen previous Dalai Lamas who came before him and were he before him. He owned Tibet. He was Tibet.

What he knew of Tibet was what his underlings chose to tell him. He was too busy with his studies to travel and visit the country that he owned.

The teenaged Dalai Lama. *(Office of Information and International Relations, Dharamsala)*

His firsthand knowledge of his country was paltry: He'd visited the three great monasteries that perched above the outskirts of Lhasa, and the Norbulinka, his summer palace—and that was about it. The rest of his life had been here, inside the dark labyrinth of the thirteen-floor, thousand-room Potala Palace, a honeycomb of mysterious corridors.

He wandered through the central section of the palace, passing great halls, cold and airless, reserved for ceremonial occasions. He passed a series of thirty chapels. He approached the mausoleums of seven of his previous selves: here he meandered through his past lives. The crypts dwarfed him, twice as high as elephants. Among the statuary, shadows expanded and danced and darted behind the flickerings of a host of votives. Everywhere he looked, precious jewels and pink gold glimmered in the semidarkness. His world was bowed heads, not faces.

One hundred seventy-five monks lived in the warrens of the west wing. In the east wing were all the government offices, a school for robed officials, assembly halls for the *Tsongdu*[1]—the rustling of robes, the clatter of tea trays, the messengers, the whisperings, the incessant prostrations at his feet—colored by the ceremonial hustle and bustle, the earnest pursuit, the prayer-making dedicated to his well-being. The Potala was a city unto itself: office complex, temple complex, apartment complex, monastic college, storehouse, armory, state treasury, mausoleum, national library, and, at the far eastern end, a prison reserved strictly for aristocratic wrongdoers.

---

[1]The National Assembly, similar to a House of Parliament. The *Tsongdu*, however, was far less influential and powerful than the *Kashag*.

It was in these insular surroundings that the Dalai Lama came to know of the world around him, as best he could. The Dalai Lama was nothing if not curious. He was particularly interested in the affairs of the outside world but—because his teachers were lamas, not political science professors—much of his curiosity went unsatisfied. As the Dalai Lama recounts in his autobiography, *I know that I grew up with hardly any knowledge of worldly affairs, and it was in that state, when I was sixteen, that I was called upon to lead my country against the invasion of Communist China.*[2]

Until now, the Dalai Lama's Regent had acted as Head of State. It was a position that, in ordinary circumstances, he would have kept until the Dalai Lama reached his eighteenth birthday.

But these were not ordinary times.

Without the Dalai Lama's consent, the twentieth century had violated his medieval world and thrown his aristocratic minions into a panic. He was suddenly bathed in the harsh light of international politics. His advisors looked to him, a sixteen-year-old, for adult council. He understood that they were loath to make important decisions. Having remembered men like Lungshar, who had dared to take the reins and had suffered the consequences, the Dalai Lama's Cabinet, not surprisingly, shrank from the accountability of decision making. Who could guide him? He was armed with little more than an atlas of the world, an atlas that none of his mentors could adequately explain. But he was fourteen Dalai Lamas rolled into one—supposedly the ultimate armament against the great army of China—and now the Tibetan government expected him to take the helm of a ship that might be already sinking.

The Dalai Lama remembers, *This filled me with anxiety . . . I was far from having finished my religious education. I knew nothing about the world and had no experience of politics, and yet I was old enough to know how ignorant I was and how much I had still to learn. I protested at first. . . . Yet I understood very well why the oracles and lamas had caused the request to be made. The long years of Regency after the death of each Dalai Lama were an inevitable weakness in our system of government. . . . We had reached a state in which most people were anxious to avoid responsibility, rather than accept it. Yet now, under the threat of inva-*

---

[2]His Holiness the Dalai Lama, *My Land and My People*, 31.

sion, we were more in need of unity than ever before, and I, as Dalai Lama, was the only person whom everybody in the country would unanimously follow . . . So I accepted, with trepidation . . .[3]

THE DALAI LAMA WAS NOT THE ONLY MEMBER OF HIS FAMILY rocked by the communist invasion. His eldest brother, well into his twenties, was the first member of the holy family to see Mao Tse-tung's true intentions.

His given name was Thubten Jigme Norbu, but in those days, he was known by his clerical title, Taktser Rinpoche.

Taktser Rinpoche was Head Abbot of the most important monastery in Tibet's northeastern frontier, Kumbum. It was so close to the Chinese city of Sining that Kumbum had always had a significant Chinese presence, as well as an enclave of Muslims called Tungans. It was remote—there had never been vanguard troops posted there by the Lhasan government—but it was extremely important in the spiritual politics of Tibet. Kumbum was the birthplace of Tsongkapa, who, centuries before, had founded the Gelupa sect,[4] the sect from which all Dalai Lamas were chosen. As such, it was rich in subsidies. It housed three thousand monks. Its golden roofs and spires, its gorgeous paintings and statuary, its magnificent library, its well-kept green and red walls—all announced its superlative worth in the arcane infrastructure of the Tibetan lamaseries.

Nevertheless, it was still an enclave very much surrounded by China.

A new China.

Kumbum was one of the first monasteries to be inundated by the Red Army. The outward benevolence that the PLA would exhibit a year later in Kham was far less apparent here. And due to the monastary's remoteness, it would be a long time before Lhasa caught wind of the turmoil.

In 1949, the moment the PLA arrived at Kumbum, they had put Taktser Rinpoche under what was essentially house arrest. Communist cadres never

---

[3]Ibid., 62.
[4]Also called the "Yellow Hats," derived from the color of their ceremonial headgear, to distinguish them from the older sects' red hats.

left his side. The Red Army demanded that the locals turn in their firearms—a shocking and unthinkable idea for Amdoans and Khampas alike.

Soon after, the age-old fabric of monastic routine of Kumbum began to disintegrate. Then the communists burned down a nearby monastery. In fear of their lives, monks began to slip away in the middle of the night. The locals' initial dissatisfaction with being under the yoke of the PLA accelerated into chaos. Finally, several nearby monasteries revolted.

The communists struck back with a vengeance. In one monastery the Chinese mobbed the chapel halls, and desecrated its sacred treasures. What they could not carry away with them they threw over the rocky precipices into the gorge beneath. Several monastery buildings were burned to the ground.

As for Taktser Rinpoche, he was constantly interrogated and now forced to submit detailed reports of all the properties of the monastery and of the nobles. He was also asked searching questions about the rank, property, and activities of everyone he knew, which laid the groundwork for future communist persecution.

Finally he was brought before Mao's newly appointed communist Governor, who castigated him for his uncompromising belief in Buddhism. Taktser Rinpoche was no fool: He knew that he drew such intense negative attention because he was the brother of the spiritual leader of Tibet. As eldest brother to the Dalai Lama, he would be of inestimable political value, if he would succumb to the communists' demands.

After nearly a year of ineluctable bullying, to no avail, the new Chinese Governor made a proposal to Taktser Rinpoche: He should go to Lhasa and personally indoctrinate the Dalai Lama. If he succeeded in turning Lhasa into a puppet of the communist party, Taktser Rinpoche would be given untold power. In his autobiography, Takster Rinpoche remembers:

"What I had to listen to was so monstrous that I had difficulty in concealing my feelings. It was nothing less than a promise to make me Governor-General of Tibet if on my arrival in Lhasa I managed to persuade the Tibetan Government to welcome the entry of Chinese communist troops into Tibet as liberators, and to accept the Chinese People's Republic as an ally.

"At this point they even let me see quite clearly that if necessary they would regard fratricide as justifiable in the circumstances. . . . They even pointed out occasions on which people had actually committed such crimes 'in the interest of the cause' and had subsequently been rewarded with high office . . ."[5]

Surrounded by the enemy, Taktser Rinpoche saw no alternative but to pretend to comply. In this way he was allowed to make the three-month journey to Lhasa without a Chinese escort. The PLA invasion had gone no farther than Chamdo, so Lhasa and all of Central Tibet was still free of Chinese occupation.

The meeting between the two brothers took place on the top floor of the Potala. The Dalai Lama listened in silence. For the first time, the teenager understood the lengths to which the Chinese would go in order to secure a Marxist state.

Taktser saved the worst—the assassination plot—for last:

"Dared I take such terrible and blasphemous words into my mouth in the presence of the Dalai Lama? But seeing my hesitation my brother ordered me to continue and hold back nothing . . . When I had at last finished my story the Dalai Lama remained silent for a long time, sunk in thought. . . . With a movement of the hand as though to dismiss an evil spectre he indicated that I should rise. We looked into each other's eyes for a moment or two, and behind those thick lenses I saw nothing but sympathy, love and concern for me . . ."

"My brother thanked me warmly and then I left. . . .

"I walked down the stone steps of the Potala with a great feeling of relief . . .

"I was grateful when attendants helped me to mount my horse . . .

"I turned my head and looked back at the Potala towards the window of the room in which the young ruler of my country now sat thinking over the new anxieties that I had been instrumental in bringing to him."[6]

THE MEETINGS AND DEBATES OF THE KASHAG AND TSONGDU IN 1950 intensified. They no longer felt that Tibet was capable of dealing with the communists by themselves. Clearly, they needed outside assistance— even the staunchest isolationists could now see it.

[5]Thubten Jigme Norbu, *Tibet Is My Country*, 222.
[6]Ibid., 228.

The *Kashag* decided to send an appeal to the nascent United Nations, which, at that time, was located in Lake Success.[7] It was a bold move on the *Kashag*'s part: Until now, Tibet had been disdainful of the organization. The very able and intelligent Shakabpa, one of the few Tibetans who had a fundamental grasp of international politics, was assigned the task of posting the appeal from Kalimpong, India, just across the border.[8]

The appeal arrived at the United Nations on November 13, 1950, and the Secretary General's office—unclear as to whether or not Tibet had an international identity of its own—had no idea what to do with it. In the first place, the appeal arrived without a member nation of the United Nations as its sponsor—a prerequisite before it could be added to the agenda. In the second place, the appeal had originated from India, not Tibet. How could the United Nations be certain it was authentic? And in the third place, its origin seemed to be from a nongovernmental source. India and Great Britain, had they chosen to do so, could have clarified the nongovernmental origin of the appeal. They knew quite well that all official Tibetan messages were sent from Kalimpong, because of communications limitations in Tibet.[9]

Not wanting to make waves with Mao Tse-tung, neither India nor Britain chose to come forward with this crucial information.

The appeal was about to be dismissed when an unlikely source came to Tibet's defense: El Salvador. By sponsoring Tibet's appeal, the tiny country forced India and Great Britain to weigh, at this critical juncture, their own political interests against their historical and moral obligations to their old ally, Tibet.[10]

It also helped the Chinese to clarify the extent to which they could strong-arm their way into Tibet without outside objections. After the PLA coopted Ngabo and secured Chamdo, there was nothing, militarily, to stop them from continuing west and occupying Lhasa. Winter was setting in, so, logistically, given the altitudinous and snowbound terrain, it was ill-advised to resume an advance. But there was another reason their forty thousand troops did *not*

---

[7]While the headquarters was being erected in New York City, the center of operations, from 1946 to 1950, was in Lake Success, located in nearby Long Island.
[8]Within Tibet, there was no extant postal system equipped to handle foreign correspondence.
[9]Melvyn Goldstein, *A History of Modern Tibet, 1913–1951*, 712.
[10]Ibid., 714.

march to the capital: For propaganda purposes, they preferred to force the Tibetan government to the negotiating table. The only way the communist occupation could proceed without rocking the international boat was for the world press to perceive their presence as a "peaceful liberation." Their propaganda served them well.

INDIA FRETTED. WHEN NEHRU MADE INQUIRIES INTO CHINA'S IN-tentions, the Chinese simply told him what they knew he wanted to hear: that their presence was nonaggressive, philanthropic, and, above all, temporary. But as the months passed, the Chinese presence looked more and more like a permanent installation. When Nehru dared to voice his concerns, Beijing responded with blistering alacrity: ". . . the problem of Tibet is a domestic problem of the People's Republic of China and no foreign interference shall be tolerated."[11] Mao was telling Nehru to mind his own business, but he was also insinuating, on a personal level, that Nehru was Great Britain's and America's water boy: ". . . with regard to the viewpoint of the Government of India on what it regards as deplorable, the Central People's Government of the People's Republic of China cannot but consider it as having been affected by foreign influences hostile to China . . ."[12]

IN THE MEANTIME, THE UNITED STATES, THE WORLD'S NEW WATCH-dog for communist expansionism, was certain that, on some level, it should have its hand in the Tibetan issue. But since Britain, America's closest ally, had had dealings with Tibet in the past and, as a result, had a better "read" on the situation, it seemed prudent to follow its lead.

The problem with following Britain's lead was that Britain did not want to lead. Great Britain was no longer so great. It had, more or less, been booted out of Central Asia, and this was no time to reverse policies and become proactive. It is true that it was an uneasy disinclination: There is evidence that the British Foreign Office at this stage wanted, on some level, to support

---

[11]International Commission of Jurists, *The Question of Tibet and the Rule of Law,* 132–33.
[12]Ibid.

Tibet's claim of independence. In a telegram sent to the British high commissioner in India, the Foreign Office wrote, "We consider that Tibetan autonomy is sufficiently well established for her to be regarded as a 'state' within the meaning of the United Nations Charter. My immediately succeeding telegram gives our views on the legal aspect: these are also for your information only at this stage and not for communication to Government of India. Whether we shall be prepared to support this interpretation of Tibet's international status in the course of preliminary debate in United Nations on validity of her appeal remains for decision. *Assuming that India takes this attitude we should be prepared to do so too,* though the implications are far reaching . . ."[13] Whatever its private assessment of the Tibetan situation may have been, Britain was determined not to interfere with, or go counter to, the newly independent Indian government's position on Tibet.

In other words, Britain now regarded Tibet as *India's* problem and it strongly urged the U.S. State Department to think likewise. If, however, America was determined to assist Tibet politically or militarily—which really seemed ill-advised—it would, at the very least, be in its best interests to first get India's blessing. After all, any material assistance to Tibet would have to travel over Indian territory, which, if discovered by the Chinese, would imply there had been Indian complicity.

AMERICA HEEDED BRITAIN'S WARNING. IT APPROACHED INDIA FOR counsel and suggested that the United States was considering assisting the Tibetans with military supplies.

India went on the defensive and (just as Britain had foreseen) pleaded with the Americans to think twice. China was extremely touchy when it came to the Tibetan issue. How would it react if it found out that the Indian Government had tacitly approved American assistance to Tibet? This would confirm the communists' paranoid view of imperialistic intrigue in Tibet. Please, India begged America, if you get involved you will only create problems for us.

---

[13]FO371/84454, telegram from the Commonwealth Relations Office in London to the United Kingdom high commissioner in India, dated November 10, 1950 (author's italics).

In January 1951, Loy Henderson, the American Ambassador in India, wrote to the Secretary of State that the Government of India was hopelessly opposed to helping Tibet and that, in view of this fact and India's "anxiety not to offend Peking, it would not be easy to prevail on [India] to extend further assistance or to permit armed shipments through India for Tibet."[14]

IN THE END, THE MEMBERS OF THE UNITED NATIONS LOOKED TO India for a definitive assessment. Had Tibet been invaded? Was Tibet an independent nation?

India advised the General Assembly that Tibet was nothing more than a suzerainty of China, adding that, in any case, the potential crisis in Tibet had now been allayed: The PLA troops had proven this by going no farther than Chamdo. Furthermore, India had received assurances from Beijing that all issues with Tibet were in the process of being settled peacefully. In conclusion, the Government of India had no misgivings about China's intentions in Tibet.

On the basis of India's breezy analysis, Tibet's first appeal to the United Nations was shelved.

ON NOVEMBER 17, 1950, IN LHASA, A CEREMONY WAS HELD IN THE Potala to formally proclaim His Holiness the Dalai Lama the temporal head of Tibet. Nehru sent the Dalai Lama a message of felicitations.

International guests included representatives of India, Nepal, and the Chogyal of Sikkim. In spite of considerable pomp, it was a joyless celebration. The Dalai Lama remembers that day:

"Kham and the entire military force stationed there were lost; the United States and Britain had refused to accept Tibetan delegations seeking diplomatic and military assistance against the Chinese; the United Nations was unwilling to consider China's invasion of Tibet; India would not offer strong military and diplomatic support; only a few thousand troops were available

---

[14]New Delhi Embassy to U.S. Department of State, January 12, 1951, FRUS, 1950, vol. VI, 618.

to protect the road from Chamdo, and it was likely that the Chinese would be able to march into Lhasa whenever they chose."[15]

Taktser Rinpoche, who had so recently been encouraged to murder his brother, stood by in attendance. Everyone knew that he had to flee Tibet before the Chinese inundated Lhasa.

NOTICEABLY MISSING FROM THESE HISTORIC PROCEEDINGS WAS Ngabo Ngawang Jigme.

It wasn't because Ngabo had been banned from the Lhasan court for his shameless performance in Kham. The court had been given to understand that Ngabo and his underlings had been detained in Chamdo by the PLA "for a period of study." In other words, they were being brainwashed.

Was Ngabo entirely won over by the communists? Perhaps not, at least at this point. But, like all intelligent yes-men, he realized the full extent to which his personal well-being was dependent on his collaboration with his new "comrades." The day after his capture, he was "encouraged" by his captors to make a public speech. (Meanwhile, by that time, the PLA had marched into Chamdo—its sheer overwhelming numbers allowing it to quickly squelch local unrest.) In Ngabo's speech, he didn't exactly praise the communists, but he did, for all practical purposes, deny that there had been any significant Tibetan resistance:

"The people of Tibet had many doubts about the Chinese Communists . . . We tried to contact the Communist Party but this proved fruitless so we tried to defend our territory by placing guards on our borders *but we did not attack the Chinese*. . . . That is all I can say."[16]

And for the moment, that was all that was required of him by the communist propaganda machine. The Chinese spin on Ngabo's (and his various subordinates') reeducation was promptly featured in Chinese newspapers:

---

[15]His Holiness the Dalai Lama, *My Land and My People*, 56.

[16]Ngabo's speech as quoted in Melvyn Goldstein, *A History of Modern Tibet, 1913–1951*, 742. Author's italics.

The officers and men of the Tibetan army agreed that life during the
period of study was the most pleasant of their lives . . .

During the day and even at night they could be heard singing happily or chanting litanies. At the conclusion of the course of study, many
of the officers and men said that they had been like blind men in the
past and that their eyes were not opened, and that they now realized
that the Tibetan people must drive away the imperialists and return to
the big family of the motherland if they wanted to be liberated . . .

They hoped that the radiance of Chairman Mao would soon be shed
over Lhasa and all Tibet.[17]

With or without Mao's "radiance," Ngabo hadn't a clue as to what was
happening in Lhasa. The PLA had confiscated Ngabo's radio, thus amputat-
ing any outside contact. He had no idea, for instance, that the Dalai Lama had
just been officially installed as the Head of State. In fact, he worried that
Lhasa might be panic-stricken and that the Dalai Lama might have fled for
India. When he and his thirty-six subordinates were finally allowed to contact Lhasa, their report was addressed to "whoever is in power in Lhasa."[18]

Ngabo's letter began by praising the communists' civility. The Chinese
were not the enemy, he vowed; but even if they were, it was pointless to overlook their powerful army. What the Chinese really wanted was an agreement—a peaceful agreement—signed by the Tibetans, stating that China
was, basically, bringing Tibet back into the fold of "the Motherland," which
was and always had been China's legitimate right. If His Holiness the Dalai
Lama would endorse such an agreement, the Tibetan people would not suf-
fer, the *khim zhi* (wealthy family estates) would not be dismantled, and the
monastic orders would remain unharmed. Ngabo's summation: There was
every reason to sign an agreement and no reason not to.[19]

The *Kashag* wasn't buying it. Signing such an agreement would be paramount to signing away their country. And anyway, with or without an agreement, what was to prevent the PLA from moving west toward the capital?

[17]"The Graces of Mao Are Higher Than Heaven," in *Tibet 1950–67*, 731.
[18]Tsering Shakya, *The Dragon in the Land of Snows*, 49.
[19]Ibid.

Perhaps the army was already marching toward Lhasa. *Whoever is in power in Lhasa:* Wasn't it obvious? Didn't Ngabo's salutation prove that the Chinese expected the Dalai Lama to go into exile?

Whatever Ngabo's aim—and there were many who believed he had been recruited by the Chinese long before the fall of Chamdo—the Dalai Lama's inner circle took Ngabo's letter as a poorly disguised ultimatum. The *Kashag* went into that rarest of things, speed mode. They devised a plan to remove His Holiness from Lhasa. There was not a moment to lose. They would resettle him in the mountain town of Yatung, just fifteen miles from the Indian border and seventy miles from Kalimpong.

Since there was no telling how long they would be in Yatung (or across the frontier), the first order of business was to ship down a large quantity of silver and gold from the Potala Treasury.[20] The next day, hundreds of pack animals were seen being laden in front of the Winter Palace. The ruling class watched in alarm. Suddenly, dozens of caravans materialized, carrying aristocrats' personal wealth, either to their country estates or to safe havens in India. It was an evacuation. Only a skeletal government would remain in the capital. Anticipating citywide panic, the Central Government did not advise the common townspeople of the move until the last possible moment.

In the meantime, the *Kashag* was resolved not to burn bridges. They ordered Shakabpa—who had sent the first appeal to the United Nations and was still residing in Kalimpong, India—to send a second appeal to Lake Success. The appeal went out on December 8, 1950. Shakabpa was also instructed to send out feelers to India and America to ascertain what, if any, kind of support would be forthcoming should the Dalai Lama defect to a foreign country.

The *Kashag* then assembled a small delegation to travel to America to present, in person, their case to the international community.

WHILE THE ARISTOCRATS WERE PACKING THEIR TRUNKS, MISSIVES from Ngabo kept arriving in Lhasa. The communists wanted the negotiations for an agreement to take place in Chamdo. Since Ngabo was already in

---

[20]Approximately five million U.S. dollars; Warren W. Smith Jr., *Tibetan Nation*, footnote, 305.

Chamdo, and since he was the one Tibetan most familiar with the communists, Ngabo graciously offered his services to act as the negotiator.

The *Tsongdu* debated what do with this offer. If Tibet refused, what would be the consequences? Ngabo had not elaborated on this crucial point.

Those opposed to an agreement argued that the Chinese promise of a "peaceful liberation" was a bold-faced lie—like "honey spread on a sharp knife."[21]

Those members of the *Tsongdu* in favor of signing an agreement with the communists—and this seemed to be the prevailing disposition—argued that Tibet should, at all costs, avoid a showdown with China.

As for Ngabo's offer to be chief negotiator, that was a clearer issue. No one in the Tibetan government wanted the mantle of leadership. Why not Ngabo? It was true that he had made a muddle of the Chamdo conflict, but his status as a prisoner-associate of the Chinese seemed to put him in the position of being a budding expert on the communist position—or so went the rationale among most of the Lhasan officials.

In retrospect, it may seem incredible that the *Kashag* and the *Tsongdu* would have gone along with Ngabo's self-appointed nomination but, on the other hand, it may have been less a matter of trusting Ngabo and more a matter of *dis*trusting their own paltry qualifications to deal with the outside world. It bears repeating that, prior to the Chinese invasion, Tibet was in an almost perfect state of isolation. Among the political elite, there were less than ten men who had traveled to a foreign land.

THE UNITED NATIONS RECEIVED THE SECOND APPEAL FROM TIBET and, again, didn't know what to do with it. This time, however, the State Department saw Tibet's perseverance as an encouraging sign and set up a research team to see how the United States could legally justify supporting Tibet as a nation independent of China. They also wired India for advice.

Once again, India shunned Tibet's appeal.

But America was no longer so easily mollified. The State Department turned to the British Embassy in Washington with an aide-mémoire profess-

---

[21]A popular Tibetan saying.

ing its desire to take a more active role in supporting Tibet: "It is believed further that, *should developments warrant, consideration could be given to recognition of Tibet as an independent State.* . . . the US Government recognizes the *de facto* autonomy that Tibet has exercised since the fall of the Manchu Dynasty . . ."[22]

Great Britain, staunchly backing up India, remained unmoved. In the end, America again found itself reluctant to move against Anglo-Indian inertia, particularly in light of the rapidly deteriorating situation in Korea, which was consuming the minds of U.S. officials.

The United Nations shelved the Tibetan appeal for a second time.

THE DALAI LAMA TRIED TO MAKE SENSE OF INTERNATIONAL politics, but it just seemed to defy logic. What was the United Nations for, if not to defend hapless countries like Tibet? The teenage leader became disillusioned, if not disgusted, with the mysterious mechanizations of Lake Success:

We had put our faith in the United Nations as a source of justice, and we were astonished to hear that it was on British initiative that the question had been shelved. . . . The attitude of the Indian representative was equally disappointing. He said he was certain a peaceful settlement could be made and Tibet's autonomy could be safeguarded, and that the best way to ensure this was to abandon the idea of discussing the matter in the General Assembly.

This was a worse disappointment than the earlier news that nobody would offer us any military help. Now our friends would not even help us to present our plea for justice. We felt abandoned to the hordes of the Chinese army.[23]

Tibet scrapped the idea of sending a delegation to Lake Success. Its only option seemed to be to seek negotiations with the communists.[24]

Ngabo was selected to be chief negotiator. Two other Lhasans—Sampho Tenzin Dhondup and Khenchung Thupten Legmom—were selected to complete the delegation. They were sent to Chamdo to join Ngabo. Sampho and

[22]DO 35/3094, as cited by Tsering Shakya, *The Dragon in the Land of Snows,* 60–61. Emphasis added by Shakya.
[23]His Holiness the Dalai Lama, *My Land and My People,* 65.
[24]Roger E. McCarthy, *Tears of the Lotus,* 62.

Khenchung took with them a letter signed by the *Kashag* and the Dalai Lama that outlined the terms that Ngabo must insist upon, which included:

1. Insist that there is no imperialist influence in Tibet.
2. Agree to seek assistance from China, as in the past, in case of any foreign attack upon Tibet.
3. Demand the return of Tibetan territories in Kham, Golok, and Amdo.
4. Demand the withdrawal of the PLA from Tibetan territory.[25]

Did the *Kashag* really believe, in writing these demands, that the Chinese would simply roll over and give in?

With the international community having abandoned them, the Tibetans had little or no leverage. Perhaps the *Kashag* was merely stalling for time until they had escaped to Yatung.

The *Kashag* had also sent with the two delegates a private letter to Ngabo. There was nothing ambiguous about its contents: On *no* condition was Ngabo to make any decisions or sign any documents without first receiving approval from the *Kashag* and the Dalai Lama.[26]

ON THE EVENING OF DECEMBER 20, THE DALAI LAMA LEFT LHASA. To avoid panic in the streets, he and his entourage left at night, disguised as commoners. Author Lowell Thomas Jr. describes the arduous trek south:

"Blizzards swept across the plateau as the caravan journeyed south. The Dalai Lama used his sedan chair mainly when entering a settlement where he would be called upon to accept official greetings. On much of the journey he rode a horse or mule, as did his family and the officials who accompanied him. Often he would dismount and walk for long distances. If the Dalai Lama

---

[25]Lu'o Yus-hung, *Bod zhi-bas bcings'-grol skor gyi nyin-tho gnad bshus* (Diary of Peaceful Liberation of Tibet), SCHT, vol. 1 (1951), 188. As cited by Shakya, *The Dragon in the Land of Snows*, 62.

[26]U. S. Ambassador in India to the Secretary of State, June 11, 1951. FRUS, 1951, vol. VII, 1707. Also, Heinrich Harrer told Loy Henderson: "With great reluctance the Dalai Lama is sending the present mission to Peking. He has not given this mission any plenipotentiary powers since he fears that . . . it might yield to pressure." U.S. Ambassador in India to the Director of the Office of South Asian Affairs, March 29, 1951. FRUS, 1951, vol. VII, 1611.

walked, everyone in the caravan also walked; thus even the most pampered officials arrived quite fit in the Chumbi Valley."[27]

They arrived in Yatung on January 7, 1951, and set up a provisional capital. The Dalai Lama used nearby Dungkar Monastery as his temporary home. All was quiet. Winter snow closed in the mountain passes, caravan traffic stopped, and the teenager spent the majority of each day in meditation.

But outside his rooms, the corridors were alive with passionate disagreement.

Among the members of the *Kashag* and the *Tsongdu*, there were many who were adamantly opposed to the Dalai Lama traveling further—that is to say, crossing the border into India and going into exile. What assurances did the Dalai Lama have of receiving any assistance from India and other foreign powers? What did the Dalai Lama or anyone else in Yatung, for that matter, know about living in a foreign country?

A message was sent to Kalimpong. Every Tibetan living in the Indian border town, including Shakabpa, must immediately come to Yatung to discuss their experiences abroad.

Shakabpa's input, once he arrived, was bleak. He particularly advised the Dalai Lama against putting too much faith in Nehru. Nehru, he said, was much more interested in having China as his friend than Tibet. It was as simple as that.

There was, however, one ray of hope that arrived in Yatung that winter.

A message was relayed to Yatung from the U.S. Embassy in New Delhi. It expressed the State Department's sympathy for the plight of the Tibetan people in general and, in particular, its willingness to extend material assistance to Tibet—provided there was evidence of "Tibetan resistance to aggression."[28]

U.S. officials waited anxiously for a reply. It never came. A second message was sent to Yatung in the spring, on April 4, 1951. Again, no response from the Dalai Lama.

The Tibetans had not replied because they didn't know how to—at least as one voice. Delegations from the three great monasteries in Lhasa—Sera,

---

[27]Lowell Thomas Jr., *The Silent War in Tibet*, 99–100.
[28]New Delhi Embassy to Department of State, 28 June 1951, National Archives, 793B.00/6-2851. Warren W. Smith Jr., *Tibetan Nation*, 292.

Drepung, and Ganden—arrived in Yatung and further intensified the unsettling atmosphere. They implored His Holiness to return to the capital immediately—what was all this talk about him moving to India? Others, including members of the Dalai Lama's family, vehemently disagreed: The only way Tibet's independence could be protected was if His Holiness *escaped* to India and waited until a more auspicious political climate made it feasible for the young leader to return.

AND THEN THERE WAS THE CONTENTIOUS AND CONFUSING AND distracting matter of the negotiations with China.

The two Lhasan delegates reached Chamdo in mid-February only to learn from Ngabo that the Chinese had changed their minds. Chamdo was out. They were going to relocate the negotiations to Beijing.

The news was relayed to Yatung and the reaction was one of deep distress. This whole "agreement situation" seemed to be receding farther and farther toward the distant horizon, away from the people who should be at the helm. How could the Dalai Lama, sequestered in a snowbound outpost, hope to control events taking place in Beijing?

Waylaid by his obstreperous court, the Dalai Lama selected four more delegates to join the other three already in Chamdo. And again, His Holiness sent a personal note to Ngabo reminding him that the delegation was not authorized to make any important decisions in Beijing without first consulting the *Kashag* and His Holiness the Dalai Lama.[29]

UNDER HEAVY PLA GUARD, NGABO AND HIS SIX UNDERLINGS arrived in Beijing in the third week of April.

Ngabo disobeyed the Dalai Lama's orders even before the talks began. He confided to his fellow delegates that he "believed that they should not refer important issues back to Yatung but should take the responsibility upon themselves."[30]

[29]Tsering Shakya, *The Dragon in the Land of Snows*, 64.
[30]Sampho Tenzing Dhondup, in an interview with Melvyn Goldstein, *A History of Modern Tibet, 1913–1951*, 760.

His reason for contravening the Dalai Lama's explicit orders? Many of the Dalai Lama's advisors—especially the clerical officials—were woefully ignorant of the modern world. Nothing would be agreed upon as long as they quibbled among themselves. Therefore, as the leader of the delegation, Ngabo "would take full responsibility for this action."[31] The other delegates agreed to keep the Dalai Lama and the *Kashag* out of the picture, so long as Ngabo swore to shoulder any potential blame.

Ngabo gave them his word.

BEIJING, APRIL 29, 1951.

The negotiations were held in the cavernous hall of the old Japanese embassy, in which the Chinese and Tibetans faced each other from opposite rows of gargantuan divans.

The first matter of importance, the Chinese announced, was whether or not Ngabo had full authority to sign an agreement. All eyes, Tibetan and Chinese alike, were on Ngabo. Ngabo assured the Chinese that he had full authority.

The Chinese then asked him whether he had the authority to write, "With all the power and authority represented by Ngabo Ngawang Jigme." Again, Ngabo answered in the affirmative.[32]

Then Ngabo glissaded into his opening speech. This was his strong suit: his oratory artistry. He avowed that Tibet's historical relationship with China had been one of priest and patron, nothing more. Tibet was a peaceful nation. There was no need to keep PLA troops within its borders.

The Chinese interrupted Ngabo: Chinese historical sovereignty over Tibet was a fact and nonnegotiable. As for Ngabo's opinion about the deployment of Chinese troops in Tibet—the Chinese didn't care what Ngabo thought. What Ngabo was expected to do, *would* do, was to stop talking nonsense, quit wasting the party's time, get his head out of the clouds, listen up, and agree to everything—*everything*—the Chinese proposed.[33]

This, then, was the opening day of the so-called negotiations.

---

[31]Ibid., 760.
[32]Ibid.
[33]Ibid.

. . .

MEANWHILE, IN THE SUBCONTINENT, LOY HENDERSON, THE AMER-
ican ambassador to India, was unusually impressed by a meeting he had just
held with Heinrich Harrer. Harrer had arrived in Delhi from Yatung. The
future author of *Seven Years in Tibet,* and a personal friend of the Dalai Lama,
he had accompanied the teenage "god-king" from Lhasa in December.
Harrer's meeting with Henderson was an important one. America, for the
first time, was able to obtain reliable intelligence on the thinking of the
Tibetan Government and, more important, on the Dalai Lama's personal
ambitions. Harrer told Henderson that the Dalai Lama had agreed to the delegation in Beijing with great reluctance, that the Dalai Lama had serious misgivings about returning to Lhasa any time in the foreseeable future, in spite
of the fact that many of his monk officials were adamant he return to the
capital and negotiate with the Chinese; and that—bottom line—the boy simply didn't know which way to turn for advice.

Already sympathetic to the Tibetan plight, Henderson was convinced it
was time to initiate *direct* contact with His Holiness. He submitted a copy of
a letter (addressed to the Dalai Lama) to the State Department, suggesting it
be sent secretly to His Holiness on plain paper and without any formal
authorization from the American government.

The letter was approved by the State Department and whisked off to Yatung.
It outlined several points, including the following:

1. The Peiping Communist regime is determined to obtain complete
   control over Tibet. No concession made to that regime by His Holiness can change this determination. The Chinese Communists prefer to gain control through trickery rather than through force. They
   are therefore anxious to persuade His Holiness to make an agreement which would allow them to establish a representative in Lhasa.
2. The establishment of a representative of the Peiping Communist
   regime in Lhasa would serve only to speed up the seizing of all of
   Tibet by the Chinese Communists.
3. Until changes in the world situation would make it difficult for the

Chinese Communists to take over Tibet, His Holiness should in no circumstances return to Lhasa or send his treasures or those of Tibet back to Lhasa . . . Any treasures which might be returned to Lhasa would eventually be taken over by the Chinese Communists.

4. His Holiness should not return to Lhasa while the danger exists that by force or trickery the Chinese Communists might seize Lhasa. He should leave Yatung for some foreign country if it should look like the Chinese Communists might try to prevent his escape.

5. It is suggested that His Holiness send representatives at once to Ceylon.[34] These representatives should try to arrange with the Government of Ceylon for the immediate transfer to Ceylon of the treasure of His Holiness. They should also try to obtain permission for His Holiness and his household to find asylum in Ceylon if His Holiness leaves Tibet. After the GOC [Government of Ceylon] has granted permission for asylum, His Holiness should ask the GOI [Government of India] for assurance that if he and his Household should leave Tibet they could pass through India to Ceylon.

6. If His Holiness and His Household could not find safe asylum in Ceylon he could be certain of finding a place of refuge in one of the friendly countries, *including the United States,* in the Western Hemisphere.[35]

Ambassador Henderson was wooing the Dalai Lama, and it would not be inappropriate to liken the boy's dilemma to a maiden with two suitors. One suitor, the United States, was inviting him to elope. The other, China, was hoping that seduction would do the trick; but if it didn't, there was always a shotgun wedding.

In hindsight, the better choice may seem obvious, but, at the time, there was an additional component that must have weighed heavily on the conflicted Dalai Lama. China's intention (remember the proposed fratricide) was clearly odious but, at least, it was a *known* dynamic. On the other hand,

---

[34]Present-day Sri Lanka, off the southern coast of India.
[35]FRUS, vol. VII, part 2 (1951), 1612–13. Author's italics.

what did His Holiness really know about the motivation behind America's courtship? Enticing as Henderson's letter may have been, it didn't come with any guarantees. The absence of a letterhead on the stationery and the absence of a signature at the bottom of the page (precautions taken by the United States government lest the letter fall into the wrong hands) could only have left the boy-leader to ponder America's sincerity.

Inexperienced in international politics but wise beyond his years, the Dalai Lama decided to hedge his bets.

Everyone assumed the negotiations in Beijing would drag on for months; Ngabo was a clever man who had some experience with the communists: There was still the possibility that Ngabo might be able to hammer out an agreement that was not too disadvantageous for the Tibetan nation. And if the negotiations broke down, well, at least the Dalai Lama was close to the Indian border and had purchased extra time in the bargain.

On May 21, the Dalai Lama wrote a reply to Henderson's letter. In it, he stated that, at present, negotiations were proceeding in Beijing. If the talks broke down, he would contact Henderson in the hopes that "the USA would do its best to help."[36]

The Dalai Lama *assumed* the negotiations were proceeding. In truth, he had no idea what was going on in Beijing. The provisional government in Yatung had not heard one word from Ngabo since the negotiations had begun.

IN BEIJING, THERE WAS NOTHING EVEN REMOTELY RESEMBLING A dialogue—never mind negotiations—taking place.

Instead, the "discussions" were an endless succession of intimidating, table-thumping, don't-make-us-angry, fit-throwing diatribes designed to reduce the Tibetan team to absolute submission. According to author T. N. Takla, "The Chinese were polite when the Tibetans were not saying anything; when the Tibetans tried to say anything, the Chinese got very angry."[37] And the

---

[36]Ibid., 73.

[37]"Conversation with Yapshi Sey, Phuntsok Tashi, Brother-in-Law of the Dalai Lama," American Consul, Calcutta, to the Department of State, August 18, 1951, National Archives, 793B.00/8-1851 from Takla's "Notes on Some Early Tibetan Communists," *Tibetan Review*, vol. 11, no. 17, 1969, 7–10.

communists' anger took a sinister turn: "Do you want a peaceful liberation or a liberation by force?"[38] According to the Dalai Lama, *Our delegates were not allowed to make any alterations or suggestion. They were insulted and abused and threatened with personal violence, and with further military action against the people of Tibet . . .*[39]

There was not a proposal on the table. There was an ultimatum on the table, and a document to be signed by the Tibetan delegation. The Tibetans could make it easy on themselves by agreeing with the Chinese that the seventeen clauses were impeccable as presented to them. There was no need to waste time mincing words about revisions. Sign now and the radiance of Mao would shine down upon them.[40]

Even the name of the document was ironic: "The 17-Point Agreement." Briefly, the points were:

1. Tibet would drive out the imperialist forces from its borders and return to the big family of the Motherland.
2. Tibet would invite the PLA to enter Central Tibet and consolidate the national defense in Lhasa.
3. Tibet had the right to exercise autonomy under the guidance and leadership of the communists.
4. The communists would not alter the existing political system of Central Tibet, including the powers of the Dalai Lama and various other Tibetan officials.
5. The status, functions, and powers of the Dalai Lama and of the Panchen Lama would be maintained. (The Panchen Lama, a Tibetan incarnate of profound importance among Tibetans, was, in terms of spiritual status, second only to the Dalai Lama. Mao had adopted, politically, the current young Panchen Lama, housed him in a mansion in Beijing, and now demanded that the delegation accept him

---

[38]Ibid.

[39]His Holiness the Dalai Lama, *My Land and My People*, 66–67.

[40]"Conversation with Yapshi Sey, Phuntsok Tashi, Brother-in-Law of the Dalai Lama," American Consul, Calcutta, to the Department of State, August 18, 1951, National Archives, 793B.00/8-1851, from Takla's "Notes on Some Early Tibetan Communists," *Tibetan Review*, vol. 11, no. 17, 1969, 7–10.

as the real incarnate—although the Dalai Lama never had. Mao's idea was to develop the Panchen Lama into the Dalai Lama's political rival. According to historian Warren Smith Jr. the potential rivalry "between the Dalai and Panchen Lamas symbolized the disunity of Tibet, a disunity which [the communists] were determined to exploit to the fullest extent."[41]

6. The status of the Dalai and Panchen Lama would reflect the "amicable relations" they enjoyed in previous incarnations.

7. Buddhism would be protected. Beliefs, customs, and habits of Tibetans would be respected. Monasteries would be protected. The communists would not interfere with the incomes of the monasteries.

8. The Tibetan army would be reorganized and eventually be absorbed into the PLA.

9. The communists would develop the spoken and written language and school education of Tibetans.

10. The communists would develop Tibetan agriculture, industry, and commerce.

11. In matters related to various reforms in Tibet, there would be no compulsion on the part of Beijing. The local government of Tibet would carry out reforms of its own accord, and when the people raised demands for reform, they would be settled by means of consultation with the leading personnel of Tibet. (This is the key article within the 17-Point Agreement, which gave the Chinese complete political control over Tibet. As Warren Smith explains: "Under Chinese control, 'demands' for reforms could be raised by a variety of persuasive and coercive methods; the nature of those reforms would be whatever the Chinese, not the majority of Tibetans, desired. Every aspect of Tibetan 'autonomy' within the Chinese state and Tibet's future would be determined by the Chinese rather than Tibetans. Further, Tibetans would find that, by the Chinese interpretation of Tibet's 'return to the Motherland,' Tibetans had not only lost their independence, but their very identity; Tibetans were

---

[41]Warren W. Smith Jr., *Tibetan Nation*, 294–95.

no longer just Tibetans, but were now to be defined as Chinese of the 'Tibetan minority nationality.' ”[42])

12. Tibetans who had been sympathizers of the *Kuomintang* or the imperialists, once reformed, could continue to hold office in Tibet.
13. When the PLA entered Central Tibet, the troops would take nothing from the local Tibetans without first purchasing it at a fair price.
14. Beijing would conduct all external affairs of Tibet.
15. In order to ensure the implementation of the agreement, Beijing would set up a military and administrative committee and a military area headquarters in Central Tibet.
16. Military and administrative costs for the PLA would be paid by Beijing. The Lhasan government would assist the PLA in the purchase and transport of food, fodder, and other daily necessities.
17. The agreement would come into force immediately after signature and seals were affixed to it.[43]

Ngabo and his fellow delegates signed the agreement on May 23, 1951. Far from lasting for months, as the Dalai Lama had anticipated, the meetings took less than four weeks.

When the Chinese ordered the Tibetan delegates to affix their respective seals to their signatures, the Tibetans replied they had not come with seals (for the obvious reason that they had not been given the authority to sign treaties). This produced but a momentary problem for the communists. They simply created forged seals that were then used to "legitimatize" the proceedings.

The next day, the Chinese held a celebration in the Imperial Palace overlooking Tiananmen Square. Ngabo met Mao Tse-tung. Again, Ngabo was asked if he had been given full authority to sign the treaty. Again, Ngabo answered in the affirmative. He was then "invited" to give a speech, likely written by the Chinese. It was full of the usual rhetoric associated with communist propaganda. The Beijing press hailed the speech as brilliant. Ngabo ended his recitation with this:

---

[42]Warren W. Smith, Jr., *Tibetan Nation*, 304
[43]Ibid., 298–301. (The seventeen points have been paraphrased by the author.)

May 23, 1951: Ngabo (center) signs the 17-Point Agreement in Beijing without the Dalai Lama's authority to do so. *(Office of Information and International Relations, Dharamsala)*

"Today we fully recognize that only with the leadership of the Central People's Government and Chairman Mao Tse-tung and the unity and cooperation of all fraternal nationalities throughout the country can we drive out our common enemy, the aggressive imperialist forces, consolidate national defense in the Southwest [Tibet], and build up the prosperous and happy big family of our motherland."[44]

---

[44]"Head of Tibetan Delegation on Peaceful Liberation of Tibet," NCNA, May 27, 1951, in *Survey of China Mainland Press.*

. . .

TWO DAYS LATER, ON MAY 26, NGABO WENT LIVE ON RADIO Peking and announced to the outside world that Tibet had signed the 17-Point Agreement:

". . . The local government of Tibet shall actively assist the People's Liberation Army to enter Tibet and consolidate the national defense . . .

"The Central People's Government shall have centralized handling of all external affairs of the area of Tibet . . .

"In order to ensure the implementation of this Agreement, the Central People's Government shall set up a Military and Administrative Committee and a Military Area Headquarters in Tibet."[45]

It was a jaw-dropping revelation. Mao had achieved a masterful victory. He had avoided the international stigma of armed conflict inside the borders of Tibet. He could now bring into Tibet as many PLA troops as he deemed

Unbeknownst to the Dalai Lama, Ngabo and Chairman Mao were clinking glasses in Beijing over the illegal signing of the 17-Point Agreement. *(Collection of the author)*

---

[45]Roger E. McCarthy, *Tears of the Lotus*, 65–67.

necessary. It made no difference that Ngabo had exceeded his authority. The international community would conclude that Tibet—for whatever reasons—had officially agreed to become a part of China.[46]

IT WAS EARLY SUMMER IN SOUTHERNMOST TIBET. THE TRAIL north of Yatung wound through peach and walnut trees. Tender fields of barley bent in the breeze. After several hundred yards, the trail gained altitude under a sky daubed with rain clouds scudding past the sun. The trail followed a rushing stream protected by willows—past a moraine of boulders—past cliffs with sacred carvings—up an incline entwined with yellow clematis—across an alpine valley dotted with yak herds. At this altitude, white tents were pitched where nomads and monastics enjoyed a picnic. The trail continued: past colonies of wild strawberries, iridescent dragonflies, and rain-soaked rose thickets drooping under the weight of their own white blossoms.[47]

Overlooking this vista, the large pile of Dungkar Monastery, the Dalai Lama's retreat, pierced the sky.

The Dalai Lama didn't see the view below him. He stared out his window dumbstruck. The radio was crackling in the background. He had just heard Ngabo's speech from Beijing:

It was a terrible shock when we heard the terms of it. We were appalled at the mixture of Communist clichés, vainglorious assertions which were completely false, and bold statements which were only partly true. And the terms were far worse and more oppressive than anything we had imagined.[48]

Should he renounce the agreement? Should he flee to India? What were the ramifications if he did? Would the rest of the world believe him? Would the communist army retaliate? All eyes were on him, including those of the abbots who were pleading with him to return immediately to Lhasa and reconcile with the Chinese.

But India was only a day's ride away.

---

[46]Ibid.
[47]Fosco Maraini, *Secret Tibet,* 115.
[48]His Holiness the Dalai Lama, *My Land and My People,* 67.

. . .

AMERICA HAD ALSO BEEN CAUGHT OFF-GUARD BY NGABO'S RADIO
broadcast. Something was amiss. The United States refused to believe that
the Dalai Lama had simply given away his country. They assumed the document had been signed under duress and without his authority. They hoped
the Dalai Lama would protest by going into exile.

Key to seeking asylum, however—at least from an American point of
view—was that the Dalai Lama first publicly disavow the 17-Point Agreement. According to Roger E. McCarthy, the CIA agent who would later work
with the Tibetans, "There was a flurry of exchanges between Yatung, Calcutta, New Delhi and Washington addressing the possibilities of exile, assistance, support at the United Nations and related issues. [Taktser Rinpoche]
was heavily involved, urging his young brother to leave Tibet."[49]

Taktser Rinpoche had already fled to India to escape the Chinese. In June,
he traveled from Kalimpong to Calcutta. There he met with the U.S. consular
officer. Concerning Ngabo's provocative radio broadcast, Taktser assured the
American that:

1. Neither the Tibetan government nor the Dalai Lama approves of the
   so-called agreement.
2. It is likely that the Dalai Lama will publicly disavow the agreement
   before the arrival of the Tibetan and Chinese delegations, which
   were currently on their way to see the Dalai Lama in Yatung.
3. The Dalai Lama was definitely going to leave Tibet, although he
   might not have time before the Chinese reached Yatung.
4. The Dalai Lama would probably find it awkward to remain in India,
   in view of the strained relations between India and Tibet. He would
   prefer to receive asylum from the Americans.[50]

The United States was delighted to hear this and felt empowered to inform
the British Foreign Office that America no longer cared to appease India. If

---

[49]Roger E. McCarthy, *Tears of the Lotus*, 66.
[50]FRUS, vol. VI, part 2 (1951), 1719.

diplomatic relations suffered, so be it. America had vowed to counter communist aggression, wherever it occurred, and it meant to be true to its word.[51]

Not surprisingly, America's revised position was met with Anglo-Indian scowls. All along, the sole advice given by the GOI to Tibet had been to go along with the Chinese. Now India felt slighted by the Dalai Lama because he had approached America first about the possibility of repudiating the 17-Point Agreement. Sir G. S. Bajpai, India's Secretary General in the Ministry of External Affairs, complained that, given this slap in the face, "Tibet could hardly expect a great deal of sympathy from the GOI" and indicated that he was inclined to wash his hands of the whole affair.[52]

THE TIBETAN DELEGATION IN BEIJING REMAINED IN CHINA UNTIL the end of June.

On July 1, 1951, six of the seven members were flown to Calcutta. (Ngabo remained behind in Beijing with his new Chinese associates.) Three days later, the six-man delegation left Calcutta for Yatung, where they would meet with the Dalai Lama.

A Chinese delegation, headed by General Chang, who would command the PLA once it arrived in Central Tibet, flew into Calcutta a few days later. He, too, was on his way to Yatung to meet with the Dalai Lama.

In Yatung, the tension was palpable. By then, the Tibetans had received guidelines from the United States. They could invalidate, on legal grounds, the agreement, provided that: (1) duress had been applied to the delegation, and (2) the delegation had exceeded its instructions or acted at variance with them. If the Tibetans renounced the treaty on these grounds, His Holiness could go into exile (along with a hundred-plus entourage) with America's blessing, and some sort of Tibetan military resistance (backed by the Americans) could be mounted against the communists occupying Tibet.[53]

---

[51]FO371/92997, telegram from the United Kingdom Embassy in Washington, D.C., to the British Foreign Office, dated June 25, 1951. As cited by Goldstein, *A History of Modern Tibet, 1913–1951*, 786.
[52]DO 35/3097, 85.
[53]Melvyn Goldstein, *A History of Modern Tibet, 1913–1951*, 779.

Unfortunately, the robed faction who insisted on the Dalai Lama's return to Lhasa was gaining ground. They simply couldn't comprehend why, if unprovoked, the communists would go out of their way to destroy the Buddhist system—in spite of the Thirteenth Dalai Lama's warnings. Besides, the thought of living abroad as impoverished exiles—no estates, no subsidies— horrified a majority of the aristocrats who hoped against hope that the communists would somehow uphold the Tibetan socioeconomic system.[54]

Those who advocated exile and the repudiation of the 17-Point Agreement were led by Phala (the Lord Chamberlain and the Dalai Lama's closest advisor), Shakabpa, Taktser Rinpoche, and other members of the Dalai Lama's immediate family. But they found themselves biting their tongues when His Holiness suddenly announced that—whatever he decided to do—he would not make up his mind until *after* General Chang had arrived in Yatung a few days hence. The Dalai Lama remembers:

A pact with America or anyone else meant war. America was thousands of miles away . . . China had numerical superiority. . . . There was a likelihood of years of struggle . . . I therefore concluded that the best course of action was to stay put and await the arrival of the Chinese general.[55]

Meanwhile, more American communiqués were shot off to Yatung, ever more demonstrative of Washington's commitment to Tibet. The State Department simply couldn't understand why the Dalai Lama was stalling.

The acrimony of the ongoing debate in Yatung became unbearable. Although the vast majority was in favor of the Dalai Lama returning to Lhasa, the anti-communist faction refused to back down.

Finally, the three head abbots demanded that the State Oracle be brought in and that the spirit of the goddess Palden Lhamo be consulted and appealed to for divine intervention.

The Oracle made his entrance in full regalia.

He went into a trance and advised the Dalai Lama to return to Lhasa.

The Dalai Lama was unwilling to accept this and defied precedent by demanding a second possession.

Again the State Oracle decreed that he should return to Lhasa.

---

[54]Ibid., 800.
[55]His Holiness the Dalai Lama, *Freedom in Exile: The Autobiography of the Dalai Lama*, 65.

The Nechung Oracle: Many of Tibet's most crucial political decisions were determined by his visions. *(Ilya Tolstoy, Collection of the Academy of Natural Sciences of Philadelphia)*

Still the teenager was not convinced.

When it became apparent that the Dalai Lama might reject the oracle's advice—something unthinkable—the high lamas from the major monasteries admonished him: "If you do not accept the direction of the gods on high, how can you expect to be accepted as their representative on earth?"

The Dalai Lama could no longer object. He announced that he would return to Lhasa.[56]

ON JULY 16, GENERAL CHANG AND ASSOCIATES ARRIVED IN Yatung.

The Dalai Lama remembers: *I was not looking forward to it. I had never seen a Chinese general, and it was a rather forbidding prospect. Nobody could know how he would behave—whether he would be sympathetic, or arrive as a conqueror . . .*

When the time came, I was peering out of a window to see what he looked like. I do not know exactly what I expected, but what I saw was three men in gray suits and peaked caps who looked extremely drab and insignificant among the splendid figures of my officials in their red and golden robes. Had I but known, the drabness was the state to which China was to reduce us all before the end, and the insignificance was certainly an illusion.[57]

---

[56]George Patterson, based on a letter he received from His Holiness the Dalai Lama, *Tibet in Revolt*, 84.
[57]His Holiness the Dalai Lama, *My Land and My People*, 69.

General Chang, who was surprisingly civil, urged the Dalai Lama to tele-graph Mao Tse-tung—to tell him that he accepted the 17-Point Agreement. The Dalai Lama declined. He rejected this idea on the grounds that the *Tsongdu* should first have to ratify the decision in Lhasa. The Dalai Lama pro-posed an alternative plan: He would wire Mao and promise him that he had decided to return to Lhasa so that he could discuss the terms of the agree-ment with the National Assembly.

It was agreed that the Dalai Lama's group and General Chang's group would travel separately to Lhasa. The Dalai Lama's contingent would go first.

Those last days in Yatung—the last time, for many years, that the Dalai Lama would experience life without a communist presence—were not with-out hope. While officials were busy packing, the Dalai Lama concentrated on his daily practice of meditation, which always renewed him. The tension that had filled the halls of Dungkar Monastery dissipated under the relief that, finally, decisions had been made.

The seasons were changing, too. There was a new crispness in the air. The green barley fields were now tinged with gold.

Much had changed in the nine months since the Dalai Lama had come to Yatung. He had arrived here as a reluctant teenager.

The Dalai Lama would return to his capital as a reluctant man.

On September 6, 1951, the Dalai Lama reentered his capital. Three days later, three thousand troops of the PLA's Eighteenth Route Army tramped into the city. Tubas blared, drums rumbled, portraits of Mao and Chou En-lai mounted on pikes bobbled between phalanxes of China's red flag. The people watched in silence as something entirely new was introduced into their world: twentieth-century noise. Chinese technicians strung electrical wires from building to building. Loudspeakers were installed on street cor-ners. Lhasans cocked their ears. After an overture of popping and hissing, Tibetans got their first taste of electrified propaganda. Even from his aerie in the Potala, the Dalai Lama could not escape the continuous caterwauling of the loudspeakers. The holiest city in Tibet was now also the most jarring.[58]

At the end of September, the *Tsongdu* convened to discuss whether or not they would ratify the 17-Point Agreement. Three hundred men attended. The

---

[58]Lowell Thomas Jr., *The Silent War in Tibet*, 108.

September 9, 1951: The PLA parades into Lhasa, marking the start of its occupation. *(Collection of the author)*

Beijing delegation—including Ngabo, who had just recently arrived in the capital with a PLA entourage—was seated in a separate area of the assembly hall.

What possible explanation, the Assembly demanded, could Ngabo offer for the travesty that had occurred in Beijing?

Ngabo moved to the center of the room. He began by making it clear that, while in China, he had accepted no bribes. Then, for an hour and a half, he artfully argued that the status and the power of the Dalai Lama would not be altered by the 17-Point Agreement. Nor, he continued, would it harm the religious and political systems of Tibet. Was not the *Tsongdu* behaving just a little bit hysterically? Did they not appreciate the array of improvements they were about to enjoy under the benevolence of Chairman Mao? The donations to Lhasa's monasteries would be unprecedented. Lhasa would have a modern hospital. There would be schools for everyone. There would be modern roads and electricity throughout the city. This was Lhasa's great opportunity and it would be tragic not to accept Mao's generosity. It was time Tibet joined the modern world. Chairman Mao would show them the way.

Ngabo's oration was precisely what the aristocracy wanted to hear. As long as the privileged class's lifestyle was to be protected, what did they care about the mumbo-jumbo of a piece of paper signed in Beijing?

The most vocal supporters of Ngabo's speech, however, came from the abbots of the three leading Lhasan monasteries. They convinced themselves that Mao was interested in only a symbolic claim over Tibet. If it were true that the monastic system would be protected by communists, then that meant the clergy's power and wealth would also be safeguarded. The rest was immaterial.[59]

The sad truth was that, in the fall of 1951, self-interest among the Lhasan hierarchy was the rule, not the exception. Few cared about the outside world, and even fewer cared if Tibet was regarded, internationally, as part of China or not.

Self-interest also informed the commoners of Lhasa. Although they had no power or wealth, they were not unduly bothered by the presence of the PLA, as long as the communists left them alone. The commoners' idea of independence was contingent upon their freedom to keep their own culture, the heart of which was Buddhism, to support the monastic system and, above all, to respect the sanctity of His Holiness the Dalai Lama, an emanation of the Bodhisattva Chenrezig. If the communists weren't going to tamper with Buddhism, as long as there was enough to eat, why put up a fuss?

ON OCTOBER 24, 1951, THE DALAI LAMA WROTE TO MAO TSE-TUNG:
"The Tibet Local Government as well as the ecclesiastic and secular people unanimously support this agreement, and under the leadership of Chairman Mao and the Central People's Government, will actively support the People's Liberation Army in Tibet to consolidate national defense, drive out imperialist influences from Tibet and safeguard the unification of the territory and the sovereignty of the Motherland."[60]

At last, Mao Tse-tung's shotgun wedding was concluded. In the following years, whenever he was challenged by the outside world, he would waive his marriage license with a condescending smile.

Whether anyone liked it or not, the emanation of Chenrezig now wore a red star on his forehead.

---

[59]Tsering Shakya, *The Dragon in the Land of Snows*, 90.
[60]*Tibet: Myth vs. Reality*, Beijing Review Publication, 1988, 134.

Yama, Lord of Death, with his sister consort *(Jamyang of Amdo)*

4

TREACHEROUS WATERS

Death was an amorous monster named Yama. He had the head of a wild bull. His penis was fully erect. His sister-consort—less grotesque but equally wrathful—wrapped her legs around one of Yama's massive thighs in tantric desire. His skin was midnight blue—hers was azurite. Their combined energy produced a hellish halo of fire that roared all around them. In their combined ecstasy, they trampled a bull that was in the act of sexually assaulting a human corpse.

Yama did not always exist.

Legend had it that there once was an old ascetic who, in search of nirvana, had meditated in a cave for fifty years. One night, moments before his enlightenment, two thieves burst into his hideaway with a stolen yak. Without seeing the old man, they hacked off the head of the bull. The ascetic said nothing. Turning around and realizing that they were being watched, the robbers drew their swords and advanced on the witness of their crime. The old man pleaded for his life. The thieves mercilessly decapitated him.

The ascetic didn't die.

He rose, snatched up the bull's head, lowered it onto his own headless shoulders, and transformed himself into Yama.

Consumed with vengeance, Yama ate the thieves and drank their blood from cups made of their skulls. Then he rampaged through the countryside laying waste to the villages and murdering all the inhabitants therein. Fearing that Yama would destroy the entire human race, the Tibetans made an appeal to Manjushri, the Bodhisattva of Wisdom.

Unlike the United Nations, Manjushri granted the Tibetans' appeal.

Manjushri sought out Yama's underworld lair—down into the very depths of the earth—and waged war on him. A frightful transformation ensued: Manjushri assumed an expanded mirror image of Yama. In this new incarnation, Manjushri was called Yamantaka.

Yamantaka sprouted thirty-two arms, eighteen legs, and nine heads—all engulfed in raging flames. When Yama saw this multiple version of himself, the shock killed him.

In this way, it is said that Death was scared to death.[1]

Yamantaka left Yama in his hell realm with a redefined role. Yama was now the *Protector* Regent of Death—he who eternally monitors the endless series of reincarnations—change that is illusory and therefore nonexistent.[2]

From the Buddhist perspective, there is nothing ironic about this anomaly. Everything in death is life. Everything in life is death. Everything is impermanence. Everything is change. But above all, everything is illusion. Death is just the interval between the past life and the future life—a dream— a watery reflection of the moon.

FOR TWENTY-YEAR-OLD ATHAR, THE NOVICE MONK FROM LITHANG, life meant promise in 1952. He had been selected to become a *shusor*'s assistant. A *shusor* was a merchant-lama who conducted business on behalf of monasteries. It was a tremendous boon for a peasant boy, and an opportunity to travel. Athar said good-bye to his mother and joined up with the *shusor*'s tea caravan. They were taking the tea to Lhasa to sell it for what they

---

[1]Yamantaka is Sanskrit for "Killer of Death"; "Dorje Shin-je" in Tibetan.
[2]Pema Wangyal of Dolpo, interview with the author.

hoped would be a sizable profit. Being on the open trail was a dream come true for Athar. That he arrived in Lhasa just in time to witness the initial influx of communist troops contributed to the excitement of his adventure rather than creating any apprehension.

This was before there were any roads—no trucks yet. But there were thousands of communist foot soldiers and hundreds of mules to carry their equipment. It was a very impressive sight. And I suppose their great number was supposed to impress us—all the best equipment, very good uniforms, all sorts of automatic weapons—some of the bigger weapons had to be carried on poles supported by pairs of soldiers. I just couldn't believe such power—we Khampas loved guns, of course.

The people of Lhasa didn't know what to think. It was frightening to them and very confusing. After the troops came, the price of the goods in the marketplace started going up very quickly. Chinese nonmilitary also came from Mainland China in large numbers: shopkeepers, shoemakers, and small-time businessmen. The Lhasans wondered if they were going to have a way to make a living.

Another thing that struck me was the many loudspeakers all over town. They were practically on every corner. You could never really get away from them: "Hail to the liberation of the Tibetans! The 17-Point Agreement will solve all the problems of the Tibetan People!" —that sort of Chinese propaganda.

My shusor *hated what was happening. He kept saying, "They are turning Lhasa into a Chinese city." We spent four months in Lhasa, which I loved because it gave me time to visit all the holy sites. I didn't understand or care what the Communist troops meant to Tibet's future. But my* shusor *did.*[3]

By the beginning of 1952, more than twenty thousand Chinese troops had been deployed to the Lhasan area. The army was very careful not to set up camp in the city proper. They were intent on downplaying the idea of foreign occupation. But that did little to allay the concern of the average Lhasan. For one thing, the immediate impact on the environment was dramatic. Overnight, Lhasa's population doubled. The tens of thousands of ponies, camels, and yaks accompanying the PLA took over the nomadic herds' traditional grazing land surrounding Lhasa. Fuel was also a problem. And since there were still no roads for transporting goods from Mainland China, the

---

[3]Athar, interview with the author.

PLA troops were utterly dependent on Tibetan surplus. A popular song heard on the streets was, "*They come here with nothing but chopsticks and empty bowls.*"[4]

The peasantry suffered the brunt of this strain. S. Sinha, the Indian consul in Lhasa and witness to the upheaval, described the economic structure of the country as "badly shaken," adding that it had "already affected the livelihood of the poor man, whose share of food and daily necessities has been ruthlessly whittled down."[5]

For all of Mao's talk of liberating the common man, his initial concern in Lhasa was not in winning over "the little guy." Unlike among the Chinese peasants, there was no preexisting desire among the Tibetan masses to be "liberated from their oppressors." Winning over the peasantry would have to come later.

Mao outlined for his generals the way to overcome the unique Tibetan problem:

"We have no material base in Tibet. In terms of social power they are stronger than us, which for the moment will not change. [Therefore make] every possible effort to use all suitable means to win over the Dalai Lama and a majority of the *upper strata* and isolate the minority of bad elements in order to achieve long-term goals of transforming Tibetan economy and polity gradually without spilling blood."[6]

Mao defined the upper strata as falling into three (sometimes overlapping) groups: the monastic hierarchy, the aristocracy, and the wealthy merchant-traders.

The monastic hierarchy: Although Mao openly despised religion, he instructed his generals to make large donations to lamasery events, feign reverence for holy artifacts, and to distribute silver dollars to the robed congregations. The Chinese even founded the Chinese Buddhist Association, which would soon boast the inclusion of high-ranking lamas.

The aristocrats: Mao authorized Chinese officials to pay the bluebloods handsomely for rentals or sold properties. Let the aristocrats think they were

---

[4]Ibid.
[5]FO 371-99659; MR, December 15, 1951.
[6]Mao Tse-tung as quoted by Dawa Norbu, "The 1959 Tibetan Rebellion: An Interpretation," *Congressional Quarterly*, no. 77 (1979), 77–78. Author's italics.

smarter than the Chinese who were eager to cough up exorbitant sums. Here, too (Mao advised), flattery would work wonders. Endless successions of fawning banquets were lavished on the nobles with the assurance that their superlative position in society would remain unchanged. Introduce them to modern technology. Spoil them with niceties. Phonographs became popular, and Bing Crosby crooned "White Christmas" from the balconies of the rich.

The wealthy merchants-traders: Mao suspected this group would be the easiest to win over, simply by dramatically increasing profits on their goods. India manufactured many items the Chinese needed but which were difficult to obtain in Mainland China. As a result, the caravans that moved along the trade trails began to bring in thousands of loads of a variety of products—from pickaxes and shovels, to cigarettes, cotton fabric, and sugar.[7] Another godsend for the merchants was the demand for their leading export—wool, which, prior to the Chinese invasion, had been in a serious slump.

Athar remembered the boon to his boss's business:

Everything changed overnight for all the Tibetan businessmen. My shusor's original plan had been to take the money we made in Lhasa and purchase coral and serge to bring back to Kham. Instead, we went to India to buy tools for the Chinese. Even though he hated the communists, he said it would be much more profitable to concentrate on their money.[8]

Administratively, Mao's goal was purely subversive. Modest reforms to the political structure—and then less modest reforms—would eventually make current Tibetan governmental structures redundant and obsolete. A master of "divide and conquer," Mao also saw value in "duplicate and conquer." The Education Committee, for instance, was organized to create new schools—a smart move inasmuch as education, up until now, had been traditionally left up to the monasteries and not supervised by the Central Government. The Education Committee was a big Chinese hit. Leading Tibetan households—including members of the Dalai Lama's family—were easily recruited, leaving Lhasan officials out of the loop and wondering why they hadn't thought of creating civilian schools long before.

---

[7]Lowell Thomas Jr., *The Silent War in Tibet*, 122.
[8]Athar, interview with the author.

Militarily, Mao's plan followed the same idea. The Chinese established the "Tibetan Military District Headquarters" in Lhasa, which was, essentially, a new Tibetan army designed to take over the old Tibetan Army when the time was right. Of the ten Command Leaders appointed to the "Tibetan Military District Headquarters," only two were Tibetan, and one of those was China's star collaborator, Ngabo. He was given the title "First Deputy Commander." When he appeared in the review stands at the inaugural ceremony—to the shock of the Tibetan troops—he wore the full regalia of a Chinese military officer.

By March of 1952, the Chinese generals felt the time was right to pressure the *Kashag* to hand over the Tibetan army. The *Kashag* was horrified but didn't know what to do. They asked the two Prime Ministers for advice. (These men had been appointed to govern Lhasa while the Dalai Lama was in Yatung in 1951. They proved to be able administrators and hard-line nationalists. They had gone on record as being against the 17-Point Agreement and they had also insulted the PLA generals by refusing to attend their social events.) The anti-communist Prime Ministers came up with a cunning idea: Rather than hand over their troops to the Chinese, they disbanded the entire Tibetan army, save three regiments.

The Chinese were furious. To underscore their fury, three thousand additional troops were brought into Lhasa. Correctly assuming that the Prime Ministers were at the bottom of this trickery, the Chinese generals demanded that the *Kashag* force the Prime Ministers to resign. Eventually, the pressure became too much. In order to avert an armed confrontation, the Dalai Lama felt he had no choice but to let the Prime Ministers go.

In terms of morale, real damage was done by their dismissal. The Prime Ministers had been wildly popular at a time when Tibet was in dire need of patriotic administrators. To make matters worse, the Tibetan food surplus had been appropriated by the PLA and now the public—for the first time in memory—was on the verge of famine.

The mood on the streets of Lhasa, already grim, got grimmer.

At the end of March, S. Sinha wrote in his monthly report to India:

"Rising prices, shortage of essential supplies, increased death from small-pox and influenza epidemics have all gravely stressed the underlying political imbalance in the country. . . . Starvation has weakened resistance to disease and many have died in the last month . . ."[9]

Kirti Lhundop, one of the thousands of young men who had been dismissed from the Tibetan army, was among those wandering the streets looking for food.

He was also searching for answers:

Now that I was an ex-soldier, I didn't know what to do. I had no skills other than fighting. I couldn't go back home [Lhoka, the district south of Lhasa] *because I knew there were no jobs there. All the other disbanded soldiers had the same problem. We were hungry. We had no place to go. We were very angry. And we decided to do something about it.*[10]

Kirti was one of many young men who joined a group called the *Mimang*.[11] The purpose of the *Mimang* was to protest the Chinese occupation and organize anti-Chinese activities. They made posters, which they plastered up and down the narrow streets of Lhasa demanding the expulsion of Chinese troops. They took a petition to the *Kashag*. They complained that there was no reason for so many Chinese soldiers to be stationed in Lhasa. No one was threatening to attack Tibet, so what were twenty thousand troops camping outside of Lhasa for? It wasn't imperialists who were starving the Lhasans. It was Chinese.

I have to say that we were as angry with the Kashag *as we were with the Chinese. They were not standing up to the Chinese. If they had been, there would have been no need for the* Mimang. *Anything the Chinese wanted, the* Kashag *just gave to them. The low price of* tsampa—*the main staple of our diet—was something Tibetans had always counted on. Now you could barely find it. Really, we Tibetans never had much, but this was the first time our country had experienced famine. And the Chinese troops just kept coming in. The rich Tibetans weren't doing anything to help us, either. Everyone was watching their own back, and that was as far as it went.*[12]

---

[9]FO 371-99659; MR, April 16, 1952.

[10]Kirti Lhundop, interview with the author.

[11]Full name *Mimang Tsongdu*, literally, the "delegation of the people."

[12]Kirti Lhundop, interview with the author.

The *Mimang* decided to confront the source of the problem, the PLA. Hundreds of young dissidents surrounded the house of General Chang Guohua, the Chinese commandant of the PLA. The general emerged from his house to see what the demonstration was about. They demanded that the general take his communist army and return to his own country. Guohua felt blindsided and not a little vulnerable. The guards stationed at his home were, until now, more for show than anything else. As he listened to the Tibetans' complaints, he made a mental note to increase his defenses. From then on, all Chinese residences would be heavily guarded.

A curfew was placed on Lhasan natives. The *Mimang* ignored the curfew. They smeared offal on pictures of Mao Tse-tung. They wrote anti-communist songs that the townspeople heartily adopted and sang openly on the streets in a kind of jaunty protest that went a long way in boosting morale.

The *Mimang*'s next target was Ngabo:

After Ngabo started the habit of wearing a Chinese officer's uniform, we hated him. He symbolized everything the Mimang thought was wrong with Tibet. We wanted to kill him, and we would have, but there were always too many Chinese guards around him. One night, we surrounded his house and screamed our protests. He didn't come out and there were too many guards for us to do anything other than yell, but at least we were letting him know what we thought of him.[13]

As the communists were beginning to learn, occupying a foreign country was one thing. Making the Tibetans accept Chinese occupation was quite another.

The Ngabo incident was reported to the Central Committee in Beijing. Mao was not overly concerned. He told the generals that the unrest was only natural. And it wouldn't go away until the PLA could provide its own food and supplies—something impossible to achieve until the roads to Lhasa, currently under construction, were completed. So far, the citizens were only vocally confrontational. Therefore, he advised:

"For the time being leave everything as it is, let this situation drag on, and do not take up these questions until our army is able to meet its own needs through production and wins the support of the masses a year or two from

---

[13]Ibid.

now. In the meantime there are two possibilities. One is that our united front policy towards the upper stratum . . . will take effect and that the Tibetan people will gradually draw closer to us, so that the bad elements and the Tibetan troops will not dare to rebel. The other possibility is that the bad element, thinking we are weak and can be bullied, may lead the Tibetan troops in rebellion . . . our army will counter-attack in self-defense and deal them a telling blow. Either will be favorable for us."[14]

The Chinese generals didn't follow Mao's plan to the letter, however. They ordered the *Mimang* to disband, which, they would soon learn, only fanned the budding insurgents' fire.

According to Kirti, the banning of the *Mimang* simply drove them underground and encouraged them to recruit additional support:

Many of the guys in the Tibetan army, whose regiments hadn't been disbanded, sympathized with us. We were all brothers, and some of them managed to smuggle weapons to us from the Tibetan arsenal. Anti-Chinese posters continued to pop up on the streets of Lhasa—that was us—only now we understood a little bit better Chinese propaganda and we attacked their propaganda word for word. One of their signs quoted Mao on the "materialism of imperialist forces." When we finally understood that word—materialism—we wrote signs that read, "Communism is materialism, not Buddhism!" We heard that sign, in particular, made the generals angry.[15]

Kalsang of Lithang, nephew of Gompo Tashi, joined the *Mimang* movement:

The Mimang *was quite a controversial movement with many of the Lhasa political leaders because power, in the traditional Tibetan government, was handed down within the same families, from one generation to the next. Naturally, they tried to hold on to their power and the* Mimang *tried to go around them. This is what you should understand: The* Mimang *was not just anticommunist; we were also pro-democratic, which scared the ruling class because many of them were becoming friendly with the communists and making money off of them.[16]*

---

[14]"On the Policies for Our Work in Tibet," Directive of the Central Committee of the CPA, from *Selected Works of Mao Tse-tung*, Beijing, 1977, vol. V, 73–76.
[15]Kirti Lhundop, interview with the author.
[16]Kalsang Gyatotsang, interview with the author.

The Dalai Lama's mother and his two older brothers,
Takster Rinpoche and Gyalo Thondup. *(Office of Information and International Relations, Dharamsala)*

Not all of the elite, however, were in bed with the Chinese. A significant number decided it was time to cut their losses, especially after the dismissal of the Prime Ministers. Under the guise of going on pilgrimages to holy sites in India, they feigned reluctance in having no option but to give up their official posts. Their real destination was Kalimpong, where there was already an enclave of Tibetan nobles waiting to see the communists' next move. Among the nobles was Gyalo Thondup, the Dalai Lama's next-oldest brother, who would soon become the single most important contact for the CIA. Gyalo would establish households in both Kalimpong and Darjeeling.

May 23, 1952.

The first anniversary of the signing of the 17-Point Agreement was celebrated by a big parade in Lhasa. The Chinese had a lot to celebrate.

Internally, the local Tibetan government had effectively been neutralized. Except for the Dalai Lama, the country was virtually without native leadership, and he was but a teenager. After the removal of the Prime Ministers, the policy of the *Kashag* was reduced to avoiding any action that might offend China and avoiding any action that might offend the Tibetan people. The *Kashag* was impotent.

BY THE END OF 1952, THE CHINESE HAD MANAGED TO PARTIALLY alleviate the famine by creating the Grain Procurement Board, organized to import large quantities of food and other goods from India. The success of the board was evidenced by a reduction in displays of public anger. As Mao had predicted, out-and-out insurrection was thwarted by a decent flow of food supplies, and the *Mimang*'s activities ebbed for the time being.

Another thing that helped the Chinese's relations with the locals was the introduction of technological developments. Small-scale hydroelectric plants were built. Newspapers printed in Tibetan were published in Lhasa every ten days and became very popular. For the first time the literate could read a censored version of international news.

Most of this activity was concentrated in the Lhasan District, but remote villages saw the advantages of modern technology as well. Medical dispensaries began popping up in the hinterlands, introducing modern means of treating illnesses for free. One illness in particular had reached epidemic proportions—syphilis.

Author George Patterson, who was in southern Tibet in 1950, relates that, according to some accounts, 90 percent of the adult Khampa lay population suffered from venereal disease: "I was rather hesitant about accepting such a percentage at first, but during my travels I found that, as far as any generalization can be made on Tibet, the figure was probably correct."[17] He treated hordes of patients with neoarsphenamine and maphenchlorsine and attributed the widespread practice of polygamy (both polyandry and polygyny) and extramarital sex as part of the problem. But he also concluded that the Khampa term used for syphilis—*gya-nad* ("Chinese illness")—shed considerable light on the subject:

"Either the Chinese soldiers brought it to Tibet during their campaigns or the Tibetan muleteers picked it up on their visits to the Chinese border. The

---

[17]George Patterson, *Journey with Loshay*, 88.

muleteers traveling continually from China to India would easily pick it up and then the nationally practiced promiscuity would accelerate the spread. There was certainly a high percentage of sterility and also of infant mortality. Many of the ordinary Tibetan women expected to lose two babies out of three, and this was not due only to carelessness on their part, for both men and women here were very fond of children."[18]

In any case, modern medicine was perhaps the most effective way the PLA had to assuage unrest among the *shi tsang*—the Chinese epithet for Tibetans, which meant "barbarians."

The *shi tsang* were impressed only to a point, but, by the end of 1953, the Chinese felt they had made substantial headway. Internal opposition in Lhasa had been significantly reduced. With food back on the table, open hostility was merely sporadic. Internationally, there was a growing willingness to believe that Tibet was merely a section of China that had been reabsorbed.

In fact, as far as The Chairman was concerned, the single most outstanding problem remaining in Tibet—and it was a big one—was Tibet's direct trade relationship with India, a relationship the two countries had enjoyed for centuries. This was a constant and growing irritation to Mao, because it blocked China from having complete control over Tibet's economy.

It was time for Mao to call on his old friend Nehru.

DECEMBER 31, 1953. BEIJING. NEGOTIATIONS BEGAN BETWEEN MAO and Nehru over India's trade relationship with Tibet. No one in Lhasa knew a thing about it. Neither the *Kashag* nor the Dalai Lama was informed of the meeting.

The resultant treaty between India and China came to be known as the Panchshila Agreement.[19]

Basically, the pact formalized all Indian trade with Tibet by having India *bypass* Tibet and go directly through Chinese channels. The pact helped to

---

[18]Ibid.
[19]Hindi for "five principles"; in English, the treaty was entitled "Agreement Between the Republic of India and the People's Republic of China on Trade and Intercourse Between Tibet Region of China and India."

solidify China's control over Tibetan economics, but politically, it was a far greater victory.

The wording of the treaty acknowledged India's unequivocal acceptance of China's sovereignty over Tibet. Tibet was referred to merely as "a region of China." This phrase was extremely important—critical, in fact—because it was the *first* instance of international recognition of Chinese sovereignty over Tibet.

Nehru, with dreams of pan-Asian peace dancing in his head, boasted that by signing the treaty, India had done "nothing better in the field of foreign affairs."[20] He also boasted that the agreement secured China's acceptance of the Sino-Indian border as established by British Raj decades before.[21]

Not everyone in the GOI was pleased with Nehru's negotiations—especially with Nehru's acceptance of Tibet as "a region of China."

Acharya Kripalani, a member of the Indian Parliament, denounced the treaty:

"I consider this as much a colonial aggression on the part of China as any colonial aggression indulged in by Western nations. The definition of colonialism is this: that one nation by force of arms or fraud occupies the territory of another nation. In this age of democracy when we hold that all people should be free and equal, I say that China's occupation of Tibet is a deliberate act of aggression."[22]

Heartening words to Tibetan sympathizers, perhaps, but of little use to Gyalo Thondup, the Dalai Lama's next oldest brother, and the growing number of dissidents who had moved out of Tibet and reassembled in the Indian border town of Kalimpong.

Athar had several opportunities to be in Kalimpong with his *shusor*'s caravans. He remembered the outpost as bustling with money, opportunity, and political intrigue:

The place was always crowded with pack mules and ponies, and Bengalis, Tibetans, Bhutanese, Nepalese, Marwaris,[23] *and Chinese, too—lots of money*

---

[20]Tsering Shakya, *The Dragon in the Land of Snows*, 119.

[21]Ibid.

[22]Chanakya Sen, ed., *Tibet Disappears: A Documentary History of Tibet's International Status, the Great Rebellion and Its Aftermath*, 120.

[23]A people originally from Rajasthan.

changed hands in Kalimpong. And lots of information. If you had money to begin with, you could make a lot of money in Kalimpong very quickly. But no one trusted anyone.

When the Tibetans in Kalimpong heard about the Panchshila Agreement, it was like the Indians had slammed the door in their faces. The Tibetans in Kalimpong were very anti-Chinese and now—if they had to do business with India through their enemy, the Chinese—well, you can see that it was a big problem for them and only increased their hatred for the communists. The talk on the streets was, "What else will Nehru do to help Mao? Will he seize our assets, since we're in Indian territory? Will he turn us over to the Chinese as illegal émigrés?"[24]

Kalimpong became a political hotbed. B. N. Mullik, chief of Indian Intelligence (and extremely pro-communist), visited Kalimpong four months after the signing of the Panchshila Agreement to take a "reading" of the mood in the border town. Though he had little sympathy for the Tibetan issue, he characterized the Kalimpong Diaspora as "shocked and anguished."[25]

THE AMBULANT ATHAR DIDN'T REALIZE IT AT THE TIME, BUT HIS job placed him in a special category of Tibetans—those who had a wider view of the changes and growing unrest over vast and varying districts of Tibet.

And no change was more dramatic or more essential to the Chinese occupation (and the eventual subjugation of the Tibetans) than the building of roads through Tibet. Although the goods Athar carried varied from trip to trip, the route remained fairly fixed: from Lhasa to Kalimpong to Dartsendo, Markham, Ba, Lithang, and, finally, back to Lhasa. The Dartsendo-Lhasa leg took him directly along the Chinese construction—what was to become the highest road in the world, a 1,413-mile wonder of modern technology that crossed twelve major rivers and fourteen mountain ranges at an average altitude of thirteen thousand feet above sea level:

---

[24]Athar, interview with the author.
[25]B. N. Mullik, *My Years with Nehru: The Chinese Betrayal,* 180.

Before the Chinese road was built, driving caravans of yaks and ponies and mules was a dangerous business—especially when you had to cross water—and there are many dangerous rivers in Tibet. There were things you wanted to know before you herded your animals through a river. How deep was it? How swift? Where was the best place to enter? Where was the best place to exit? Rivers were the homes of the nagas, water spirits who could cause you much harm if you didn't treat them with the proper respect. They could join forces with Yama and cause you to die. They could drown you. And we Tibetans didn't swim, because we had always been warned that it was best not to disturb the nagas. Well, as it turned out, dealing with the Chinese was like dealing with the nagas. Very risky.

Each time we made the circuit, the Chinese roads and bridges got closer to completion. They weren't paved but they cut across high passes and deep gorges—this was a really big change in Tibet. We were very impressed. And thousands of Tibetans were helping to build the roads. In the beginning, the Tibetans were

Tibet road crews carving out the precipitous Chinese Dartsendo-Lhasa highway. *(Collection of the author)*

paid very well. The Chinese employed over thirty thousand laborers on the road projects. Most of these guys were just farmers or nomads who had never had cash in their lives. They loved their jobs. This was the best thing that had ever happened to their families.

Even my shusor *was happy with the new roads. We could make the circuit so much faster. The military didn't bother us too much either. They needed us. We were bringing them goods. Oh, they would check our documentation or inspect our goods. But we weren't running guns or anything like that, so they didn't give us much trouble. My* shusor *made fun of them behind their backs. He called them "yadmo-yadmo," which means "yes-yes" in Tibetan, because they were always making big smiles at us and making a big show of what friends they were.*

But that changed. By 1954, I don't think anybody was calling the Chinese "yadmo-yadmo"—*never again.*

The [Tibetan] road crews became very unhappy. They would come up to our caravan and complain that the Chinese were cutting their wages. Each time we came, they had cut the wages a little bit more. When the Tibetans complained to their employers, the Chinese told them it was time to forget about money and to "think of the good of the Motherland." Many of the nomads just threw down their shovels and walked home—wherever that was, and many times it was very far away.

We traders also saw profits fall. By 1954, when much of the roads had been completed, they started to pay us less for the goods we brought from India. Then they started lecturing us—that we should be giving our profit to the Chinese government as a patriotic act! Also, the number of Chinese truck caravans grew—they became the yak caravans' competition. And the trucks were always given priority along the roads. We would have to herd our yaks to the side while the trucks passed. On my last caravan with the shusor, *there were many security checks along the way and many delays at these checkpoints.*

You know, now that I think about it, we called the roads "magmi-lamka"—"military roads" in Tibetan—so I guess we had some understanding that Tibet was turning into one big military base for the Chinese. Then, after the Chinese started taxing our goods so heavily that we could no longer make money, and we just gave up—that was when we realized how stupid we had been all along. It was our caravans that had helped build their military road—the very thing that was ruining our business. We had been tricked, and the time had come for us to pay for our stupidity.[26]

The road crews were beginning to understand as well. The drastic wage reductions caused a mass exodus from the Chinese roads precisely at the moment when the projects were nearing completion. No amount of cajoling would induce the Tibetans to return to the road crews.

So forced labor was introduced.

According to Lowell Thomas Jr., "Seven thousand men for the Lhasa airport; twenty thousand for the western reaches of the Shigatse-Gartok road; eight thousand for the roads of the Chumbi Valley; five thousand to clear timber for a Chinese rest camp in the forested hills to the east of Lhasa; more thousands for the forts and landing fields of south-west Tibet and all along the Indian border . . . the workers were summarily called up and dispatched to any area where they were needed. They might be required to go great distances on foot to reach their assigned work area."[27]

Incidents of labor-related deaths increased and so did Tibetan hatred. According to Thomas, on one section of the road in Kham, "two elderly men, who made up part of a group of ninety workers conscripted from a village, died of exhaustion during their term of labor. They were working many days' journey from home, and the Chinese overseer troops would not allow the bodies to be taken back for traditional disposal and the religious rites, all-important to an auspicious rebirth. When the village work group returned home, bearing this news, the people were at first sick with grief. Two nights later, however, they attacked the camp of a military patrol near the village. Three Chinese soldiers were killed."[28]

The communists were perfectly capable of crushing minor flare-ups, but a major political situation was beginning to take shape that was far more dangerous, and a doctrinal travesty to boot: The peasantry, the so-called downtrodden masses—the very group who were supposed to naturally embrace communism—were the Tibetans who were now most willing to kill Chinese.

Kalsang of Lithang put it this way:

---

[26]Athar, interview with the author.
[27]Lowell Thomas Jr., *The Silent War in Tibet*, 139.
[28]Ibid., 140–41.

Even if they had been our friends—which, of course, they weren't—it wouldn't have lessened our resentment. You don't know what it's like to have a foreign power occupy your country. But if you've ever had a relative or good friend stay too long in your house, you know how you begin to resent every little thing they do.[29]

Another Khampa put it more succinctly:

"They were like bull elephants bedding wherever they pleased."[30]

By the middle of 1954, China had a stranglehold on Tibetan commerce, transportation, and communications. In addition to road construction, Chairman Mao could boast new military installations, airfields, and communications facilities.

Having established physical control over the colonized nation, he could finally concentrate on what he did best: *political* coercion.

The Chairman rolled up his sleeves.

He understood that the key to Tibet was the Dalai Lama. Since it was out of the question to openly oppose him, the next best thing would be to subvert him. Mao was remarkably optimistic about the latter. He reasoned that, although the Dalai Lama was intelligent, fiercely patriotic, and devoted to his people, he was nevertheless inordinately young, ignorant of the outside world, and therefore impressionable—nothing a little reeducation couldn't remedy. Why not whisk him off to Beijing for an extended visit? In Beijing he would be separated from his people by thousands of miles and by centuries in time.

So Mao devised a pretext. He invited the Dalai Lama (along with a four-hundred-person entourage) to be an honored guest at an important celebration in Beijing—the framing of the new Chinese constitution. For his part, the Dalai Lama liked the idea. He saw it as an excellent political opportunity:

I was still greatly disappointed at [the Communists'] *complete disregard for the interest and welfare of our people. I thought I ought to meet the highest authorities in China, and try to persuade them to carry out the promises they had made in the agreement they had forced on us.*[31]

[29]Kalsang Gyatotsang, interview with the author.
[30]John F. Avedon, *In Exile from the Land of Snows,* 43.
[31]His Holiness the Dalai Lama, *My Land and My People,* 78.

. . .

IN ACCEPTING THE INVITATION, HOWEVER, THE DALAI LAMA HAD failed to take into account public reaction.

Tibet panicked.

Lowell Thomas Jr. relates the story:

"Immediately a storm of almost hysterical protest came from every corner of the country. Monasteries, large and small, dispatched fast couriers to Lhasa with messages pleading with the Precious One to remain with his people. At emergency meetings of the *Mimang* opinions were unanimous: the Dalai Lama must not go to China. . . . Khampa chieftains from the east [Gompo Tashi included] galloped into Lhasa, their swords drawn, to proclaim their loyalty to the God-King and to state their opinion that he should not leave the Holy City."[32]

Most Tibetans—ever suspicious of Chinese, particularly when they went into their *yadmo-yadmo* mode—did not believe that the Dalai Lama could be going to Beijing of his own free will. According to Thomas, "A wave of grief swept through the country. Few believed that the Fourteenth would ever return, and they mourned for him as though he were already dead. Thousands of people who lived near Lhasa dropped their work and made toward the Holy City, presumably hoping for a final glimpse of the Precious Protector."[33]

The nineteen-year-old would not be dissuaded. He left the Potala on July 11, 1954. On his way to the ferry outside of town (at the northern shore of the Kyichu River), the crowds went wild. The loudspeakers called for calm but the thousands of Tibetans were inconsolable.

Thomas continues: "The Chinese seemed stunned by the display of emotion and reverence. . . . The troops especially were confused. They had been ordered to act with the utmost restraint. The people, however, showed complete indifference to the bayonets. Many threw themselves into the street, and their prostrate bodies had to be lifted out of the way. Thus the procession inched along, and hours were required to get through the city."[34]

---

[32]Lowell Thomas Jr., *The Silent War in Tibet*, 155.
[33]Ibid.
[34]Ibid., 156.

When the procession reached the ferry and His Holiness was lowered to the ground, people moaned and pulled at their hair.

He walked down a white carpet and boarded several yak-skin coracles that had been lashed together for his transportation. The conveyance pushed off and the image of the Dalai Lama slowly retreated into the distance. All eyes were on a yellow silk parasol that was held above the Precious One. To many, it appeared the Kyichu River was pulling their leader down into its treacherous depths.

Thomas concludes: "In a final paroxysm of despair a group from the crowd suddenly rushed forward and broke through the guards. At first the Chinese thought the crowd was beginning to attack. Instead the people threw themselves from the stone embankment into the river to drown. Their action signaled a wave of suicidal frenzy in the great throng. Crowds pushed frantically toward the river. More troops were called hurriedly to line the embankment and to prevent the crowds from reaching the water. Some of the people tried to throw themselves onto the bayonets. The soldiers struggled with the people and kept most of them away. Other soldiers in boats, however, had to drag people forcibly from the water."[35]

And suddenly the Dalai Lama was gone from view.

The Lhasans looked at one another in an almost drugged disbelief. Zombie-like, they returned to a dead city. Kirti Lhundop called it *"a town of hungry ghosts. Do you know about the hungry ghosts? In Tibet, we believe that when you die, you enter the* Bardo.[36] *Yama watches over the Bardo and sends you onto your next life, which, depending on your karma, can take place in one of six realms: the god realm, the demigod realm, the human realm, the animal realm, the hungry-ghost realm, and the hell realm. Hungry ghosts are those who are so attached to their past life that they cannot let go of it. Nothing in the present satisfies them. They eat without satisfying their hunger. They drink without satisfying their thirst. Water only makes them thirstier. They are trapped. Nothing, no one can help them. That was Lhasa, after His Holiness left town."*[37]

---

[35]Ibid., 156–57.
[36]Sanskrit; literally, "space" or "interval."
[37]Kirti Lhundop, interview with the author.

. . .

THE BEIJING OF 1954 WAS A DAZZLING EXPERIENCE FOR ANYONE who had never been outside Tibet. To many of the Dalai Lama's entourage, entering the famed capital was like being ushered into the god-realm. Chairman Mao made sure the Tibetan dignitaries were lavished with all the amenities available to the communist elite. They would be feted for nearly a year.

Of all the Tibetans, the Dalai Lama had the least amount of time to enjoy the luxuries proffered. Mao was determined to keep the Dalai Lama on a tight schedule. The young man experienced his first train ride, his first airplane flight, and his first view of the buildings and transportation systems of a modern city. He participated in political sessions wherein he learned the fundamentals of Marxism. He met many foreign dignitaries (although real interaction was blocked by his ever-present Chinese escorts), including Nehru and Khrushchev. He saw all the trimmings of twentieth-century technology: factories with production lines, hospitals, schools, and universities.

So, too, did the fourteen-year-old Panchen Lama—spiritually, the second most important figure in Tibet and, politically, Mao's puppet.

"Divide and conquer" was now applied to the two holy men: It was Mao's intention to compromise the Dalai Lama's standing among his people by elevating the status of the Panchen Lama—both politically and spiritually— to equal footing. This was in direct contradiction of the traditional Buddhist ranking: As far back as the sixteenth century, whichever lama was older would automatically serve as tutor for the younger—though *always* with the understanding that the Dalai Lama retained temporal and spiritual superiority.

Mao's scheme was complicated but not original. Mao borrowed, or rather inherited, the idea from his predecessor, Chiang Kai-shek.

In 1923, the previous, Ninth Panchen Lama, convinced that the Thirteenth Dalai Lama was persecuting him, fled to Beijing for the protection of Chiang Kai-shek's regime. He died in Jyekundo in 1937, under mysterious circumstances, never to return to his ancestral seat, Tashilhunpo.[38] The *Kuomintang* saw the Panchen Lama's death as an opportunity to aggravate an

---

[38]Located in Shigatse, southwest of Lhasa.

already existing power struggle between Tibetan factions: Although the rec-ognized reincarnation of the Panchen Lamas had to be approved by the Lhasan government, the *Kuomintang* circumvented tradition by "discover-ing" their own Tibetan candidate. They proclaimed their new Panchen Lama in Beijing, in 1949.

A few months later, when Mao sent Chiang Kai-shek running to Formosa, he regarded the eleven-year-old Panchen Lama, ensconced in luxury in Bei-jing, as part of his political inheritance. (The Lhasan government refused to accept the boy as the Tenth Panchen Lama. But in 1951, when Ngabo signed the 17-Point Agreement, he was also automatically "certifying" that the boy in Beijing was, in fact, the real Panchen Lama—a key point in the agreement and a major victory for the communist regime.)

In 1954, Mao may have been able to fabricate political status for the Panchen Lama, but he had no control over the youth's natural gifts and flaws. The Panchen Lama was good at parroting standard-issue communist slo-gans, but he was no born leader. Whereas the Dalai Lama's intelligence was indisputably top-notch, the Panchen Lama was rumored to be rather slow-witted. To make matters worse, according to Lowell Thomas Jr., Mao failed to take "full advantage of their opportunity to educate him adequately . . . he seemed to have been taught little except that he was a person of almost lim-itless importance. When he was not paid the deference that he had been taught was due to him, he did not become angry or petulant; he was merely reduced to utter confusion."[39]

Whatever his shortcomings, the Panchen Lama deserved—and received—sympathy rather than criticism from the slightly older Dalai Lama. And some-thing else developed between the two young men that Chairman Mao had not counted on: The two teenagers developed a sincere regard for one another. This would come back to haunt Mao later on.

Nevertheless, Mao had to create absolute parity between the Panchen and Dalai Lamas. It was a crucial element in his long-term plan to crush Tibet.

In fact, the real reason the Dalai Lama had been brought to Beijing was so he could be induced to endorse Mao's new pet project for Tibet: PCART.

---

[39]Lowell Thomas Jr., *The Silent War in Tibet,* 116.

PCART stood for "Preparatory Committee for the eventual establishment of the Autonomous Region of Tibet." It was an important-sounding name, but PCART had nothing to do with autonomy. It was Mao's next step in destroying the last shred of independence still existing in Tibet.

And this was where the Panchen Lama's elevated status came into play: Mao was planning to assign the Panchen Lama a commanding position within PCART.

On the surface, PCART seemed to indicate that Tibet

The Panchen Lama, Mao Tse-tung, and the Dalai Lama in Beijing for the unveiling of PCART. (© *John Ackerly, Tibet Images*)

would avoid the more draconian "democratic reforms," of the kind the Soviet communists instituted when they invaded Mongolia in the 1930s: the denunciation and eradication of Buddhism; the ridicule of the intelligentsia, scholars, and high lamas; the surrender of all property, personal belongings, and individual liberty.

According to Roger E. McCarthy, Mao "managed to convince the Dalai Lama that China would not dispatch more military forces into Tibet to achieve what China wanted. . . . PCART was described to the Dalai Lama (by Mao) as an organization designed to *expand* the authority of the Dalai Lama and to increase the numbers of Tibetans in his government."[40]

In reality, PCART was conceived as a giant wedge to be driven into, and fatally crack, Tibet's governing system.

The Dalai Lama would be named "Chairman," which meant he would control Central Tibet. General Chang Guohua, the PLA Commander in

---

[40]Roger E. McCarthy, *Tears of the Lotus,* 86. Author's italics.

Lhasa, would be named "Vice Chairman," which meant he would control Eastern Tibet. The Panchen Lama would be named the other "Vice Chairman," which meant he would control Western Tibet. And the ever-available Ngabo would hold the nonterritorial office of Secretary General.

Divide and conquer.

The Dalai Lama suspected that PCART was a ruse. But he also believed— or, at the very least, ardently *wanted* to believe—that his many private conversations with Mao Tse-tung (and his resultant assessment that Mao was sincere and even kind) would somehow prevail in Tibet's favor. Much later, he would comment on his naïveté:

To give membership to these separate newly invented regions was an infringement in itself of the Chinese agreement not to alter the political system in Tibet or the status of the Dalai Lama. And the choice of members already had the seeds in it of failure. But people in desperate situations are always ready to cling to the slightest hope, and I hoped—in spite of my gloomy experience of Chinese political committees—that a committee with forty-six Tibetan members and only five Chinese could be made to work.

So I set off for home, very anxious to see what had been happening there, and trusting that we could make good use of this last degree of freedom.[41]

The Dalai Lama left Beijing in March 1955. His wishful thinking would be brief.

ONE OF THE DALAI LAMA'S FIRST STOPS, ONCE HE REENTERED Tibet, was his birthplace in Amdo, as well as the nearby monastery of Kumbum, from which his brother Taktser had escaped five years before.

Whatever nostalgia he may have felt was quickly erased. Something was seriously wrong in Eastern Tibet. Something had happened here that had not happened in Central Tibet. What, he wanted to know, was going on?

A clutch of Chinese cadres accompanied him almost everywhere, greatly reducing his opportunity of speaking privately with local Tibetans—but he could see the effects of repression in their faces nonetheless:

---

[41]His Holiness the Dalai Lama, *My Land and My People,* 96.

I asked them if they were happy and they answered that they were 'very happy and prosperous under the guidance of the Chinese Communist Party and Chairman Mao Tse-tung.' But even while they said it, I saw tears in their eyes, and I realized with a shock that even to me they were afraid to answer the question except by this Chinese Communist formula.[42]

What had happened in Amdo was a culmination of six years of increasingly harsh treatment by the communist cadres. Here, more than anywhere else in Tibet, the changes were devastating. The cadres were exasperated by the noncooperative attitude of the Tibetans: These Amdoans were stupid, obstinate, ungrateful, and deliberately antagonistic to the party line! Very well, they would go into "tough-love" mode and see how the Amdoans liked it. They introduced severe land reforms and insupportable tax hikes. And when that didn't seem to improve the Tibetans' attitude, the Chinese went after the religious leaders. Widespread persecution of the monks and nuns soon followed.

One event in particular, prior to the Dalai Lama's arrival, had enraged the communists. It involved the various tribes of the Golok people.[43]

Of all the Tibetan tribes, the Goloks had, perhaps, garnered the most notoriety. Their name meant "backward head," or "bellicosity," which, historically, had been directed primarily at the Central Government in Lhasa.[44] Nevertheless, they threw off the yoke of anyone—Chinese, Mongolian, or Tibetan—who tried to conquer them.[45] Their lifestyle was nomadic, so the boundaries of Golok were ill-defined but, generally, their territory extended northeast of Jyekundo and south of Kumbum, encompassing the multiple sources of the Yellow River along the Sino-Tibetan border. They had their own distinct dialect that Central Tibetans found almost impossible to understand. They were fierce, rugged, and good-looking. Fond of sable-trimmed hats, the men had aquiline noses, high cheekbones, and curly black hair that fell in tangled masses over their shoulders. The women were equally handsome and independent. The women's gypsylike costumes were distinguished by large silver

---

[42]Ibid., 97.
[43]Although a census had never been taken, it was estimated that the Golok tribes consisted of nearly one hundred thousand individuals.
[44]John F. Avedon, *In Exile from the Land of Snows*, 234.
[45]Their revolt against both countries, in 1807, is described in Warren W. Smith Jr.'s *Tibetan Nation*.

Golok monks. *(Joseph F. Rock, Collection of the Royal Botanic Garden, Edinburgh)*

plates attached to the back of their heads.[46] Everyone agreed, however, that their outstanding quality—men *and* women—was absolute fearlessness.

The communists were about to get a close look at the Goloks' legendary fearlessness. In 1954, some overzealous PLA troops burned several Golok monasteries to the ground. The sacrilege was too much for the devout Goloks. They called for an all-out war, which took the Chinese by surprise. The Goloks waged guerilla campaigns in which they took advantage of the mountainous terrain of their homeland. They waited until the PLA were drawn deep into their traps and then they slaughtered the godless enemy to a man. Many of the local monks were only too happy to lend a helping hand.

Infuriated, the communists rounded up several Amdoan leaders and ordered them to meet with the Golok chiefs and abbots and demand that they turn in their weapons. The Amdoans tried to reason with the Chinese: The Goloks would never allow themselves to be disarmed. They would die before they would submit to disarmament and they, the Amdoan leaders, would be the first to be murdered by the Goloks for having suggested such a fantastical idea.

The Chinese would hear none of it and told the Amdoans (at gunpoint) to proceed as ordered.

It was not to be. Rather than face death at the hands of the Goloks, the Amdoans defected south, where they eventually joined the growing population of malcontents in Kalimpong, India.[47]

---

[46]William Woodville Rockhill, *Land of the Lamas,* 181, 188.
[47]George Patterson, *Requiem for Tibet,* 147.

As for the Goloks—nomads and monks alike—they mounted their horses and rode to hideouts in the hills, biding their time and organizing themselves for further strikes against the despised Chinese.

THE TIBETAN TOWNS ALONG THE EASTERN FRONTIER WERE filled with similar stories of resistance.

The Dalai Lama heard these stories as he traveled south into the Khampa region. Here, too, the tales of communist savagery began to take on an all-too-familiar pattern.

This was a real eye-opener for the Dalai Lama. Either his Lhasan advisors hadn't known of these events, or simply hadn't cared enough about the plight of the Eastern Tibetan tribes to inform His Holiness. Now he was learning firsthand. And—most startling of all to the Dalai Lama—these tribes were speaking of openly confronting the enemy. This was a revolutionary idea to the young leader.

In my 1999 interview with the Dalai Lama, he told me that the Central Government had always thought in terms of *negotiations* with the Chinese. The *Kashag* had never even mentioned independence as a realistic option:

In 1955, when I came back from China, I spent more than two months on the road. I stopped at every town, city, monastery, and at each place I gave teachings. There was a very strong anti-Chinese feeling—that was very clear. Then, in the Derge area, I spent two nights in the private residence of a Khampa leader. He [and other Khampas] spoke about the independence of Tibet!

At that time, my mind was going in a different direction. Because of my meetings with Mao in Beijing, I was quite hopeful [about PCART]. But then the Khampa leader mentioned independence—openly!—his intentions of independence for Tibet—including all of Kham and Amdo—I was quite surprised! What I saw, among these Khampas, was not only their negative feelings about China, but also that they were nurturing an idea of an independent Tibet.[48]

This idea of unity must have reverberated in the Dalai Lama's mind when he headed further south, deep into the heart of Kham.

---

[48]His Holiness the Dalai Lama, 1999 interview in Dharamsala with the author and Roger E. McCarthy.

. . .

ATHAR, WHO WAS TEMPORARILY BACK IN LITHANG WITH HIS
mother, heard that the Dalai Lama was on his way to Dartsendo. It was very
exciting news for the entire region:

*The China-Lhasa road had finally been completed in 1955, a month or two
before the Dalai Lama reached Dartsendo on his return trip from China. But
right after it was finished, there was a major earthquake in the area. Large sections of the road in Kham were completely destroyed, and the Chinese couldn't
decide which way His Holiness ought to return to the capital.*

*Three high lamas from Lithang were sent to Dartsendo. Since the Chinese
road was ruined, the Lithang people hoped the Dalai Lama could use the opportunity to visit our monastery, which had been built by the Third Dalai Lama.
We had a very personal connection with all the Dalai Lamas. The Seventh and
Tenth Dalai Lamas had come from Lithang, as well as many of the high lamas
in the Gelupa monasteries of Lhasa. So you could say that, spiritually and politically, we were connected to the Dalai Lama's rule.*

*The PLA had some idea of this connection—especially the political part—
and they didn't like it at all. They hated the idea of His Holiness going to
Lithang. They viewed Lithang as enemy territory. They said, "You people from
Lithang are bad because you are always causing problems for us. You are like
wild cowboys. You are rough. You steal from our garrisons. You ambush our caravans. All you know how to do is fight and rob. You even put your best guns on
your altars! How can we trust you with the care of the Dalai Lama? You are the
worst troublemakers in Tibet!"*

*Of course the Dalai Lama was much safer with us than the Chinese, but the
lamas didn't say that. Instead, they suggested that the Dalai Lama could go to
Minyag Gangkhar. There was a pretty good mule trail from Lithang to Minyag
Gangkhar, so people from Lithang could see the Dalai Lama after all. The Chinese agreed, but they had no idea how many would come!*

*Thousands showed up! There wasn't anybody left in Lithang. They were all in
Minyag Gangkhar!*

*His Holiness gave teachings for three days. It was the most important event of
our lives. We Khampas were so happy that His Holiness was back on Tibetan soil
that we cried openly.*

The Chinese soldiers were very nervous, and more troops were rushed in, in case there was any kind of trouble. I think the PLA were putting on some sort of act. When had any Dalai Lama ever been harmed while traveling through Kham? The only people who would have harmed the Dalai Lama in Kham were the Chinese. And the Chinese knew that very well. They hated us because the Dalai Lama was so safe in Kham. I'll tell you one thing about the Chinese though: They were right about the people from Lithang being the worst trouble-makers in Tibet. They were about to find out how bad "bad" could be.[49]

ON JUNE 29, 1955, THE DALAI LAMA REENTERED HIS CAPITAL AFTER a year's absence. It was seething with newly organized resistance. Even before the Dalai Lama's return, the communists had put PCART into action. Changes were happening all over town, but the most inflammatory were taking place within the hallowed walls of the three great monasteries of Lhasa. The Chinese had decided to audit the lamaseries. From here on, the abbots would be expected to keep detailed accounts of their possessions, receipts, and expenditures. The reason behind the auditing was the growing menace of the (supposedly disbanded) *Mimang*. It was largely the monasteries that supported the *Mimang,* and the communists knew it. By keeping financial tabs on the religious institutions, they hoped, they could disrupt support of the miscreants.

A booklet had recently surfaced, crudely printed and passed from hand to hand in the back streets of Lhasa. It warned that, whatever the Dalai Lama might say in public in praise of the communists, the people should not believe it, because *He has no option but speak what is written for Him. Do not be discouraged nor be disillusioned nor lose your belief in Him.*[50] The booklet also gave an update of the crimes perpetrated by the communists in Amdo, Golok, and Kham.

The booklet—obviously written by the *Mimang*—brought up an important question: Who was actually producing these booklets? The answer was equally obvious: The only printing houses in all of Tibet were housed inside monasteries.

[49]Athar, interview with the author.
[50]Tsering Shakya, *The Dragon in the Land of Snows,* 139.

For the first time, the monasteries were openly characterized by the Chinese as insurgent. Reaction was swift. Tibetans regarded the monastic system as sacrosanct; communist control and disrespect of the clergy was intolerable and in direct violation of the 17-Point Agreement. The people flooded the streets in angry demonstrations. Some protests were spontaneous but others were well organized. Officials' houses were stoned. Increasingly virulent posters appeared all over Lhasa. Small PLA patrols were ambushed.

The violence culminated during *Losar,* the Tibetan New Year celebrations. An unscheduled parade of *dob-dobs,* or "warrior monks"—the elite and fearsome security force for monasteries—demanded the Chinese cease snooping around the "treasures of the monasteries." (Treasure might mean golden statues and priceless books, but there was no one in Lhasa who didn't know that it also meant the vital cache of guns and ammunition locked up in all monastic storerooms.)

Khampa monks belonging to the elite force the *dob-dobs.* The swords and clubs were not for show. *(Joseph F. Rock, Collection of National Geographic Society)*

The public outcry was of such unprecedented vehemence that the Chinese were truly shocked and forced to reconsider. They didn't dare risk an open confrontation with the clergy—not yet—not until their other reforms were fully operational. Reluctantly, temporarily, the cadres backed off the monastic institutions.

Still, the Chinese failed to understand the profound role the monasteries were playing. Put simply, the trans-Tibetan network of religious enclaves was the pony express of the resistance movement. Using the six-thousand-plus monasteries scattered throughout Tibet like so many relay stations, the burgeoning resistance could gather reports of incidents of injustice and/or newly deployed PLA troops quite expeditiously—wherever they occurred in the vast country. Also, lamas "going on pilgrimages"—a time-honored tradition, unexceptional and familiar to everyone—provided the perfect guise for spies on the move.

Some monks took a more direct approach. They "gave back their vows" to the monasteries, the formality of renouncing one's monkhood.

Kalsang of Lithang was one of them:

It was getting very hard, as a monk, to just sit back and watch what was happening to Kham. The slightest provocation by the Chinese was met with more and more hostility. It seemed clear to my entire family that it was only a matter of time before there would be a major uprising. My uncle, Gompo Tashi, got word for me to come to Lhasa, where things were really getting tense. When I arrived, I was very surprised: There were many hundreds of Khampas already there, waiting for the word to fight. That's when I took off my monk's robes forever, like many other monks who had escaped to Central Tibet.[51]

WHAT PRECIPITATED THIS INFLUX OF KHAMPAS, AMDOANS, AND goloks was the "democratic reforms" that, unlike in Lhasa, were in full swing in Eastern Tibet.

Conscripted labor has already been mentioned, but other reforms in the east were tearing the natives apart. Over twenty thousand Tibetan children had been separated from their families in order to be "educated" as wards of

---

[51]Kalsang Gyatso, interview with the author.

the state in a newly created network of minority schools.[52] In Amdo, especially, roads and land reform had totally disrupted the nomadic way of life. The loss of political independence, the confiscation of land and property, the subversion and constant ridicule of their culture and religion and the increased menace of foreign troops threw nomadic life into a tailspin.

But the greatest miscalculation perpetrated by the Chinese was their not-so-subtle move for gun control. Chinese delegations descended on Khampa villages with the news that all weapons must be identified by type and owner. This was the last straw. No Khampa believed that it would stop there. Overnight, guns were squirreled away in safe places. A Khampa's gun was the quintessential component of his worth as a protector of his family, home, and religion—no possession was more jealously guarded. If the Chinese wanted the Khampas' guns, they would have to fight for them, which was exactly what many Khampas were in the mood for anyway. No action so unified the Tibetans as the threat of disarmament. Tribes who had seldom, if ever, joined forces with neighboring tribes, now met secretly to find ways to face the Chinese with a united front. And many monks, like Kalsang, said good-bye to their robed brothers to join the resistance—or rather said hello to them, because their fellow monks had also "returned their vows" to the abbots.

HOW COULD BUDDHIST MONKS BECOME WARRIORS?

Perhaps the iconography of Buddhist painting supplied the answer, in part.

Manjushri, the Bodhisattva of Wisdom, the deity who had transformed himself into Yamantaka in order to kill Death, was painted in the temples holding a holy book[53] in one hand and, in the other, a flaming sword. Cutting through ignorance was an act of courage and, some said, mental violence.

Another example was King Gesar.

King Gesar, it will be remembered, pictured in full armor riding into battle on his warhorse, was said to have killed the enemies of the *dharma*—thousands of them—with ruthless abandon.

---

[52]John F. Avedon, *In Exile from the Land of Snows*, 44.
[53]The *Prajnaparamita*, "transcendent knowledge" in Sanskrit: Buddha's teachings on emptiness, transcending the fixation of subject, object, and action.

Vajrapani, the Bodhisattva who represented the embattled aspect of the guardians of faith, was envisioned as a pugnacious god furiously engulfed in flames.

There was no dearth of examples.

In a world where metaphors and wondrous otherworldly events were a working reality—where potentially demonic and plague-inducing goddesses lurked in the rivers and lakes; where serpent-tailed Rahula held dominion over a hostile sky; where brigands could ride into your tiny village and take your earthly possessions and hack your family to pieces if you weren't prepared to defend yourself; where life was a compendium of a million past lives, a million future lives, and all the karma accrued therein; where violence was *never* a good thing, but an inevitable phenomenon along the savage journey to Enlightenment—war against enemies of the dharma was a personal choice and not to be judged. If a life taken would spare a hundred—if the death of a human engaged in negative activity would benefit all sentient beings—then was there not a karmic trade-off?

Violence could not be rewarded.

Never.

You sucked it up and accepted the penalty for your transgressions. If you were relegated to the hell realm in your next life because you *took* life in this one, so be it. That's what you deserved.

But you could also hope that if you helped others at the expense of your own karma, the extenuating circumstances of your *motivation* might, in the end, weigh in your favor. Tibetan history was littered with examples of monks taking up arms when Buddhism was perceived as being threatened.

And finally, from a military personnel standpoint, when defending the faith, monks could be the most magnificent of soldiers. Lowell Thomas Jr. describes the monks as "superbly disciplined. They could subsist on a meager diet, and the rigors of their duties gave them muscular strength and amazing stamina."[54] And because of the unparalleled communication network between monasteries, "the average lama had a clearer picture of the enemy's strength and deployment and was in a better position to plan effective tactics"[55] than any layman.

---

[54]Lowell Thomas Jr., *The Silent War in Tibet*, 183.
[55]Ibid.

Good or bad, monasteries had always been potential armies. It was like looking at the reflection of the moon in a lake. The moon was not really in the lake, but then again, the moon was in the lake.

LITHANG, 1955.

The monks finally experienced the full brunt of Chinese hatred. Athar remembers:

In 1955, several communist leaders came to Lithang Monastery and announced that all arms had to be surrendered. They knew we had large stores of weapons and ammunition. They said, "All property now belongs to the communists. Tibet is now China and you must learn how we Chinese live." Everyone in the Lithang area was forced to go to communist meetings . . . so many meetings! And they got uglier and uglier. But the monastery would not give up its weapons.

Then one day, all the high lamas were dragged out into a courtyard, and all the townspeople were forced to watch at gunpoint. The Chinese were screaming at our lamas, and you should understand how shocking this was to the people who revered them as their spiritual guides. The Chinese yelled:

"For five years we have been trying to civilize you but you are still just like animals. You do not think like us. So now you must make a choice. Either you take the White Road or the Black Road. If you surrender your arms and property peacefully, that is the White Road. If you make us fight you—and you will lose—that is the Black Road."

One of the older lamas stepped forward and said:

"What is there to decide? Our own families will not give up what is theirs and has always been theirs. You Chinese did not give us our property. Our forefathers gave us our property. Why should we suddenly have to hand it over to you, as if it was yours in the first place?"

After that meeting, there was no doubt in anyone's mind that big trouble was waiting for us.

Lithang was marked.

You could see it in the eyes of the Chinese.[56]

---

[56]Athar, interview with the author.

The historical Buddha at the moment of Enlightenment under the
Bodhi tree in Bodhgaya, India *(Jamyang of Amdo)*

5

BLOODBATH AND THE
BODHI TREE

Gompo Tashi likened the beginnings of the resistance as gusts of wind: *...Slowly building in size and strength, as they became a howling storm; it was like a gigantic storm one could see forming on the distant horizon in the east that would gradually come closer and closer until its full fury was felt.... And in the meantime, the tribal leaders were organizing and communicating.*[1]

One such gust appeared at the 1956 New Year's celebration in Lhasa. The annual parades gave the Tibetans a political opportunity to curse the Chinese occupation. These demonstrations were, in part, spearheaded by three *Mimang* leaders: Alo Chonzed, Bumthang, and Lhabchug. The communists reacted by demanding the arrest of the ringleaders. After considerable stalling, the *Kashag* submitted to the Chinese demand. The patriots were thrown into prison.

---

[1]Gompo Tashi, *Four Rivers, Six Ranges,* 72.

Their incarceration, however, generated an electric rallying point for local hostilities. Even worse, while imprisoned, Lhabchug unexpectedly died. The Chinese claimed Lhabchug perished of natural causes, but Tibetans suspected foul play. The public outcry was deafening. The communists didn't want martyrs on their hands. They quickly decreed that the remaining two *Mimang* leaders would be released and banished from Tibet. But the damage had been done. The public did not and would not forgive. Alo Chonzed, in particular, had been enormously popular with the people. The communists could physically eject him from Tibet, but the memory of Alo remained a bitter presence. And it wasn't just the Chinese who, from a public relations viewpoint, suffered. Much of the peoples' fury was directed at the members of the *Kashag* as well. They, too, had blood on their hands. It was they, after all, who buckled under the Chinese demand and offered up Lhasa's finest like a trio of sacrificial cows. Once again, the cowards at the top were handing over Tibet, a little piece at a time. In explaining how he regarded the political hierarchy, Kirti Lhundop said: *Loving the Dalai Lama was simple. Hating the Chinese was simple. But the* Kashag *and the aristocrats up there in the Potala? Every time I passed* [the Potala] *my stomach got tight. I felt ashamed.*[2]

ABOUT THE SAME TIME, IN THE LAWLESS DISTRICT OF GOLOK, THE gusts of dissent took a more violent turn.

Mao had promised on Beijing radio that, eventually, he would move ten million Chinese into the Tibetan region. Since the Goloks' territory abutted the Sino-Tibetan border, they were the first to experience "population transfer." Mao resettled thousands of Chinese farmers into the heart of the Goloks' grazing land. Unlike Lhasans, however, Goloks were not demonstrators. Spontaneously and simultaneously, from all directions, laymen and monks readied their weapons and attacked newly arrived Chinese farmers without mercy.

The PLA struck back.

Three thousand Chinese troops marched into the disputed area with orders to disarm the Goloks. The Goloks responded with a blood-curdling

---

[2]Kirti Lhundop, interview with the author.

war cry and engaged the enemy in a two-day battle. News of the battle reached other Golok camps; within hours, a much larger expedition of local tribes was organized. Nearly two thousand mounted Goloks—accompanied by Muslim guerillas who also lived in the region—galloped to the nearest Chinese garrison. Armed with swords and muzzle-loading rifles, they surprised the garrison in a predawn attack and massacred most of its eight hundred Chinese troops. The Goloks' losses were small, and they captured an excellent supply of arms in the process.

Victory was short-lived.

An even larger contingent of Chinese fanned out, stole the Goloks' herds, burned their settlements and monasteries to the ground, and slaughtered several thousand Golok men, women, and children in the process. The survivors escaped to the hills. Filled with grief at the loss of their families, their homes, their way of life, the Goloks vowed to live only to murder Chinese— no matter how long it took—every last one of them.[3]

The rest of Tibet would not know of the Goloks' plight until long after the fact. Once again, the lack of a modern communications network would shackle the Tibetan resistance's ability to address outrage. As for the outside world, it would be years before they learned of the Golok revolt.

DEEP IN SOUTHERN KHAM, THE SITUATION WAS EQUALLY VOLATILE.

The revolt began with the tribals of Changtreng,[4] who refused to cooperate with Chinese land reforms. When cadres accompanied by PLA escorts entered Changtreng to force the issue, the Khampas struck back by killing the Chinese to a man.

The PLA exacted revenge by moving in an enormous contingent of troops, thereby laying siege to Samphe-Ling, the main monastery of Changtreng. Now even more defiant, the Khampas blocked the brook that provided water to the Chinese camp, situated less than a mile from Samphe-Ling.

---

[3]Lowell Thomas Jr., *The Silent War in Tibet*, 187.
[4]A day's ride south of Lithang.

By the end of February, the three thousand monks in Samphe-Ling had taken in thousands of local inhabitants. Some were refugees; others were there simply to fight and protect their beloved monastery.

One day, a Chinese plane flew very low over Samphe-Ling. It dropped leaflets. The leaflets warned the Khampas to surrender before it was too late. The Tibetans refused.[5]

Tinzing Jyurme, a nineteen-year-old monk of Samphe-Ling, recalled:

The monastery was built well and could withstand pre-twentieth-century attacks. But, of course, the Chinese had mortar shells. It didn't matter, because the Chinese knew if they attacked from the ground they would sustain heavy casualties themselves. Finally, a single plane came out of the clouds and bombed and leveled Samphe-Ling. So many monks and men and women and children were killed within a few minutes! I don't think anyone ever knew how many, but at least a thousand—maybe two thousand. Those that survived were either arrested by the PLA or fled to the mountains in the west, and then on to Lhasa. I was one of them who escaped.

But not the rest of my family.

My family was particularly unlucky. My father and my uncle had been two of the main troublemakers. The Chinese captured them. All of my family's land and possessions was confiscated. My mother and little brothers and sister were thrown out onto the street like beggars. My father and uncle were beaten repeatedly in the town square and then locked inside a big storehouse that had somehow survived the bombs. Over a hundred men from Changtreng—including many lamas—were kept there . . . terrible conditions . . . no windows . . . no medical care, and they were all beaten on a regular basis, with many broken bones and internal injuries. At one point, my father refused to denounce the head abbot, so he was left without food for eight days. He was imprisoned for one and a half years like that—always half-starved. Then he was relocated—like many of the monks and laymen—ten kilometers away, where he became a forced laborer in the road crews. He lasted for another three years on the road crews, until he died of exhaustion.

---

[5]Tsering Shakya, *The Dragon in the Land of Snows*, 140.

As I said, I managed to escape, but the rest of my family was restricted to the Changtreng boundaries and also forced to do hard labor. Every night after work, they were forced to attend communist indoctrination meetings called thamzings.[6] The thamzings were really awful —the worst thing the Chinese ever did to us Tibetans. The Chinese built a wooden platform in the town square, and each night they would drag a different "wrongdoer" up onto the platform so that everyone could see him ... or her.

Chinese cadres preparing Tibetan woman for *thamzing*. *(Office of Information and International Relations, Dharamsala)*

Usually they had been beaten before they were put up on the platform so that they would look submissive. They had to keep their heads down so that they looked shameful. If they looked up, they would get a rifle butt in the side of their head. They had signs hanging from their necks that labeled them "enemy of the people." The local people were then forced to accuse their neighbors and loved ones up on the platform of being "enemies of the people." If they didn't say bad things, they would be the next ones up on the platform. In this way, Tibetans were encouraged to spy and say bad things about each other. Everyone became paranoid of their neighbors. No one trusted anyone else. There were so many

---

[6]Literally, "struggle." *Thamzing* is a "peculiarly Chinese invention combining intimidation, humiliation, and sheer exhaustion. Briefly described, it is a political and physical gang-beating of one man by many, in which the victim has no defense, even the truth ... no victim can hold out for long. ... There is never any time limit to a Struggle. ... After three or four days the victim begins inventing sins he has never committed, hoping that an admission monstrous enough might win him a reprieve." Bao Ruo-wang, *Prisoner of Mao*, 59.

beatings in the village courtyard . . . and torture sessions . . . and executions. One of my older brothers was tortured and beaten to death on that platform. My other three siblings didn't die there but they died of a combination of thamzing beatings and malnutrition while imprisoned.[7]

THE NYARONG DISTRICT WAS FARING NO BETTER. NYARONG WAS the home of Aten, the opium dealer. There, the Chinese "democratic" reforms were rejected with equal fury:

Chinese soldiers accompanied by civil officials proceeded from village to village, demanding the surrender of weapons. They then held thamzings. Village headmen, lamas and prominent citizens were denounced, beaten, humiliated and sometimes executed. The whole area was rocked by these events, and any last illusion of compromise or peace was shattered when the Chinese turned against the tribal leaders whom they had previously honored and feted. Gyurme, an important tribal chief, was one example. He was away on business at Dartsendo when a number of Chinese soldiers came to his house and demanded that they—his mother, wife, young son and an old family retainer—surrender all weapons. When the Chinese were told that there were no guns on the property, without a single warning, the Chinese shot every one of them dead.[8]

A fiery young woman by the name of Dorjee Yudon, who knew the family who had been executed and whose husband, also a tribal leader, was away on business in Dartsendo at the time, flew into a rage. On behalf of all innocent families in Nyarong, she vowed to fight back. She called for a meeting of the men who were under her husband's jurisdiction. She ordered them to ready their firearms.

Jamyang Norbu writes: *She dispatched letters all over eastern Tibet, urging the people to rise against the Chinese. Dressed in a man's robe and with a pistol strapped to her side, she rode before her warriors to do battle with the enemy. She ferociously attacked Chinese columns and outposts everywhere in Nyarong.*

[7]Tinzing Jyurme, interview with the author.
[8]Gompo Tashi, *Four Rivers, Six Ranges,* 82.

The remaining Chinese soldiers and officials retreated to the Castle of the Female Dragon, where they proceeded to hold out.

The castle was stormed, with Dorjee Yudon herself leading the charges. But the great walls of that old castle were built to withstand such attacks, and without artillery (which the rebels did not have) were well nigh impregnable. Casualties soared. Finally Dorjee Yudon decided to lay siege to the castle.

By now the whole countryside was in ferment, and many other villages and tribes rose up to fight. Dorjee Yudon's task at the castle was proving to be difficult. The Chinese garrison was well stocked with food and ammunition, and they also had a spring of clear water within the walls.

After a month, six hundred troops from the Eighteenth Division arrived from Kanze to relieve their beleaguered comrades in the castle. Dorjee Yudon met them at Upper Nyarong and managed to defeat them. About four hundred Chinese soldiers were killed, but two hundred managed to break through the siege lines and enter the castle.

However another column of about fifteen to twenty thousand soldiers poured in from Drango and Thau in the east. Dorjee Yudon was forced to give away, and the siege was lifted. Yet the fighting accelerated and lasted for a month, after which the superior numbers and arms of the Chinese began to tell.

The Chinese suffered heavy losses, about two thousand dead and many more wounded. Two hundred officers were also killed. Their bodies were buried with much ceremony outside the old castle.

Finally the Chinese regained some measure of control in the country, and the rebels had to take to the hills, where they initiated a relentless guerilla campaign. Day by day, their numbers swelled.[9]

Nothing is known about Dorjee Yudon's demise, although one source heard a rumor that she had been shot between the eyes by a Tibetan—what Westerners would call a bounty hunter—for a sizable Chinese reward.[10]

IN DERGE, REVOLT BEGAN BECAUSE THE CHINESE BUNGLED A PLAN to deceive the local hierarchy.

---

[9]Jamyang Norbu, *Horseman in the Snow*, 96–97.
[10]Sonam Namgyal, interview with the author.

The communists summoned two hundred leaders from the Derge District to convene at a local fortress,[11] ostensibly to discuss the matter of "democratic" reforms. Once the Khampas were secured inside the fortress, five thousand PLA troops surrounded the hill. For two weeks the Tibetans were held prisoner. Daily they were belittled, screamed at and threatened, because they refused to embrace Mao's dream. On the fifteenth day of detention, the Khampas decided to pretend to endorse the Chinese demands. Three days later, the prisoners realized that the guards of the fortress had become inattentive. That same night they escaped into the surrounding mountains. Having tasted Chinese treachery firsthand, Derge's organized guerilla resistance was assured, the Chinese themselves having turned the Khampa establishment into a vengeful posse of outlaws.[12]

AS FOR THE LITHANG PEOPLE, WHAT THE CHINESE CALLED "THE worst of the troublemakers," the uprising began during a religious ceremony in the spring of 1956. Chinese cadres attempted to arrest high-ranking lamas, and a showdown ensued.

The PLA particularly wanted to capture the head abbot of Lithang, Khangsar Rinpoche. He had refused to hand over the wealth of the monastery. But according to one Tibetan source, the Chinese singled out Khangsar Rinpoche because he had been openly anti-communist for years.[13]

Whatever the underlying reason, the laymen and the monks alike decided that it was time to dig in and fight. Athar reports:

We had nothing to lose and maybe a small chance to win if we fought. One thing was certain: If we just gave up, we would be killed or turned into slaves.

A messenger rode into town saying that the PLA was on the move, heading toward Lithang in great numbers—perhaps as many as twenty-five thousand troops. All the people rushed around, gathering up their hidden weapons. Some of the wealthier families, like Gompo Tashi's, had their own private armories. And of course the monastery had big stockpiles.

---

[11]In the village of Gyamda, halfway between Derge and Chamdo.
[12]John F. Avedon, In Exile from the Land of Snows, 44.
[13]Tenzing Tso-chak, interviewed by Fred Lane in "The Warrior Tribes of Kham," Asiaweek, March 2, 1994.

One of our local leaders, Yunri Ponpo,[14] collected many nomads to help us. Yunri Ponpo was a friend of mine. He was young, about twenty-five, and not big for a Khampa, but everyone respected him—he never stepped away from a fight. He was a little crazy and one of the best riders and marksmen in the region. By that time, he and his men had already gone on many incursions to rob Chinese garrisons and to attack small groups of PLA, and of course the Chinese knew all about him and wanted him dead. While they sent out search parties to kill him, Yunri Ponpo took his men and collected two thousand more nomads to come to Lithang—which we really needed.

The PLA heard about this and decided to kill Yunri before he got back to Lithang. Because Yunri was so popular, the Chinese hoped that killing him would scare us—they thought we would be too shaken to continue fighting. So they set up an ambush about a day's ride from Lithang. It was a narrow pass and they figured he would be coming back that way, since, from the south, it was wide-open plain . . . no cover. The problem for the Chinese was that they didn't know what he looked like. Yunri Ponpo didn't know anything about this, and he and his men rode right into the Chinese trap. It was a shoot-out. When the smoke cleared, a few of Yunri Ponpo's men had been killed, but many more Chinese were murdered. But the Chinese saw it as a victory because they were convinced that they had killed Yunri Ponpo. They made an announcement that Yunri Ponpo was dead, but the truth was that they had only killed his servant. When they found out their mistake and that he had been spotted a day later in Lithang, they were mad as nagas.

Yunri and his men made camp just below town. He called a meeting inside the monastery on the hill. He told the lamas about the ambush and said, "Tomorrow or the next day the Chinese will come here and we must fight. There can be no more waiting. You know what they did in Changtreng. That is Lithang's fate as well. They tried to kill us yesterday and they mean to destroy this monastery and everything in it."

Lithang was the biggest monastery in Kham. It was built up the hillside and was protected all the way around by a twenty-foot-tall wall. There were eight gates. The first thing the monks did was to lock and guard the gates. Overnight, the monastery turned into a military headquarters.

---

[14]His full name was Yunri-Pon Sonam Wangyal.

Yunri Ponpo, patriot of Lithang.
(Collection of Athar Lithang)

On every rooftop, lamas and monks—nearly five hundred of them—stood guard looking out over the valley and the river that went down through it out into the plain. The word spread quickly that Lithang was going to fight. Thousands of local people got their guns and came to the monastery ready to fight alongside Yunri Ponpo and the monks. Four nomad leaders brought hundreds of families each. Farmer leaders brought in many more hundreds of families. Lithang monastery was like a city, it was so big, but there had never been that many people inside its walls at one time—at least, as long as anybody could remember. Everybody helped. Women brought in water. Children helped with the barricades. There was fear but there was also happiness because the Lithang people were finally doing something.[15]

Dorje Sherap, another young monk from Lithang, picks up the narrative:

The next day the PLA moved across the plain. From the monastery you could see for over fifty miles. I don't know how many thousands came, but they set up camp in a way that stretched out very far—probably to show off their numbers. The soldiers went to work digging trenches . . . to let everybody know that they weren't going anywhere. They brought all kinds of automatic weapons and big artillery that was pointed at the monastery. The resistance had nothing like that—just different kinds of rifles, many of them antiques—and our stock of ammunition was not very good. But we had enough food to last for a long time. If the Chinese wanted a siege, that was fine with us.

The siege lasted for one month and twenty-seven days. Sometimes they would attack, but we always killed more of them than they did us.

---

[15]Athar, interview with the author.

Also, some of the Khampas managed to sneak through enemy lines at night and dam up the stream that ran out of the hills next to the monastery so that the PLA would have nothing to drink. When the Chinese sent a group of soldiers up the canyon for water, we could pick them off, one by one—no problem. After nine days of this, a few of us sneaked back through enemy lines and reopened the dam. The Chinese were really thirsty by now. They rushed up through the canyon to get water. And in this way, we killed a very large number of Chinese guys.[16]

Again, Athar:

There was a high lama who for several years had been collaborating with the Chinese. He had been in the communist camp all this time. After nearly two months of the siege, the Chinese sent him up to the monastery to talk. He said, "Airplanes are not far away. If you do not surrender tonight, tomorrow this monastery will be bombed and destroyed. Trust me. It is going to happen. It would be better if you do something tonight. Either surrender, or try to escape . . . there is no other way. You must do something to save yourselves."

After he left, airplanes circled over Lithang and then flew away. It was clear that the lama wasn't lying.

Yunri Ponpo had a big meeting that afternoon. After the sun went down, at least half of the laymen and their families, and also many of the monks who had kept their vows, slipped away out a back gate.

But Yunri Ponpo said, "I will never leave this monastery. It's better to die here than to give in to the Chinese." Some of his men tried to persuade him to leave. They told him that if they left now, they could fight another day from a different place. But Yunri Ponpo said, "No. Wherever we decide to go, we are all going to die from Chinese bullets. If we surrender, they will kill us. I'm finished running. Everyone else can escape if they like, but I'm staying here."

The next morning, the Chinese began by shelling the walls of the monastery. By ten o'clock, they had broken through and the PLA came pouring through the holes. They were everywhere. And there was shooting from all directions. For about thirty minutes, you were as likely to be killed by a Tibetan as a Chinese. So many soldiers on both sides were killed. Artillery bombed many of the gompas and smaller chapels. Tibetans were scattered through the alleys and streets— soldiers lying facedown in their own blood.

---

[16]Dorje Sherap, interview with the author.

Yunri Ponpo and some of his men were in a big chapel about halfway up the hill. They killed as many PLA as they could before their ammunition ran out. Rebels who were scattered about in other buildings also ran out of ammunition and they threw their guns out the windows. They came out unarmed, their hands up. Everything quieted down. The shelling stopped, the rifles quit firing.

Finally, Yunri Ponpo sent a messenger out of his chapel and told the PLA that he was prepared to surrender but only if he was allowed to personally surrender to the commanding general of the Chinese.

Now this general had a strange appearance. He had black moles all over his face and he had webbed fingers—just like a duck. Tibetans called him "Ga-lag," which means "hands of the duck." Yunri Ponpo said, "I am Yunri Ponpo and I will surrender only to Ga-lag." And Ga-lag was very happy to hear this. When he heard this, he ran over to Yunri Ponpo's building.

In the meantime, Yunri Ponpo prepared himself for his death. Like all Khampa warriors, he wore a gua around his neck with sacred prayers and pictures to pro-tect him from enemy bullets. I was told that inside his gua he had a picture of the Jowa.[17] He took the gua off so he wouldn't be protected from the enemy. Then he put on a traditional Tibetan jacket with very long sleeves that hung way down past his hands. And up his right sleeve, he secretly held a pistol.

General Ga-lag met Yunri Ponpo outside the gompa. Everyone was watch-ing. The general treated him with great respect. He said, "You are famous among your people for being a strong leader, but now you must come with me to the building where I have jailed other Tibetans like you. There you will be able to rest."

Yunri Ponpo said, "Well, up to now I have never been to a Chinese jail and I don't intend to start now." He brought out his hidden pistol and pumped six rounds into the general. They say that for a minute everyone just stood there in silence—in shock, I guess, to see their commander murdered right under their noses. Then they all turned on Yunri Ponpo and opened fire for a long time. They say that when the gunfire ended, Yunri Ponpo didn't even look like a human being. He didn't look like anything.

---

[17]Jowo Rinpoche, the holiest statue of the Buddha in Tibet, located in Lhasa.

The communists' plan immediately changed. They stopped looking for survivors or even the snipers that were still hidden. The Chinese vacated the compound. And then the planes flew in.

Three Russian Ilyushin-28 warplanes circled and, just as the high lama had promised, bombed Lithang. By the time they had dropped all their bombs, nothing was left . . . totally gone in a matter of minutes . . . all the ancient texts, the famous art, the holy relics, the stupas, the largest statue of Buddha in Tibet . . . everything was gone.

I don't know how many people died over the two-month siege—I've heard from three thousand to five thousand people.

Anyway, those same bombers flew to other monasteries that day, in the Ba and Markham area, and destroyed them just as they had destroyed Lithang.

The only reason I'm here to tell about it is because I was in Lhasa at the time. I knew things were getting bad in Kham, of course, but I had no idea it was going to be that bad. Then, one day I was walking down a street and an announcement came over the loudspeakers. Lithang had revolted and had been leveled. That's when I knew I could no longer keep my monk's vows. I had to fight.[18]

THE CONTEMPORARY READER MAY WELL QUESTION WHY THE IN-ternational community was not doing something to stop or, at the very least, protest this series of massacres. The answer is, the outside world simply did not know. In the 1950s, there were no foreign camera crews or reporters allowed within the occupied nation. The only news leaking out of Tibet was from the south, across the Indian border. The dissident enclave of Tibetans living in Kalimpong were only too happy to relay the horrifying events. A few foreign journalists stationed in India (including George Patterson, who will be discussed later) occasionally referenced the rumors. The problem was they were *just* rumors, impossible to prove. When the foreign press sought to verify the alleged atrocities through the GOI, Indian officials repeatedly denied the reports. According to them, all potential news items disseminated from Kalimpong, an anti-communist haven for political insurgents, were auto-

---

[18]Athar, interview with the author.

matically suspect. Besides, when the GOI questioned Beijing about the rumors, the communists dismissed the reports as reactionary propaganda. That was good enough for Nehru and his pro-communist underlings. Like the U.N. resolutions, the truth of the Tibetan revolt couldn't get past the Indian border. The isolation that had protected Tibet for so many centuries had, in the twentieth century, become Tibet's worst nightmare.

1956 BECAME THE YEAR, IN GOMPO TASHI'S WORDS, *WHEN MOST Tibetans finally understood that the promises made by the Chinese were not worth even the breath used while talking or listening to them. Democratic reforms? Land reform? Assistance? Progress? The translation of those terms was quite simple: violence, and threats, and starvation . . . and death . . . all in the name of socialism on the path to Chinese communism. It was clear that the Han intended to inhabit and totally control Tibet, and we Tibetans were to all but disappear. This was Mao Tse-tung's interpretation of welcoming Tibet to his so-called family.*[19]

Kham, Amdo, Golok—every village had its own version of oppression and, as likely as not, the citizens of those respective villages would tell you it was *their* region where the uprising began. In a way, all of them were correct. The overlapping of rapid-fire events and spontaneous revolt against those events was such that a single identifiable moment was irrelevant. The point is that, within a few weeks, resistance in Eastern Tibet became the "howling storm" described by Gompo Tashi.

The Chinese reaction was as swift as it was atrocious. Wives, daughters, and nuns were raped—in many cases, repeatedly. Celibate monks were forced to have intercourse. In one documented case in Amdo, the Chinese turned a monastery into a horse stable, brought in prostitutes, and, at gunpoint, demanded that the monks take them. When they refused, two of them were crucified. When another monk protested, the Chinese chopped off his arm above the elbow. "Buddha," they laughed, "would give him back his arm."[20]

[19]Gompo Tashi Andrugtsang, quoted in Roger E. McCarthy, *Tears of the Lotus,* 103–04.
[20]*United Asia: Survey on Tibet,* 191.

Tibetans were dismembered, vivisected, beheaded, burned, scalded to death, dragged to death by horses or vehicles—abused in every way. In another incident in Amdo, three high lamas were beaten and then dropped into a pit. The Chinese forced the local people to urinate on their spiritual leaders. Then they ordered the lamas "to demonstrate their religious powers by flying out of the pit. They were finally shot."[21]

Parents were shot in the head by their traumatized children.

Other children were dragged away from their homes—many mere infants—and relocated to state-run schools and orphanages, while their parents were doomed to malignant labor camps.

The sacred (and many times priceless) images found in monasteries were desecrated, shipped off to China, or destroyed on the spot. Sacred books were used as toilet paper. Monasteries were turned into barns and pigsties. Others, like Lithang Monastery, were simply blown to bits.

In the aftermath of the bombing of Lithang, surrounding nomad encampments were machine-gunned and bombed from the air. The governor of Lithang was tortured to death in front of a local crowd who were forced to watch at gunpoint. Hundreds of monks were killed by firing squads. Countless thousands of natives then disappeared into labor camps.[22]

In the Amdoan village of Doi, three hundred landowners were assembled and shot in the back of their heads. The townspeople were commanded to watch, then warned that the same fate awaited them if they continued to oppose the introduction of socialism.[23]

Abbots were inspired at gunpoint to eat their own feces in front of their horrified followers. "Where is Buddha now?" they were taunted by the Chinese. According to the International Commission of Jurists report, "By late 1956 the Chinese were even sterilizing males in some areas, and forcing Tibetan women to bear children fathered by Chinese. . . . The inhabitants of a remote village called Patung Ahnga were assembled and forced to watch twenty-five wealthy people being publicly burned to death. In another village called Jeuba men and women had to watch twenty-four parents being killed by hav-

---

[21]Ibid.
[22]*Tibet: The Facts*, report prepared for the United Nations Commission on Human Rights, 15–16.
[23]Michel Peissel, *Cavaliers of Kham*, 55.

ing nails driven into their eyes—because they had refused to send their children to Chinese schools."[24]

The horrors went on and on. The Han Chinese introduced whole new worlds of cruelty. And there was no one to stop them. If ever there was a hell on earth, it was in Eastern Tibet in 1956.

AT FIRST THE GUERILLAS FOUGHT IN A KIND OF FRENZY OF HATRED and revenge. Their forays, although demoralizing to the Chinese, had little strategic effect and often resulted in greater losses to themselves than to the enemy. Before long, however, the attacks became more organized. The natural aptitude of the Tibetans for tactical surprise and their ability to use their terrain effectively began to count. Moreover, communication between the larger bands—with the help of the monastic orders—was established and the leadership improved. The resistance worked out elementary systems of supply. The monasteries and the *Mimang* helped with arms and intelligence. And, above all, the people remained loyal to the insurgents and rarely betrayed them to the enemy.

An example of this loyalty and grassroots resistance was the role women—whose husbands had been obliged to go into hiding—played in the villages and hamlets now left void of male protection. Nawang Chenmo, a Khampa rebel, remembers:

Traditionally, Khampa warriors always took their women and children with them when they were on the move—even if it was during a time of war. But in those early days of the uprising, there really wasn't time. We were called outlaws and we had to move constantly and quickly. But our women were of great help to us. They were the ones who kept us informed. They knew our hiding places and, at night, they would sneak up into the mountains where we were grouped and update the positions of the PLA. They also came up with a clever way of communicating with us in the daytime. When we approached our villages, we always knew if the communists were around, because our women would hang

---

[24]Statements by witnesses called before the International Commission of Jurists, 1960; quoted from Noel Barber, *From the Land of Lost Content*, 42–43.

red clothes—and only red clothes—out to dry. I don't think the Red Chinese ever *caught on to the women's trick.*[25]

Men, as well as women, who were not actually fighting, nevertheless made a huge contribution to the rebellion. They continued to produce the food, fodder, and livestock, without which the resistance could not have lasted for a week. They also provided shelter. They risked their families' lives by doing this, but, such was their rage, it didn't deter them. They also sharpened their reconnaissance abilities and passed on valuable information about the movement of the PLA troops.[26]

By the fall of 1956, tens of thousands of Tibetans in Eastern Tibet were engaged full-time in guerilla fighting against the Han Chinese. In thousands of square miles of Tibetan territory, and even in the lands beyond the Drichu River under direct Chinese administration, no Han dared set foot without backup. Only the strongest Chinese bases were safe from attack. Patrols more than a day's ride from these centers were almost sure to be ambushed. And, most important, traffic through the Kham region of the Chamdo–Lhasa road was becoming so hazardous that the Chinese were compelled to move their supply trains in convoys of forty to fifty trucks. Each vehicle carried several heavily armed soldiers. The convoys moved slowly, because around the next curve the drivers might find a blown-out road, the rubble of a man-made landslide, or an ambush of desperate Tibetans seeking revenge. The Chinese truck drivers gave this no-man's-land a nickname: The Road of Death.[27]

According to Roger McCarthy (who, years later, debriefed the leaders of the resistance), the rebels were guided by the *Mimang* and rapidly organized themselves into small fighting units throughout the country:

"Their quick and determined attacks on horseback resulted in many Chinese garrisons in the east being overrun and demolished. With swords and rifles the Tibetans attacked the Chinese posts. . . . Some parts of Kham and Amdo were described as being covered with smoke and fire for weeks from the fighting and the destruction of Chinese camps. The Chinese infantry

---

[25]Nawang Chenmo, interview with the author.
[26]Lowell Thomas Jr., *The Silent War in Tibet*, 188.
[27]Ibid., 190–91.

soldiers were no match for, nor were they able to resist, the swift surprise attacks of the determined and vengeful cavalry units. The wild charges on horseback by the Khambas, the Amdos and the Goloks, firing their rifles and wielding their swords, had not been experienced before by the Chinese and they fled in huge numbers. And they died in large numbers. And many of their installations were totally burned."[28]

The men who had survived Lithang, for instance—now full-fledged freedom fighters—had regrouped in the east, halfway between Lithang and Dartsendo, in the village of Nyagchuka. They commenced to ambush soldiers traveling on the PLA supply route—as many as two hundred PLA troops were killed at one time. A month later, the guerillas attacked a PLA depot. Kunga Samten Dewatshang remembers:

Taken by surprise, the guards were overpowered and nine hundred sacks of grain were seized. This was distributed amongst the guerrillas. Acting on information received from their scouts . . . forty guerrillas ambushed a PLA convoy which was carrying ammunition from Nyagchuka . . . about twenty-five loads of ammunition were captured, of which four were cannon shells. . . . In the meantime, another group . . . attacked a Chinese bank at Goku. The PLA soldiers stationed there were overwhelmed and the bank was destroyed.[29]

These same Khampas then sent two couriers to Lhasa with letters describing in detail the destruction that was going on all over Eastern Tibet. Athar describes:

One letter was addressed to the Kashag. It said, "Please, send us ammunition and guns, or send us military backup, or get us help from the outside—maybe America, the land of freedom—because, otherwise, there will be nothing left of our country."

The second letter went to the three main monasteries in Lhasa—Drepung, Sera, and Ganden—and it said, "We people from Lithang had a great monastery just as great as your monasteries. Many of your families were from Lithang. Now the monastery is nothing but dust and broken rock. Take care! The monks who weren't shot or tortured to death, have given back their vows and taken up arms

---

[28]Roger E. McCarthy, *Tears of the Lotus*, 104.
[29]Kunga Samten Dewatshang, *Flight at the Cuckoo's Behest*, 111–12.

Khampa warriors from Lithang.
(Collection of Athar Lithang)

because they have no other choice. Don't believe what the communists are say-
ing to you. You will face the same fate in Lhasa as we have in Kham. It would be
better if you armed yourselves and fought now, than wait until it is too late.
Please believe us. The communists only plan to destroy you."

    The third letter went to Gompo Tashi, who was in Lhasa. The letter said,
"The communists have bombed and destroyed everything. There is nothing left
of Lithang, Changtreng, Ba, Markham, and many other places. They have killed
so many people, including high lamas—shot in the head right in front of us.
Now you must stop doing business and try to find out how to stop the Chinese.
Your family, the Andrugtsangs, is the most important family in Kham. With all
your connections with the Tsongdu *and the* Kashag, *you must do something,*
please, for your people."[30]

---

[30]Athar, interview with the author.

Phala, Lord Chamberlain. *(Collection of Athar Lithang)*

To the amazement of the Khampas, except for the letter delivered to Gompo Tashi, the letters fell on deaf ears.

LHASA, 1956.

Phala Thupten Woden, the Lord Chamberlain and the Dalai Lama's closest advisor, controlled all access to His Holiness. Whatever news Phala received about the uprising in Eastern Tibet was carefully filtered before reaching the Dalai Lama. The urgent request that had been sent by Athar and other young rebels was not passed on to the Dalai Lama.[31]

Phala blocked the Khampas because he feared that if the Dalai Lama were to meet with them, the Chinese would implicate His Holiness in the Khampa uprising. Clearly, Phala was sympathetic with both the *Mimang* and the Khampa leaders, but his overriding concern was that the revolt in Eastern Tibet might spread to Lhasa and that the Chinese would subsequently crush it with the ferocity they had illustrated in Kham, Amdo, and Golok. The best consolation Phala could offer was to urge the Khampas to be patient. He advised them that, in order for revolt to be a success, *We would need to take the egg, without frightening the hen.*[32]

The number of refugees pouring into Lhasa from Kham, Amdo, and Golok increased daily, and a large number of them naturally gravitated toward the

---

[31]Phala, "The Phala Papers," 32. A published interview, in Tibetan, with the ex–Lord Chamberlain by the Government-in-Exile, Dharamsala, 1984. This document is referred to, among the Tibetan Diaspora, as "Phala's Autobiography." Although there are autobiographical components, it is more accurately described as a recorded debriefing of Phala by Dharamsala officials. The document was translated into English for the author by Tashi Chutter in New Delhi.

[32]Phala as quoted by Athar, interview with the author. Also found in "The Phala Papers," 33.

Mimang. In addition to this huge influx, there were now over forty thousand Chinese troops swarming the capital and its environs. Once again, food and fuel supplies became a major issue. The resultant bitterness turned Lhasa into a very short fuse indeed. More and more, the disenfranchised—particularly those who were members of the *Mimang* still stinging from the banishment of Alo Chonzed—looked to Gompo Tashi Andrugtsang for leadership.

GOMPO TASHI'S ATTRIBUTES WERE MANY. THOUGH JUST TURNING fifty, he was strong and fit. He was fiercely patriotic, intelligent, personable, and had an almost legendary reputation for having fearlessly trounced marauding bandit gangs in his youth back in Lithang. But beyond his warrior reputation, his access to the Lhasan elite made him the ideal candidate for leader of the resistance: He was extremely generous to the monastic institutions, inordinately diplomatic (for a Khampa) with ranking members of the Central Government, and, although he enjoyed the reputation of a man who had traveled to the outside world—a glittering rarity in Tibetan society—he was equally equipped to look a Khampa square in the eye and talk to him like a brother. All of these attributes would serve him well.

Athar recalls the first meeting he attended with Gompo Tashi at the helm. It was with several hundred Lithang compatriots who, by that time, had fled to Lhasa:

We were all of the mind to go back to Lithang and join the resistance there. But Gompo Tashi really objected. "No, that is useless," he told us. "What can a few hundred warriors do there? We have to centralize a fighting force, and the best place we can do that is from here, in Lhasa. Also, we must stop thinking only of Lithang. We must now start thinking of the entire Tibetan nation.

"The first thing we need to do is to conclude whatever business ventures we have going on. After all, our homes are no more, many of our relatives are no more, our center of worship is no more—we really have nothing to lose—better to liquidate our assets and turn them into weapons and ammunition. The second thing we must do is to get expert training from outside Tibet: that will be the task of the youngest and strongest men."

We saw that Gompo Tashi's idea was the better one. We told him we were with him.

He then selected two small groups of young men to leave Tibet. One group was to go to Taiwan, because, at that time, the exiled Nationalists were the number-one enemy of Mao. One of the guys in that group was my best friend, Tsewang Dorje—an old buddy from childhood.

The second group—the group I was in—was to go to India. There were twenty-seven of us. We crossed the high passes in southern Tibet and entered India. We arrived at Kalimpong soon afterward, where some of Gompo Tashi's family, including his nephews Wangdu and Kalsang, were waiting for us.

That was October 1956.[33]

AT THE SAME TIME, THE DALAI LAMA WAS ALSO PREPARING TO GO to India.

Nehru had formally invited His Holiness to attend the 2,500th anniversary of Buddha's birth. The Dalai Lama was more than receptive to the idea. Not only would it provide the opportunity to go on pilgrimages to some of the Buddhist holy sites, it would offer him the opportunity to speak to Nehru about the upheaval in Eastern Tibet as well and, in general, renew his contact with the outside world. And, he hoped, he would be out from under the eye of the Chinese:

I knew I was still inexperienced in international politics, but so was everyone in our country. We knew other countries had faced situations like ours, and that a great fund of political wisdom and experience existed in the democratic world; but so far none of it had been available for us, and we had to act by a kind of untrained instinct. We desperately wanted sympathetic wise advice.[34]

One item he particularly wished to be advised on was the wisdom of his remaining the secular head of Tibet:

I was very despondent. . . . So far, all my attempts at a peaceful solution of our problems had come to nothing, and with the Preparatory Committee [PCART] a mere mockery of responsible government I could see no better hope of success in the future. Worst of all, I felt I was losing control of my own people. In the east they were being driven into barbarism. In central Tibet they were

---

[33]Athar, interview with the author.
[34]His Holiness the Dalai Lama, My Land and My People, 110.

growing more determined to resort to violence: and I felt I would not be able to stop them much longer, even though I could not approve of violence and did not believe it could possibly help us. . . .

Thus I began to think it might be in the best interests of Tibet if I withdrew from all political activities, in order to keep my religious authority intact. Yet while I was in Tibet, I could not escape from politics. To withdraw, I would have to leave the country, bitterly and desperately though I hated that idea.[35]

Of course, it wasn't just a matter of the Dalai Lama accepting Nehru's invitation. The Dalai Lama couldn't travel to the next district unless he first obtained permission from the Chinese authorities. Permission to travel was something they did not easily grant.

The communists, who wanted complete control over the Dalai Lama, hated the proposed trip. It forced them into a no-win situation: If they denied the Dalai Lama permission, they would be accused of holding the Dalai Lama captive (which, of course, they were), yet if they granted him passage to India, they risked him coming into contact with anti-Chinese factions and—even worse—he would be free to seek asylum in India or elsewhere, if that was what he secretly had in mind.

The communists finally relented when, in October, the GOI extended a second formal invitation—this time with the inclusion of the Panchen Lama. At least the younger lama could be counted on to represent China's presence in Tibet in a favorable fashion. General Chang gave the Dalai Lama the green light, but not before lecturing him as if, according to the Dalai Lama, *I were a schoolboy. . . . he warned me that if any of the Indian leaders asked me about the Indo-Tibetan frontier, I was only to say that this was a matter for the Foreign Office in Peking. I might also be asked, he said, about the situation in Tibet. If newspapermen or junior officials asked me, I was to say that there had been a little trouble, but everything was normal now. If it was Mr. Nehru or other high officials of the Indian government who asked, I could tell them a little more—that there had been uprisings in some parts of Tibet.*

The final part of this lecture was a suggestion that if I was likely to have to make speeches during the celebration, I had better prepare them in advance in

---

[35]Ibid., 107–08.

Lhasa. I was in fact expecting to make a speech at the Buddha Jayanti,[36] and before I left Lhasa a draft was written for me by Ngabo, as Secretary-General of the Preparatory Committee, in consultation with the Chinese. I rewrote it entirely after I came to India.[37]

The Dalai Lama's entourage left Lhasa on November 19. The Panchen Lama's left from Shigatse a few days later.

KALIMPONG: GIVEN THE UPHEAVAL INSIDE EASTERN TIBET, THE twenty-seven Khampas handpicked by Gompo Tashi were hard-pressed to cool their heels in the Indian outpost. Their main ambition was to fight the Chinese. What were they doing in Kalimpong? No one had really told them much. They were young, strong, hot-blooded—some were still teenagers— and completely unskilled in sitting still while war was being waged back in their homeland.

Gyalo Thundop understood their impatience. When they complained to him, he suggested that they travel, en masse, to New Delhi to meet representatives of the Indian government. Athar remembers:

Our main purpose as a delegation was to inform the Indians what the communists were really up to in Eastern Tibet. Gyalo told us that Nehru still believed all the communist propaganda that there was very little trouble in Tibet.

So we documented as best we could all the bombings, murders, tortures that had taken place up until that time.[38]

They descended on the capital and created street protests against the Chinese:

We were in our traditional Khampa clothes, and I guess we looked pretty wild. Our pictures were in the newspapers. Anyway, we were finally invited to go to Mr. Nehru's house. When he met us, he started laughing at us. He thought we were very funny-looking. He couldn't stop laughing at our fur hats and boots and big knives. "Just like American cowboys," he kept saying.

---

[36]The Buddha's birthday celebration.
[37]His Holiness the Dalai Lama, *My Land and My People*, 111–13.
[38]Athar, interview with the author.

The meeting didn't last long and Mr. Nehru never bothered to tell us what he thought about the Chinese atrocities. And I don't know if he ever read the document we presented to him. He didn't read it while we were there, although that is what we hoped he would do. And I don't think he listened. I think he thought of us as clowns.[39]

By now, the Dalai Lama's two older brothers—Gyalo Thondup and Taktser Rinpoche—identified by Chinese spies as having had contacts with Washington, London, and the *Kuomintang*, had also arrived in Delhi in anticipation of the Dalai Lama's arrival.

The Chinese's worst fears came true the minute the Dalai Lama descended from the plane in Delhi. (He had been flown in from the Bagdogra Airport in Sikkim.) He was greeted by a host of international dignitaries and, in effect, was treated like a head of state. The Dalai Lama recounts:

At the airport, the Vice President, Dr. Radhakrishnan, and the Prime Minister, Mr. Nehru, were waiting to welcome me. The Chinese Ambassador, who was in the plane with me, insisted on introducing me, first to them and then to the members of the diplomatic corps. He took me along the line, presenting the officials of many countries. We came to the representative of Britain; but what was going to happen, I wondered, when we came to the representative of the United States? It was a delicate exercise in diplomatic manners. At the crucial moment, the Chinese Ambassador suddenly vanished like a magician, and I was left face-to-face with the American.[40] *Somebody from the Indian Foreign Office tactfully stepped in and introduced me.*[41]

Perhaps even more galling to the communists was the embarrassing treatment of the Panchen Lama. The Indians regarded him as a secondary figure of the Buddha Jayanti. Nehru no doubt had a fairly clear understanding of the Panchen Lama's status among his own people and—Brahmin to the bone—Nehru snubbed him accordingly. He moved the Dalai Lama into his personal guesthouse, while the Panchen Lama was lodged elsewhere. He received the Panchen Lama *only* at public ceremonies, while he conducted numerous private meetings with the Dalai Lama. The Panchen Lama also later complained

---

[39]Ibid.
[40]Ambassador Loy Henderson.
[41]His Holiness the Dalai Lama, *My Land and My People*, 115–16.

The Dalai Lama's 1956 visit to India. To his left is the Panchen Lama, to his right Chinese Premier Chou En-lai, Nehru, and Indira Gandhi. *(Mark Riboud/Magnum Photo Agency)*

that, on the pilgrimage junket, he and his "entourage had to sleep on the trains sometimes because they were not provided with housing."[42]

The Dalai Lama had the opportunity to sit down with Nehru and outline his concerns over the Chinese presence in Tibet—the violence in Eastern Tibet, his fear that it would spread to the Lhasa area and, above all, his wish to remain in India, at least until the Tibetan situation improved. Sarvepalli Gopal, one of Nehru's deputies, recounts:

Nehru listened patiently and told the Dalai Lama that there was nothing the Government of India could do. Tibet had never been recognized as an independent country. The best hope for Tibet was to try to work within the 17-Point Agreement.[43]

As always, Nehru's priority was peaceful coexistence between India and China, yet, in truth, his Gandhi-inspired idealism was getting a bit ragged

---

[42]International Commission of Jurists, *The Question of Tibet and the Rule of Law,* 183.
[43]Sarvepalli Gopal, vol. 3, 1984, 36; as quoted by Shakya, *The Dragon in the Land of Snows,* 152.

around the edges. With ever-increasing frequency, many of his advisors pointed toward the Indo-Tibetan border—now an Indo-*Chinese* border—with newly constructed roads suitable for the deployment of army vehicles. What was to stop the Chinese from moving into Indian territory and claiming it as their own? The Chinese had made assurances to the contrary, but it remained a serious threat Nehru should not overlook. Other advisors noted the increased chumminess between China and Nepal, a clear indication that China had no intention of allowing India to encroach upon the Himalayan kingdom. China, Nehru's advisors warned him, smiled at India with clenched fists.

Nehru broached these concerns to the Chinese Premier, Chou En-lai. He reported what the Dalai Lama had told him about the troubles in Tibet and the young leader's disinclination to return home anytime soon. According to author H. G. Parthasarathi, Chou En-lai responded that the idea that China could "introduce communism into Tibet was rather fantastic, because Tibet was very backward and as far removed from communism as any country could be."[44]

This, of course, was exactly what Nehru wanted to hear. It appealed to his snobbery as well as his ardent wish to make the Tibetan situation just—somehow—go away.

THE DALAI LAMA ALSO HAD A CHANCE TO SPEAK TO CHOU EN-LAI, who presented a different persona. He feigned sympathy for the Dalai Lama's situation. He even agreed with the Dalai Lama that the Chinese had made some mistakes in Eastern Tibet.

According to the Dalai Lama, *He said he would report what I had said to Mao Tse-tung, but I could not tie him down to any definite promise of improvement.*[45]

The Dalai Lama held most of his meetings at his temporary residence in Nehru's guesthouse. Not all of the Dalai Lama's meetings, however, were with high-ranking officials. Athar and his group of Khampas were granted an audience. Athar recounted the horrors taking place in Eastern Tibet, and the Dalai Lama responded with great sympathy:

---

[44]H. G. Parthasarathi, ed., *Jawaharlal Nehru, Letters to Chief Ministers, 1947–1964*, 228–29.
[45]His Holiness the Dalai Lama, *My Land and My People*, 118.

The Dalai Lama told us, "I am so sorry. I know you have big problems, but don't worry." And he gave us a big prayer.

Then we followed His Holiness to Bodhgaya. The Dalai and Panchen Lamas made big ceremonies for thousands of worshippers. We Khampas got more good prayers from him but there was not another chance to speak to His Holiness about the situation in Kham.

But we got to speak with Taktser Rinpoche, his oldest brother, in Bodhgaya. He said that he and his other brother, Gyalo Thondup, had spoken with Chou En-lai in Delhi and that they had spoken very openly about the terrible way the Tibetans were being treated by the Chinese, and that Chou En-lai had promised things would get better in Tibet. Taktser told us not to worry and, most importantly, to be patient.

He also did something in Bodhgaya that we thought was very strange. He took pictures of us with his camera. Not group photos—separate photos of each one of us. He said he wanted them as souvenirs, but we thought that was kind of strange for an incarnate lama. Why would he want pictures of some rough Khampas?[46]

The Dalai Lama's pilgrimage to Bodhgaya and other holy places in northern India was more than just a source of inspiration for him. The serenity of Bodhgaya in particular acted as a panacea to his state of mind. Whatever else the Dalai Lama was, he was a young monk who ardently wanted to *be* a monk—to advocate nonviolence—but who, nevertheless, felt constantly thwarted by the mantle thrust upon him: professional politico in charge of a war-ravaged nation. The political context of this trip, therefore, has never been the whole story. The *religious* significance of the Dalai Lama's pilgrimage to Bodhgaya influenced, to some extent, his future actions.

Bodhgaya is the site of the Buddha's Enlightenment. The symbolic importance of visiting Bodhgaya can be equated to the Judeo-Christian pilgrimage to Jerusalem or the Muslim's trip to Mecca—though the similarity stops there. Unlike Jerusalem and Mecca, Bodhgaya is neither a city nor a political hub. Its setting on the banks of the Niranjan River is remote, bucolic, and resolutely serene.

Twenty-five hundred years ago, Buddha traveled through this area practicing various austerities without the desired spiritual results. After six years, he

---

[46]Athar, interview with the author.

came to believe that physical deprivation could never lead to realization. He abandoned his half-starvation diet by thoroughly enjoying a rich milk-rice meal, after which he sat under a great bodhi tree[47] in Bodhgaya. There he announced that he would not move until he had attained Enlightenment. Many temptations followed, introduced by Mara, Lord of Illusion. Mara, symbolizing the delusions of one's own mind, tried tirelessly to distract Buddha from his purpose, but to no avail. Buddha touched the earth, calling it to bear witness to the countless lifetimes of virtue he had already achieved. Mara, in a final showdown, unleashed an army of demons concocted to distract and mislead Buddha. But Buddha's compassion prevailed. He transformed the demons' arrows into flowers, thus achieving perfect Enlightenment.

Bodhgaya, site of Buddha's Enlightenment under the bodhi tree. *(John Huntington/Crystal Mirror Series, Volume Nine: Holy Places of the Buddha)*

The bodhi tree that now grows in Bodhgaya is probably the fifth generation of the original.[48] Its broad canopy is overshadowed by the 170-foot tower to the east of it—the Mahabodhi Temple—an elongated pyramid heavily encrusted with stone carvings. The original building is believed to date three centuries before the birth of Christ.

The Dalai Lama explains the spiritual significance of Bodhgaya:

Every devout Buddhist will always associate Budh Gaya with all that is noblest and loftiest in his religious and cultural inheritance. From my very early youth I had thought and dreamed about this visit. Now I stood in the presence of the Holy Spirit who had attained Mahaparinirvana, the highest Nirvana, in this sacred place, and had found for all mankind the path to salvation. As I stood

---

[47]Pipal tree, *Ficus religiosa.*
[48]It is popularly hailed as the "oldest continually documented tree in the world."

there, a feeling of religious fervor filled my heart, and left me bewildered with the
knowledge and impact of the divine power which is in all of us.

But while I was still on my pilgrimage, having traveled on to Sarnath, a mes-
senger came to me from the Chinese embassy in Delhi. He brought a telegram
from General Chang Chin-wu, the Chinese representative in Lhasa. It said the
situation at home was serious; spies and collaborators were planning a huge
revolt; I should return as soon as possible. And at [Bodhgaya] itself, one of my
Chinese escorts gave me a message that Chou En-lai was coming back to Delhi
and was anxious to see me. So after a few more days, I had to drag myself back
to the world of politics, hostility and mistrust.[49]

Ardently believing in Buddha's doctrine that one should always follow the
path of peace, the Dalai Lama relinquished the clarifying embrace of Bodhgaya and returned to the shadowy riddles of Delhi intrigue.

THE DALAI LAMA'S MEETING WITH CHOU EN-LAI MIRRORED HIS
previous one, with the Dalai Lama repeating all he had described before. But
this time, the Chinese Premier's response was smoothly dismissive: [Chou
En-lai] *answered that Mao Tse-tung had made it perfectly clear that "reforms"*
would only be introduced in Tibet in accordance with the wishes of the people.
He spoke as though he still could not understand why Tibetans did not welcome
the Chinese.[50]

Meanwhile, Kalsang, the nephew of Gompo Tashi, was in India to secretly
make contact with the CIA in Calcutta:

My older brother Bhugan Gyatotsang wrote me and told me about the bomb-
ings of Lithang, Samphe-Ling, and other Khampa centers. He recorded all the
atrocities, including all of the resistance leaders who had been captured by the
Chinese.

Gompo Tashi contacted me and told me he had been in close contact with
Gyalo Thondup, who had been in contact with the Americans. I was chosen to
take my brother's information and other documents and see the Americans in
Calcutta with an update of the current situation. I was very impressed by the

---

[49]His Holiness the Dalai Lama, *My Land and My People*, 121.
[50]Ibid., 122.

professional secrecy of the Americans. Before I finally met my contact, I was switched from three cars, one after the other. I had to lie down in the back seat. The windows in these cars had been painted dark to maintain secrecy. My contact was "Mr. Mark," but I don't think "Mr. Mark" was his real name.[51]

MEANWHILE, THE RESISTANCE IN LHASA WAS GAINING HEADWAY. In the last days of 1956, Gompo Tashi laid out the groundwork for an organized underground army:

On the pretense of undertaking a business trip, three of my men proceeded to [Kham], with a message from me to various leaders in the area. The message read:

"For some time you people have been rebeling against the Red Chinese. The time has now arrived to muster all your courage and put your bravery to the test. I know you are prepared to risk your lives and exert all your strength to defend Tibet. I also know that the tremendous task that you have undertaken is a noble cause and that you will have no regrets despite the ghastly atrocities committed by the enemy. In this hour of peril, I appeal to all people, including government servants, who value their freedom and religion, to unite in the common struggle against the Chinese. Messages are being sent to people in other parts of Tibet and the neighboring countries, such as India, to explain that the Tibetans now have no alternative but to take up arms against the Chinese."[52]

THE DALAI LAMA KNEW NOTHING ABOUT THIS. In any case, he was preoccupied by a more immediate and personal dilemma: The time had come for him to decide to either return to Lhasa or to go into exile. On the one hand, Chou En-Lai and Nehru were adamantly opposed to his exile and insistent that the problems in Tibet were but temporary. On the other hand, his brothers and many members of his entourage—including members of the *Kashag*—begged him *not* to return to

---

[51]Kalsang Gyatotsang, interview with the author.
[52]Gompo Tashi Andrugtsang, *Four Rivers, Six Ranges*, 58.

Tibet. They argued that he might be killed if he returned. Besides, his entire family was now in India. What about the safety of his family if they returned? Curiously, the one person who seemed to straddle the issue of the Dalai Lama's return to Lhasa was Mao Tse-tung.

At the Second Plenum of the Eighth Central Committee, Mao addressed the Tibetan situation metaphorically: "You can't [create] a husband and wife simply by tying two people together. If a person no longer likes your place and wants to run away, let him go."[53]

Quite an idea for someone who had organized the Dalai Lama's shotgun wedding only two years before. Perhaps the political worth of the Dalai Lama had simply diminished in the philanderer's eyes, because Mao added, almost whimsically: "I will not be sad if we lost Dalai."[54]

The Dalai Lama had one final meeting with Nehru.

The Prime Minister reiterated Chou En-lai's assurances that China was only interested in improving Tibet's backward economic and social status. He also said that Chou En-Lai had admitted to mistakes but that these could *only* be rectified if the Dalai Lama returned to Lhasa.

So what would it be? Nehru wanted to know. Return or exile?

I remember telling Mr. Nehru in that final meeting that I had made up my mind to go back to Tibet for two reasons: because he had advised me to do so, and because Chou En-lai had given definite promises to me and my brothers.[55]

With that, there was but one last item for Nehru to clear. The Dalai Lama wished to visit Kalimpong before returning to Tibet. Chou En-lai had hated the idea and had warned him not to go, because the resident malcontents might persuade him to change his mind and remain in India.

Surprisingly, though, Nehru didn't object. He even promised the Dalai Lama that the GOI would make all the arrangements and would look after him in the frontier hill-town.

---

[53]John K. Leung and Michael Y. M. Kau, *The Writings of Mao Zedong, 1947–1976*, vol. 2, 170.
[54]Ibid.
[55]His Holiness the Dalai Lama, *My Land and My People*, 123.

. . .

THE DALAI LAMA ARRIVED IN KALIMPONG ON JANUARY 22, 1957. Athar's gang of "funny-looking Khampas" was close behind. In their own mind, they had become the Dalai Lama's unofficial bodyguard and they were united in their determination to keep him from returning to Lhasa, so convinced they were that he would be imprisoned or murdered by the Chinese. They presented their fear to Gyalo Thondup. According to Athar, *Gyalo dismissed our worries as if he had something more important to think about. He told us to sit tight and not leave Kalimpong—that we would be receiving orders from him in a matter of days. He wouldn't give us any details and, of course, it was not our place to question the brother of His Holiness the Dalai Lama.*[56]

While the young Khampas milled about the streets of the caravan town, disgruntled and impatient, the Dalai Lama held numerous meetings behind closed doors. Once again, the debate over his return heated up. His family members and most of the Tibetan officials pleaded with him to stay in India.

Ngabo was there. He argued for the Dalai Lama's return to Lhasa. Who, he wanted to know, would take care of the Dalai Lama and his entourage if he went into exile? There was no indication the GOI wanted to help nor, for that matter, any other foreign government. Besides, had the Dalai Lama considered how he would be treated as a private citizen? Could he really tolerate not being lavished with the attention due his high station?[57] (This was an eerie remark that echoed a rather snide comment Marshal Ho Lung, an associate of Chou En-lai's, had recently made to the Dalai Lama: *The snow lion looks dignified if he stays in his mountain abode, but if he comes down to the valleys he is treated like a dog.*[58])

Taktser Rinpoche stepped into the argument—apparently without thinking first: He told Ngabo that he was completely misinformed. There *was* a foreign government that had offered to help the Dalai Lama.

Really, Ngabo asked, and who might that be?

---

[56]Athar, interview with the author.
[57]T. N. Takla, "Notes on Some Early Tibetan Communists," *Tibetan Review*, vol. 11, no. 17, 1969, 7–10.
[58]His Holiness the Dalai Lama, *My Land and My People*, 122.

The room grew quiet. Taktser changed the subject, but everyone knew that he could only be referring to the Americans.[59]

Only Taktser Rinpoche and Gyalo Thondup knew the extent to which the Americans were poised to help. Just down the street, right there in Kalimpong, the first Khampa recruits were about to be selected to train with the CIA.

Athar remembered:

We were just waiting and waiting. When was Gyalo going to tell us what he had planned for us? What had the Dalai Lama decided? Was he going or staying? One day, someone told us that there was a big disagreement between the Lhasan officials and the Dalai Lama, and so the two oracles [Nechung and Gadong] *had been brought in to make a final decision. Both oracles told His Holiness to return to Lhasa.*

That was very bad news to us. Very bad. We thought it was a terrible mistake!

We decided to do something to prevent the Dalai Lama from going—to take it out of his hands. Now by that time, there were about one hundred of us Khampas just killing time in Kalimpong. Our plan was to leave Kalimpong and reenter Tibet. We would go up into the Chumbi Valley, where the Dalai Lama had stayed in 1951. We would engage the PLA in fighting. Make a big fuss! Then we would ride to Lhasa and make even bigger problems. The idea behind all this was to block the main road to Lhasa and thereby make it impossible for His Holiness to return to the capital. Mr. Nehru would see that it was impossible for the Dalai Lama to travel north and then he would change his mind and beg the Dalai Lama to stay in India.

We sent messengers with our plan—one letter went to the Lhasan government and the other to Gompo Tashi. But the government wrote back, "No, no! Don't do this! If you start trouble in Lhoka and if there is an uprising in Lhasa, the PLA will use it as an excuse to really crush us. They will bomb Lhasa and many thousands of people will die and we are not strong enough to defeat the Chinese!" They were very upset with us.

So we cooled down and dropped the plan.

It's a good thing we did, because a few days later—one night—Gyalo and Jyantsa Khenchen [the financial minister of Lhasa], *collected some of us guys*

---

[59]T. N. Takla, "Notes on Some Early Tibetan Communists," *Tibetan Review*, vol. 11, no. 17, 1969, 10.

for a meeting. Gyalo told us to forget all of our plans—that we were going to be helped by the Americans very soon. Then, on the 20th of February 1957, Gyalo Thundop brought six of us together and announced that we were to leave on a very secret mission that very night. The five he chose besides me were Lhotse, Tsewang, Gompo Tashi's nephew Wangdu, Dedrup, and Dreshe. We were not to tell anyone in Kalimpong. Gyalo really emphasized that. There were spies all over Kalimpong, he said, Indian spies, Chinese spies, and Tibetan spies. We were not to even discuss it with each other. The six of us didn't care about any of that. We were just excited that, finally, we were going to get to do something to hurt the Chinese. The Americans were our heroes. They had all the best weapons. Nobody could beat the Americans. We were very excited.[60]

UNAWARE OF THE CIA PLAN, THE DALAI LAMA MADE PREPARATIONS for the journey back home. While in India, he had been feted and moved about in automobiles, trains, and airplanes—all the sorts of niceties available outside of Tibet. He would return to his homeland on horseback and, when the terrain became too steep, on foot. The Dalai Lama almost welcomed the physical discomfort awaiting him. At least politics would be put on hiatus:

I was weary of politics. Political talks had taken up most of my time in Delhi, and cut short my pilgrimage. I had begun to detest them, and would gladly have retired from politics altogether if I had not had a duty to my people in Tibet . . .

It was snowing hard in the mountains. I had to wait nearly a month before the way to Tibet, across the Nathu-la, was open.

At last the weather improved and the way was open. At the top of the Nathu-la I said good-bye to the last of my friends from India and Sikkim. As I walked across the top of the pass, into Tibet, I saw that among the little prayer flags which Tibetans always like to fly in high places, enormous red flags of China had been hoisted, and portraits of Mao Tse-tung.[61]

Even the highest Tibetan mountain peaks were no longer Tibetan.

---

[60]Athar, interview with the author.
[61]His Holiness the Dalai Lama, *My Land and My People*, 125.

. . .

LHASA.
During the Dalai Lama's absence, Mao had dispatched an additional forty thousand troops to Tibet, bringing the total to well over two hundred thousand.[62] The Dalai Lama immediately set about registering protests over the many atrocities he had been briefed on during his Indian trip. The Chinese commander he confronted pretended to be shocked. He disavowed any knowledge of misdeeds in the eastern provinces. He wanted to know specific details. He asked the Dalai Lama to tell him the names of the Chinese allegedly involved: the dates, the precise times, locations, details of the charges, names of witnesses, etc. Unable to provide all the criteria demanded by the general, the Dalai Lama found his complaints dismissed.[63]

More than once, while the Dalai Lama had been in Beijing in 1954, Mao Tse-tung had insisted that they write often and keep in touch. Taking him at his word, the Dalai Lama now decided to contact Mao directly. He wrote a letter itemizing all of his misgivings and objections, and posted it to Beijing.

Chairman Mao did not reply.

The Dalai Lama wrote a second letter.

Again, silence from China's capital.

And again, the Dalai Lama sent off a third letter with the same disappointing results.

Either Mao never received the letters or, in his hectic schedule, was simply not motivated enough to respond.

WITH NO ONE TO CURTAIL THE CHINESE WRATH IN KHAM, THE dreaded *thamzings* became ever more brutal. Now the wives and daughters of the accused men were forced to take part in the public accusations. Gompo Tashi writes:

They [the women] *were stripped of their clothing in the presence of all, and*

---

[62]Roger E. McCarthy, *Tears of the Lotus*, 128.
[63]Ibid., 117.

*if the man refused to "confess" to the charges, the women were raped in front of
the man. There were always enough Chinese soldiers present who had not been
with a woman for a long time and who were more than willing to follow orders
and participate. There were even cases of the man being forced to have intercourse with his wife in front of the others, after which he would be executed, and
his daughters and wife then given to the Chinese soldiers.*[64]

Nuns were not exempt.

*There were many cases where monks were disrobed and forced to have inter-
course with disrobed nuns, with the Chinese cadre then disdainfully proclaim-
ing that such is the religion of the Tibetans and the so-called vows of chastity.
Then these monks would usually be executed and the nuns given to the Chinese
soldiers. In many areas very few females escaped being raped, regardless of age,
and often they were repeatedly raped before being killed.*[65]

For most Tibetans, in 1957, the serenity of Bodhgaya was very far away
indeed.

---

[64]Gompo Tashi Andrugtsang, quoted in Roger E. McCarthy, *Tears of the Lotus,* 122.
[65]Ibid.

Flag of the *Chushi-Gangdruk (Collection of the author)*

6

GOMPO TASHI
AND THE CIA

Labor prisons, firing squads, torture, the murder of family members, the slaughter of lamas—by 1957, Eastern Tibet was a free-fall zone of Chinese occupation. For most Khampas, Amdoans, and Goloks, the last ray of hope was anchored to the safety of His Holiness the Dalai Lama. And now, on top of everything else that had been yanked away from them, the communists wanted to confiscate their weapons. No way. As Gompo Tashi put it: *How could the Dalai Lama be protected if we had no weapons to protect him with?*[1] Khampa guns, Tibetan Buddhism, and Chinese butchery became inextricably entwined.

Gompo Tashi may have had many problems in 1957, but recruiting volunteers for his nascent resistance army was not one of them. What did it matter if they died fighting? What was their alternative? With or without Gompo Tashi, the resistance already existed and would continue to grow. The

---

[1]Gompo Tashi Andrugtsang, quoted in Roger E. McCarthy, *Tears of the Lotus,* 148.

only thing lacking was someone to organize the scattered resistance into a unified force.

One of Gompo Tashi's problems—a problem that would never go away—was the Central Government's fear of upsetting the Chinese. Every time he approached Phala, Lord Chamberlain, the answer was always the same: "*This is not the time. This is not the course of action that we should be taking. We need patience.*"[2]

Looking back at early 1957, Gompo Tashi regarded his personal activities—especially his futile meetings with various members of the Central Government—as wasted time. Not everyone would agree. Roger E. McCarthy, the young American who had been tapped to organize and manage the newly created CIA Tibetan Task Force, and who subsequently interviewed Gompo Tashi three years later, respectfully disagreed that the general had been wasting time:

Gompo Tashi was doing no such thing. He was traveling and talking to monasteries, rallying different tribes in both Kham and Amdo—and in the process of doing this, he also put together an update on terrain features, with an eye to fighting in areas in the east and south, which proved to be very advantageous to him later on. This may have been a fortuitous add-on to what he originally planned to do, but he accumulated a lot of valuable information under the guise of "pilgrimage." He even went down into India, which turned out to be advantageous, because, along the way, he discovered who had stocks of ammunition and arms for sale—obviously all black market.

He had also been in steady contact with the Dalai Lama's brothers, Gyalo Thondup and Thubten Jigme Norbu [Taktser Rinpoche]. They, in turn, were talking to the Americans from an early point on. Gyalo, in particular, instigated first contact in Calcutta in either '51 or early '52. And, of course, Gyalo was in touch with other expatriates—as well as the refugees coming into India—an exodus that started in 1952–53. All through the 50s, Gyalo was accumulating crucial information, but few listened to him—or cared.[3]

Gompo Tashi did care, and regularly communicated with Gyalo.

---

[2]Ibid.

[3]Roger E. McCarthy, interview with the author, based on McCarthy's CIA debriefing of Gompo Tashi Andrugtsang, 1959.

Gompo Tashi was also good friends with Phala and never gave up trying to convince him that resistance was the only answer.

Who was Phala? It was said that, as Lord Chamberlain, he was the Dalai Lama's closest advisor. But where did Phala stand on the issue of organized resistance?

Roger McCarthy describes Phala as *part and parcel of almost everything. He was the man that the Dalai Lama—particularly at that age—was dependent upon for advice, guidance, and valued opinion.*[4]

And yet, because he was the sole buffer between the rebels and His Holiness, it has never been entirely clear what information was and was *not* passed on to the Dalai Lama. Certainly, Phala was sympathetic to the resistance. Since 1952, Phala had been kept informed by both of the Dalai Lama's older brothers on various correspondence and negotiations with the State Department and the CIA.[5] In addition, as an ardent nationalist, he had tried to persuade the Dalai Lama to seek exile in 1950, and resumed the argument when the exile question again arose in 1957, in Kalimpong.[6]

Nevertheless, wherever his sympathies may have lain, Phala's first priority was to protect the Dalai Lama from harmful associations. It is not impossible, then, that, on occasion, he might have simply not relayed requests from the rebels in order to ensure that the Dalai Lama would remain blameless should the Chinese later make inquiries.[7]

Whatever Phala's personal feelings may have been, Gompo Tashi finally realized he would have to organize the resistance without the blessing of His Holiness. McCarthy, in recounting his 1959 debriefing of Gompo Tashi, says that, in the end, *Gompo Tashi told me that he could not really understand but, finally, simply decided to pursue what he knew in his heart to be the right course of action.*

And fortunately, President Eisenhower, reading reports that were coming in and realizing that the Tibetans were going to support the resistance regardless of

---

[4]Ibid.

[5]John Kenneth Knaus, *Orphans of the Cold War,* 96, 135, 143.

[6]Kenneth Conboy and James Morrison, *The CIA's Secret War in Tibet,* 68.

[7]Roger E. McCarthy, the creator of the CIA Tibetan Task Force, in an interview with the author, said that, in retrospect, one of the great mysteries of the resistance was Phala's role: "The very sad part of this whole story is that no one went to talk to Phala after [the Dalai Lama escaped in 1959]. I have kicked my rear end many times for that . . . Phala was an incredible source for everything."

U.S. help, decided that the least America could do was to give them the assistance and wherewithal to do as much as they, the resistance groups, could do on their own. To simply abandon them at that point, in Eisenhower's estimation, would have been unconscionable.[8]

And so, while Gompo Tashi organized resistance inside Tibet, the CIA began working more closely with the Dalai Lama's older brothers. McCarthy continues:

An order was sent out from Washington to the Far East Bureau to immediately select a handful of Tibetans for "external training as a pilot team that would infiltrate their homeland and assess the state of resistance." The U.S. objective was to destabilize China, and it was for this reason that it abandoned diplomatic initiatives in favor of a covert mission. In other words, the Dalai Lama's position—whatever that may have been—was no longer an issue.[9]

The first CIA agent to sit at the Tibetan desk was John Reagan. When he received the order to exfiltrate six Tibetans, Reagan flew to India to oversee the operation in concert with Gyalo Thondup.

Is it possible that the Dalai Lama did not know? Again, McCarthy:

The Dalai Lama writes in his book that he did not. As an opinion, I don't know which way to come down on this, given Phala's role. It's hard to believe that this would have been done without his tacit blessing. On the other hand, he may have given an approval without knowing what he was really approving.

As for Gyalo, I don't think he would have proceeded [with the CIA connection] without some kind of approval. Whether or not Phala played a part in this approval is second-guessing.[10]

Given the propensity for secrecy among the Dalai Lama's advisors—particularly among the members of the paranoid *Kashag*—withholding information from His Holiness did not seem unlikely. An accurate portrait of the *Kashag* would be to paint them tiptoeing down the shadowy corridors of the Potala, mouths sealed and index fingers jammed against their lips. "Shhhhh" was the mantra of Lhasan politics.

[8]Ibid.
[9]Ibid.
[10]Ibid.

What is crystal clear is that Gyalo and Gompo Tashi were the men who selected the first six men to train with the CIA—as they did for most, if not all, the trainees that followed.[11]

For Athar and his five Khampa buddies, the endless waiting in Kalimpong was almost over.

IN THE MEANTIME, BACK IN LHASA, GOMPO TASHI HAD DEVISED an ingenious method of garnering funds for the resistance, without the Chinese or the Lhasan government catching on—and without compromising the Dalai Lama's safety.

There was a special religious ceremony performed on behalf of the Dalai Lama—a "long-life" ceremony—that involving offering gifts and prayers to His Holiness. The event was called *Tenshuk Shapten* and, traditionally, the person sponsoring the ceremony would, out of necessity, need to travel across the country collecting donations.

For some time, Gompo Tashi, out of sheer devotion, had been considering mounting such a tribute. But as the resistance began to take shape, he also realized that gathering donations for a *Tenshuk Shapten* would provide the perfect cover for organizing resistance without raising Chinese suspicions.

He met with prominent merchants and lamas in Lhasa and announced his *Tenshuk Shapten*. And what would be his gift to the Dalai Lama?

A magnificent, jewel-encrusted golden throne.

Naturally, it would require the help of many people throughout the country.

The donations poured in, both in money and gems. There were eye-widening quantities of gold, silver, diamonds, pearls, onyx, coral, and turquoise. Women donated their personal ornaments. Even beggars offered what they could. Forty-nine goldsmiths, five silversmiths, nineteen engravers, six painters, eight tailors, six carpenters, three blacksmiths, and three wel-

---

[11]Ibid. In an aside, McCarthy added, "A couple of those who have written about Tibet have said that parachuting back into Tibet was a question asked by the CIA. It was *not* asked by any of us connected with the project. We never raised the question, neither at Camp Hale nor did I ask it on Saipan. Parachuting was an assumption and a given simply because there was no other way for them to get back into the tribal area of Tibet. They came and were described to me as having been 'handpicked,' and, to me, that always had the connotation of their being a rather select group."

ders, in addition to thirty general assistants, were hired to combine their talents to create the masterpiece.[12]

And while the artisans pooled their talents, Gompo Tashi traveled to Lhokha, Kongpo, and Kham, ostensibly collecting donations but, in reality, collecting resistance leaders from all over the south of Tibet. When he returned to Lhasa he had, in his wake, twenty-seven tribal chiefs ready to do his bidding.

Under the cover of darkness, they converged on Gompo Tashi's stately house in Lhasa.

Thupten Dargyal, a twenty-year-old from Kongpo, was there that night, along with his wealthy merchant father:

The meeting at Gompo Tashi's house began as a kind of party—everyone was discussing the building of the golden throne. Then Gompo Tashi got serious and quieted everyone down and he gave a speech about what we men had to do. He said, "Our way of life has been ridiculed, our religion attacked, and our countrymen killed. Who can say they don't also have designs against His Holiness the Dalai Lama? We must unite and forget our petty personal interests."[13]

Gompo Tashi then asked the men to gather around his private altar. In front of a large painting of Palden Lhamo, the patron goddess of Tibet, and an autographed photograph of the Dalai Lama, he made the men take a sacred oath. The men swore that from here on out they would dedicate their lives to fighting the Chinese until there was an end to communist occupation.

Their secret organization would be *Chushi-Gangdruk*—an ancient name for Kham, meaning "four rivers, six ranges"—in other words, "all of Kham," or "unity."[14]

Drawupon was also there that historic evening. His physical appearance had changed as much as his hometown of Jyekundo. Now in his twenties, he was well over six feet tall, with massive shoulders and the sad eyes of a man who had seen far too much sorrow for his years. As for Jyekundo, it, too, car-

[12]Gompo Tashi Andrugtsang, *Four Rivers, Six Ranges*, 52.
[13]Thupten Dargyal, interview with the author.
[14]The four rivers are the Nyalchu, the Dzachu, the Drichu, and the Machu. The six ranges are Duldza Zalmogang, Tshawagang, Markhamgang, Pobargang, Mardzagang, and Minyagang. Later, the *Chushi-Gangdruk* would also be called the "National Volunteer Defense Army," in order to include all districts of Tibet, but *Chushi-Gangdruk* has remained the more popular name.

ried the sadness of a Tibetan city buried under the presence of the PLA. Drawupon's father had died in 1952, leaving his son to deal with the communists. The "reforms," the *thamzings,* and all the other horrors had forced Drawupon to flee west with a small army of rebels.

That night at Gompo Tashi's, however, Drawupon was anything but despondent:

Joining the Chushi-Gangdruk *was the answer to all my prayers. Gompo Tashi's views were my people's views. What was the point of trying to negotiate with the Chinese? That had taken us nowhere. And we were convinced that the Americans were behind us and that—somehow—over a period of time, we would succeed in driving out the PLA. We were united in this optimism. We never looked back from that time on. Gompo Tashi had provided us with a way, a path. We believed in him completely. At last we could hold up our heads.*

The Chushi-Gangdruk *created a flag for itself. Across a yellow background, there were two crossed swords—both unsheathed and one on fire.*[15]

Though simple in design, the flag spoke volumes. The yellow background was the color of their religion, symbolizing their intention of defending Buddhism from the Chinese. The flaming sword was the weapon of Manjushri, the Bodhisattva of Wisdom, which could sever the roots of ignorance. Ignorance was the cause of communism. The naked sword symbolized the Khampas' bravery *and* their heritage—it was the only weapon they knew how to make with their own hands.

It was time to put their flag into action.

KALIMPONG. FEBRUARY 20, 1957.

Athar, Wangdu, Lhotse, Tsewang, Dedrup, and Dreshe, six brawny Tibetans dressed in calf-length *longhis*—light cotton wraparound skirts worn by Indian laborers—squatted in the darkness of a lonely road.

That day, Gyalo Thondup had told us not to wear anything Tibetan, Athar remembers. He said, *"Don't bring any money and don't bring your knives or anything personal that might identify who you are." Well, we didn't have any proper identification, so that was no problem, but none of us felt good about*

---

[15]Drawupon, interview with the author.

traveling without our knives. We didn't argue. We ate a big dinner and, after dark, we slipped out of town to a place called "The Ninth Mile." That's where we were supposed to be picked up.

At nine o'clock, Gyalo pulled up in a jeep. He was behind the wheel and his attendant, Gelung, sat next to him. Gyalo brought Gelung because he spoke Hindi, which would be useful later on. Gyalo told us guys to be very quiet. We drove south without talking—down to Siliguri, where we stopped for a break. We ate chapattis and potatoes without saying one word.

Gyalo left us at Siliguri. We had a new driver for the rest of the way, which was almost to the East Pakistani [present-day Bangladesh] *border.*

From there, we went on foot. Gelung led the way down a small path that went through a tea plantation. He was using a compass, which I had never seen before. We walked for several hours in the jungle and, during the hike, Gelung showed us how to use the compass and explained why it was useful.

Our objective was to find a big river that marked the Indian–East Pakistani border [Kamlui River]. *We walked for two hours before finding it. The river was very deep. It took us another hour to find a crossing that was shallow enough for us, because only one of us could swim. Luckily, the land was very flat and the river was peaceful. We locked hands and waded across. We didn't mind getting soaked, because even in the middle of the night it was very, very hot.*

Once we got to the East Pakistani side of the river, we walked inland and came to a narrow road. We had been instructed to wait there.

The moon was out, so we could see if anybody was approaching. A little bit later, we saw a guy walking toward us. He was definitely armed and, at first, we thought he was Indian, which really put us on our guard. But then Gelung got up, clicked a signal with his flashlight and got the appropriate signal clicked back at him, and we knew he was Pakistani.[16]

We followed the Pakistani down the path, then turned down another path and met up with more Pakistanis who were waiting for us with a Tibetan— someone we knew—Jentzen Dhondrup, the cook of Taktser Rinpoche. This really surprised and pleased us. He praised us for reaching our goal safely, and then

---

[16]Athar, interview with the author. At that time, America's relations with the East Pakistanis were much better than with the Indians. Given Nehru's anti-American proclivity, it was paramount from the CIA point of view that the Indians remain ignorant of the Tibetan exfiltration.

explained how an American was waiting for us in a house down the road. This was where Gelung's responsibility for us ended, so we said good-bye and continued on with Jentzen.

There was a jeep hidden in the bush. It was brought out and we drove in that for about a half-hour before reaching a small building, which was an East Pakistani checkpost. Inside was an American, sound asleep snoring.

We had never seen an American before. He had brown hair, blue eyes and a big nose. And he was hairy and we thought this was very funny. We made a joke about how the Chinese had an American imperialist in their backyard and didn't even know it. He woke up and was very kind to us. He shook all of our hands, made us tea and served us fancy biscuits. [The American in question was CIA officer Edward McAllister. He was posted in Karachi and tasked with penetrating the local Chinese community.]

After a while, two jeeps pulled up outside. The American got in one of them and we Tibetans got in the other and drove for another six hours. I remember how thirsty we were. Even though we had been to Delhi and Bodhgaya and Sarnath, we Tibetans weren't used to hot weather. We had to stop several times— whenever we came close to a river—so that we could have a drink. Every time we stopped, I thought, "There really are a lot of people involved in this thing!"

Finally we reached a house near a big city railway depot [on the outskirts of Dacca]. *We were brought Indian food and left to rest for a while.*

So then we were taken to the big railway station. Pakistani guards surrounded us so that it looked like we were prisoners being escorted onto the train. I guess, in that way, no one would ask any questions. They put us in a first-class car with no other passengers. We were very impressed: very fancy. And then someone brought us water with ice in it. We were so amazed: Here we were in the hottest place on earth—where had they found ice in such a place?

We traveled by train a long time. And then we were transferred to a covered truck—again, for a long time—and finally we reached an airport with an American plane and staff waiting for us. [The plane was a C-118, part of the Kadena, Okinawa, fleet organized for unconventional operations and given the impossible name "332nd Troop Carrier Squadron, Medium (Special)"] *We were hurried up the back stairs of the plane. All the window curtains were pulled down and we weren't allowed to pull them up. We took off almost immediately.*

You should understand how strange and exciting it was to be in a plane. Even though we couldn't see much—and we never saw the pilot or crew—the noise of the engines and the feeling in our stomachs when we took off made us joke that we were in the god-realm. And if you think about it, the speed of a plane really isn't human.

There's this Buddhist story about a man being taken across the ocean by sim-pos—goddesses with blue eyes. And we could peek and see that we were flying over the ocean [the South China Sea]—*this was also the first time that we had seen an ocean—and it was such excitement for us and we joked with each other that we were being taken across the ocean by simpos.*

We flew into a big military installation in Taiwan [actually, it was Okinawa]. *No one told us that, but we kind of guessed that, because along with the American jets—they were everywhere—there were also lots of Chinese people and Chinese writing on the buildings* [the people and writing were Japanese].

We were put in a building on top of a hill that overlooked a military camp. Two things happened there—one that made us angry and one that made us happy. We were angry because we were taken to a hospital and told to take our clothes off for a physical. First, we were very healthy and strong guys and we thought it was a waste of time. Second, Tibetans don't go walking around naked. But they insisted that this was part of the physical. The thing that calmed us down and really made us happy was that Taktser Rinpoche walked in. To have the Dalai Lama's brother with us just changed everything in our minds. By then he had been living in America and he spoke English very well and he was going to act as our translator. Anyway, we calmed down after he arrived and we passed the physical. We spent the next week being interrogated by the Americans—I guess they were CIA. These interrogations were conducted separately, with Tak-tser acting as our translator. We had to tell every detail about our families and ourselves.

From there we were flown to Saipan, although none of us knew it at the time. Until just recently, I thought we had trained on the island of Guam. It was all very strange and new to us. And of course we had no idea what to expect once we stepped off the plane. Nobody had told us anything except that we were going to learn how to fight like Americans.[17]

---

[17]Ibid.

. . .

ROGER E. MCCARTHY HAD BEEN HURTLED INTO A SIMILARLY
foreign situation:

There wasn't much time to prepare for the Tibetans' arrival. What we got, in the
way of instruction, was a cable from CIA headquarters that there would be a pro-
gram involving Tibetans: A pilot group of six would be arriving in early or mid
April. The group was to be given across-the-board training, meaning that it was not
just paramilitary, but also intelligence, communications, etc. The idea would be to
organize this group into at least two teams, which were to be, on completion of
training, reinfiltrated into Tibet by parachute in the fall of 1957. Once back in
Tibet, they would be relied upon for messages to be sent back and forth using agent
communications in the form of RS-1.[18] *We were also advised that Thubten Jigme*
Norbu [Taktser Rinpoche] and his previous manservant, Jentzen, would be accom-
panying them as translators. How we trained them was left to us. And the only
reading material on Tibet that I could find before the arrival of the group was a copy
of Heinrich Harrer's Seven Years in Tibet—*the only Tibetan book we had in the*
Saipan library—so it became my Bible until I could get additional data sent in.[19]

McCarthy had grown up in the Finger Lakes district of upstate New York
and graduated from Syracuse University in three and a half years. His ruggedness was surpassed only by his intelligence. He had graduated with the
idea of joining the FBI, but he and a fraternity brother had been encouraged
by a former OSS officer faculty member at Syracuse to contact the CIA.

McCarthy joined the CIA in 1952 and, after a concentrated training
period, arrived in Taiwan in early June of the same year. He received additional training in 1955 and 1956, was rapidly promoted, and, in 1957, transferred to Saipan along with his new bride who also worked with the Agency.[20]

There were instructors on Saipan that were more senior than myself—
including more than a couple of former OSS men. Ordinarily, when a special and
high priority project such as this came in, it would have been given to a more

---

[18]An old WWII system for Morse code, which consisted of a radio transmitter and a hand-cranked
generator.

[19]Roger E. McCarthy, interview with the author.

[20]Roger E. McCarthy, letter to the author. McCarthy's wife worked in the psychological and propaganda training section, having previously worked in the Tokyo Station after graduating from Purdue.

Roger McCarthy on Saipan in the 1950s.
(Collection of Roger E. McCarthy)

senior instructor. This was only five years into my CIA career; I was the grand old age of thirty.

Actually, it was more by default that I got the Tibetan assignment. The older guys didn't want it. They were afraid that it was going to be a disaster. In fact, one of those senior instructors still owes me a couple of cases of beer on a bet that we made whether [the Tibetan project] would succeed or not.[21]

I must say that it was not a very impressive group that got off the airplane. Of course, in their defense, it had been a long trip from East Pakistan and they were obviously exhausted.[22]

In fact, the Khampas had just flown into the twentieth century.

Oh, the changes they were experiencing were unbelievable. We're talking about Tibet, a country where the average altitude is fourteen thousand feet, as opposed to Saipan, an island a few feet above sea level. From cold and dry— Tibet—to hot and humid—Saipan. And unfortunately, the only thing we could provide for their comfort was electric fans in their small dorms. The heat of the day alone was a huge adjustment for them, as was the heavy training schedule they had. But they were incredibly adaptable men.

Training included Morse code, cut numbers, radio signal plans, the U.S.-made RS-1 crystal-operated radio transmitter and receiver . . . encoding and decoding using one-time pads, use of telecodes (Tibetan telecode was developed during the training), map and compass reading, small arms up to and including

---

[21]The wagerer in question was Eli Popovich, who was in charge of the paramilitary section when McCarthy arrived, but would soon be transferred elsewhere.
[22]Roger E. McCarthy, interview with the author.

*60-mm mortar and 57-mm recoilless rifles, fragmentation and incendiary gre-
nades, fire and movement tactics . . . offensive and defensive ambushes, an array
of simple sabotage techniques, use of demolitions, Molotov cocktails, booby traps,
unarmed and hand-to-hand combat, cross-country and night movement, observation, casing, authentication, elicitation, information collection, reports writing, tradecraft techniques, resistance organizations, sketching, preparation of
drop zones, parachute ground training, simple psychological warfare techniques,
first aid, simple disguise techniques, and physical fitness.*[23]

The Khampas' facilities consisted of two Quonset huts.[24] One contained
sleeping quarters where the six trainees bunked along with Jentzen. The
other contained a classroom (which doubled as a mess hall), a kitchen, and a
laundry room. There was also a private bedroom and bath for Taktser Rinpoche, as befitted the older brother of the Dalai Lama.[25]

Taktser Rinpoche became, in essence, McCarthy's crash-course in all things
Tibetan:

The Chushi-Gangdruk *was not known by me or anyone else on Saipan—not
until after Taktser's arrival and subsequent conversations with him. He was the
primary translator and interpreter for the training of the group. . . . We learned,
somewhat tardily, that until the creation of the* Chushi-Gangdruk, *the different
tribes in Kham and Amdo seldom worked together in a coordinated effort. It was
a different world and a different mind-set. But when religion and freedom
became the primary concerns, brought on by the Chinese invasion, then all the
tribes began to take note of each other.*

*Taktser was, and is, a very gentle person—almost too gentle in the sense that
he didn't readily understand our sense of urgency. That was a little frustrating.
However, he did most of the classroom work and all of his (and Jentzen's) stories
of Tibet were very educational.*[26]

Only days into the training did McCarthy begin to understand the true
mettle of the Khampa warrior. No physical challenge was too great, and their

---

[23]Roger E. McCarthy, *Tears of the Lotus*, 240.
[24]A prefabricated building with a semicircular roof of corrugated metal, which curves down to form
the walls.
[25]Roger E. McCarthy, interview with the author.
[26]Ibid.

attitude was open, fun-loving, and gregarious—all except for Tsewang, who seemed either shy or a little withdrawn:

I believe it was the second or third day after their arrival. Early in the morning, about five-thirty A.M., we were out for the morning run. We noticed that Tsewang was quieter than the others, and later that morning he mentioned that he had stomach pains. The Tibetans thought it was probably because of the change in diet. However, his pains didn't go away. It finally got to the point that we did a hands-on examination and learned that it was the appendix area that bothered him, and that the area was hot to the touch. The attending medic[27] said we should bring Tsewang into the medical facility on the base, and we did, around midnight.

The doctor confirmed the problem and opened him up. There was nothing left of the appendix but tiny pieces scattered throughout the cavity. The doctor shook his head, completely astounded. He suspected that the eruption had taken place at least two days before Tsewang landed on Saipan! How he had managed to deal with the pain with such stoicism was beyond anyone's comprehension.

The doc and medic had just begun to remove the pieces with tweezers—a difficult task in itself. To make matters worse, while they had Tsewang wide open, the main power on the base went out. The doc and medic put on miners' caps and, with the help of a flashlight and a backup security light, they removed all the pieces they could find given the poor lighting. The doctor then emptied almost all of the sulfa packets that could be found in the Dispensary into the cavity—he literally salted the whole area with it. He said, "If Tsewang has not had any antibiotics before, there is a chance. I give him a fifty-fifty chance of survival."

A week later, Tsewang was running again with the others in the morning. No aftereffects. No infection. It was as if nothing had ever happened—except he did become a different person in that he was no longer quiet. He became active, he asked questions, and it became clear that he, like all the others, had a great sense of humor.

Loosened saltshaker caps (so that buddies would inadvertently dump the contents on their food) were indicative of the gentler side of their playfulness. But their pranks could also get rugged.

---

[27]Gus Ormrod. He paid a daily visit to the trainees and was present during live-fire and demolition field training.

The Tibetans always got even with one another—one "revenge" after the next. They played rough. And close friendships, such as Athar and Lhotse's, did not inhibit thoroughly rowdy scuffles. Athar broke Lhotse's finger while disarming him in an unarmed-combat exercise. Bloody noses and lips, and a generous supply of bruises were commonplace and not worth comment.[28]

Nor were the Khampas shy about tussling with the CIA team, if invited. Harry Mustakos, contact man between Headquarters and the Tibetan project, decided one day to test the legendary skill of Khampa swordplay. He tossed a short traditional Tibetan blade to Lhotse and challenged him.

It turned out to be a bad idea. *A few seconds later, Mustakos found himself bleeding from a nick on his hand and without the knife he started with—plus Lhotse's knife poised to do serious damage. The other trainees thought the incident funny, as did I and the other instructors. Afterward, Mustakos agreed with me that it would be best if he concentrated on the administrative requirements and left all the instruction needs to me.*

And then there was demolition training: *For the Tibetans, demolition training was like "happy hour," no matter the challenges of properly setting long or short fuses, or the various explosives of charges to be used. The bigger the bang and the more damage that the explosives achieved the better! More than once we had to call in the base fire department to put out fires created by the trainees (and instructors) in the training area, and the numerous WWII Quonset huts that had populated the training area became fewer as they became "targets."*[29]

"Joyous effort," to borrow a Buddhist phrase, was also exhibited during ambush exercises. *This became fun for the two (separated) groups, for each got to work against the other. Using M-80s to simulate a large charge, the Tibetans were to sneak up and secretly place booby-traps. They enthusiastically booby-trapped each other all over the place—including doors, tables, the dining area, bathrooms, in the vehicles, along trails and footpaths—everywhere imaginable. They were not short on imagination. At one point, Wangdu, Gompo Tashi's nephew, requested that special training be given on readily portable nuclear weapons of some kind. He was quite disappointed when I told him that we did not have nuclear bombs in our possession or curriculum.*

---

[28]Roger E. McCarthy, interview with the author.
[29]Ibid.

Demolition exercise conducted for the Tibetan trainees on Saipan. *(Collection of Roger E. McCarthy)*

Nevertheless, and not surprisingly, given their upbringing, rifle and handgun range work was a snap for them. In discussions with them as to what weapons were commonly found in Tibet, I think we were all amazed at the "Heinz 57" description answers. Their marksmanship was always impressive despite the array of weapons presented.

And in spite of their antics, they were very disciplined. They understood the value of intelligence nets—what would work, what couldn't work. Somewhat skeptical at first, they adapted very quickly and understood the necessity and advantage of small-unit tactics. Their attention to detail during observation exercises was superior. In fact, I don't know of any subject in which they ever failed. Nor were they afraid to ask questions. To my surprise, they quickly learned how to read and use maps, a skill few can claim. (From simple coordinates concepts to eight digit accurate grid coordinates and transposing the resultant coordinates into accurate insertions in the one-time pad system to be used, as well as the need for properly and accurately orientating the antennas to communicate by the RS-1 radio according to the signal plans provided by Washington—all six did very well.)

Also, to various degrees, they became adept in communications techniques that, at that time, amounted to Morse code, signal plans, and taking care of the radios and various pieces of equipment, including the frequency-controlled crystals. (Wangdu was the exception: he was totally uninterested in learning communications. He figured that was something his servant, Dedrup, was going to pick up for him.[30])

Water exercises did not come easy for them. Only one of the six could swim. Nevertheless we went paddling in the nearby ocean with lightened combat loads inside the reef in six-man rubber boats, using compass and maps to locate the right landing spots. This included two or three night "infiltrations" and "exfiltrations" exercises after the trainees had become somewhat adept in handling the paddles. I do remember that all six enjoyed splashing about in the pools formed inside by the coral reef, but understandably, none were interested in venturing into the breaking waves just beyond the reef.

Basically, we fell in love with these guys. The Tibetans distinguished themselves from the other nationalities that I had worked with. There was their obvious high spirit, dedication, self-discipline, and a degree of self-confidence. They were brave, honest, and strong—everything one respects in a man.

But there was something else about them—hard to explain.[31]

FOUR DECADES LATER, I ASKED ATHAR, DURING OUR FIRST INTER-view, what it had been like to suddenly be so far from Tibet. He shrugged and answered:

Well, we had already lost our homes and many people in our families. Many of our loved ones we had seen die, some in great agony. And there was nothing we could do about it. I don't think you've experienced that. These are things you don't forget, but they do kill the idea of home. Those that were alive were scattered in the mountains fighting the Chinese—or in Lhasa, or trying to get to Lhasa, or imprisoned, or in labor camps, or trying to escape to India. What homes do you

---

[30]As will be seen, this was to have serious consequences once the team was re-infiltrated into Tibet.
[31]Roger E. McCarthy, interview with the author.

mean? We didn't have homes to go back to. And anyway, Mr. Roger kept us very busy and we had the brother of the Dalai Lama with us and the Americans were helping us so much . . . I thought about home all the time but it was a place of the past. Wherever I was, it became home for that day. Saipan was our home. We called it "Dursa," by the way, which means "Island of the Dead" in Tibetan. We were told that in World War II, a big battle had taken place there.[32]

There were skeletons all over the beaches where we trained: everywhere, especially in the caves along the beach. We joked that there were more dead guys than alive guys on Saipan. There were also unexploded bombs the size of men, half-buried in the sand. Sometimes, we were put on the bomb-search details. We were given small red flags to take with us; if we discovered bombs, we attached the flags to nearby trees so the Americans could later remove the explosives and detonate them beside the ocean. The whole island would shake.

But what I most remember was a rock cliff overlooking the ocean where, we were told, many Japanese had committed suicide by leaping to their death. That made me think about home. Khampas were committing suicide back in Tibet—something that was rare before the communists came—even monks were jumping into the rivers so that they wouldn't be forced to denounce or kill their lamas. By then, Tibet was "Dursa," too.[33]

Athar, Lhotse, Wangdu, Dedrup, Tsewang, and Dreshe were given American nicknames—Tom, Lou, Walt, Dan, Sam, and Dick, respectively. They would train on the island for five months.

MEANWHILE, WHILE THEY WERE LEARNING THE WESTERN TECH-niques of war, Eastern Tibet continued to sink under the weight of Chinese oppression.

According to Michel Peissel, "Mass executions took place and terrible tortures were inflicted, tortures of the most sinister kind, many recorded in the

---

[32]Toward the end of the war, the Americans had needed Saipan as a staging base to bomb Japan. The struggle for possession of the island became one of the most violent conflicts in the Pacific. In 1944, the U.S. Navy brought in more than five hundred vessels. It took a month of continual bombing before they were able to put seventy-one thousand troops ashore. Nearly thirty thousand Japanese died in the process. A year later, the "Enola Gay," the B-29 that dropped the bomb on Hiroshima, took off from Saipan's sister island, Tinian.

[33]Athar, interview with the author.

reports of the International Commission of Jurists. Children were forced to shoot their parents, monks were wrapped in wool, covered with kerosene and set on fire, while the Chinese mocked the living torches and told them to have Lord Buddha intervene for them."[34]

A massive migration of Eastern Tibetans headed west, to the capital. Lhasa, home of the Dalai Lama, was their last hope.

And many arrived at the capital just in time for *Tenshuk Shapten* and the unveiling of Gompo Tashi's golden throne, offered to the Dalai Lama on July 4, 1957. The remnants of the Tibetan army marched, the monks blew their long trumpets, dancing troops performed in the streets and, everywhere, giant pots of smoldering juniper branches filled the air with resinous perfume.

Gompo Tashi remembers: *The throne was placed in one of the balconies of the Norbulingka Palace,*[35] *and when the Dalai Lama sat upon it there was general rejoicing. . . . The officials of the Dalai Lama decided that the throne should be kept in the Potala and the ceremony repeated every year, when the Dalai Lama would sit on the throne and receive the people in audience.*[36]

Such were the last shreds of optimism still clinging to the well-wishers of the Dalai Lama's reign.

Gompo Tashi and the principal leaders of the *Chushi-Gangdruk* continued to hold their meetings without the Chinese catching on—a remarkable feat given the increasing number of spies now firmly sequestered within the main monasteries and within the offices of the Potala. According to McCarthy, under Gompo Tashi's guidance, *the leaders agreed on the areas in the provinces where each would operate; they completed drafting their organizational plans, including designating the officers who would hold the key positions, and they listed the many things that needed to be done before the* Chushi-Gangdruk *could become effective. These included obtaining weapons and ammunition, horses, pack animals, food for fighters and animals, training areas, and selecting likely targets to hit, such as storage areas used by the Chinese, and locations of smaller enemy units. They also exchanged information on*

[34]Michel Peissel, *Cavaliers of Kham: The Secret War in Tibet,* 87.
[35]The Dalai Lama's summer residence, several miles west of central Lhasa and just north of the Kyi Chu River.
[36]Gompo Tashi Andrugtsang, *Four Rivers, Six Ranges,* 54.

escape routes that could be used in situations where it was necessary to avoid or escape from the Chinese.[37]

And then the leaders gathered their rebel forces and headed back to the hell-realm of Kham, Amdo, and Golok.

The men they enlisted along the way were not short on motivation. They, too, had lost everything. Insubordination was practically nonexistent. They took oaths never to reveal their camps to anyone, even under torture. A brotherhood was born that had never been known by the tribals in the days before the communist occupation. Fellow guerilllas were the only family left to them. And although they had no army uniforms, they didn't need outfits to illustrate their grim unity. You could see it in their set jaws—their desire to kill every Chinese in Tibet.

[37]Roger E. McCarthy, *Tears of the Lotus,* 135.

Guru Rinpoche (Padmasambhava) *(Jamyang of Amdo)*

7

TIBETANS FROM
THE SKY

Before Buddhism, Tibetans worshiped an animistic and shamanistic religion called Bon. It was a heavily populated pantheon of gods and goddesses who were largely hostile to the human race. Animal and human
sacrifice were necessary to appease the deities, and the high priests kept a
close watch on their demands through sorcery, divination, ophiolatry,[1] can-
nibalism, and many other forms of primitive mysticism. Buddhism had traveled up from India, from time to time striking a chord with the royal courts,
but the Bon-pa priests, jealously guarding their inherited power, made sure
the foreign religion was kept at bay, partially by blaming natural catastrophes
on the kings' dalliances with Buddhism.

In the mid-eighth century, the greatest warrior-king of Tibet, King Trhisong Detsen, challenged the Bon hierarchy by importing the most famous

---

[1] Worship of snakes. Tibetan Buddhism embraces serpent deities as well. The *nagas,* serpent spirits, as
described by Athar, rule the rivers and lakes in Tibet.

Buddhist mystic of the subcontinent. His name was Guru Rinpoche (or Padmasambhava, as he was known in India).[2] He was of royal blood, many believed him to be the "Second Buddha," and, several centuries later, King Gesar would be identified as an emanation of Guru Rinpoche.

Guru Rinpoche was, among other things, a warrior for Buddhism. It was said he could transform himself into monstrous manifestations should non-Buddhist forms encroach upon the dharma. As he traveled across the Himalaya and toward King Trhisong Detsen, who awaited his arrival in the Yarlung Valley—the valley from which all Tibetan kings hailed—Guru Rinpoche melted snow-massed mountains, caused alpine lakes to boil, pierced demons' eyes, flew into the sky, created avalanches, arrested the wind, and, one by one, subdued the Bon retinue of deities, ultimately transforming them into "protector deities" of the Buddhist faith, thus creating what was to become the uniquely Tibetan register of Buddhist deities.[3]

The stories surrounding "the Second Buddha," as fantastic as they may sound to the contemporary reader, are taken in all seriousness in Tibet. What is historically irrefutable is that Guru Rinpoche was a real personage who, some twelve hundred years ago, came to Tibet at King Trhisong Detsen's bidding. The two famous men met at Samye, some sixty kilometers southeast of Lhasa, situated along the wide sandy shoals of the Tsangpo River (known as the "Brahmaputra" in India). Together they established Tibetan Buddhism by building its first monastery. The first generations of Tibetan monks were ordained at Samye Monastery. Eventually, it became the most important academic hub in Asia—a center of a systematic translation effort unparalleled in history.[4]

---

[2]Padmasambhava means "lotus-born" in Sanskrit, an idea charged with Buddhist significance. The lotus symbolizes absolute purity—a flower conceived in sludge, yet managing to emerge untainted by its murky origins. Buddha adopted the lotus as a metaphor for a kind of immaculate conception: The practitioner of Buddhism begins his or her metaphysical journey swamped by worldly suffering, but if motivation is correct and skillful means are perfected, he or she will journey upward and eventually reach the open sky of Enlightenment. Padmasambhava is usually depicted seated on a lotus rising up out of a magnificent lake.

[3]A detailed account of Guru Rinpoche's activities in Tibet can be found in Mikel Dunham, *Samye: A Pilgrimate to the Birthplace of Tibetan Buddhism.*

[4]Crystal Mirror Series, vol. V, 12: "Through the close collaboration of panditas and Tibetan lotsabas, the entire Vinaya was translated within a single generation, together with nearly 750 Sutras, Dharanis, and sastras, including all the major Prajnaparamita Sutras and the extensive Ratnakuta and Avatamsaka Sutras."

In the 1950s, Samye was still a major center for all four schools of Tibetan Buddhism.[5] The Dalai Lama's chief oracle had ancient ties with Samye and, for all Tibetans, it was a primary "power spot" much frequented by pilgrims.

In 1957, the number of people in the CIA who knew of Samye's existence or, for that matter, the relevance of Guru Rinpoche in Tibet's history, was zero.

IN SAIPAN, THE TRAINING OF THE SIX KHAMPAS WAS PROGRESSING at a remarkable rate. Nearly fifty years later, McCarthy still marvels at the amount of training that he and his team crammed into five months before air-dropping the trainees back into Tibet:

Had I known then what I know now, I would have also supplied them with a chapel or at least an altar. Taktser Rinpoche conducted prayer meetings approximately twice weekly—either in the early mornings or late evenings, but neither he nor any of the Tibetans asked for anything to support their Buddhist practice. The Buddhist system doesn't really call attention to itself. And when the distinctive beach formation south of Samye was selected as one of the locations designated for reinfiltration, none of the Tibetans mentioned its incredible spiritual significance, or in any way clued us in.[6]

WHILE MCCARTHY WAS TRAINING THE KHAMPAS, A CHANGE OF guard was taking place in Washington. Frank Holober replaced John Reagan as head of the Tibetan project. A brilliant linguist and Harvard graduate, Holober's first task was to write a basic plan out of which the new program would proceed:

I was looking for the operational potential—the human potentials in these warriors. We already recognized that we were dealing with people who were more deserving than some of the people we had been working for. They were truly involved in trying to protect their way of life, their country, and were willing to fight for it. The Tibetans had this great spirit: "Give us the tool, and we'll

---

[5]The four schools are Nyingma-pa, Kagyu-pa, Sakya-pa, and Gelug-pa.
[6]Roger E. McCarthy, telephone conversation with the author.

Frank Holober, who wrote the basic plan for the CIA's Tibetan Task Force. (*Collection of Mrs. Lee Holober*)

do the job." They weren't asking the CIA to do the job for them, which is what we got from a lot of the groups we were working with. We wanted to work for the Tibetans. In Kham, Amdo, and Golok, the Tibetans were born to the saddle, well trained with guns, in possession of guns—they were ready to go. It was just a matter of adding to that: training, helping to organize, and giving them some better arms and ammunition.

But it was all exploratory. What did the CIA know about Tibet? Not very much. There weren't even good maps. We didn't know what the situation was inside. It's true that we had people outside, like Gyalo Thondup and Taktser Rinpoche, who had some sort of correspondence going back and forth by courier, but it was hit or miss. The intelligence was almost nonexistent.

The basic plan was to create a self-contained unit. And if you got it approved, the money would flow and everything else would fall into place. In the meantime, Roger McCarthy was waiting in Saipan, wondering when this damn report would get done so he could get things moving.

Politically, there was already CIA support in place for the Dalai Lama—personally and for his government. Nobody at the Agency wanted the Dalai Lama to have such financial difficulties that he was handicapped in getting his message out.

I think the first cost estimate I put in there was $500,000. How I arrived at that figure, I no longer recall. The allocation of money was not specific. Well, the distribution of moneys had already started, really. I think we were already giving out $180,000 a year to Gyalo Thondup, who had set up an account. The finance people handled that: They just put it into his account to do whatever he

*wanted to do with it and we just trusted him to do the right thing. I think he did.
I know he was investing part of it. One time I remember having a conversation
with Gyalo and he wanted my advice on good stocks to buy.*

*As for the Dalai Lama . . . well, all along, the Agency knew that we were not
going to be able to recruit the Dalai Lama. He was not going to be an agent for
the CIA. But there was an international gap in leadership of Buddhists worldwide. There were a lot of Buddhist countries. And there were a lot of strong
movements—especially in Japan. (Inter alia, I discovered later that we had a
special "in" with the Buddhist organization in Japan.)*

*But the point is, the Agency was hoping that the Dalai Lama would somehow
fit into this international void and sort of be acknowledged as the "Pope of the
Buddhists," if you will—in effect, broaden the anti-communist aspect of Buddhism everywhere. We didn't feel that we could actually ask the Dalai Lama to
do this, of course, but it was the Agency's hope that he, of his own volition—by
virtue of his position and the fact that he had endured such suffering at the
hands of the Chinese—that he would eventually occupy that position, which
would, in turn, help us in our international anti-communist program, including the United Nations and elsewhere. We were prepared to use our media assists
if the Dalai Lama would show a little initiative along those lines. As it turned
out, he never did.*

*Regardless, the plan was approved. In essence, it had been approved even
before I had written it. When the report finally landed on the appropriate desk,
the Agency said, "Well, Frank, it's about time," and BAM—they put the chop on
it and away we went.*[7]

THE PRIMARY OPERATIONAL GOAL WAS TO CREATE TWO TIBETAN
teams that would be parachuted back into Tibet. One team would be dropped
into Kham, not far from their home village, to support the rebels there.
Wangdu, Dedrup, Dreshe, and Tsewang were selected for that group. Wangdu
was a natural leader but his communications training was the weakest of the
six. This would be offset by the exceptional skills of Dreshe, the trainee from
Bathang.

---

[7]Frank Holober, interview with the author.

The smaller team, comprised of Athar and Lhotse, would be dropped in somewhere in the Lhasa area to make contact with Gompo Tashi and Phala. Both men were adept communicators and more familiar with the Lhasa area than the others.[8]

Athar balked when he learned that he and Lhotse would not be dropped in Kham. It was Taktser Rinpoche who broke the news to him. Athar's initial response was one of anger:

I had agreed to train so that I could kill Chinese. Well, Kham was where the fighting was, not Lhasa. Besides, I didn't know any of the high-ranking officials in Lhasa. What could I do there? Also, I thought of the Lhasa officials as cowards—always doing exactly what the Chinese told them to do. I was afraid that some of the Lhasa officials might betray us to the communists—tell them that we were American-trained spies.[9]

It was only after he learned that he was to make contact with Gompo Tashi that Athar calmed down.

McCarthy had difficulty convincing all six Tibetans of the advantage of small unit tactics. Khampas had grown up believing in "safety in numbers":

The five-man fire team was stressed as the basic organization for guerilla warfare practices. The Khampas accepted the necessity and value of the setting up of good ambushes, as well as the concept of "quick hit and quick withdrawal," but they told us that five-man teams would not be readily accepted by their colleagues inside Tibet. This turned out to be correct: About the best compromise the trainees could muster, after they returned to Tibet, was to employ fifty-man groups, for the most part—a serious and often fatal mistake. The tribal use of larger forces (a hundred or more)—a Khampa and Amdoan tradition—was not about to be readily changed by the trainees. That the Tibetan resistance had already enjoyed stunning successes in defeating the PLA forces in 1956–57, using their cavalry tactics and large numbers, had only cemented the Eastern Tibetans' thinking that this was the way to victory.[10]

---

[8]Roger E. McCarthy, interview with the author.
[9]Athar, interview with the author.
[10]Roger E. McCarthy, interview with the author.

. . .

NEITHER THE CHINESE NOR THE AMERICAN PUBLIC HAD ANY idea that the CIA was training Tibetans. It would be a successfully guarded secret for nearly two decades.

MEANWHILE, INSIDE TIBET, RESISTANCE FIGHTERS WERE STILL engaged in combat in every district of Kham, Amdo, and Golok.

They wore no official uniform other than their traditional *chubas,* draped Khampa-style and hiked at the waist higher than those worn in Lhasa. For the most part, they lived in their saddles, raiding, besieging, running, and hiding. They set up their *magars* (resistance camps) beside lonely monasteries or villages overlooking strategic trails. Many women followed the rebels, but, by that time, many others had already been killed, abducted, or simply left behind, their fate unknown. And, as McCarthy points out, the Chinese feared the disenfranchised warriors all the more for this:

Every desolate gorge, every secluded river crossing, every isolated path through the conifer forests became the backdrop for potential ambush. And the Chinese knew, all too well, that these rebels—who had lost everything—never took prisoners.[11]

IN EARLY OCTOBER, THE SIX TIBETANS PREPARED FOR THEIR final training before returning to Tibet. They were flown to the island of Okinawa, where they would be given their practice dives.

Jim McElroy, a former rigger in the paratroops, was in charge of airborne support in Okinawa. McCarthy informed McElroy that the training jumps would be unconventional: They would be made *without* reserve chutes, because the Khampas' actual reinfiltration into Tibet would be made without reserve chutes. McCarthy's reasoning behind this decision was twofold:

The small reserve would be of little or no use at fourteen thousand feet, and at best the Tibetans would be seriously injured if the reserve were pulled; and

---

[11]Ibid.

secondly, it was far more practical to give the jumper a chest pack containing a weapon (folding stock), some ammo, money (Tibetan, Nepalese, and gold coins), some emergency rations, maps, compass, signal plans and crystals for radio operators), a knife, and a small flashlight.

McElroy was skeptical about jumping without a reserve parachute, but when I boarded the plane without a reserve for the demonstration jump, he mumbled a bit, and then removed his reserve as well.[12]

The six Tibetans watched the demonstrations from the safety of the tarmac. The first demonstration, conducted out of a C-119, went according to plan, both instructors making textbook landings.

However, McCarthy's next jump demonstration, from a B-17, was less pretty:

Once again, Jim and I jumped without reserves. Just after we exited the plane, we saw a red flare fired from the ground. (This signal, which indicated that the winds were too high for a safe jump, was, of course, not much help if you had already jumped.) McElroy and I exchanged suitable comments and maneuvered for a landing. He headed for a tarmac near some storage buildings. Thinking better of a cement landing, I opted for some nearby rice paddies. The ground wind speed was a concern, so I decided to try to make a running landing. All was going well until I finished running across one paddy and started to run on the next one; unfortunately, it was about a foot lower than the first one, and I went sprawling, facedown. With the wind pulling my parachute, I then went headfirst through the low dirt-wall separating paddies. Fortunately, my football helmet took the shocks, and I was finally able to grip the quick release and the air spilled out of the canopy. The Tibetans had converged on me by that time, and all were bent over with laughter as they helped me out of the paddy. The front of my fatigues, my face, my arms were covered in muck. Meanwhile, McElroy had managed to land close to one of the outbuildings, which successfully blocked the wind; he came away with a couple of scrapes. Given the wind gusts, which were thirty by that time, we were lucky . . . but we had demonstrated the features of the T-10[13] *and the blessing of a helmet.*[14]

---

[12]Ibid.

[13]Type of parachute, considerably customized for Tibetan conditions by McElroy. For a detailed description of the modifications, as well as relevant aeronautical information, see McCarthy's *Tears of the Lotus.*

[14]Roger E. McCarthy, letter to the author.

All six trainees made three familiarization jumps—without reserves—while they were on Okinawa, both in the night and the day. Athar's only comment concerning this potentially lethal adventure was: *Well, we were used to heights.*[15]

McCarthy confirms their fearlessness, with Dreshe seeming to be the exception:

The first jumps went smoothly for the trainees, except that the last of the Tibetans to jump, Dreshe, sat down on the edge of the open door of the C-119, rather than exiting, as he should have. He was in a somewhat curled position, his eyes tightly shut, with his head tucked down and arms crossed in front of him, exactly as though he had actually exited. I was immediately behind him, so I simply reached down, lifted him by the collar of his jumpsuit and "helped" him exit. I followed him out of the aircraft. All the others had exited as though they had jumped numerous times before. Most of them even used the toggles to "steer" on this first jump. I talked to Dreshe afterward about his "sitting" in the door, but he assured me he was not afraid of jumping, was simply nervous, and in his mind had "jumped" OK. I was a bit dubious, but accepted his statement and reassured him that the parachute would always work.[16]

If Athar thought parachuting an unremarkable experience, he was far more impressed by CIA instructions concerning his tasks, once he and Lhotse returned to the Lhasa area. Their first mandate was to make contact with and debrief Gompo Tashi. What was the size and state of the *Chushi-Gangdruk*? How organized were they? What sort of firepower and funding was available to them? What kind of equipment did the *Chushi-Gangdruk* most need?

Their second mandate was to meet with Phala, Lord Chamberlain. The CIA wanted Phala's assessment of the political situation in the capital. How much pressure were the PLA generals exerting on the Dalai Lama? What was the Dalai Lama's personal position regarding the communists? What was the *Kashag*'s position? Which of the Dalai Lama's advisers could be trusted and which were suspect? What was the mood of the Tibetan people? If, indeed, they despised the Chinese occupation, what were they prepared to do in order to free themselves of the communists?

---

[15]Athar, interview with the author.
[16]Roger E. McCarthy, interview with the author.

Their third mandate was to make a reconnaissance, as best they could, of the PLA in and around Lhasa. What were their numbers and locations? What kind of vehicles and tanks did they have? What airfields had they constructed and what kind of planes could be landed on these airfields? What was their air power? What roads and bridges had been constructed and where were their locations? What were the details of communist mistreatment and torturing of Tibetans? How was the PLA affecting the Tibetan economy? Had the PLA taken the entire Tibetan food surplus? And, most important, to what extent was the Dalai Lama in danger? Were the communists prepared to kidnap him, to kill him?[17]

With the exceptions of Gompo Tashi, Phala, and Gyalo Thondup, Athar and Lhotse were to trust no one. They were to tell no one about their training. Many Tibetan lives could be at stake. Athar's anticipation grew with every added instruction:

The closer we got to reinfiltration, the more excited we got. We had so much new equipment and we couldn't wait to get back and use it on the Chinese. Unfortunately, just a few days before we were to fly back to East Pakistan, there was an accident.[18]

The six trainees were on the firing range, testing various pistols to determine their individual preferences. Tsewang was testing a Canadian 9-mm. One of the instructors shouted something, Tsewang turned to see what was wrong and, at the same moment, accidentally pulled the trigger of his 9-mm.

McCarthy was off to the side when he heard the round go off. He ran toward them and recounts what he saw:

None of the trainees appeared to be hurt but I noticed that they were all looking at Tsewang. I yelled for Gus, the medic, and rushed over to Tsewang, who by then was staring at the Corcoran jump boot on his right foot. I noticed the lace had been broken, and saw some blood starting to ooze from the small hole under the lace. I cut his fatigue pants leg from ankle to thigh and, together with Gus, we managed to remove his boot and blood-soaked sock. From the blood pumping from the wound, it was obvious an artery had been hit. Gus tried to stem the flow of blood by using a pressure point on Tsewang's upper thigh, but was unable

---

[17]Athar, interview with the author.
[18]Ibid.

to slow it down. He removed his belt from his khaki shorts and made a tourni-
quet while I successfully exerted my weight—at 6'1"and 205 pounds, I was
much heavier than what the slightly built Gus could bring to bear—on the pres-
sure point. Together we secured the tourniquet and a military ambulance rushed
him to a nearby military hospital. Jentzen went along as translator.

I sat for a while with the trainees, wondering to myself what else could possi-
bly go wrong.

We then returned to the safe house on Base. Two or three hours later, Tsewang
limped in with Gus and Jentzen. Incredibly, X-rays showed that no bones had
been broken or shattered in the foot, so the doctors had simply extracted from the
wound the bits of leather and lace that had gone into his foot. (To have a bullet
go through your foot without striking any bone is all but impossible, but in
essence, Tsewang had accomplished his second miracle—the first having been
his recovery from the burst appendix on Saipan.)[19]

Tsewang assured his buddies his foot was fine. But it was obvious to all
that his injury would not be healed in time for their reinfiltration into Tibet.
There was no way he would be cleared to jump from a plane. That meant that
there would be one less member in Wangdu's group, a fact that was disheart-
ening to all.[20]

In the meantime, there was one last item given to the trainees before their
departure: the "L" tablet.

The "L" tablet was a cyanide ampoule nestled inside a tiny box cushioned
with sawdust. Should critical injuries be sustained while parachuting, or
should other more compelling emergencies arise, such as being captured by
the Chinese, suicide could be achieved within seconds. McCarthy explains:

The TDS (Technical Services Division) had provided the "L" tablets. I ex-
plained to the trainees that the capsule could be placed in the mouth, or swal-
lowed, and if the capsule was not deliberately broken then it could be re-used . . .
but once broken by the teeth, it was then a matter of simply inhaling deeply and
death would quickly follow. I demonstrated the "in the mouth" part while talk-
ing about how the capsule should be used, to show the trainees that the tablet
would not easily break, and could be removed from the mouth if so desired. All

---

[19]Roger E. McCarthy, letter to the author.
[20]Athar, interview with the author.

the trainees decided to have the capsule taped to their arms or legs. (This choice was offered to all subsequent trainees prior to parachuting into Tibet. The aircrews were also offered the option. I do not recall any of them choosing not to take the capsule with them.)[21]

The CIA umbrella cryptonym for clandestine assistance to Tibet was STCIRCUS. In keeping with this theme, STBARNUM was used to indicate overflight activities, including the airdrop of the six Tibetans. (Overflights were planned at CIA headquarters in the Air Operations division, headed by Gar Thorsrud.) Pinpointing the location of the drop zones was a problem. Apart from a few World Aeronautical Charts (WAC), primarily of use to flight crews, there were no reliable maps of Tibet. (Maps from U-2 overflights would not be available to the CIA for another two years.)

According to McCarthy, the only operational maps of the drop zones in Tibet were from a collection of old English hand-drawn maps and photos from the days of the McMahon line.[22] One of the most informative photographs was of the Tsangpo River, sixty kilometers southeast of Lhasa. The river was wide, and the low-lying sandy dunes were even more expansive—an easily identifiable drop zone, especially in the moonlight. No one paid any attention to the monastery nearby. This would be a night mission for the obvious reason of avoiding Chinese (as well as Indian) detection. And at that time, known ground-based navigational aids—including reinfiltration drop zones—were few and far between.

The second airdrop site—for Wangdu's group—was determined not by old photographs but by the information provided by the Khampa trainees themselves. Molha Khashar was Wangdu's hometown, a tiny village near the much larger Lithang. Current reports indicated that the Lithang district area was still one of the most hotly disputed areas in Kham. Wangdu's group would have to be prepared for the possibility of firefight the moment they touched ground.

The all-important supply bundles, also to be dropped from the planes, were now ready. They contained Tibetan clothing and accessories—including

[21]Roger E. McCarthy, letter to the author.
[22]Ibid. McCarthy is referring to the British military expedition that reached Lhasa in 1904. It was Thorsrud who came up with the photographs.

boots and hats, prayer beads and Tibetan knives. (These had been obtained by Wangdu's brother, Kalsang, who had sent them to the CIA from Darjeeling.) Along with special food rations, there was an assortment of foreign-made handguns, ammunition, cameras, compasses, pencils, pencil sharpeners, binoculars, signaling mirrors, first-aid equipment, native medicines, sunglasses, cloud coverage cards, map-grid cards and maps. Once the men had safely landed, the procedure to be followed was to bury the parachutes and the jump equipment, change into Tibetan clothing, cache all else that was not necessary or needed right away, such as the back-up RS-I radio equipment, and to proceed with their respective missions, making sure the location of the items cached was well remembered by team members.[23]

When it was finally time to leave Okinawa and return to Tibet, Tsewang had no choice but to say good-bye to his teammates. The plan was for Tsewang to join his team later, overland, once his foot healed. Dreshe, Wangdu, Dedrup, Athar, Lhotse, McCarthy, McElroy, and Jentzen climbed aboard a B-17, the "Flying Fortress" of World War II fame—only this bomber had been stripped of all its American markings. It was painted black.

Their destination was Kurmitola, an old World War II airfield located just outside Dacca, East Pakistan. The airfield would be the two Tibetan teams' staging base.

The Khampas did not bother with the oxygen masks until the bomber reached well above eighteen thousand feet, at which point McCarthy insisted they go on oxygen. They seemed oblivious to the turbulence and the thin air. They talked, they sang and sipped tea as if they were already back home, comfortably arranged around a campfire.

At the staging base, the Pakistani Army provided for everything, including cots and mosquito nets, which the army set up for the Tibetans on the tarmac.[24]

October, 1957. Night of the full moon. The Tibetan calendar was lunar, and it seemed fitting, in Athar's mind, that the Americans were paying heed to the old lunar cycle. Before leaving Okinawa, Taktser Rinpoche had told the

---

[23]Ibid.

[24]Ibid. When McCarthy mentioned the East Pakistanis' helpfulness, he explained, "Those were the days when the U.S. had good relations with Ayub Khan, head of West and East Pakistan, thanks in large part to the affable Agency officer, Walter Cox, who was a friend of Ayub Khan's."

young men that the airdrop was timed with an auspicious date. The full moon made it even more auspicious.[25]

But the auspicious date came and went.

An overcast sky moved in, and the mission had to be postponed for three nights. Finally, on October 20, the last night of the full-moon cycle, the clouds parted and the team prepared to go. There would be no Americans on the flight. Polish and Czech expatriates manned the unmarked aircraft. The CIA had trained them in Germany for deep-penetration missions into Eastern Europe. If something went terribly wrong and the plane went down, the Americans would simply deny all knowledge of them.[26]

Secrecy was of paramount importance. The plane would have to overfly Indian territory without Indian permission, and the problem with that was that Calcutta had radar. This was circumvented, according to Conboy and Morrison, by Gar Thorsrud: "Gar Thorsrud had already done his homework and knew that the Indian system had no compensation feature and could be defeated if the B-17 used the Himalayan massif as a radar screen. Flying north over Sikkim, the crew would go as far as the Brahmaputra [Tsangpo River near Samye] for the first drop, cut east across the Tibetan plateau to Kham [near Lithang] for the second drop, then veer southwest through Indian territory back to East Pakistan."[27]

There were other dangers, however, as James Glerum, who served under-cover with the CIA's Far Eastern air operations, explains:

Penetrating a denied area is never easy . . . But in this case, the ranges, the altitude, the lack of navigational aids for much of the mission made it to me a very challenging operation.[28]

Lawrence Ropka, the Air Force navigator detailed to the project as flight planner, adds:

The major challenges were, first and foremost, equipment. We had none. The airplanes did have a crude radar but there were no other means of navigation other than celestial and dead reckoning . . . and, of course, eyeball navigation:

---

[25] Athar, interview with the author.
[26] William M. Leary, "Secret Mission to Tibet: The CIA's Most Demanding, Most Successful Airlift," *Air & Space*, Dec. 1997–Jan. 1998.
[27] Kenneth Conboy and James Morrison, *The CIA's Secret War in Tibet*, 61.
[28] Quoted in William M. Leary, "Secret Mission to Tibet."

looking out the window and trying to determine your position relative to various terrain features. There were no radio beacons. There was nothing.[29]

As McCarthy escorted his trainees to the unmarked aircraft, he wished them luck:

By now, it was easy to regard the Tibetans as our brothers. Our good-byes were heartfelt.[30]

The two teams boarded the black bomber chanting the mantra of Vajrasattva, the Bodhisattva of Purification:[31]

OM BADZAR SATWA HUNG

OM BADZAR SATWA HUNG

OM BADZAR SATWA HUNG

Athar remembers:

The plane seemed to go straight up after takeoff. It was really something to see the Himalaya from the sky. The moon was out. The snow on the mountains was blue.[32]

Despite the altitude, the Tibetans required no oxygen.

The anonymous bomber made its approach over the Tsangpo River. The sandy tract, captured in the old photograph, came into view. Athar and Lhotse stood up. They said a hasty good-bye to Wangdu, Dedrup, and Dreshe. Athar and Lhotse's radio and other gear were tied to a three-hundred-foot line; the line, in turn, was secured to Athar's midsection. When the aircraft descended to about one thousand feet above ground level (fourteen thousand feet), the bundle was pushed out of the exit. Athar then followed the line out of the plane. Lhotse jumped immediately after, following Athar's direction with his toggle cords. He could see the Tsangpo glistening below them.[33]

We could also see the famous golden roof of Samye.

They say that when Guru Rinpoche was deciding the proportions of the

---

[29]Ibid.

[30]Roger E. McCarthy, conversation with the author.

[31]Athar, interview with the author.

[32]Ibid.

[33]Conboy and Morrison, *The CIA's Secret War in Tibet*, 62.

The main temple of Samye. *(Collection of the author)*

monastery, he flew up into the sky and pointed with his tse-sum.[34] *The sun was behind him and it cast the shadow—like a pointer—of his* tse-sum *on the ground. That was how King Trhisong Detsen, who was on the ground, marked off Samye's boundaries. Lhotse and I were exactly where Guru Rinpoche would have been in the sky. It was strange and very special. Later, we talked about floating above Samye many times.*[35]

When the team landed, the wind was blowing hard off the surface of the Tsangpo. The river was particularly wide at this juncture, a watery barricade that took pilgrims several hours to cross by coracle. After ridding themselves

---

[34]"Khatvanga" in Sanskrit: a ritual trident usually depicted as resting in the crook of Guru Rinpoche's left arm.
[35]Athar, interview with the author.

of their parachute harnesses and the 9-mm Sten submachine guns strapped around their chests, they broke open their supply bundle, changed into the *chubas* that Kalsang had sent to Okinawa from Darjeeling, buried most of their supplies in the sand, and bedded down for the night.[36] The CIA agents didn't sleep for long. Athar says that, before the sun came up, they headed away from the river up to a hill where they tried using the wireless:

The light of the radio came on, but just a little bit, not like when we had practiced with it on Saipan. Maybe it was because we couldn't crank it hard enough. But just in case it was broken, we hid that one, dug up the other one and took it with us. We headed toward the village built around the eastern entrance to Samye Monastery. No one paid any attention to us. Samye is so used to traders and nomads and mendicant monks that we were just two more pilgrims. It was easy because we were pilgrims. There were little shops where we bought food, and also khatas and yak butter to be used as offerings to the various altars in Samye. While we were shopping, some of the villagers were gossiping about hearing an airplane the night before. Someone said that the plane must have been the Chinese. Lhotse and I looked at each other, and then agreed with the villagers. "Yes, it must have been Chinese."

Samye is enclosed by a huge circular wall. We began by doing chora[37] *around the outside of the wall. We then entered by the main gate and went into the main chapel and left offerings. We did* chora *on all three floors. Then we went to the chapel of Pehar, who is the protector deity of Samye, and made offerings to the memory of friends and family who had been killed by the Chinese; then we went back to the village where we made arrangements to buy a horse.*

Then we made the four-hour walk to Chimphu, which is a holy hill[38] northeast of Samye. There are many monks and nuns who live in caves toward the top of Chimphu. We left butter, tsampa, and brick tea at the entrances of these little caves, because the people inside never leave, or at least not for many years.

---

[36]Kenneth Conboy and James Morrison, *The CIA's Secret War in Tibet*, 63.
[37]A Buddhist ritual and a kind of walking meditation, in which the practitioner circles buildings, monuments, and chapels while intoning mantras.
[38]The top of Chimphu is 17,500 feet—no "hill" by Western standards. In such an altitudinous world, Tibetans (as do the Nepalese) often reserve the word "mountain" for peaks over 20,000 feet.

(Tibetans always help people who are really practicing Buddhism. We believe that we gain merit in this way.) Chimphu is famous because Guru Rinpoche practiced in these caves and many great teachers achieved enlightenment there. While we were up there, we ran into three young monks who were from Chatreng—very near Lithang. The monastery at Chatreng had been bombed at the same time as Lithang. It was no problem getting them to help us crank the radio and, in this way, on Chimphu hill, we finally got through to the Americans.[39]

Athar and Lhotse informed the Agency that they had arrived safely and that they were preparing to leave the airdrop for Lhasa.

They headed back down to Samye and picked up their newly purchased horse.

The vast area south of Samye was called Lhoka. The topography was varied: rugged mountains, narrow gorges, forests, fertile valleys, alpine lakes, as well as wide-ranging tracts, barren and uninhabited by man. Lhoka was also where the ancient kings had built a string of forts, east to west. Ruins of these citadels still rose across jagged ridges. One of the first things that the Chinese had accomplished in the early '50s was to establish garrisons in Lhoka in or around the region's great forts. Also, there was a rough trail that meandered south through Lhoka's forests, and the Chinese had already begun exploiting it for timber. They transported this much-needed resource to Lhasa where there were many building projects in progress.[40]

Athar and Lhotse, however, were about to discover that the *Chushi-Gangdruk* had taken back Lhoka from the communists in a series of bold attacks. The CIA trainees' spirits soared as they worked their way west across terrain now controlled by their rebel brothers. In fact, they were to learn, Gompo Tashi's men now controlled Central Tibet all the way to the Indian border! Athar and Lhotse made a *puja* with incense, thanking the gods for helping them vanquish the enemies of Buddhism.[41] Had they known what to look for, they might have seen *Sputnik,* the first satellite launched into outer space, gliding like Rahula across the turquoise sky.

---

[39]Athar, interview with the author. Athar's use of the Chatreng men raises an interesting question. If he and Lhotse were "to trust no one" as mandated by the CIA, how did they explain the radio to their newly made friends? Unfortunately, the author failed to ask that question when he had the opportunity.
[40]Michel Peissel, *Cavaliers of Kham,* 108.
[41]Athar, interview with the author.

. . .

MEANWHILE, AFTER THE "FLYING FORTRESS" HAD CIRCLED SAMYE and dropped Athar and Lhotse, the B-17 banked to the east and headed for Lithang with the second team. Wangdu, Dedrup, and Dreshe were not as lucky as Athar and Lhotse. By the time they arrived over Kham, a dense cloud system had enveloped all of Eastern Tibet.

The Czech and Polish crew shook their heads. This part of the mission had to be aborted. They returned to Kurmitola with the second group of Tibetans. Wangdu and his team members got more bad news when they regrouped with McCarthy on the East Pakistan tarmac: Unfavorable weather predictions over Kham precluded additional tries for the remaining days of full moon for the month. McCarthy had no alternative but to fly the team back to Okinawa and attempt reinfiltration later, when the full-moon cycle came around again in November.[42]

During the following month in Okinawa, the Tibetans' morale went from low to high. The news that Athar and Lhotse had successfully reinfiltrated put everyone in a celebratory mood. Also, Tsewang's foot healed rapidly: McCarthy told Tsewang that he would be allowed to parachute with the rest of the team on the November run. McCarthy recalls that even Dreshe seemed to have regained his sense of humor, which had been declining ever since the six men had left Saipan for their parachute training on Okinawa.[43]

In November, Wangdu, Tsewang, Dedrup, and Dreshe were flown back to Kurmitola where, with the support of the Pakistani Army personnel, preparations were quickly finalized. Weather forecasts were favorable. McCarthy remembers:

Wangdu was particularly animated and entertained us with a "hand-shaking" pantomime of himself as he parachuted to ground and fixed his location by simulated use of map and compass. Little did he know then that he would soon have good reason for being very nervous.[44]

"Big Mac" Korczowski, the Polish loadmaster for the flight, hustled the Khampas aboard. McCarthy waved good-bye. The moon came out. The B-17

[42]Roger E. McCarthy, letter to the author.
[43]Ibid.
[44]Ibid.

lumbered up into the starry sky and nosed toward Kham. The radio operator kept McCarthy advised of the designated checkpoints along the way. Cloud coverage along the route prevented the crew from locating the exact location that Wangdu had wanted, but the decision was made to jump anyway—as it turned out, some six miles from Wangdu's home village.[45]

When the B-17 returned to the airbase in Kurmitola, McCarthy rushed to the plane to congratulate the Polish-Czech crew. He peered through the "joe hole." His jaw dropped open in disbelief:

Dreshe was sitting close by without his parachute and canvas bag. "Big Mac" approached and apologized, saying that Dreshe had hyperventilated when it came time for him to jump. "Big Mac" had pulled him away from the "joe hole" so that Wangdu, Dedrup, and Tsewang could make their jumps.

I'm sure Dreshe saw me wince with shock. That Dreshe had the primary radio and signal plan on him had been forgotten by "Big Mac," but it was far too late to remedy that. I remember feeling that my reaction was like receiving a hard blow to the body, for it meant that Wangdu would be without that which Dreshe did best: the ability to communicate. Without the primary "commo" plan, it would be a miracle—his third—if Tsewang, with a bandaged foot, managed to make contact with us.

I helped Dreshe from the plane, for he was still in some distress.[46]

WANGDU'S TEAM DESCENDED ON A HILLSIDE FORESTED WITH PINES. Thousands of Chinese were known to be in the area. The team hid their excess equipment and climbed to the top of a nearby prominence in an effort to find their bearings. All was not peaceful in the darkened forests of Kham. They heard gunfire not too far away. Nervously, they bedded down for the night.

It was not until the next morning that Wangdu realized the plane had overshot its target by a good six miles. He and his two companions headed back south toward Wangdu's home village. That afternoon, while walking a ridge, the team ran into a nomad moving a herd of Khampa ponies. Wangdu

---

[45]Ibid.
[46]Ibid.

asked the man if there were any rebels in the vicinity. The nomad nodded. "Lots of Chinese, too," he added. He agreed to lead the team to the rebels' *magar*.

Just as it was getting dark, Wangdu's team emerged into a clearing where the rebels were camped. There was a moment or two of uneasiness and suspicion. But soon the two groups converged on one another with open arms. Among the rebel band was a warrior by the name of Bhugan Gyatotsang. Bhugan was Wangdu's older brother.[47]

The Khampa boys were home.

DECEMBER ARRIVED IN OKINAWA WITHOUT NEWS OF THE SECOND team. The long stretch of silence cast a shadow over McCarthy's Tibetan Task Force. Dreshe, however, the best radio operator and the one trainee who had failed to jump, did his best to remain optimistic about his missing teammates. Whether or not a signal from Wangdu's team was received, McCarthy decided to reinfiltrate Dreshe overland at the soonest possible date. It would be up to Dreshe to find his way to Wangdu's team somewhere in the Lithang district.

Right before Christmas 1957, the radio suddenly crackled:

Tsewang came on the air loud and clear. He signaled they were well and "free of control." Obviously he had sorted the problems involved, including using the secondary radio, the back-up signal, the right crystals, the right one-time pads, and oriented the radio's antenna correctly. I wondered only who had cranked the hand generator besides Dedrup . . . very likely fellow Khampas.[48] I remember saying that Tsewang's message was the best Christmas gift I could possibly get.[49]

In follow-up messages, Wangdu reported large resistance forces in the area—between five and ten thousand Khampas. Firefights, ambushes, and larger confrontations were cropping up all over the mountains and gorges of Eastern Tibet. Wangdu indicated that he was now in command of an "army" of freedom fighters. He requested immediate airdrops of arms and ammuni-

---

[47]Kenneth Conboy and James Morrison, *The CIA's Secret War in Tibet*, 65. Also Athar, interview with the author.
[48]Roger E. McCarthy, letter to the author.
[49]Roger E. McCarthy, telephone conversation with the author.

tion. The problem was that, in his enthusiasm, Wangdu failed to pinpoint locations for the airdrops. McCarthy radioed back, requesting precise coordinates. Again Wangdu answered that he needed airdrops, but failed to include the crucial information as to where, exactly, the CIA was to drop the loads. McCarthy repeated his previous request.

And then, there was no response from Wangdu's team.

The New Year came and went. Additional messages from inside Tibet were zero. In the meantime, jump-shy Dreshe had been reinfiltrated, overland, from East Pakistan. Dreshe radioed that he had made it to Tibet and that he was heading north toward Lithang, where he would locate and link up with Wangdu's team.

Then there was silence from Dreshe as well.

The CIA had no choice but to assume the worst. Wangdu, Tsewang, Dedrup, and Dreshe—two-thirds of McCarthy's trainees—were listed MIA. It would be a year and a half before the Americans found out what had happened.

BY THE BEGINNING OF 1958, THE CHINESE HAD COMMITTED EIGHT PLA divisions and at least 150,000 men in Eastern Tibet alone. The revolt in Amdo, especially, had reached its apex. The land reforms introduced in 1956 had ignited the uprising, but it was only now that the full impact of those reforms was felt by many of the nomadic tribes. According to Warren Smith Jr. "Some nomadic areas of Amdo were reported to have been virtually emptied of men, all having fled or been killed or imprisoned. Most of the population of the Sokpo (Mongol) was reportedly massacred."[50]

In another Amdo district, near Lake Kokonor, more than a thousand monks of Trakmar Monastery were herded into the monastic quadrangle and riddled by the fusillade of machine guns hastily mounted to the courtyard wall. And at the monastery of Labrang, the PLA evicted the three thousand monks living there, even though the monastery had not participated in the revolt. In fact, the majority of Amdoan monasteries were evacuated, looted of any valuable assets, then systematically torn down, the lumber and stone used to construct PLA barracks or homes for Chinese settlers imported from the

---

[50]Warren W. Smith Jr., *Tibetan Nation*, 442.

Mainland. Like the monks, many Amdoans were sent to labor camps where two-thirds of them eventually perished. New ways of killing laymen became commonplace in Amdo: scalding, vivisection, and throwing people from airplanes.[51] But, perhaps most tragically of all, truckloads of Tibetan children were hauled off in order (so went the Chinese logic) that parents could better concentrate on their labor contributions to the "Motherland." Mothers who objected were unceremoniously thrown into the nearest river. All told, according to the International Commission of Jurists (the Geneva-based human rights–monitoring organization composed of fifty member nations), approximately fifteen thousand infants and children were forcibly removed from Tibet, the fate of these children still unknown.[52]

BY THE BEGINNING OF 1958, ATHAR AND LHOTSE HAD MADE CONTACT with Gompo Tashi a few miles outside of Lhasa. They told him they had orders to speak with Phala, but Gompo Tashi advised them that, given the preponderance of Chinese spies, it was risky and would take some time to arrange. While waiting, the CIA trainees temporarily settled in the village of Pempo, twenty-six kilometers northeast of the capital. There they resumed radio contact with the CIA. They observed and reported back to Washington the status of Damshung airfield. Then, disguised as pilgrims, they stayed at Drepung monastery for a week, then shifted to Sera Monastery, all the time gathering information for the Agency.

Finally, in February 1958, their meeting with Phala was held at Norbulingka. Athar told Phala that the United States was open to establishing direct contact with him and providing a considerable amount of aid. Phala's reaction was noncommittal. They then asked Phala for permission to have an audience with the Dalai Lama, but the meeting never happened.

In the meantime, Eastern Tibetan refugees kept pouring into the Lhasa area—more each day. Then in April, even more Tibetans flooded the capital for the annual religious celebrations.

---

[51]John E. Avedon, *In Exile from the Land of Snows,* 48.
[52]Warren W. Smith Jr., *Tibetan Nation,* 442.

According to McCarthy, *Gompo Tashi arrived with a party of some 300 from Eastern Tibet. It was a brazen act on his part, for by this time the Chinese had become suspicious of him and would have arrested him if they had anything more than suspicions. But they were still not sure . . . he was 53, thus in their mind too old to fight, and, to their knowledge, had so far only traveled extensively on religious pilgrimages and had continued his trade caravans. Again, under cover of the religious celebrations, Gompo Tashi completed plans with more than 20 other resistance leaders who had arrived in smaller groups.*[53]

In May, the Chinese inaugurated a census of the thousands of squatters who had recently encamped in the Lhasa Valley. Refugees were required to prove their name, age, birthplace, father's name, and provide three copies of his or her photograph. These were documents that few, if any, Tibetans owned. Nevertheless, such documentation was now necessary if the Eastern Tibetans wished to remain in the Lhasa area. Gompo Tashi describes the reasoning behind the communist census:

The Chinese believed this would afford them the control and safety that they wanted. They had become increasingly concerned about the rumors that the Tibetans had resolved to fight . . . Gunshots had been heard in Lhasa for many weeks, and the Chinese believed that these came from resistance forces in the area. Some of the shots were from Tibetans attacking Chinese patrols . . . and some were from nervous Chinese on guard duty outside of Lhasa shooting at just about anything they heard . . . But many of the shots were fired by two or three Tibetans firing different weapons from different positions to upset the Chinese as part of the psychological warfare that had been devised by the resistance leaders. These nightly firings had the Chinese nerves very much on edge, and the previous tranquility of Lhasa was no more. These new restrictive orders by the Chinese served only to further anger Tibetans from the provinces. The orders were futile, for it did not take long before "travel" documents, even those requiring a signature by a Chinese, could be duplicated or, if necessary, obtained for a small amount of money. And there were many ways into Lhasa that the Chinese could not control.[54]

---

[53]Roger E. McCarthy, *Tears of the Lotus,* 138.
[54]Quoted ibid., 141.

Bathang Regiment's version of the *Chushi-Gangdruk* flag, decorated with a tiger, snow lion, dragon, and garuda. *(Collection of Athar Lithang)*

MEANWHILE, BY JUNE 1958, TWENTY THOUSAND TO THIRTY THOU-sand members of the *Chushi-Gangdruk* had joined forces in Lhoka. The success of their many engagements with PLA troops was gaining momentum.

They were also moving closer to Lhasa—this in spite of being outarmed by the Chinese. The reason for this was, in part, because they were beginning to better equip themselves by raiding Chinese garrisons and capturing guns and ammunition from fallen PLA troops. Gompo Tashi personally contributed to the effort by buying Russian-made guns of both short and long range. From India, Nepal, Sikkim, Bhutan, Pakistan—and even China—he was able to purchase additional rifles and pistols.[55]

---

[55]Ibid., 143.

Having concluded this business, Gompo Tashi hopped on his motorcycle (also imported from India) and headed south for Lhoka to join up with his army:

I had decided that [my motorcycle] *was the most secure way, for it was not likely that a bored, half-asleep Chinese guard would concern himself with a lone motorcyclist—nor could he have stopped or caught me even if he wished. I then headed for Lhoka on horseback. On the way we were joined by hundreds of others who were on their way to join the volunteer army.*[56]

Athar and Lhotse—having accomplished all that they could in Lhasa—were two of those volunteers.

THE MILITARY SCENE IN LHOKA, UTTERLY CONTROLLED BY THE rebels, was nothing short of spectacular. Gompo Tashi described the meeting of so many different tribal groups as "a confluence of rivers." They met above Yamdog Yutso Chinmo Lake. There were over five thousand cavalry from central Tibet alone. [We] *paraded proudly on our horses in four lines abreast, each of us dressed in our traditional tribal clothing, and with rifle and sword.*[57] The troops offered piles of incense. The blue smoke spiraled up and out over the open countryside. Toward the front of the rebel cavalry, a horseman carried a portrait of the Dalai Lama. Thousands of champing steeds pranced through the valley, their pride and optimism as vast as the sky above them. And at the vanguard of the procession, the yellow crossed-swords flag of the *Chushi-Gangdruk* snapped in the wind.[58]

Gompo Tashi's military review was less than a hundred miles from Chinese-occupied Lhasa.

FURIOUS OVER REPORTS OF THE FREEDOM FIGHTERS' GROWING army, the generals in Lhasa demanded that the Dalai Lama send the remnants of his Tibetan Army to Lhoka, to attack the *Chushi-Gangdruk.*

---

[56]Quoted in Roger E. McCarthy, *Tears of the Lotus,* 143.
[57]Ibid.
[58]Ibid.

1958: The *Chushi-Gangdruk* on parade at Headquarters in Lhoka. *(Collection of Athar Lithang)*

The Dalai Lama flatly refused, pointing out, quite realistically, that the troops would, in all likelihood, simply *join* forces with the *Chushi-Gangdruk*. He did agree to call on the rebel army to lay down their arms and return to Eastern Tibet, but he knew that the request would be ignored. (It will be remembered that, for several years now, the *Mimang* had distributed booklets instructing Tibetans to suspect "official" proclamations delivered by the Dalai Lama as having been made under Chinese duress. It was a political warning now widely embraced as a "given" among the citizenry.) As was to be expected, the rebels' reaction was to respectfully ignore the Dalai Lama's request, responding that, in any case, Eastern Tibetans had no homes to return to.

The communists were livid and launched an international smear campaign.

From 1958 onward, the New China News Agency floated fabricated dispatches of Khampa misdeeds including the theft, plunder, rape, and murder of fellow Tibetans. The Khampas were accused of, among other things, desecrating monasteries and raping nuns. (These atrocities, of course—

Chushi-Gangdruk in Lhoka. *(Collection of Roger E. McCarthy)*

happening with appalling regularity—were perpetrated by the accusers.)
The Chinese went further: they dressed troops in Khampa disguises and then
sent them out on raiding parties to steal locals' horses and goods. Those Chinese caught in the act were unceremoniously shot by the *Chushi-Gangdruk;*
but Gompo Tashi could see that precautions must be made: In the future,
those Khampas who approached locals with requisitions for animals and
food were to present official documents, signed by their commanders."[59]

There was, however, a kernel of truth in the Chinese indictment. There
were a number of Amdoan and Khampa renegades roaming the countryside,
taking advantage of the general upheaval in Lhoka and reverting to their
ancient tradition of banditry. Gompo Tashi addressed the problem by
encouraging locals to capture the miscreants and, if they refused to surrender, to kill them on the spot.

---

[59]Ibid.

Having made this point clear, we dispatched soldiers in groups of 50 to 100 men to those areas where these wandering bands were most likely to be . . . The Chinese also learned of our efforts and about what we had told the people. . . . actually it was the Chinese that were paying the renegades and bandits to cause problems.[60] (Roger McCarthy would later comment on Gompo Tashi's Code of Conduct in Lhoka: *Gompo Tashi had no compunction whatsoever to execute traitors. There was example after example of traitors who—well, he just blew their asses off—or disfigured them to the point that it would have been better had they died.*[61])

Another ruse of the Chinese: Some of the Chinese soldiers attempted to join the *Chushi-Gangdruk* as spies. Their efforts backfired.

Gompo Tashi found it child's play to establish which Chinese sincerely wished to join the rebels and which were merely spies. The *Chushi-Gangdruk* executed most of them. A few of them weren't, perhaps, as lucky: They were stripped naked, their faces branded, and then sent back to the enemy camp *with fewer fingers and ears than they had earlier.*[62] Not surprisingly, the PLA decided to stop the spy effort.

What is surprising is the number of Chinese who sincerely defected— either by rallying to the Tibetan cause, or by going AWOL, or even out of fear of being murdered by their own officers. Regimental control often crumbled when the high-pitched war cries of the Khampas echoed through the canyons. As Gompo Tashi put it, *Unless their forces were much larger than ours, the Chinese soldiers usually chose to run rather than fight, for they especially feared our swords and our marksmanship. It surprised us to often see some of the Chinese officers shoot their own men when they would run from us. The officers were usually in back of the soldiers—not leading them—probably to make sure that the soldiers did not run away.*[63]

IN THE MEANTIME, THE CIA RADIO OPERATORS IN WASHINGTON were kept abreast of the dramatic Lhokan buildup of rebels from Athar and

---

[60]Ibid.
[61]Roger E. McCarthy, letter to the author.
[62]Quoted in Roger E. McCarthy, *Tears of the Lotus,* 146.
[63]Ibid.

Lhotse. The team requested more supply drops. A precise locale for an air-drop, however, was not forthcoming, which—as in the case of Wangdu's team—created a dilemma on both sides. The Agency decided that they needed to meet with Athar in person before acting on further requests. They arranged for Athar to rendezvous with them in India.

On a borrowed horse, Athar rode ten days to the Sikkim border, escaped a PLA ambush, and continued on to Darjeeling where he teamed up with Gyalo Thondup and his personal assistant Lhamo Tsering.[64] Eventually, Lhamo Tsering would become the CIA's main operative in India.

From Darjeeling, Gyalo, Lhamo Tsering, and Athar headed south, to Calcutta. There, they were driven—while lying low in the back seat—to a safe house, where Frank Holober was waiting.

Holober had a long list of prepared questions for Athar.

I had my eyes opened, concerning the extent to which the Tibetan people had already rebelled. It was very extensive, and the numbers amassed in Lhoka was alarming. What the Agency had in mind was for the rebels to operate as guerilla units and, politically, to organize underground so that they didn't stick up like nails to be hammered back down into the wood by the PLA. The CIA plan had been to form cells, from village to village, so that, if the time ever came when we wanted to stage something really big, we could give the signal and everybody could jump up at once. And in the meantime, we had dropped two teams back into Tibet, who were trained to spread that kind of doctrine.

But I began to realize that it just wasn't in the nature of the Khampas to behave that way. If they saw something they didn't like, they were going to mount a horse, wave a gun, and say, "Let's go hunt us some communists!"

So after I had questioned Athar, I turned to Gyalo Thondup, the Dalai Lama's brother, whom I had never met before. I wanted to find out from him what he thought about his ability to control that kind of situation from the Indian side of the border.

My recollection is that Gyalo hemmed and hawed a lot.

It wasn't my intention to pin him down, really. I think I already knew what the situation was, and the limitations therein. For Gyalo, on the outside, to con-

---

[64]Kenneth Conboy and James Morrison, *The CIA's Secret War in Tibet*, 73.

trol the movements of the guerilla activity on the inside just was not feasible. But it was a point I wanted to raise with him anyway, just for the record.

Well, with or without the CIA, the resistance was going to continue. So, ultimately we decided to proceed with limited material support and to train a second group of Tibetans.[65]

AUGUST 4, 1958.

The leading expatriates in Kalimpong, headed by Gyalo Thondup, met at his home to draw up a third appeal to the United Nations.

The following day three hundred copies were posted to various membernations of the United Nations, as well as international political and religious organizations. The appeal declared Tibet's independence, denounced the savage repression perpetrated by the Chinese, and begged for international intervention. Along with the appeal, a separate report summarized Chinese atrocities to date, including "the use of poisonous gas, the desecration and plundering of monasteries, the slaughtering of monks, women and children, and at least 15,000 deaths and tens of thousands of homeless refugees."[66]

Nehru, anticipating outrage from the Chinese, moved swiftly to counteract the effect of the appeal. All Tibetans in the Kalimpong-Darjeeling area were warned that if they issued additional public statements, they would be summarily expelled from India. Nehru also issued twenty-five personal warnings to various leading expatriates living in Kalimpong.[67]

Later, the Indians would deny that they had tried to censor the Tibetans in Kalimpong. B. N. Mullik, Director of the Indian Intelligence Bureau and apologist for Nehru's regime, in particular, asserted that it was the *Tibetans* in Kalimpong—not the Indians—who had wanted to keep the Tibetan situation a secret from the international community. Why? Because, according to him, the expatriates were either too ignorant or too stupid to understand what was going on: *They* [the Tibetans in Kalimpong] *were uncertain about the attitude of the Government of India and were afraid that they themselves*

---

[65]Frank Holober, interview with the author.
[66]George N. Patterson, *Requiem for Tibet,* 160.
[67]Ibid., 161.

might be accused of complicity and so they kept quiet. But the main reason [that they didn't speak out] *was they did not properly grasp all that was going on in Tibet.*[68]

The truth is that there were few—if any—people on the planet who had a better grasp of what was going on in Tibet than the dissidents in Kalimpong. Far from discounting the stories, the Kalimpong exiles were the chief promulgators of the rebellion. (Mullik contradicted his own theory by characterizing the Kalimpong Tibetans as "a nest of spies."[69])

In the event, the Tibetans, while stunned by the Indian demand that they shut up, were not unduly surprised. The Indians had been either censoring or denying their reports since 1951. Many took this latest insult as their cue to preempt the GOI threat of expulsion by simply leaving Kalimpong of their own free will. They headed north across the border to join their brothers-in-arms and to die with them, if that was to be their fate.[70]

Meanwhile, among the nest of spies, there was a sizable contingent of Chinese spies who—as Nehru had feared—were infuriated by the appeal that had originated from Kalimpong. They complained to Beijing that Nehru was either unwilling or unable to contain his disruptive refugees.

THE CHINESE IN LHASA WERE NO LESS OUTRAGED BY NEWS OF THE Tibetans' third appeal to the United Nations: They now openly blamed the Dalai Lama and the *Kashag* for the *Chushi-Gangdruk's* presence in Lhoka. This was the Dalai Lama's reaction:

The revolt had broken out in the district they [the Chinese] *themselves had controlled for seven years; yet now they furiously blamed our government for it. Their complaints and accusations were endless, day after day: the Cabinet was not trying to suppress the "reactionaries," it was leaving Tibetan armories unguarded, so that "reactionaries" could steal arms and ammunition. . . . Like all invaders, they had totally lost sight of the sole cause of the revolt against*

---

[68]B. N. Mullik, *The Chinese Betrayal: My Years with Nehru*, 215.

[69]George N. Patterson, *Requiem for Tibet*, 160.

[70]Ibid.

them: that our people did not want them in our country, and were ready to give their lives to be rid of them.[71]

Up until now, the Chinese epithet "reactionaries" had been directed at the Khampas, Amdoans, and Goloks. But by mid-1958, the slur was expanded to include Central Tibetans as well. The Dalai Lama feared that all signs pointed to a Lhasan showdown:

The Chinese were arming their civilians and reinforcing their barricades in the city. They declared that throughout the country they would only protect their own nationals . . . everything else was our [the Kashag's and the Dalai Lama's] responsibility. They summoned more meetings in schools and other places, and told people that the Cabinet was in league with the "reactionaries" and its members would be dealt with accordingly—not merely shot, they sometimes went on to explain, but executed slowly and publicly.[72]

General Tan, head of the PLA in Lhasa, spoke at a Tibetan women's organization and admonished them with a grim metaphor: "Flies gathered around carrion; the way to get rid of the flies is to get rid of the rotten meat."[73]

When hearing this, the Dalai Lama sighed:

The flies, I suppose, were the guerrilla fighters; the rotten meat was either my Cabinet or myself.[74]

ATHAR RODE BACK INTO LHOKA. AS HE RETRACED HIS TRACKS, IN search of Lhotse—his best friend, his brother, his fellow Saipan graduate—he thought about his meeting with Frank Holober. The one dark spot in the debriefing had been when he learned the CIA had received no messages from Wangdu's team since before Christmas. I just hoped that it was the radios that had died, not the guys. Anyway, there was nothing I could do. Kham was a long way from Lhoka. News traveled very slowly back then. And besides, I was very optimistic when I returned to Tibet. Things were going well. The meeting in

[71]His Holiness the Dalai Lama, My Land and My People, 132.
[72]Ibid., 133.
[73]Ibid.
[74]Ibid.

Calcutta had gone very well. America promised me airdrops and it was up to Lhotse and me to radio the CIA the correct coordinates for the designated zones. This was something I could do and I was very happy. We were going to get additional arms and ammunition which was what we needed most. With American airplanes supporting us, it felt like we really had a chance.[75]

In 1958, the world was rapidly changing. Khrushchev became the new dictator of the USSR. Charles de Gaulle became President of France. Alaska became the forty-ninth state in America. Boris Pasternak refused the Nobel Prize. Vladimir Nabokov's *Lolita* scandalized a puritanical public. Stereo records went on sale for the first time. Elvis Presley was inducted into the army in Memphis, Tennessee. The world had its eyes on the sky. America's Vanguard spaceships—one after another—were launched on the screens of a million TV sets, only to lean over and explode in front of an increasingly disappointed audience. France bombed Tunisia from the sky. Howard Johnson set an aircraft altitude record in his F-104—27,810 miles. Pan Am flew its first transatlantic jet trip from New York to Paris. *Sputnik III* orbited the planet.

And in a lonely campsite on a remote plateau in Lhoka, Athar and Lhotse, now reunited—they, too, considered the stars. *We talked about how much had happened to us. We talked about the simpos taking us to Dursa* [Death Island] *and then dropping us back down again, at the exact same spot where Guru Rinpoche had flown above Samye. We really felt that the gods were with us, that with American airplanes supporting us, we were going to take back Tibet.*[76]

---

[75]Athar, interview with the author.
[76]Ibid.

Palden Lhamo, protectress of Tibet, the dharma, and the Dalai Lama *(Jamyang of Amdo)*

8

POISON EATERS

Palden Lhamo had never been so needed or vigilantly attended to with ritual and prayer. She was the frenzied enemy of evil, the security guard for the dharma, and, above all, the personal Protectress of the Dalai Lama. Because she was the special defender of His Holiness, it followed that Palden Lhamo also protected the city in which he lived, as well as the Lhasan government over which he ruled. Theology and politics were ineluctably entwined in the image of Palden Lhamo and, in 1958, she galvanized the Tibetans with her implied patriotism.

Although beautiful in her peaceful manifestation, Palden Lhamo was usually portrayed as terrifying and hideous. Her steed was a white mule with a third eye on his left flank—echoing his mistress's third eye of all-knowing wrath. Together they stormed the skies above a sea of blood.

Palden Lhamo's hair was on fire. Snakes, flayed human skins, and skulls were her adornments. From her girth dangled dice with which to decide the fate of mankind. Raised in front of her sagging breast was a skull brimming with blood and human entrails. And above her head flew a parasol of peacock feathers.

The ancient observation that peacocks consumed a variety of herbal poisons, apparently without harmful effects, had not been lost on Buddhist iconographers. Tibetans believed that peacocks transformed these poisons into the glamorous hues of their iridescent plumage—a metaphor for the Buddhist practitioner's ability to transform Attachment, Anger, and Ignorance—the Three Spiritual Poisons—into Enlightenment.[1]

But why did Palden Lhamo have dice as part of her armor? Did that not imply a connection to Yama? The Lord of Death was judge and jury for one's future reincarnations. To be born into the human realm (as opposed, say, into the animal realm or the hungry ghost realm) was a precious gift. If, in addition, one had come into this rebirth with attributes such as wealth, power, or superior intelligence, then this lifetime was especially auspicious. But here was the catch to getting a great roll of the dice: An auspicious human life form automatically came with the moral responsibility of helping *other* sentient beings less fortunate. To ignore this responsibility—to live a life of myopic self-interest—was to defile one's karma, perpetrate one of the gravest transgressions a Buddhist could commit, and guarantee that one's next incarnation would be vomitous; a freefall down into the very depths of the hell realm. That was Yama's way. And patriotism was Palden Lhamo's way. The ultimate bodyguard for Tibet, Palden Lhamo, held Yama's dice. Do the math. They were connected. Politically, Palden Lhamo was the wrathful antidote to communism; morally, she held the dice; emotionally, Palden Lhamo carried all the weight of a national flag.

BUT TO SUGGEST THAT TIBETANS ACTED HARMONIOUSLY AND IN concert with one another is misleading. With the exception of Gompo Tashi's forces fighting in Lhoka—by 1958, over eighty thousand rebels in Lhoka marched under the *Chushi-Gangdruk* flag[2]—resistance to the Chinese occupation may have looked more like a free-for-all than anything else. Those

---

[1]Pema Wangyal of Dolpo, interview with the author.
[2]Roger E. McCarthy, interview with the author.

who lived in isolated pockets—and this still made up the vast majority of Tibetans—fought as best they could without any notion of what was going on elsewhere in their country. Even Gompo Tashi, one of the few well-informed men in Tibet, was constantly on the move and had little or no idea of what was going on in the capital at any given moment. Many times couriers from Lhasa would ride the trails for two weeks before catching up with him. By that time, their "updates" were, at best, of limited value and, at worst, strategically misleading. One can only imagine how many times Gompo Tashi gathered in the reins with one hand, snatched a proffered report with the other, scanned the contents, then "divined" what had most likely transpired in the interim since the ink had dried and the trail dust had accumulated on the courier's dog-eared missive.

The *absence* of an overview: In 1958, what did average Tibetans really comprehend about the events going on around them? They understood that they hated China, distilled by years of grinding communist occupation. They understood that they wanted their country back, which is to say they wanted their lives back. But what information—good hard facts—was available to them to determine how best to solve their problems? Even the matter of deciding to fight the Chinese was not as simple as it sounded: Picking up a rifle was one thing, knowing where to aim was another.

Except for the chosen few, the CIA's involvement was top secret. The nation at large had every reason to feel a keen sense of international abandonment. There was no modern communications network. Tibetan newspapers were available only in Lhasa and they were worthless, because the journalists were collaborators and the editors were communists. For the rest of the country, current affairs was strictly word of mouth. A man with firsthand news could spread his knowledge only as far as his legs were willing or able to take him. What happened in one valley was unknown in the next valley over. Tibet was a million-and-one informational cul-de-sacs. There were no timely radio reports to put it all together. There was no electricity—never mind nightly television commentaries to shed light on, or make sense of, the ongoing crisis. The only embedded journalists in Tibet would have been Chinese, reporting to officials in Beijing, not to Tibetans and certainly not to the outside world. The Western press heard rumors that there was unrest inside Tibet, but the only way of verifying it was through the Chinese and Indian governments. The Indians downplayed the rumors while the Chinese admitted to a few disturbances but insisted they were an internal problem—a concern for the Chinese Central Government and no one else.

Stranded and ignorant of events beyond the closest village, many Tibetans simply placed their hopes in the higher powers of Palden Lhamo and the Dalai Lama. And since the Dalai Lama lived in Palden Lhamo's Holy City, Tibetans trekked toward the capital in greater and greater numbers—and in blind faith. Others, having lost even that dim hope, headed south to India but, otherwise and on every other level, with little sense of direction.

Still, in Tibet's darkest hour, there were many Buddhists who saw quite clearly the course they should take—the straight and patriotic path of helping fellow Tibetans.

Kalsang Gyatotsang, for instance—brother of Wangdu and Bugan and nephew of Gompo Tashi—was in Darjeeling trying to keep the lines of communication between Tibet and the CIA open. He hadn't heard from his brothers since Wangdu's radio had gone dead months before. But he waited with a modicum of hope, ready to do whatever the Americans asked of him in the meantime.

Taktser Rinpoche, who visited his brother in Kalimpong soon after the first six CIA trainees had been reinfiltrated into Tibet, witnessed firsthand the surprising influx of refugees pouring into Indian border towns. He decided to focus on that aspect of the crisis. Funded in part by the CIA, he flew to Europe, then New York, to secure donations from various institutions and welfare organizations, thus creating the first assistance program for Tibetan refugees. Soon after, the vanguard consignments of tents, blankets, and tinned foodstuffs were sent off by the World Church Services and arrived in India for Tibetan refugees. Taktser Rinpoche then moved to Seattle, where he accepted a position in the Far Eastern Institute.[3] The CIA would soon be sending American agents to the institute to learn Tibetan.

During 1958, Gyalo Thondup continued to be in communication with Gompo Tashi and worked with the Americans from his Kalimpong and Darjeeling homes. Among other things, he focused on assembling new candidates for what would be, he was hopeful, an ongoing CIA training program.

---

[3]Thubten Jigme Norbu, *Tibet Is My Country*, 247.

In fact, he had been culling and cultivating potential leaders as early as 1956. One teenager, Tashi Chutter, recalls how he was brought into Gyalo Thondup's plan:

I was from a small village in Kongpo. I grew up on an estate owned by the Dalai Lama's family; only two days ride from the Indian border—very remote. Anything that happened beyond our village was, by and large, a mystery to me. In 1956, when I was nineteen, an attendant of Mr. Gyalo Thondup came to my village and selected three boys to return with him to Siliguri, Darjeeling, to learn English. I was one of the selected. That was when I first met Lhamo Tsering who was, at that time, learning how to use a wireless. Even then, Gyalo was working with the resistance, although none of us students knew it at the time—nor were we aware that helping the resistance was the purpose of our education. Gyalo was preparing for the future—especially if, one day, His Holiness fled Tibet. English translators would be essential for communicating with the outside world. And very few Tibetans, besides Gyalo, understood this.

To show you how ignorant I was, I'll tell you a true story. Soon after we arrived in Darjeeling, a very sophisticated, well-dressed Lhasan visited our school. When he came into our room, we assumed that this grand personage must be Mr. Gyalo Thondup, the elder brother of His Holiness. So we fell to the floor and made prostrations. One of the officials yelled, "What are you doing? Stop prostrating! Get up! This man is Gyalo Thondup's tailor!" He had come to measure us for new clothes. The next day, the real Gyalo Thondup arrived. He was very dignified, handsome, and gentle with us. For the next three years, we learned English, geography, and mathematics from Anglo-Indian tutors from the British St. Joseph's Academy, with no idea that we would eventually be trained by the CIA.[4]

Phala, Lord Chamberlain, was kept apprised of Gyalo Thondup's activities and young trainees, but apparently left the Dalai Lama out of the loop.

Even Cyclone was doing his part for the Tibetan nation, though the CIA—had they been aware of his existence—neither would have understood nor appreciated his efforts: Cyclone prayed for peace. Now, as a young lama at Riwoche Monastery, he saw the gradual ruthlessness of the PLA unfold in Kham but never gave up the belief that meditation, proper motivation, and

---

[4]Tashi Chutter, interview with the author.

the evoking of deities such as Palden Lhamo and Guru Rinpoche were the best channels through which to foil the communists. Nevertheless, the immediate danger to his family was closing in on his practice. Aba, his father, paid a surprise visit to him in 1958. The purpose of Aba's visit was to receive a prediction from the monastery's oracle. The oracle told him that if he and his family didn't leave Tibet "by the end of the Pig Year" (1959), they would lose their lives. Before returning home, Aba ordered Cyclone to be ready to leave Riwoche at a moment's notice. The family was going to make a run for it. He had heard that India was allowing refugees to cross the border—but who knew how long that would last?[5]

Of all the Tibetans so far discussed, Athar and Lhotse were perhaps the most optimistic and ebullient in the fall of 1958. In September, they returned to the area south of Samye, near a desolate lake that was designated as the first airdrop zone for CIA arms supplies. The plateau encompassing the lake was forlorn, windy, and, even by Tibetan standard, isolated. But Athar and Lhotse didn't feel deserted. The Americans had adopted them, were supporting their cause, and, most important, putting their money where their mouth was. The proof was in the sky above them: first came the rumble, then the plane itself, then the fantastical appearance of olive-green parachutes popping open all over the sky, swaying back and forth, delicately floating down toward the lake and finally hitting ground along the rocky shoreline.[6] Once the bundles were free of their canopies, Athar and Lhotse unwrapped twelve thousand pounds of glistening resistance tools: Lee Enfield .303 rifles, 60-mm mortars, 57-mm recoilless rifles, 2.36 bazookas, great caches of grenades, .30 caliber light machine guns[7]—a treasure trove from the United States, to be sure. But Palden Lhamo was also thanked.

For the next six months, Athar and Lhotse's job would be to distribute weapons, not use them—a little bit of a drawback, but they didn't really mind. They were supporting the resistance in a way that no other Tibetans could. The next airdrop, at the same lake, occurred in November. The reports

[5]Goser, Cyclone's younger brother, telephone conversation with the author. (Real name withheld by request.)
[6]The isolated lake was called Drigu Tso.
[7]Roger E. McCarthy, *Tears of the Lotus*, 242–43. In a follow-up letter to the author, McCarthy added, "The aircraft used were C-118s with American crews, after which we obtained C-130s for the overflights."

they sent back to the CIA stated that the *Chushi-Gangdruk* was playing havoc with the PLA in Lhoka. And although Athar and Lhotse wouldn't meet up with the main fighting arm of the *Chushi-Gangdruk* for several months, the news coming in from Gompo Tashi's myriad company commanders, who rendezvoused with Athar and Lhotse to pick up arms and ammunition, was filled with Tibetan victories on the Lhokan battlefields.[8]

In the Battle at the Nyimo River, for instance, Gompo Tashi and his men had turned a potential disaster into triumph. The PLA, numbering well into the thousands, surprised the *Chushi-Gangdruk*. Armed with cannons, automatic weapons, and grenades, they kept up a constant fusillade of gunfire and shelling. Realizing that to remain where they were would be fatal, but not having the option to retreat, Gompo Tashi decided to simply hack his way through the Chinese ranks:

As the buglers in our camp sounded the signal to attack, I led seventy horses on to the field. Galloping at full speed, we charged the enemy like wild animals, fighting them hand to hand. The Chinese were unable to resist the onslaught and withdrew to a nearby village. We pursued them and battled in and around the village until they retreated further and took shelter in the houses.

Most of them had taken refuge in two large houses that contained an office and some telegraph equipment. We shot down every door and window in these houses and eventually had to burn them, as this was the only way to destroy the Chinese who were hiding inside . . . I believe at least 700 Chinese were killed in this battle and many more were seriously wounded.[9]

Time and again, the psychological advantage of the *Chushi-Gangdruk* prevailed in spite of the numerical odds against them. At the Battle of Jhang Yangpa Ching, with nearly ten thousand PLA troops in the immediate area, Gompo Tashi simply terrified his way into victory. Not only were he and his men protected by Palden Lhamo, they played the priceless card of having nothing to lose:

We were left with no alternative but to advance and attack the Chinese, even if it meant fighting to the finish. We gathered our forces and promptly mounted a furious charge on horseback. The unexpected weight of the attack, accompa-

---

[8]Athar, interview with the author.

[9]Gompo Tashi Andrugtsang, *Four Rivers, Six Ranges*, 77–78.

nied by our unearthly battle cries, created utter [panic] *among the Chinese ranks. They fell rapidly back in disorder . . .*[10]

Meanwhile, other commanders of the *Chushi-Gangdruk* had taken their troops east of Lhoka. The Prince of Derge, for instance, had led his men into Kongpo, the district separating Lhoka from Kham proper. (The prince's family estate was long gone by 1958. It had been usurped by the PLA, rendering the royal family penniless, without homes, and with numerous family members imprisoned.) Now, at the age of twenty-one, the prince had been promoted to commander of the Derge division of the *Chushi-Gangdruk*. Following Gompo Tashi's orders, he engaged his troops in carefully choreographed hit-and-withdraw missions focusing on isolated contingents of PLA, as well as small convoys and storage facilities. Kongpo would be his field of operations for many months to come.[11]

Drawupon, the boy-turned-chief from Jyekundo, now a twenty-six-year-old commander, was also ordered to lead his troops east. Gompo Tashi's plan was for Drawupon to return to his home district to spearhead Jyekundo resistance. It was a long journey: a two-month ride from Lhoka. Unfortunately, like so many missions in 1958, Drawupon's was forced to change course after his rebels encountered the sheer number of PLA troops in Kham:

We were halfway back to Jyekundo, one month into the trip, when I learned from a large group of nomads that Jyekundo was overrun with a very large contingent of Chinese. With my small group, it was unrealistic to think that we could do much damage at the time and, probably, we would end up serving as target practice for the PLA. Fighting was going on everywhere, so I altered my plans. I concentrated on convincing small factions that I met along the way to join forces with my own and simply forget about home districts but rather take a stand wherever and whenever we met the enemy.[12]

Drawupon's burgeoning army moved north. By the time they got to the Goshun District, they numbered almost fifteen thousand Khampas. This number included the Khampas' families, which made mobilization all the more difficult. But that was the ancient way. Warriors traveled with their

[10]Ibid., 79–80.
[11]Donyo Jagotsang, interview with the author.
[12]Drawupon, interview with the author.

women and children. For a while their firefights with the PLA were success-ful but, by October 1958, the Chinese had sent in huge backup forces to destroy Drawupon. Even more alarming, reconnaissance planes could be heard flying overhead. Cloud cover protected the rebels for the time being. Drawupon ordered his troop to split into four different groups to make detection from the sky less easy. Even so, the slow-moving *Chushi-Gangdruk*, made even slower by livestock and family, were eventually located.

Drawupon remembers when the bombing began:

They not only dropped bombs on us, but they also dropped rocks the size of a man's fist from the open doors of the planes. It sounds strange, but, really, we feared the rocks more than the bombs. You couldn't hear the rocks falling. You would look around and suddenly there was someone on the ground with his head split open.

Wherever we traveled, the planes kept track of our movement.

One morning the planes found my particular group as we worked our way through a deep ravine. Two aircraft bombed our line, which was very spread out. Many of us—the stronger of us—were able to scramble up the sides of the sur-rounding cliffs, but many others were not. In the panic, everyone just ran for cover wherever they could find it. Many were injured or killed—especially the older members of our families. And there was nothing we could do to help them until the Chinese flew away.

We didn't have any anti-aircraft guns or anything like that. But some of us were lucky enough to get up on top of a hill. The planes made a big turn and headed back for a second strike. They were coming in very, very low. It almost looked like their wings were going to be snagged by the cliffs.

One of the planes came right by us on the tip of the hill. The plane was so close that we could see right into the pilot's window. Understand, we were eye-level with the pilot! Looking at that Chinaman's face, we just emptied our guns into his cockpit, and the next thing we knew, the engine sputtered—pha-pha-pha— and then it crashed a few hundred yards beyond us.

We ran down and surrounded the wreckage. The pilots were dead, but there were three survivors who tumbled out. We gunned them down when they tried to come out.[13]

---

[13]Ibid.

Inside the wreck, Drawupon and his men found machine guns—more powerful than they had seen before—bullets three-inches long. There was also a cache of bombs. The rebels tried unsuccessfully to remove the machine guns from their mounts. The sun was sinking fast, so they decided to come back to the wreckage the following morning and, in the meantime, join the others who were now tending to the dead and wounded. As the sky darkened, the fatigue of being on the run for many days caught up with them. Without bothering to post guards, the rebels bedded down and fell asleep. It was a fatal mistake.

During the night, PLA ground troops, in great numbers, returned to the area of the downed aircraft. By daybreak, they had the area surrounded without the rebels knowing. Drawupon's army awoke to the chatter of machine guns firing on them from all directions. No sooner had they mounted their horses—those that weren't riddled with bullets—than bombers swooped in from the east. Drawupon described it as a kind of living hell:

Hundreds and hundreds of Khampas—including many women and children—died in the first hour alone. I tell you that women and children were killed. But what does that mean to someone who wasn't there? Our women. Our children. Not your children. Maybe, if the world had seen what happened that day in Goshun Gorge—you know—like the television news these days on the BBC—if the world had seen what they did to us, I think we might have gotten help from the outside world. Only Americans were trying to help us. Where was India? Where was the United Nations?[14]

The only people who weren't gunned down that day were the ones quick enough to scramble up through the ravines. Everyone else was rounded up and shot. Drawupon, who managed to escape to high ground, gazed back on the carnage below. In addition to the hundreds of family members left where they had fallen, herds of horses and livestock lay slaughtered in the gorge. Several months later, Drawupon would learn that similar carnage had befallen the other groups caught by the PLA in Goshun. Of the original group of fifteen thousand, only about four thousand managed to reach the safety of Lhoka.

---

[14]Ibid.

It was a different Drawupon who, two months later, returned to Lhoka and entered Gompo Tashi's *magar:*

I guess I was happy to be back in Lhoka. I was alive. We had lost so many relatives and friends in the few months we were gone. I know I wasn't the same guy when I got back to Lhoka. I was only twenty-six, but I didn't feel young.[15]

OTHERS FLEEING KHAM AND AMDO HAD SIMILAR STORIES OF horror—journeys that began as organized ventures but dissembled into chaos. Aten, the opium-trader from Kanze, who, until now, had managed to evade the communists' wrath, was finally labeled (as were all the other leaders of Kanze) an "enemy of the people."

Under cover of darkness, Atan, his two wives, and daughter fled Kanze without any clear-cut idea of where they were going.

Soon after, he and his family joined a rebel band. At first, they were a small force of ten men with only four rifles between them. But as was the case all over Tibet, small groups sought out other groups and formed larger cells of resistance. His group quickly grew to forty families. Six weeks later, it had grown to three hundred families. Initially, they had attempted to join forces with a Golok cavalry, which—so they had heard—numbered ten thousand guerillas. Their constant firefights with PLA forces, however, forced Aten's group to drift south toward the Derge region. Within a day or two, they would reach one of the most famous monasteries in Kham: an enclave of a thousand monks, called Dzogchen.

Unknown to Aten, Dzogchen Monastery had recently been overrun and commandeered by three hundred PLA troops. The PLA officers had moved into the *labrang,* the private residence of the Head Abbot, Dzogchen Rinpoche, who was subsequently moved out and placed under house arrest on the top floor.

Overnight, the monastery was turned into a hell realm. By day, the common monks were given axes and forced to cut down the surrounding forest, and by night, they were subjected to *thamzings.* The sacred images of the

---

[15]Ibid.

temples were destroyed. The monks were forced to walk on the Holy Scriptures and perform other acts of sacrilege.

As if their torment wasn't bad enough, an officer told the monks that, the following day, Dzogchen Rinpoche would be subjected to *thamzing*. The monks could take no more: Slavery and humiliation they could handle, but not the mistreatment of their High Abbot. The monks had no guns, but they did possess swords, knives, and the axes that the Chinese themselves had given them to cut trees. Axes and swords would have to do: They were determined to save Dzogchen Rinpoche. They stormed the *labrang*. They murdered the guards outside with their blades, burst inside, and hacked their way up the stairs. It was dark in the building and there was a great deal of shouting and confusion. The Chinese soldiers panicked and started to shoot indiscriminately. It was pandemonium.

The monks managed to reach the top floor, stabbing, clubbing, and axing all Chinese who were foolish enough to try to stop them. At the height of the massacre, a flying axe seriously wounded Dzogchen Rinpoche. The monks picked him up and carried their abbot down the stairs and back outside. Then they locked the doors from the outside so that the remaining Chinese could not escape. They built a bonfire against the side of the *labrang* and burned the Chinese troops alive.

The monks armed themselves with the arms and ammunition of the dead Chinese. They carried Dzogchen Rinpoche up the mountain trail, fleeing before other PLA troops came by and discovered the carnage.

It was during their escape that Aten and his troops encountered the monks from Dzogchen Monastery. Aten helped them hide in a remote monastery some miles off. There, Aten helped the monks nurse their wounded until Dzogchen Rinpoche succumbed to his axe wound. The next day, Aten broke camp and led his army west, toward Lhasa. Those of the Dzogchen monks who were well enough to travel, took off their robes, scooped up their PLA rifles, and followed Aten west, where they would eventually join the ranks of the *Chushi-Gangdruk*.[16]

---

[16]Jamyang Norbu, *Horseman in the Snow*, 118–24.

. . .

BY THE WINTER OF 1958, THE REBELS' SUCCESS IN LHOKA HAD
reached its zenith. Gompo Tashi's men were now fighting within thirty miles of
Lhasa. Time and again, the psychological advantage of the rebels prevailed in
spite of the numerical odds against them. PLA troops fought because they were
told to. The *Chushi-Gangdruk,* on the other hand, had intensely personal scores
to settle with the enemy. When they drew their swords, they had an image of a
raped wife or a murdered father to urge them on. And unlike the Chinese soldiers, they possessed the ultimate trump card: They had nothing left to lose.

News of rebel victories to the south reached Lhasan ears in concentric
waves of contagion. More and more Tibetans in the capital were firing off
their rifles as if to echo the guns of their heroes in Lhoka. Sporadic gunfire
became a nightly occurrence. Some said the culprits were drunken Khampas.
Others said they were nervous PLA guards. Probably it was both. There were
now approximately fifteen thousand refugees in the environs of Lhasa. They
moved about the city fully armed and with trigger-happy eyes.

It was a recipe for disaster. The Chinese, who were mostly stationed in several camps outside of Lhasa proper, were increasingly nervous whenever they
were assigned patrol duty in town. So far, they had been ordered not to start
anything that might be interpreted by the crowds as aggression. But how long
could they keep it up? The mood in the streets was ominous in spite of the
PLA's uncocked rifles. It was true that there were the aristocratic collaborators who still felt the only way to protect their wealth and privilege was to
placate the communists, but they were the only Tibetan contingent in Lhasa
that the Chinese felt they could rely on. And even that was small consolation,
since the number of the wealthy continued to dwindle—many having decided to slip away from Lhasa for the safety of Kalimpong, and taking with
them as much of their assets as possible. To make matters worse—at least
from the Chinese point of view—it was evident that there was a growing faction of Dalai Lama loyalists (including, perhaps, members of the *Kashag*),
who, in spite of the Dalai Lama's plea for nonviolence, were pro–*Chushi-
Gangdruk.* No doubt these Lhasans were being influenced, in part, by reports
of Gompo Tashi's victories. But the sheer number of Tibetans now living in

Lhasa, including the thousands of Eastern Tibetans—freedom fighters one and all—created a brew of belligerence that had never before been witnessed in the congested streets and alleyways of the capital. The proliferation of fire-power and the close proximity of the various factions was enough to create a powder keg. Little wonder the Chinese were getting paranoid.

And no one sensed the danger more acutely—nor walked the political tightrope more carefully—than Phala, Lord Chamberlain:

> The Chinese were monitoring my every move. In spite of such risks, I never-theless did my best to ensure that our relationship with the Khampas did not deteriorate. They wanted to talk directly to His Holiness, but I deflected their efforts by telling them that that would only tip off the Chinese . . .
>
> I did not discuss these matters with the Kashag. There was no time and the utmost secrecy had to be maintained. It wasn't that I didn't have faith in the Kashag, but if I proposed these matters to them, the Kashag would weigh the pros and cons and it would take too much time to make decisions, especially since they had to face the daily brunt of the Chinese. At the same time, the Kashag had full faith in me, and that I would promote beneficial actions.[17]

Apparently, Phala was the Maestro of Concealment. It would seem that practically every conversation he had, from the end of 1958 onward, was uttered to someone sworn to secrecy. One can only wonder how he managed to keep all the truths and half-truths compartmentalized. Just before the beginning of 1959, for instance, Gompo Tashi somehow managed to evade the notice of the Chinese and secretly rendezvous with Phala.[18] Gompo Tashi proposed that the *Chushi-Gangdruk* should raid the arms depots in Lhasa, right under the eyes of the Chinese. Phala persuaded Gompo Tashi that that would only create a catastrophe for the *Kashag* and the Dalai Lama:

> Instead, I suggested to him that he raid the [Chinese] arms depot in Shang of U Tsang, which he did soon after.[19]

The raid was one of the *Chushi-Gangdruk's* finest military moments—if not the most daring: It was literally under the nose of the Chinese generals,

---

[17]Phala, "The Phala Papers."
[18]Neither Phala nor Gompo Tashi ever revealed where or how this meeting took place.
[19]Ibid.

Shang being a mere twenty-five miles from the main force of the PLA, that is to say, Lhasa. Michel Peissel describes the raid:

... *Two thousand Khampas guerrillas attacked the three thousand men of the garrison of Tsetang* [Shang], *the largest Chinese outpost on the south banks of the* [Tsangpo River].... *After six hours of heavy fighting, the Khampas broke into the garrison; the Chinese scattered, most to be mowed down, others to be caught by patrolling horsemen who ran them to the ground, or rushed them to a watery death in the turbulent* [Tsangpo River].[20]

The fury of the Chinese generals, once they heard of this major military embarrassment, can only be imagined. Not only had they lost a huge cache of weapons and ammunition but, more important, they lost face as well. The crowds in Lhasa were exhilarated and ever more bold in their defiance of the Chinese occupation.

IN THE MEANTIME, BY THE BEGINNING OF 1959, ATHAR AND LHOSE were working overtime, designating and securing airdrop zones, and then reporting back to the CIA the condition of resistance tools once they had been dropped. The CIA's overflight operation was now in full swing. In all, approximately forty loads were successfully airdropped into the Tibetan range. McCarthy explains: *This calculates into a minimum of 550,000 to nearly 800,000 pounds of material being parachuted to the Volunteers.... This is not an insignificant accomplishment, especially under the difficult operational circumstances attendant to the clandestine and highly sensitive undertaking involved.*[21] *We had even reached the point* [by early 1959] *where we were sending in three C-130s for any one drop.*[22]

The CIA was also getting fairly good updates concerning the growing tension in Lhasa. From time to time, either Athar or Lhotse—both of whom had their own radios and could travel separately—would ride up to the hills over-

---

[20]Michel Peissel, *Cavaliers of Kham*, 112–13.

[21]Roger E. McCarthy, *Tears of the Lotus*, 242–43. In a letter to the author, McCarthy added, "The aircraft used were C-118s with American crews, after which we obtained C-130s for the overflights."

[22]Roger E. McCarthy, telephone conversation with the author.

looking Lhasa for quick surveys. The CIA was primarily concerned about the well-being of the Dalai Lama. They knew that Phala had (or was working on) some sort of contingency plan in case it became necessary for the Dalai Lama to escape. How Phala could make such a plan work, given the forty thousand PLA troops in the Lhasa area, seemed like a very daunting task indeed. Still, the Agency felt it had little choice but to place its trust in the Lord Chamberlain's abilities and hope for the best. The CIA came to the conclusion that the Chinese abduction of the Dalai Lama was a real danger, that a showdown in Lhasa might be inevitable, but that—one way or another—out-and-out revolution was not necessarily imminent, given the information so far given to them.[23]

In January of 1959, Phala probably would have disagreed with the CIA's assessment. According to his later remembrance:

The Chinese were on high alert. They came to believe that the whole of Tibet backed the Chushi-Gangdruk *and, as a precautionary measure, they dug trenches all around their camps in Lhasa. They put electric wires on top of their fences. They mounted machine guns and artillery guns on top of the posts. The situation just got worse and worse. There were many cases of stabbing and murder in the streets. The local Tibetans began to stab Chinese nationals at the slightest provocation. The general feeling was that war would erupt at any moment.*[24]

Gompo Tashi, on the other hand, seemed to have been thinking more along the CIA lines. In any case, he didn't deem it necessary to stay near the capital in case of an open revolt. By early 1959, he had taken a large contingent of *Chushi-Gangdruk* to Kongpo. This was where the Prince of Derge—at least a week's hard ride from Lhasa—was conducting his hit-and-withdraw attacks. Gompo Tashi's idea was to bring in reinforcements for the prince in order to further confuse and demoralize the PLA troops in that area. One of the fiercest conflicts yet ensued in Kongpo. It was a fifteen-day battle, with the *Chushi-Gangdruk* the clear victors.

There was one close call, however, in Kongpo. In a fierce conflict in Dhamshung, Gompo Tashi incurred multiple gunshot wounds. Miraculously,

---

[23]Ibid.
[24]Phala, "The Phala Papers."

he survived and was in no immediate danger. He held back for a few weeks while his wounds healed, but soon he sat his horse and led attacks. It would be several years in the future before his war wounds took their toll. For the present, Palden Lhamo, it seemed, was watching out for her own.

This, then, was the general picture of the resistance effort in the first two months of 1959: Several key players were outside of Tibet in touch with the CIA; Athar and Lhotse, inside Tibet, also were in touch with the Agency, but were primarily oiling the machinery of ongoing airdrops; innumerable resistance groups were fighting for their lives in Kham, Amdo, and Golok—some had assistance or leadership from the *Chushi-Gangdruk*, but others were on their own, simply trying to stay one step ahead of the PLA; Gompo Tashi and his men were in Kongpo, as were several of his commanders, while the majority of the *Chushi-Gangdruk* remained in Lhoka, where fighting was at its peak. And then there was Lhasa.

SITUATED WITHIN THE HEART OF LHASA, HEMMED IN BY THE densely clumped housing of the Barkhor (a strictly Tibetan residential area of narrow lanes), sat the holiest building in Tibet—the Jokhang. The Jokhang didn't look like a cathedral, although, essentially, that's what it was. It was a big, thickset, stone box. Neither its gargantuan doors at the front gate, nor the interior piazza—congested with the sour-smelling intermingling of beggars, monks, and pilgrims working their way into its interior—boded well for a spiritual experience. And yet, if you looked up, there was some visual promise. The metallic roof was resolutely exuberant. Its swags curved in all directions like the sails of a gilded armada. Once inside, and once your eyes adapted to the cavernous darkness of the main chapel, you began to understand the Jokhang's importance. Dominating the central altar was Tibet's most important golden statue, *Jowo Rinpoche,* "The Lord Buddha," encrusted with pearls and precious jewels. *Jowo Rinpoche* was imported from China and brought to Tibet in the seventh century. *Jowo Rinpoche's* gaze was inscrutable—one of inner focus and, perhaps, primordial patience. Whatever he was thinking, his meditative presence was so commanding that you couldn't help feeling that you were in the vortex of the Tibetan world—on all levels, dead center.

In early 1959, the Dalai Lama was temporarily staying at the Jokhang. In spite of—or perhaps because of—the political turmoil outside its walls, the Dalai Lama was preparing for his final tests for the *Geshe Lharampa* degree, the highest theological degree offered in Tibet. It was a degree he had been working toward since he was thirteen. That he was able to concentrate at all—given the friction and apprehension pervading Lhasa— was something of a miracle. But beyond that, the abbots agreed that the results of his preliminary tests were brilliant.

The communists regarded the Dalai Lama as, primarily, a political figure, and obviously paid scant attention to the Dalai Lama's religious pursuits except when matters of theology interrupted their own designs. For some time now they had been trying to extract a promise from the Dalai Lama to go to Beijing to attend the National People's Congress. The invitation seemed poorly (even oafishly) timed. When the Dalai Lama had gone to Beijing five years before, in 1954, Lhasa's reaction had been one of panic, then desolation. Of course there was always the possibility that provocation was China's goal.

Yet the Dalai Lama was resolved to complete his exams. He refused to set dates for any trips to China, or elsewhere, for the foreseeable future.

Nevertheless, at the beginning of February 1959, Radio Peking announced that the Dalai Lama had made plans to visit the Chinese capital. The "news" turned Lhasa on its head. No one was more shocked than the Dalai Lama.

Rumors began to circulate in the streets that the communists were trying to abduct the Holy One. There were ample reasons for suspicions being aroused. Recently, on four separate occasions, famous *Rinpoches* from Eastern Tibetan monasteries had been kidnapped by the PLA after having accepted invitations to Chinese social events. Three of the four *Rinpoches* were subsequently murdered, while the other disappeared in the Chinese prison system.[25] Lhasans were well aware of these treacheries, and the dark mood poisoning their city grew darker.

At the beginning of March, the Dalai Lama was preparing for his final and most important *Geshe Lharampa* examination.

In the middle of the preparations, the communists barged into the Jokhang and demanded to see the Dalai Lama:

---

[25]His Holiness the Dalai Lama, *My Land, My People,* 169.

I was told that two Chinese officers wanted to see me. They were shown in—two junior officers who said they had been sent by General Tan Kuan-sen. They wanted me to tell the general a date on which I could attend a theatrical show he had decided to stage in the Chinese army camp . . .

This visit was curious. Normally, unless the general called on me himself, messages from him were sent through whichever of my officials were most concerned . . .

So the unusual procedure of sending junior officers to see me personally, and of sending them to the temple, immediately aroused suspicion among all my people who came to know of it . . .

Nothing more was heard of this strange invitation before I left the temple for the Norbulingka on the fifth of March. My procession to the Norbulingka had always been a great occasion, and in previous years the Chinese had taken part in it, but this year everybody noticed that no Chinese attended.[26]

GENERAL TAN, THE COMMANDER WHO HAD SENT JUNIOR OFFI-cials to interrupt the Dalai Lama's examination, had, for some time been third in command of the PLA in Lhasa. Just recently, however, he had been promoted to Commander in Chief. Given the unrest in Lhasa, this was a bizarre development. As Shakya points out: "At this critical juncture the Chinese seemed to have misjudged the situation. In March the Party's Central Committee recalled to Beijing the two highest-ranking officials in Tibet. . . . They may have been recalled to discuss the deteriorating situation, but the absence of two leaders from Lhasa at such a time shows that the Chinese were unprepared for a major crisis. After nearly a decade in Tibet the Chinese leadership should have known that during *Monlam*[27] anti-Chinese activities would be at their peak."[28]

---

[26]His Holiness the Dalai Lama, *My Land and My People*, 134–35.

[27]*Monlam* translates as "the Great Prayer Festival," an occasion during which the life of the historical Buddha is celebrated. It falls on the heels of the Tibetan New Year and draws huge crowds. Even in the most peaceful times, *Monlam* had the reputation of taxing the civil authorities' ability to control the crowds.

[28]Tsering Shakya, *The Dragon in the Land of Snows*, 185–86.

In any case, General Tan seems to have had a disagreeable (if not offensive) persona. Noel Barber describes him as having "a pair of stooped shoulders, yellow teeth, extremely thin hands, and a habit of reeking with perfume. He was utterly ruthless and the picture we have of Tan is that of the dedicated party member who is also the complete boss—storming, ranting, raving, a hard, tough, professional soldier, his authority buttressed by his spies everywhere."[29] These traits would not have concerned the Beijing hierarchy, but General Tan displayed one character flaw that even Mao might have objected to: He was an alcoholic. When he was intoxicated, which seems to have been fairly often, he was said to issue orders no sober man would have condoned.[30] Whether or not dependency controlled the general's judgment, one thing was clear: General Tan was obsessed with the idea of getting the Dalai Lama to his theatrical dance performance at PLA Headquarters. He hounded the Dalai Lama. Finally, on March 7, the Dalai Lama relented and, against the advice of his inner circle, fixed the date to visit Yutok (PLA Headquarters, located along the south-central edge of the Lhasan city limits) for March 10.

The day before the dance program, on the morning of March 9, Kusung Depon, the commander of the Dalai Lama's personal bodyguards (and the husband of the Dalai Lama's sister) was summoned to Yutok. He was told that the Dalai Lama's customary armed escort of twenty-five would *not* be allowed to enter Yutok the following morning. The Dalai Lama was expected, essentially, to attend the program without retinue or protection. Kusung Depon found this unprecedented mandate not only odd but also seriously alarming. He became even more alarmed when he heard General Tan's final stipulation: The citizens of Lhasa were not to know of the Dalai Lama's visit to Yutok. Except for the *Kashag*, everyone else must be kept in the dark. All the recent rumors about the Chinese wanting to kidnap the Dalai Lama, in Kusung Depon's mind, seemed to be coming true. And he, the Dalai Lama's brother-in-law, was being asked to collaborate in the plot—just as Taktser Rinpoche had been invited to kill his brother years before. Kusung Depon calmed himself and asked why the Chinese wanted to break protocol and why they were demanding secrecy. The answer chilled him to the bone:

---

[29]Noel Barber, *From the Land of Lost Content*, 43–44.
[30]Ibid.

Will you be responsible if someone pulls the trigger?[31] That single question became the flashpoint for a political wildfire unprecedented in Tibetan history.

By sunset, there wasn't a Tibetan in Lhasa who wasn't repeating the question—*Will you be responsible if someone pulls the trigger?*—nor was there anyone who doubted what the question implied. Quite literally, the Dalai Lama was expected to walk into the enemy camp unprotected—and secretly, at that. As Lhasa went to bed that night, there was only one thing on their minds: How can we prevent the Chinese from harming (perhaps even killing) our Precious One?

MARCH 10, 1959.

By dawn, the people were already spilling into the streets. They were armed and indifferent to personal safety. By nine o'clock A.M., thirty thousand Lhasans and Eastern Tibetan refugees had moved south from the city and gathered before the sentry boxes flanking Norbulingka's front gate, as well as to the sides of the Jewel Park's lengthy perimeter walls. No one had organized them. No one had said, "Let's go to the Summer Palace and become the largest human shield in the history of mankind on behalf of the Dalai Lama." Nevertheless, that is what they had achieved in their spontaneous desire to protect their leader. Nothing would stop them, not even the Dalai Lama himself. If they had to imprison the Precious One in order to protect him, so be it. No one was getting in or out of the Summer Palace without the mob's permission.

It took a while for the true import of the protesters' action to sink in. But gradually it dawned on them that, by coming to the aid of the Dalai Lama in this fashion, they were demonstrating a far more radical departure from the norm. Half of the Tibetans in the crowd were from Kham, Amdo, and Golok: For the first time, Lhasans and Eastern Tibetans were acting as one. As they rubbed shoulders with one another, a realization crept over the crowd: They—not the *Kashag,* not the *Tsongdu,* not the abbots of the monasteries, not the aristocracy—represented the will of the country. In effect, by protecting the Dalai Lama from kidnapping, they had also kidnapped the Tibetan

---

[31]Michel Peissel, *Cavaliers of Kham,* 119.

government and the hierarchy in one glorious swoop. The idea became tactile—a formication that prickled the collective skin of the crowd: The people were now the ruling body of Tibet.

A high-ranking Tibetan official by the name of Sampho, who wanted to get inside the Summer Palace, was the first person that morning to experience the intoxication of this new political force. Sampho was foolish enough to arrive at Norbulingka in a Chinese jeep. That was his first mistake. His second mistake was in thinking that he could use his governmental status to bully his way through the mob. According to Phala, the mob turned on him:

Thinking that Sampho was a Chinese leader, the mob attacked the vehicle with stones. When Sampho jumped from the jeep, he was struck on the head with a rock. He fell to the ground unconscious. Fortunately, some Tibetan officials recognized him and he was whisked off to the nearby dispensary of the Norbulingka . . .[32]

Phakpala, the next Tibetan official who tried to make his way through the crowd, was not so lucky—nor so innocent. Next to Ngabo, Phakpala was the most notorious Chinese collaborator in Lhasa. In his mid-twenties, Phakpala was a highly distinguished lama from Sera Monastery, openly pro-communist and known to have cooperated with the Chinese generals for at least two years. It was no secret that he favored Chinese apparel and it was even said that he was allowed to keep a trunk of Chinese gowns at Yutok, which he dipped into whenever he attended Chinese parties.[33]

That morning, Phakpala left Chinese Army Headquarters on a bicycle, with the important task of persuading the Dalai Lama to attend the show—just in case the *Kashag* tried to back out at the last moment.[34] Was Phakpala so far removed from the mood of the populace, that he thought his mission had the slightest chance of success? Or was he simply convinced that no one would dare harm him because of his connections to the PLA generals? One way or another, his appearance could not have been more provocative: He

[32]Phala, "The Phala Papers."
[33]Noel Barber, *From the Land of Lost Content,* 75–76.
[34]A more popular version has it that Phakpala was on his way to assassinate the Dalai Lama, but this has never been verified.

wore a Chinese quilted jacket, sunglasses, a Chinese "dust mask" that veiled his mouth and throat, and—to finish off his outfit—a pistol thrust into his belt. He got as far as the main gate. The surrounding crush of people, not knowing if he was Tibetan or Chinese, yanked down his "dust mask." Apparently, someone recognized him and yelled out to the crowd, "It's Phakpala, the traitor!"

Phakpala panicked and grabbed for his gun. The crowd ripped him off his bicycle and threw him to the ground. A Khampa drew his sword and impaled him. The crowd finished him off with large stones, a process which—according to firsthand accounts—was grisly and took an inordinate amount of time.

The *ragyaba* (a stratum of Tibetans very low on the social register, whose traditional job was to dispose of corpses) were summoned. When they arrived, they refused to touch the corpse of a collaborator. Instead, they tied *chuba* belts around Phakpala's feet and dragged the corpse away from the gates, then down the tree-lined lane that headed back into town. A procession of vengeful Tibetans trailed behind—laughing, dancing, and in myriad ways further desecrating the hated villain's body. When the mob reached the center of Lhasa, the mutilated body was thrown across the back of a pony and paraded around, to the delight of a jeering crowd.[35]

Upon hearing of this, the *Kashag*—horrified and yet essentially quarantined inside Norbulingka—sent a senior member of the *Kashag*, by the name of Surkhang, to the top of the Summer Palace wall. Surkhang yelled down at the crowd. He implored them to calm themselves in the name of Buddha. The crowd grew silent. He promised that the Dalai Lama had no intention of going to the Yutok theatrical that day. He added that, in the place of the Dalai Lama, he and other senior members of the government would go to Yutok to explain the situation to the Chinese generals.

The crowd was only partially appeased. According to Phala's recollection, *the people said, "If this is true, let the vehicle that is to transport* Kashag *members come out of the gate empty. (Apparently, they feared that there might be an attempt to smuggle the Dalai Lama out of the Summer Palace.) So when we*

---

[35]Ibid., 84.

[Phala and the *Kashag*] *came out the main gate, we were confronted by some women who had long daggers at their waists. Backing them up were fierce-looking Tibetan youths. They warned us to speak to the Chinese without fear and not to be lured by dayangs* [Tibetan currency].[36] This must have been a profoundly humiliating moment for Phala and the *Kashag*. Not only were the armed women giving them orders—as if the ministers were nothing more than common couriers—but they also made it quite clear that they suspected the ministers of being bribable and seditious.

Shaken, the *Kashag* and Phala clambered aboard the jeep and were whisked off to Yutok. Worse was to come.

Yutok was a huge encampment with high fences, barbed wire, newly built watchtowers, and armed sentries. Once they were cleared to drive through the main gate, the Tibetans realized that, if General Tan's theatrical performance was a guise for a sinister plot, it nevertheless had been elaborately planned. Chinese children in pretty costumes were standing in line awaiting the guests. The children had flowers in their hands and were openly disappointed when they realized the Dalai Lama was not among the Tibetan officials. Preparing themselves for the worst, Phala and the *Kashag* were ushered into a nearby army guesthouse.[37]

According to Noel Barber, "Ten Chinese officers—but not General Tan—were sitting on one side of the long table, talking and drinking tea. And there was an eleventh man sitting on the Chinese side of the table—none other than the saturnine Ngabo. This was astonishing, for invariably at these conferences the opponents were arranged on opposite sides of the green table, but now Ngabo made no attempt to join the Tibetans . . . Though it had been Ngabo's task to act as a go-between at the Chinese headquarters, this was the final insult. Presumably Ngabo thought the time for keeping up pretence had passed."[38] For nearly ten minutes the Tibetan cabinet ministers were left standing. Not once did the Chinese look up to acknowledge the ministers' presence. Finally, just as the conference seemed to be breaking up, General Tan strode into the room. If the Tibetans had any hopes their dis-

---

[36]Phala, "The Phala Papers," 25.
[37]Noel Barber, *From the Land of Lost Content,* 87–88.
[38]Ibid.

cussion might be amicable, those hopes were dashed by the look on General Tan's face. He glared at the Tibetans, as if daring them to provide an adequate explanation for the insulting absence of the Dalai Lama. The beleaguered *Kashag* began with an apology. They told General Tan that the Dalai Lama had sincerely wanted to attend the dance performance, but the mob outside Norbulingka simply would not permit his exit.

General Tan said nothing but indicated with a nod that he agreed that the Dalai Lama was not to blame. Then he flew into a rage, blaming the *Kashag* and Phala for this unpardonable snub. The harangue was excruciatingly long. As the general became more worked up, he accused them of secretly supporting the *Chushi-Gangdruk,* of defying his orders to disarm the Khampas, of encouraging the refugees from Eastern Tibet to disrupt the tranquility of Lhasa—the list of insubordinate acts went on and on. Now, the general threatened, the ministers would pay. As unbearable as the general was, Phala dreaded even more the moment the diatribe was over. He felt certain that, at that point, he and the *Kashag* would, at the very least, be thrown into the army brig:[39]

Then the general turned to me. I, in particular, was to blame. Since I was in charge of security, it was my responsibility for the stoning to death of the Tibetan collaborator [Phakpala] *earlier in the day. General Tan would give me three days to find and hand over the murderers. I responded by saying that, since it had been the spontaneous action of a mob—not just one or two individuals—it would be impossible for me to pinpoint anyone in particular. And before I could say anything else against the Chinese, Surkhang stopped me.*

The Chinese got up, one by one, and rained filthy words upon us.[40]

The meeting dragged on for two more hours, during which Ngabo had not opened his mouth once.[41]

And then, just as quickly as the general's bombastic display had begun, it ended. After a moment of silence, in an off-hand manner, General Tan said they could return to Norbulingka. They were being dismissed as if they were

---

[39]Phala, "The Phala Papers," 26.
[40]Ibid.
[41]Noel Barber, *From the Land of Lost Content,* 90.

unworthy even of the cell required to imprison them. Phala was dumb-struck.[42]

The ministers were driven back to the Summer Palace. The mob—the people who had effectively usurped them of their power—silently parted and made room for the returning vehicle. In their absence, the people in the street had elected seventy members from their ranks to form a "Free-dom Committee," which would, from now on, be in charge. With the com-mittee's permission, the gates of Norbulingka were opened, the ministers were waved through, and the gates shut behind them.

Within the palace grounds, there was a well-appointed guesthouse allot-ted to senior officials, to which Phala and the *Kashag* now retreated. Over-looking a poplar grove, the building was sunny, roomy, and full of Tibetan finery. But Phala was hardly consoled. In spite of the luxury of his environs, it was still little more than a jail. Phala remembers: *For the next seven days, none of us returned to our homes. There was no sleep for us. We ate our food without tasting it. It was as if everybody was paralyzed.*[43]

BY THE AFTERNOON OF MARCH 10, THE "FREEDOM COMMITTEE" and the crowd who supported it were enveloped in a kind of euphoria. They marched to the foot of the Potala Palace. There the committee members repudiated the 17-Point Agreement before another huge crowd. They burned copies of the agreement. They cited Ngabo as the head traitor of the Tibetan nation. And then they declared war on China. The crowd roared with approval. Then the committee marched to the courtyard of the Jokhang, where their defiant speeches were repeated with equally popular results.

Significantly, the small contingents of PLA within the city limits of Lhasa made themselves scarce that day. This only added to the crowd's euphoria. "Even the Chinese are hiding!" they yelled. In one day's time, by preventing the Chinese from capturing the Dalai Lama, they had not only created a new ruling order, but thrown off the yoke of the communists as well. And now that they had found their voice, they were not about to be silenced.

---

[42]Phala, "The Phala Papers," 27.
[43]Ibid.

All day long, the Dalai Lama had been receiving updates of the unfolding rebellion. As evening approached, he decided to send an official, protected by the Dalai Lama's personal bodyguards, outside the palace walls to try to reason with the "Freedom Committee": *I sent a message saying that it was the duty of the leaders to reduce the existing tension and not to aggravate it. But my advice seemed to fall on ears that could not hear.*[44]

With thousands of Tibetans looking on, the "Freedom Committee" pointed out to the Dalai Lama's personal bodyguards that the crowd had merely accomplished what they, the bodyguards, had failed to do: to protect His Holiness the Dalai Lama from the enemy Chinese. The logic of the argument completely humbled and won over the Dalai Lama's bodyguards. They swore that, from that moment on, they would obey neither the Chinese nor the *Kashag.* As a symbol of their allegiance to the "Freedom Committee," the bodyguards discarded the Chinese uniforms they had had been ordered to wear and joined the rebels in Tibetan clothes. The crowd went wild. It was mutiny, at last.[45]

MARCH 11, 1959.

While General Tan awaited orders from Beijing, the "Freedom Committee" continued to flex its muscles.

The first thing they did was to post guards *within* Norbulingka's outer wall. More specifically, they surrounded the *Kashag's* building to prevent the ministers from leaving the palace grounds without permission. If he had any doubts before, the Dalai Lama now understood the extent to which his subjects distrusted the *Kashag:*

They [the crowd] *feared that if they did not take the law into their own hands the Government might be forced into a compromise by the Chinese authorities.*[46]

Next, the "Freedom Committee" approached the Tibetan Army—or rather the remnants of the Tibetan Army—which promptly opened the doors of its

---

[44]His Holiness the Dalai Lama, *Freedom in Exile,* 134.
[45]Michel Peissel, *Cavaliers of Kham,* 124
[46]His Holiness the Dalai Lama, *Freedom in Exile,* 134.

arsenals and distributed arms to the jubilant crowd. The army, too, had now joined forces with the rebels.

Next, the committee turned its attention to setting up barricades and armed defenses throughout the areas of the city that were in their control. A contingent of Khampas and Lhasans marched up to the top of Chakpori (Iron Hill), a steep ridge where the ancient Medical College looked down over the Vale of Lhasa. Alongside several rusty cannons (which had been set up there in a previous era), they set up mortars and light artillery.

Another contingent headed north and blocked the main road to the Chinese airport where, in reaction, the PLA moved in tanks and armored cars.

From all accounts, the Eastern Tibetans instigated the defense buildup within the city limits, which is not surprising given their prior experience of fighting the PLA in their own regions. But lest it be assumed that the Lhasan citizenry was merely following the Khampas' orders, or in any way acting under duress, it was the Lhasans who showed the Khampas where best to

Chakpori (Iron Hill), home of Lhasa's ancient Medical College, prior to its destruction. (*Brooke Dolan, Collection of the Academy of Natural Sciences of Philadelphia*)

concentrate their manpower and weapons. The Lhasan citizenry were with the Khampa guerillas every step of the way. Less well-armed than the Eastern Tibetans, they nevertheless proudly carried axes, picks, shovels and anything else that might be construed as a weapon. They, like their Eastern Tibetan counterparts, were ready for a showdown.[47] In addition, the townspeople added their own brand of resistance by persuading fellow Lhasans, who were servants, to walk out on their Chinese masters. Chinese businesses, the Chinese schools and the Chinese hospital were also boycotted. And down the innumerable streets and alleys, posters appeared denouncing the occupying forces.[48] Phala remembers some of the slurs pasted on Lhasa's walls: *"Chinese return to China!" "Tibet belongs to Tibet!" "We will wipe out the Chinese!"* The *posters also found their way to the Indian Consular Office.*[49]

All along, the Indian Consulate in Lhasa had been radioing Delhi about the increasing violence and upheaval in the Tibetan capital. The question arises: Why didn't the consul's reports find their way to foreign reporters stationed in India? Nehru not only suppressed the reports, he also privately warned the consul to "Stick to your business and do not get entangled."[50] At the same time, George Patterson, the British journalist stationed in Delhi, began to receive similar information from his contacts in Kalimpong, which he quickly and regularly relayed to his newspaper, the *Daily Telegraph.* Nehru was outraged by the resultant series of published articles. He publicly denied the authenticity of the articles and dismissed Patterson as an "absurdist" who "accepted every bazaar rumor for fact."[51] Once again, international awareness of Tibet's plight was thwarted—at least in part—by Nehru's servile relationship with Beijing. Nevertheless, the foreign press was intrigued, and worldwide speculation began to grow.

In the meantime, on March 11, General Tan sent the powerless *Kashag* an ultimatum: If these acts of Tibetan aggression—particularly the barricades that were springing up all over town—were not immediately removed, the Chinese would not be responsible for the ensuing violence.

---

[47]Ibid., 128.

[48]Lowell Thomas Jr., *The Silent War in Tibet,* 274.

[49]Phala, "The Phala Papers," 28.

[50]This was a later admission on Nehru's part, given in a speech in the Lok Sabha on May 4, 1959.

[51]George N. Patterson, *Requiem for Tibet,* 173.

The *Kashag* brought the leaders of the "Freedom Committee" inside the Norbulingka compound. They showed the rebels the ultimatum and begged them to remove the barricades so, as the Dalai Lama would later write, *that the Chinese could not find an excuse in them for more repression. But that advice had exactly the wrong effect. The leaders absolutely refused to demolish the barricades. They said they had put them there to protect the Norbulingka by keeping Chinese reinforcements out of the city, and if the Chinese wanted them removed, the obvious conclusion was they did mean to attack the Palace and capture the Dalai Lama. They also said that the Chinese themselves had put up barricades . . . and taken similar precautions to protect their Tibetan supporters, such as Ngabo. If the Chinese could use barricades to protect Ngabo, they asked, why should they object to the people of Lhasa protecting the Palace?*

This development distressed me very much. I felt it was one step more toward disaster. So I decided to speak to the people's leaders myself. I sent for them, and all seventy of them came, and in the presence of the Cabinet and other senior officials I did my best to dissuade them from their actions.[52]

The rebels were loath to disobey His Holiness, but, in the end, their instinct to protect him contravened their qualms about defiance. The "Freedom Committee" made one concession to His Holiness. They agreed to regroup at Shol, the village at the foot of the Potala Palace four miles away, as a means of dispersing the crowd surrounding Norbulingka. Despite this, tens of thousands maintained their vigil around the Dalai Lama's Summer Palace.

Like the *Kashag*, the Dalai Lama now felt powerless to do anything. Sometimes he could hear in the distance, as he strolled through his park of exotic animals and ornamental pools, the chanting of political slogans—the crowd's excitement as well as their anger wafting over the high walls of Norbulingka. At these moments, the Dalai Lama could envision nothing but tragedy in the wake of the people's passion:

Most of them had armed themselves with sticks, spades, or knives, or whatever other weapons they could muster. Among them were some soldiers and Khampas with rifles, a few machine guns, and even fourteen or fifteen mortars. Hand to hand, with fists or swords, one Tibetan would have been worth a dozen Chinese—recent experiences in the eastern provinces had confirmed this old

---

[52]His Holiness the Dalai Lama, *My Land and My People*, 151.

belief. But it was obvious that their strength was useless against the heavy equipment which the Chinese could bring to wipe them out. Practically, they had nothing to fight with except their own determination to protect me.

But within the inner walk, in the immediate precincts of the Palace, everything had the appearance of calm and peace. There were no signs of anything untoward. The garden was quiet as usual. The peacocks strutted about with their plumes held high, unconcerned about the human turmoil . . .[53]

And so, on the evening of March 11, while peacocks retreated to their roosts in the Jewel Park, the fabled city of a million votive candles transformed itself into a theater of war. The high windows of the Potala bristled with glinting rifle barrels. Iron Hill, the Medical College, became a turret tower camouflaged in prayer flags. The Jokhang became a stockade, while its most sacred occupant, *Jowo Rinpoche*, stared from under immutable eyelids of gold.

PLA troops peered from the shadows of their fixed positions: barracks to the south of town, Chinese buildings scattered within central Lhasa, and barricades along all roads that they controlled. Silently, their defenses had been fortified during the day. But with the coming of darkness, and with Tibetan laughter echoing down the streets, sandbags and barbed wire did little to calm the nerves of the foreign troops.

Fifty miles to the south, the *Chushi-Gangdruk* was busy with its own confrontations; likewise in Kongpo, Kham, Golok, and Amdo. All over Tibet, men stretched out around isolated *magar* campfires, unaware that the Dalai Lama was in a jail within a jail and that the Holy City was about to explode. Thousands of miles away, the CIA was only slightly better informed. Although Lhasa was reckoned to be in a high state of instability, no one in Washington could have predicted that, within days, there would be all-out war. Even Athar and Lhotse, who had their fingers on the pulse of Tibet as well as anyone, were not in Lhasa and therefore were unable to report the rapid unraveling of Lhasan law and order. As for the international press, they clung futilely to an Indian grapevine rotten at the roots.

Palden Lhamo had her work cut out for her.

---

[53]Ibid., 153.

March 12, 1959: Mass protests of the Chinese occupation, five days before the Dalai Lama escaped. *(Office of Information and International Relations, Dharamsala)*

ON MARCH 12, IT WAS THE WOMEN'S TURN TO PROTEST. THOU- sands of grandmothers, mothers, and daughters took to the streets and amassed at the foot of the Potala. They marched east, to the streets around the Barkhor and the Jokhang. They chanted, "Independence now!" and goaded the PLA troops who were now stationed along the way. "Go ahead and shoot us!" they taunted. "Independence now!"[54]

At the Summer Palace, more barricades were constructed while, inside the walls, members of the rebel army cleaned their guns and listened to reports coming in about Chinese movement. All morning, more and more PLA troops and equipment had appeared throughout the city and, apparently, many of them were on "sightseeing" missions. Just a mile from Norbulingka, for instance, two Chinese tanks trundled to a stop. The Tibetan crowd still surrounding the Summer Palace reported that soldiers emerged from the

---

[54]John F. Avedon, *In Exile from the Land of Snows*, 53.

tops of both tanks and began taking instrument readings—presumably for range bearing. Other Tibetans reported that they had seen several Chinese who shinnied up telegraph poles that appeared to be in good working order. They were obviously making artillery readings.[55] Hundreds of trucks were observed moving ominously toward the Potala, only to veer to the left and head down toward the Chinese camp southwest of the Summer Palace.

The sudden visibility of these various PLA maneuvers and the intent behind them became a matter of heated debate within and without the walls of Norbulingka over the next three days. The Chinese were obviously too smart to simply give away their attack plans. Still, while the rebels fortified their own positions, they argued over which PLA displays were feints, and which were the real thing. One thing every Tibetan could agree on was that they must, at all costs, protect their most important and irreplaceable asset: His Holiness the Dalai Lama.

The Chinese, too, believed in the value of the "prize."

But no one was more aware of this "prize" aspect than the Dalai Lama himself. Ironically, he was also the only person in Tibet who regarded his personal well-being as irrelevant. He was convinced that, if something didn't give soon, with or without the "prize," the Chinese would simply unleash their artillery and annihilate Lhasa:

I would indeed have been willing to go there [Yutok] *and throw myself on the mercy of the Chinese if that would have prevented the massacre of my people; but the people would never have let me do it.*[56] As for escaping Lhasa—which many advisors and family members were urging him to do—as late as March 15, the Dalai Lama dismissed the notion as repugnant and as a cowardly betrayal of his people.

Phala didn't agree. He saw the Dalai Lama's escape as the only way to continue the fight for Tibetan independence. For months he had reminded the Dalai Lama of his thoughts on this subject, to no avail. By March 15, with the buildup of Chinese *and* Tibetan forces, he worried that the chance of a successful escape had been blocked from three directions: The Chinese military, the Tibetan mob, and now the Dalai Lama who didn't want to talk about it.

---

[55]Noel Barber, *From the Land of Lost Content,* 100.
[56]His Holiness the Dalai Lama, *My Land and My People,* 155.

But what if Lhasa erupted into an all-out war? At that point, Phala felt certain that the Dalai Lama would realize he had no choice but to attempt an escape. With this eventuality in mind, Phala privately set about updating and finalizing contingency escape plans, without the Dalai Lama's knowledge:

The Dalai Lama's life was clearly in danger. Privately, I told the Kashag that we must prepare for his escape, and all agreed that the utmost secrecy was necessary. I took responsibility for the date, the manner, and the route to be taken. The less anyone knew, the better. After consulting with the State Oracle, the date was fixed on March 17. It had to be kept top secret, so even the Tsongdu was not let in on the escape plan. I arranged for horses to be quietly transferred to the other side of the Tsangpo River. Since the southern gate of the Norbulingka was void of Chinese, I decided that that would become the beginning of our escape route.[57]

He took other precautions as well. The Dalai Lama's mother and youngest brother, Ngari Rinpoche, were brought to the Summer Palace where they would remain until the night of March 17. Phala also instructed his personal tailor to create a set of ordinary soldier's clothes to fit His Holiness[58]—a crafty choice in which to disguise the nonmilitant Dalai Lama.

In the meantime, Athar and Lhotse were close enough to the Lhasa area to be able to advise the CIA that things were looking very grim indeed. The CIA felt that their only option was to wait and watch.[59]

MARCH 15, 1959.

For a moment that morning, it looked as if open war was minutes away. One hundred fifty feet from the southern wall of Norbulingka—the direction from which Phala intended to effect an escape two nights later—a platoon of Chinese soldiers arrived in what appeared to be an offensive action. In response, hundreds of Tibetan troops ran to defensive positions and took aim. *They were so close we could see their faces,* recollected Ngari Rinpoche, the Dalai Lama's youngest brother, who, against his mother's orders, had

---

[57]Phala, "The Phala Papers," 27–28.
[58]Ibid.
[59]Athar's and Lhotse's exact locations are unknown. But on the basis of a phone conversation with Roger McCarthy, the author is making the assumption that one or both of the Tibetans were close enough to Lhasa to receive accurate information and to wire Washington with valid updates.

been helping man the defense. The Tibetan troops cocked their rifles and held their breath, convinced that a firefight was about to commence. But then, obeying their sergeant's orders, the PLA troops fell in line and marched on. It was not until the PLA had disappeared from view that it dawned on the Tibetans that the Chinese had been on a reconnaissance mission to draw out the Tibetans' numbers. The Tibetans had unwittingly complied.[60]

MARCH 16.

The Dalai Lama received a letter from Ngabo claiming that the Chinese knew all about his escape plans that the PLA would capture the Dalai Lama if he tried to leave.[61] Ngabo added:

If Your Holiness with a few trusted officers can stay within the Inner Wall and inform General Tan exactly which building you will occupy, they certainly intend that this building will not be damaged.[62]

The PLA was preparing to destroy the palace. As for the tens of thousands of Tibetans outside the walls, they were expendable. What the Chinese were not willing to sacrifice, though, was the Dalai Lama, whose well-being remained of inestimable value to the communists' propaganda machine.

The Dalai Lama didn't answer Ngabo's letter. He did, however, write to General Tan, emphasizing his helplessness. He promised—as soon as the tension eased a little—to come to Yutok to join the general. And in a remarkably fawning coda, he expressed hope that the general would write to him often.

The Dalai Lama was no fool. By now he had correctly assessed his utter powerlessness to control the chaos. The best he could do was to stall for time by writing falsely conciliatory letters to the general. This, and other obsequious correspondence to General Tan would later be used by the Chinese to "prove" that His Holiness did not flee Lhasa of his own will but was, in fact, kidnapped by "Tibetan reactionaries." Many historians have faulted the Dalai Lama for these letters. And yet these missives, to some extent, succeeded in

---

[60]John F. Avedon, *In Exile from the Land of Snows*, 53.
[61]Given the events that were about to take place, Ngabo's claim to have known of Phala's contingency plan seems to have been a good guess on Ngabo's part, but nothing more than that. In the end, the Dalai Lama called Ngabo's bluff.
[62]Noel Barber, *From the Land of Lost Content*, 100.

keeping the general off-guard. In fact, the Dalai Lama's letters were an important ruse that helped to ensure the success of his escape.

On the night of March 16, Phala convened a meeting of all the patrol units stationed within the compound and along the gates to the exterior: *I told them that, from now on, while the guards were on patrol, it was mandatory to identify by name everyone who passed. I also instructed them that under no circumstances were they to use their flashlights—which might tip off Chinese spies that something was up.*[63] Phala's real reason for banning flashlights was to prevent a guard from recognizing the Dalai Lama, should the escape plan go into effect. It was a shrewd decision.

MARCH 17.

At four o'clock in the afternoon, General Tan sent his final message to the Dalai Lama.

The Dalai Lama, Phala, and the *Kashag* were seating themselves in a beautiful conference room—built by the previous Dalai Lama—with a simple altar and sumptuous *thankghas* decorating the walls. The Dalai Lama sat on a gilded platform covered in rugs. His cabinet sat in Western-style chairs. The topic of discussion was the dark connotations of Ngabo's latest letter. Just as the tea was served, they heard General Tan's message: A mortar shell exploded just outside their conference room in an ornamental pool. Soon after, a second boom rang in their ears from the direction of a bog outside the northern wall.[64]

And then there was silence. They waited. Additional shelling did not follow.

Phala turned to the shaken Dalai Lama and said, "Warning shots."

Then he added: "We must escape."

At first, the Dalai Lama didn't respond.

The decision was not a small matter; the stakes were high; the whole future of Tibet depended on it. There was no certainty that escape was physically possible at all—Ngabo had assured us it was not. If I did escape from Lhasa, where was I to go, and how could I reach asylum? Above all, would the Chinese destroy our

---

[63]Phala, "The Phala Papers," 30.
[64]Noel Barber, *From the Land of Lost Content,* 107.

*holy city and massacre our people if I went—or would the people scatter from
the Palace when they heard that I had gone, and so perhaps would some lives
be saved?*[65]

But the explosions were still ringing in his ears and, in truth, the Dalai
Lama had run out of cards to play. He agreed to make a run for it at ten
o'clock that night.

Phala ordered everyone in the room to synchronize their watches to his.
After a few more instructions, the meeting was adjourned, each man setting
off in different directions to wrap up his personal affairs.

Phala's contingency plan was quite comprehensive, down to the Dalai
Lama's personal staff:

*Without drawing attention to the fact, I sent the Dalai Lama's personal cook
out of Lhasa and instructed the cook to wait, along with his staff, at Ramagan
Ferry, where we would later meet up with him. I swore the cook to secrecy and,
as a precaution, ordered him to wear a photograph of His Holiness on top of his
head and to keep it there until further orders.*[66]

More important, he wrote the Indian Consul General, broaching the subject of exile.[67]

Finally, he sent a courier south, to notify the *Chushi-Gangdruk* to prepare
a reception committee. Important guests were on their way.[68]

ON MARCH 17, ALMOST AT THE VERY MOMENT THE DALAI LAMA'S
ornamental pool was shelled, Nehru stood on the floor of the Indian Parliament and assured its members that reports of unrest in Lhasa were "bizarre
rumors." The Tibetan problem was "a clash of minds rather than a clash of
arms," he said.[69]

---

[65]His Holiness the Dalai Lama, *My Land and My People*, 157.
[66]Phala, "The Phala Papers," 28. Keeping a photograph on top of one's head may seem, to Westerners,
a peculiar demand. In Tibet, to tap a sacred object on top of one's head is a gesture of profound
respect. Phala knew that if the cook was ever remindful of the Dalai Lama's image, the servant's
secrecy could be guaranteed—thus the mandate to keep the picture on his head.
[67]It's not clear if he received an answer.
[68]Conboy and Morrison, *The CIA's Secret War in Tibet*, 91.
[69]George N. Patterson, *Requiem for Tibet*, 173.

Nehru's assertions were duly reported on the front page of numerous Indian and international newspapers the next day.[70]

It would be Nehru's last dishonest account of the Tibetan crisis. Two days later, on March 20, the PLA would pivot their mortars and shell the Indian Consulate in the heart of Lhasa.[71]

IN THE MEANTIME, THERE WOULD BE SEVERAL GROUPS ESCAPING the night of March 17. The first included the Dalai Lama's mother and his youngest brother, Ngari Rinpoche. Both wore pants, disguised as male servants. Ngari, in his youthful ebullience, saw the event as a great adventure. He remembers what happened that night at about eight thirty:

There was a cool breeze blowing, the stars had come out and it was very peaceful. Then suddenly a burst of Bren-gun fire came from the direction of the river. The soldiers dashed out of the house and we all looked from the porch, but couldn't see a thing. Later we heard that a hundred of our troops guarding the Ramagan ferry had run into a Chinese patrol. Luckily our fire scared them off, keeping the way to the river clear.[72]

The first group slipped out of Norbulingka's south gate around nine o'clock.

The next group was of various officials who slipped out of the compound, hidden in a tarp-covered truck.

The last group scheduled to escape was the Dalai Lama and his entourage, which included Phala, the Head Abbot, and Kusung Depon, the Dalai Lama's brother-in-law and Commander of his Personal Bodyguard. Around nine thirty, Phala's spies returned from the ferry saying that the Dalai Lama's family had reached the river safely.

The Dalai Lama, clutching his official seal in his hand, prepared for his departure. He changed into the costume Phala's tailor had provided him, and then walked into his personal altar room for the last time. He sat on cushions and read from an ancient translation of Buddha's teachings, pausing for

[70]Ibid.
[71]Noel Barber, *From the Land of Lost Content*, 104.
[72]John F. Avedon, *In Exile from the Land of Snows*, 54.

a moment at a passage emphasizing the need to cultivate confidence and courage.[73]

Because of the last-minute nature of his escape and the necessity to inform as few people as possible, there would be no porters to carry the Dalai Lama's most treasured possessions. He would have to carry those himself. He picked up a cylindrical tube with a loose cloth handle and slung it over his shoulder. Inside the container was a rolled-up *thankgha* that had originally belonged to the Second Dalai Lama. The scroll painting was of Palden Lhamo.[74]

Just then, as if rallying from a long slumber, Palden Lhamo made her contribution to the escape: The wind suddenly whipped up outside. A sandstorm enveloped the Vale of Lhasa. High winds were common at this time of year, but according to those who escaped that night, this windstorm and the resultant murky veil it created were singularly propitious.[75] Who else but Palden Lhamo could have worked such magic?

The Dalai stuffed his glasses into a pocket and ventured out into the night. Phala was by his side and watched his young leader take one last look at his beloved Norbulingka:

It was the saddest sight, the most awful moment I have ever known in my life.[76]

The Dalai Lama worked his way through the blinding sand and, as he approached the south gate, took into his hands a proffered rifle. Awkwardly, he slung it over his shoulder, bowed his head against the wind and, flanked by two common soldiers, headed out the door.

Outside the walls, the throng huddled—thousands of them. According to Noel Barber, "As Phala walked through, someone in the crowd yelled, *Who are those people?* and a wag with a sense of humor cried above the wind, *It's Phala! Better not light your torches!*"[77]

Phala's earlier order had stuck. They would pass through the crowd without anyone shining light on their faces.

---

[73]His Holiness the Dalai Lama, *Freedom in Exile*, 138.
[74]Ibid.
[75]Noel Barber, *From the Land of Lost Content*, 119.
[76]Ibid., 120.
[77]Ibid., 121.

They disappeared into the brown shroud beyond.

A large patrol of rebels, who had earlier made a reconnaissance of the riverbank, now returned and intercepted Phala's group. They reported to Phala that no PLA troops were in the vicinity. Then, recognizing the Dalai Lama, they insisted that they form an additional escort. Phala was equally insistent that they should, and would, not do so:

I told them that if we all remained together, we would be far too conspicuous. It was like yelling to the Chinese, "Here we are! Come get us!" I told them to split up, and meet us at the riverbank from the other side.[78] It was a tense moment for the Dalai Lama who, without his glasses on, and with the sandstorm blowing in his eyes, was practically blind. He edged away from the group. *While I was arguing with the soldiers, the Dalai Lama secretly left without calling attention to himself and, as soon as I had convinced the soldiers to go the other way, I had to run to catch up with His Holiness. In that way we finally reached the Ramagan Ferry.*[79]

Almost on cue, the wind died down—just as the Dalai Lama and his entourage embarked in yak-skin coracles and headed across the Kyichu. In midstream, the sandy curtains of wind thinned and dropped away from one another, revealing the lights of Lhasa flickering in a recumbent background.

As the far shore drew near, the Dalai Lama could see the group awaiting him. His family, his ministers, his attendants and his tutors slowly came into view—all practically unrecognizable in their ragtag disguises.

In stark contrast—and creating a forbidding backdrop to this gathering—was a swaggering mounted guard of thirty Khampa warriors. Their ponies champed at the bits. The young men's long hair whipped like flags. Their leopard-trimmed *chubas* and fox-fur hats added to their dramatic appearance. Silhouetted against a clearing sky posed warriors armed to the teeth—proud descendants of King Gesar.

The Dalai Lama's coracle scraped into the bank and came to a halt.

The warriors dismounted. They bowed their heads and neared the Precious One with outstretched arms. Draped across their palms were white *khatas*.

---

[78]Phala, "The Phala Papers," 31.
[79]Ibid.

The Dalai Lama studied the warriors' faces. They were mostly his age and yet what dramatically different lives these men had lived. These defenders of the faith, whose eyes teared in reverence, were killers—something the Dalai Lama could never condone. Yet how could he condemn them? Whatever their transgressions, and whatever karma was accrued therein, these men had acted on behalf of his safety and the Buddhist teachings that he represented.

In spite of my beliefs, I very much admired their courage and their determination to carry on the grim battle they had started for our freedom, culture, and religion. I thanked them for their strength and bravery, and also, more personally, for the protection they had given me. . . . By then, I could not in honesty advise them to avoid violence. In order to fight, they had sacrificed their homes and all the comforts and benefits of a peaceful life. Now they could see no alternative but to go on fighting, and I had none to offer.[80]

Gunfire crackled and spattered in the distance.

It was time to mount. The reincarnate lamas, the old aristocrats, and the rugged Khampas all yanked their reins to the side, wheeled their ponies away from the haze of the city, and spurred southward into the darkness.

They rode all night with only one rest stop.

Rebel-controlled Lhoka was their destination. On the south side of the Tsangpo, the eighty-thousand-strong *Chushi-Gangdruk* awaited the solemn arrival of their leader.

SOME HISTORIANS HAVE CLAIMED THAT THE CIA WAS INSTRUMENtal in planning the Dalai Lama's escape from Lhasa. Roger McCarthy categorically denies this, not only because it isn't true but, more important, because the CIA myth robs the Tibetans—who pulled off an extremely difficult deception—of much deserved praise:

Credit must be given to the Khampa resistance as well as to Phala and a couple of officials whom Phala trusted. The CIA had nothing to do with the contingency plan, contrary to many later reports. We supported it, but it was Tibetan-created, and they should be given full credit. It is unfortunate, of course, that the Dalai Lama was unable to take any of the treasury or the most

---

[80]His Holiness the Dalai Lama, *My Land and My People*, 170–71.

sacred and absolutely essential artifacts of their religious history. Money in particular—convertible coin of the realm—could have helped the thousands of refugees that would follow him into India. On the whole, however, the Tibetans' plan worked out incredibly well. Practically no one knew about it until after the fact.[81]

Gompo Tashi was among those unaware of the escape. While the Dalai Lama set out with his Khampa bodyguards, the commander of the *Chushi-Gangdruk* was running for his life. He had led a contingent of five hundred warriors far to the east, only to incur heavy losses from PLA troops. He and his remaining men were now working their way back toward the relative safety of Lhoka, but the retreat itself was harrowing. Chinese forces had inundated the intervening area and, from the air, the crisscross of communist surveillance planes made movement in open terrain extremely risky for his cavalry. The last thing he was thinking about was the Lhasa situation. Literally and figuratively, everyone was traveling in different directions. Gompo Tashi raced westward. The Dalai Lama headed south. Athar and Lhotse rode north—rode hard—in search of the Dalai Lama.

MEANWHILE, IN LHASA, ALL BETS WERE OFF.

Already, by the morning of March 18, rumors began to circulate that the Dalai Lama had escaped, but no one could be sure that the rumors were true. What if the Chinese had captured him or murdered him? One way or another, it was time to cast off the yoke of the occupying force.

Kirti Lhundop, the ex-Tibetan Army soldier whose battalion had been disbanded years before and who had subsequently joined the *Mimang*, sensed the change:

Blinders had been torn away from the Lhasans' eyes. For years, we [the Mimang] *had been warning the Lhasans that their cooperation with the Chinese could only lead to the total destruction of Tibet. And finally, they understood. Not knowing where the Dalai Lama was . . . that was what made them understand: Without the Dalai Lama, they were in the same boat as other Tibetans. Before this, Lhasans looked down on the Khampas and Amdoans and*

---

[81]Roger E. McCarthy, interview with the author.

Goloks—maybe they still did, but now at least they understood what their fellow Tibetans had been through. Before, it had been a regional problem. Now the Chinese had a national uprising on their hands.[82]

The Tibetans scrambled to doubly fortify the Lhasan buildings that were under their control: the Jokhang, the Potala Palace, the Medical College on Iron Hill, Rangsum Ferry and, of course, Norbulingka. Traffic increased in all parts of town—the people laden with weapons and goods. Some were attempting to escape from the powder-keg atmosphere. Others were grimly digging in. In the old, residential part of town—the Barkhor—Tibetan men could be seen assessing rooftop aeries as potential snipers' nests. Below, their wives stacked bales of wet wool—wet because the added density created bulletproof barricades against Chinese machine guns, which were also beginning to sprout like weeds in residential windows throughout the city.

The whereabouts of the Dalai Lama was no less unsettling for the Chinese. Having failed to get in touch with His Holiness, General Tan feared the worst: The Dalai Lama had somehow escaped the confines of Norbulingka. Suspecting that he might have sought refuge with one of the foreign consulates in town—India, Bhutan, and Nepal—General Tan frantically asked permission to search their compounds. The three consuls respectfully denied his request.

The rumors circulating about the Dalai Lama only exacerbated General Tan's fury. The Dalai Lama was still in the Norbulingka. No, he was hiding in the Jokhang. No, the Indian Consulate had helped him escape to the south. No, he had been seen fleeing west, toward Shigatse, with Khampa warriors. And, worst of all: The Dalai Lama had secretly given himself up to General Tan in order to avert the bombing of Lhasa. The general screamed at his subordinates to bring him reliable sources.

MARCH 19, 1959.

Lhasan defiance was one thing. Jubilation was another.

There was a kind of surreal celebration surfacing in the narrow, congested streets of the Barkhor. The tang of spring was in the air. Posters calling for

---

[82]Kirti Lhundop, interview with the author.

open revolt went up while little boys flew kites between budding poplars. An Amdoan stalwart, dressed up in ancient armor, recited part of the epic *King Gesar*. When he sang the part in which Gesar bragged of his military conquests in the East—a none-too-subtle reference to the Chinese—the crowd went wild. Groups of Khampas, young and old, drank great quantities of *chang* offered to them by Lhasan ladies. Vandals smeared the ubiquitous posters of Mao Tse-tung with feces—and with fresh-faced disregard of the consequences.

General Tan responded by beefing up the troops, mortars, machine guns, and armored cars already choking the city limits.

Every gun in Lhasa—Chinese and Tibetan—was now oiled and leveled at an enemy target.

MARCH 20, 1959, THREE O'CLOCK A.M.

The Chinese—still not certain where the Dalai Lama was—again shelled the Summer Palace; only this time, unlike the two warning shots of March 17, the salvoes continued nonstop until daybreak.

No one slept that night. What if the Dalai Lama *hadn't* escaped? The same sickening thought was on everyone's mind: Each shell that exploded might be the one that killed His Holiness—the only reason to keep on living.

At dawn, the city again emptied into the streets.

Kirti Lhundop recounts what happened:

There were two kinds of Tibetans that morning: the ones who were trying to escape Lhasa and the ones who decided to stay and fight. Neither group thought we could beat the Chinese. It didn't matter to me. I didn't care. My wife and children were safe in Lhoka, with her family. My only thought was to defend the Dalai Lama if it wasn't too late. It didn't go beyond that. No organization. No plan. But there were lots of people who felt just like I did. I saw girls coming down alleyways with butcher knives. I saw old men with sharpened sticks. There were little kids armed with rocks. I saw monks with rifles and Molotov cocktails. That morning, all of us were doing the same thing: hunting Chinese. Maybe it was stupid. But it was the only way left for us—or at least for me.

Kirti had spent the night at a friend's house in the tightly compacted Barkhor District surrounding the Jokhang. As they readied their rifles and counted their precious bullets, two armed monks burst in, one of whom was Kirti's younger brother.

It was strange to see my brother out of his monk's robes. But not a big surprise. He was from Sera Monastery, and the night before the monks had opened up the Sera arsenal, which was one of the biggest in Lhasa. My little brother was very excited to fight the Chinese. I took the grenades from him because I was afraid he might hurt himself. But he knew how to shoot. The four of us decided that, as soon as the sun came up, we would go to Norbulingka to find out what was happening to the Dalai Lama. We agreed that if we got separated we would meet back at the house at the end of the day. The sun came up and we took off.

What they didn't realize was that, overnight, the Chinese had deployed great numbers of troops and equipment in a north-south barricade that successfully divided the city in half—thus anticipating Tibetans, like Kirti, and preventing them from joining the thousands already camped at Norbulingka. Kirti's group got about halfway to the Potala before people coming back from that direction convinced them to turn back, saying that the Chinese barricade was impenetrable. They were completely confused. By that time, there was shelling and gunfighting in the streets, and as far as Kirti and his buddies could tell, it was happening all over the city. A Khampa told them that Tibetans still had control of the Potala and Iron Hill, but that both places were now under heavy fire. They also heard that the shelling of Norbulingka had stopped. No one seemed to know anything about the Dalai Lama. Finally, someone told them that fighting was intensifying around the Jokhang—quite close to where they had started out that morning. They headed back toward the Barkhor District.

We turned a corner and were suddenly caught in heavy crossfire between two buildings on either side of the street. My friend and I got separated but I was still with my brother and the other monk. We headed south until we came to another intersection, northeast of Turquoise Bridge. [Not too far south of the Turquoise Bridge was Yutok, so that area was particularly concentrated with PLA forces.] *A guy I knew spotted me and yelled at me to help him. He and about ten other people were trying to strengthen a barricade. They had made a defense in front of a large house that held lots of rifles and ammunition. And so we spent some time dragging carts, boxes, sandbags, furniture—anything we could find—to help strengthen the wall. While this was going on, a woman took a bullet to the head and my brother got shot in the left shoulder, right at the base of the neck. He was bleeding very badly. He grabbed my shoulder and I helped him into a shop nearby. There was an old woman inside. She got some rags. We slowed the bleeding.*

There was an explosion outside—very close—then screaming. My brother wanted me to find out what was going on, but I didn't want to leave him. The old woman said she would watch after him. My brother told me to go on. I told him I would come back soon. And then I ran outside.

The house we had been trying to defend had been shelled. It was on fire, and it was impossible to do much about the fire, because the Chinese were shooting at us from a rooftop across the way. Three Tibetan women were shot and killed while trying to put out the fire. Everyone went running for cover. Then a guy said we should circle back around to the back of the building where the Chinese snipers were. I told that guy that I had three grenades. He and I and another guy took off together.

There was no one guarding the back of the building where the Chinese snipers were. The door was even open! I just pulled the grenade pin, threw it in, and ran to the other side of the street. We waited, but the grenade didn't explode. So I ran back over and threw in another grenade. That one exploded almost immediately. The blast threw me backward. I was stunned but OK. One guy pulled me back into a doorway across the street while the other threw a homemade bomb in the Chinese hideout. Smoke poured out of the building and we heard the snipers screaming at each other on the roof. A few seconds later we heard them coming down and then three soldiers came running out through the smoke. I was still on the ground, trying to get my head clear, but my friends leveled their rifles and—pa pa pa—killed them. A second later, two more Chinese started to come through, but they saw that it was a trap and disappeared back inside. We could hear them coughing and yelling. The guy next to me grabbed my last grenade and made a perfect throw into the hole. The whole front of the house came down—I think on top of the Chinese inside.

We took off and got into another fight one street over. That was when I discovered that I had cut my upper right arm pretty bad. Until then I thought all the blood on my chuba was my brother's. I don't even know how I did it, but I guess that maybe I got hurt when the grenade exploded. It didn't hurt that much except when I brought up my rifle to aim. One of my friends tied off my arm with a khata *and then we took off again. We got back to the barricaded house and helped the people who were putting out the fire.* There were four or five dead people in the courtyard, and others were wounded but there was little we could do about it. One woman was bleeding from the stomach. Her insides were spilling out. She begged for someone to shoot her. Someone did.[83]

The same kind of carnage was happening all over the city. Reportedly, over three thousand Tibetans were killed on March 20. Machine guns mowed down hundreds of unarmed women and children, for instance, who were marching near the transport depot. By noon, the panic on both sides was such that indiscriminate shooting became the norm.

At some point, I went back to the shop where I had left my brother. I was afraid that he might be dead. But when I got inside, I saw that he was gone. And the old woman who had helped him—she was gone, too. I went outside and asked if anyone had seen or knew where they went. No one knew anything. I thought, "Well, at least he is well enough to move." And I guessed that maybe he had headed back to the house where he had found me the night before.

After that I kind of lost track of time. I mean, I remember things, but it gets a little mixed up here. I remember taking a wounded guy's son to his cousin's house. Dead people, dead horses. Lots of carcasses. There was a very young boy who got shot in the head while peeing against a wall. He was killed instantly. I remember his bare feet crossed over each other. I almost threw up. I saw a group of women laughing in front of a house that was on fire: They told me it was the third Chinese house they had set on fire. I went by so many houses that were closed up but you could hear the people behind the doors. One minute a street was quiet, the next minute people were running and screaming. Things like that. And by then the rumor was all over town that His Holiness had escaped. There was no proof, but it's what everyone wanted to hear. So you saw dead bodies but you also saw people celebrating that the Dalai Lama was alive. People were crying. People were bragging that Khampas had taken over this place or that place. There were moments when I felt completely happy. Everywhere, people were talking about how many Chinese were being killed. But, of course, it didn't matter how many we killed, because there were always more Chinese troops to come in and take their place.

---

[83]Ibid.

Late in the afternoon, I got back to my friend's house. My brother wasn't there, and neither was my friend. And it didn't look like anybody had been there all day. My arm was starting to give me trouble by then. It was stiff. I was getting chills, too, and my head felt like it was burning up. I took off the bandages and I knew it needed some doctoring. I climbed up to the roof where the light was better so I could clean up the arm a little bit. I poured some chang on it and rubbed some herbs around the wound—I don't know what you call the herbs in English—and I put four big stitches in it with a needle and yak thread. On top of the next roof was a family just watching the town. They had a big pot of juniper branches burning, and they were doing puja to Palden Lhamo. I could see many rooftops, and there were lots of families who were just watching the war in the streets. There was smoke all over town—and I don't mean from incense. To the west, in the direction of Iron Hill—that was where a lot of the heavy shelling was going on. But there was gunfire all around. It was strange to watch it. It seemed real when you were in the streets but not so real on the roof.

When the sun went down, Lhasa got quiet. The bombing stopped. The rifle shots stopped—most of them, anyway. And that's when you could see families taking off for the country—lots of them. By then, I really felt sick. I fell asleep. When I woke up, I felt worse, and now it really hurt to raise my arm. It was dark by then. I went back out on the street to see what was going on. I met some guys who had heard that the Ramagan Ferry was still controlled by the Khampas. They said they were going to try to cross the river and join up with the Chushi-Gangdruk. I decided to go with them. I figured it was my last chance to get out of Lhasa—no one knew how long before the PLA would take over the ferry.

So that's when I left Lhasa.

I never went back.

I never saw my brother. I don't know what happened. Maybe he died in the street trying to escape. There were a lot like that. I don't know. Probably. But I never told my mother the truth—that I had been with Dorje that day or that he had returned his vows. It would have killed her. She was very proud of Dorje being a monk.[84]

The revolt in Lhasa continued for two more days. There were pitched battles, ubiquitous hand-to-hand combat, and fierce losses on both sides. There

---

[84]Ibid.

were temporary victories for the Tibetans. The Khampas foiled the PLA's attempt to rush the Summer Palace. On Iron Hill, they manned an ancient cannon that did considerable damage to Chinese troops below. They held on to the Potala. They took over the cinema and other key sites and, in spite of General Tan's armored cars that meant to retrieve Ramagan Ferry, the Khampa cavalry held off their advance.

But by the morning of March 22, the tide turned in favor of the Chinese. Their superior manpower and firing power, their endless shelling, coupled with the Tibetans diminishing food and ammunition supplies, began to tell. The night before, only a skeleton rebel force remained at the Summer Palace, now thoroughly pummeled. The bodies of the dead were heaped high and likened to "stacks of cordwood"[85]—the stench unbearable. According to one account, those who were too wounded to join the evacuation were mercifully put to death by their friends.[86] The Potala was finally lost to the PLA. The three main monasteries were blackened versions of their former selves. There was nothing left of the Medical College on Iron Hill—nothing.

The last major bastion of Tibetan revolt focused on the Jokhang, the holiest building in Tibet. Perhaps sensing the end was near, more and more Tibetans sought out the sacred landmark as their last stand. The cathedral's central courtyard and all the hundreds of chapels within were packed with the faithful who imagined that, here at least, they were safe from the communists. From the golden rooftop of the cathedral, a multitude of Tibetans could be seen circling clockwise in *chora* around the environs—an enormous human shield slowly swirling like the spread wings of a cyclone. For the PLA, the crowd—estimated to be around ten thousand Tibetans—was a logistical nightmare. According to one account, the PLA estimated that even if the fighting had suddenly ceased, it would still take another two days to escort the Tibetans outside the city."[87]

But of course, the communists were in no position (nor had they the inclination) to peacefully remove the people.

---

[85]Joe Bageant, *Military History,* Feb. 2004.
[86]Michel Peissel, *Cavaliers of Kham,* 145.
[87]Noel Barber, *From the Land of Lost Content,* 172.

At daybreak the first shells ripped through the Jokhang's ornate rooftop. Chinese machine guns mowed down the crowd in front of the holy building. Khampas struck back with their own machine guns and sword-wielding cavalry. For three hours the battle raged, the losses on both sides appalling. Finally, around noon, a Chinese tank rumbled down the street. When it reached the Jokhang, it kept going. It tore through the main gate, crunched over fallen bodies, and came to a screeching halt in the inner courtyard. The foregone conclusion—that it was only a matter of time before the PLA would prevail—had now become a smoldering reality at the doorstep of *Jowo Rinpoche.*

The violation of Tibet was complete.

In the aftermath, the number of Tibetans imprisoned by the Chinese was in the tens of thousands. The twenty-five thousand monks of the three great monasteries, those who had not been shot, were held under house arrest.

Those that had the means to escape did.

Others chose suicide.

The number of dead and wounded Tibetans was estimated at over fifteen thousand. Bodies of men, women, and children made many side streets impassable. According to McCarthy, "After the barrages of heavy fire by artillery, mortars and machine guns were finished, the Chinese then inspected

PLA soldiers capture two Tibetan officers during the 1959 revolt in Lhasa. *(Office of Information and International Relations, Dharamsala)*

each body, looking for the Dalai Lama. The wounded were simply killed or left to die as the Chinese continued their search."[88] Publicly, of course, the Chinese put a different spin on the national uprising. They contended that there was local unrest, but nothing more. In fact, Beijing refused to admit that a single Tibetan had been killed. Indeed, the Ministry of Propaganda painted a picture that suggested Lhasa had been transformed into a city of rapture. The communists' official "eyewitness" account was given by one Shan Chao. The day after the revolt had been crushed, "everywhere you could see faces bright with smiles. Practically everybody held a piece of snowy white hata [*sic*; *khata*] in his hands but no one knew who had initiated this idea. When people met us [the Chinese] on the streets, they held up their hata high and spoke the Tibetan greeting: 'Chuhsidelai!' This greeting, not normally used in daily conversations, was now on everybody's lips. It means 'good luck and good fortune.'"[89]

PHALA'S ORIGINAL ESCAPE PLAN DID NOT INCLUDE GOING TO INDIA. As the Dalai Lama rode south, he decided to set up a temporary headquarters at Lhuntse Dzong (much as he had done at Yatung in 1951). Lhuntse Dzong was a sprawling stone fort overlooking a broad valley, sixty miles north of the Indian border. It was also a stronghold of the *Chushi-Gangdruk*. The Dalai Lama felt that, as long as he remained in Tibet, the communists would think twice about reprisals to the citizens of Lhasa. As he pressed further south, however, his plan became less and less tenable.

On March 24, a courier from Lhasa caught up with him with the news that Norbulingka had been shelled throughout the night. Hours later, another, bleaker report revealed that an all-out revolt had ensued. Eyewitness reports continued to trickle in and, gradually, the Dalai Lama was able to piece together the violence done to his people and his city:

Why did they do it? They ruined the Norbulingka believing that I was still inside it, so clearly they no longer cared whether they killed me or not. After they discovered I was not there, either alive or dead, they continued to shell the city

---

[88]Roger E. McCarthy, *Tears of the Lotus*, 184.
[89]*Peking Review*, May 5, 1959, vol. II, no. 18, 24.

and the monasteries. . . . We knew, as soon as we heard the dreadful news, that there was only one possible reason for it. Our people—not especially our rich or ruling class, but our ordinary people—had finally, eight years after the invasion began, convinced the Chinese that they would never willingly accept their alien rule. So the Chinese were trying now to terrify them, by merciless slaughter, into accepting this rule against their will.[90]

ON MARCH 25, THE DALAI LAMA'S ENTOURAGE ARRIVED AT A small monastery called Chongye Riwodechen. It was there that Athar and Lhotse caught up with His Holiness.

We spoke with Phala first. He asked us what kind of protection from the Chinese we could offer him. We told him that the Chushi-Gangdruk had complete control over the area. Besides, there were no roads in Lhoka, which made it very difficult for the PLA to move in large numbers of troops or armed vehicles from the north. We also told Phala that the Americans were supplying weapons to the rebels and that they planned to train more Tibetans somewhere outside of Tibet. If the Americans could have direct contact with the Dalai Lama, things would be even better. This pleased him very much.

The next day we met with His Holiness. We asked him what his intentions were, and he answered that a provisional government was going to be set up in Lhuntse Dzong. It was very clear that he did not wish to cross the Indian border. Then we told him all about our training with the CIA, about their air-drops to us, about future CIA training, and about our RS-I radio. You could see that he was very excited about this. He was grateful for our help and gave us precious beads. After we left His Holiness, we radioed the Americans that the Dalai Lama was safe in Lhoka.[91]

AT THAT MOMENT, THE ONLY WESTERNERS WHO KNEW OF THE Dalai Lama's general whereabouts were agents of the CIA. Roger McCarthy explains:

[90]His Holiness the Dalai Lama, *My Land and My People*, 168–69.
[91]Athar, interview with the author.

After the Dalai Lama left Lhasa, Athar and Lhotse were in contact with us daily. John Greaney was at the Tibetan desk in Washington. The CIA made a conscious decision not to send any messages to the Dalai Lama for the time being. They didn't want to add any unwanted dynamics to the situation. They feared it could possibly delay the Dalai Lama's exodus. But it was an apprehensive time. Through various intercepts, the CIA learned that Mao had put out alerts to "nail" the Dalai Lama. Also through intercepts, we had discovered that an organized Chinese search was well under way, including by air. There was one thing of which we were certain: Wherever the Dalai Lama was at any given moment, the hounds were not far behind.[92]

At the same time, however, the CIA made plans to airdrop additional supplies to Athar and Lhotse. Tibet was suddenly at the top of the White House's agenda. For the next week, Athar's reports were part of Eisenhower's daily Current Intelligence Bulletins. Athar—the humble peasant from a Tibetan village—became, in the words of the CIA officer John Greaney, "the best informed person in the world."[93]

The Dalai Lama continued south with Athar and Lhotse (and their wirelesses) following in his wake. On March 27, the Dalai Lama arrived at Lhuntse Dzong. From all directions, he received bad news. From his transistor radio, he heard a Beijing newscast reporting that the *Kashag*, the *Tsongdu*, and the entire Tibetan government had been dissolved. The new leaders of Tibet were the Panchen Lama and Ngabo.

Equally distressing—and far more urgent—was information from Athar and Lhotse (supplied to them by John Greaney) revealing that the PLA were amassing troops north of Bhutan. The Chinese assumed the Dalai Lama was racing for the border. The PLA plan was to cut off all escape routes left open to the Dalai Lama. If he didn't escape now, he would lose the option altogether. The Dalai Lama decided to head south.

Before he resumed his exodus, however, he officially and publicly repudiated the 17-Point Agreement. He also repudiated the unlawful restructuring of his government and dismissed the promotion of the Panchen Lama and Ngabo on the grounds that the Chinese had no authority to do so. He signed

---

[92]Roger E. McCarthry, telephone conversation with the author.
[93]Quoted in Kenneth Conboy and James Morrison, *The CIA's Secret War in Tibet*, 92.

a document of repudiation, and copies were sent out by horseback to all the major towns of Tibet. Athar remembers that the Dalai Lama's defiance brightened the pessimistic mood of the encampment. The chanting of lamas, the blaring of horns, the crashing of cymbals, the flying of banners and flags all signaled the import of the moment, but the fact remained: The Dalai Lama's only hope was exile.

The CIA was very much relieved to hear, through Athar, that the Dalai Lama had repudiated the 17-Point Agreement. John Greaney asked Athar if the Tibetans had secured official permission from India to cross the Indian border. Athar, in turn, asked Phala. Phala admitted to a shocked Athar that no such agreement was in place.

The CIA stepped forward, as McCarthy later explained:

When it became apparent that the Dalai Lama could be turned away from the Indian border, well, the resultant action was all CIA. Usually, in situations like this, it would have gone through the U.S. Ambassador in Delhi. But the time frame was such that traffic couldn't be handled in the normal way. Top priority for the handling of this piece of correspondence was given. Specifically, it went quickly from the Agency, to the State Department, to the White House, and finally to Prime Minister Nehru. The permission to enter India got back to the Dalai Lama [through Athar] before our Ambassador in India had even been advised. Much to his displeasure, he was cut out of the loop.[94]

The terrain south of Lhuntse Dzong was some of the most difficult yet traveled by the Dalai Lama and his entourage. Two of the highest mountain passes lay ahead. The white pony that had been the Dalai Lama's transport was replaced by a *dzo* in those final days. Weakened by dysentery and the hardship of nineteen-thousand-foot mountain passes buffeted by icy winds, hounded by reports that the PLA were closing in on Tsona—an outpost very near the border—the Dalai Lama pressed on. In one of his final acts on Tibetan soil, he wrote a proclamation that, in effect, at long last paid tribute to the warriors who had fought to protect him and his Buddhist nation: He promoted Gompo Tashi, in absentia, to the highest rank of general. The proclamation read in part:

---

[94]Roger E. McCarthy, interview with the author.

"Your unshaken devotion towards the cause of Tibet's Buddhist Faith and political stability, expressed in the conspicuous gallantry and intrepidity in commanding *Chushi Gangdruk* victoriously against the spiritual foe, Communist Chinese force, will be honored hereby with your promotion to the rank of General Dzasak."[95]

BY NOW, WESTERN NEWS ORGANIZATIONS WERE PUBLISHING INformation coming down from Kalimpong. The coverage went from two paragraphs to front-page headlines almost overnight. The notion that the "Reds" were in hot pursuit of a "god-king" was just too good: The world leaned forward as if watching the last furlong of the Triple Crown.

THE DALAI LAMA NEARED THE INDIAN BORDER UNSCATHED BY the Chinese. It was time to say good-bye to his *Chushi-Gangdruk* escort and the CIA radiomen, Athar and Lhotse. Although Nehru had granted asylum to the Dalai Lama and his entourage of eighty political and religious advisors, as well as members of his family, the rebel forces would not be allowed to follow their leader into exile. When asked if this denial upset him, Athar replied:

No, not at all. We were very proud of what we had done. Think how angry the Chinese were going to be when they found out the Dalai Lama was safe in India! The Americans were helping us to fight the Chinese. Additional airdrops were on the way. What could we have done in India?

And we did something else that day that really helped His Holiness. When he left Lhasa, the only currency he had was paper Tibetan notes. They would be of no use to him in India. But Lhotse and I were carrying two hundred thousand Indian rupees, supplied by the CIA in their second airdrop. The CIA authorized us to hand them over to the Dalai Lama. This was a big help for him. That we could do this for His Holiness when he was about to enter India with nothing— it made us very proud.

We watched them head south and, when they disappeared, Lhotse and I set up the radio. We told the CIA that everything was fine, that the Dalai Lama had

---

[95]Gompo Tashi Andrugtsang, *Four Rivers, Six Ranges,* 106.

reached the border safely, and then we asked them to airdrop enough weapons for thirty thousand men. Then we headed back north, to the fighting.[96]

The rest of the Dalai Lama's escape was down a rapidly descending path into the tropical "sauna" of Assam. The foliage closed in around the entourage. Snowscapes were replaced with steaming jungles.

Late in the afternoon of March 31, the Dalai Lama, significantly weakened by his ordeal, rode into a clearing with tall bamboo gates up ahead. He dismounted his *dzo*. Gurkha soldiers offered him *khatas*. With Phala by his side, the Dalai Lama put on a brave smile and walked through the proscenium of exile.

The ruler was twenty-three years old.

---

[96]Athar, interview with the author.

A Khampa's crayon drawing of the Chinese occupation of Tibet, done at Camp Hale, Colorado, the top-secret training facility used by the CIA *(Collection of Bruce Walker)*

9

NEW HOPES AND
NEW DEVASTATIONS

The odds had always been against Tibet.

When the Chinese invaded in 1950, they brought with them the might of modern warfare, a means of communication, and a bottomless well of manpower. By 1959, that advantage had been increased a hundredfold. In the interim, the roads, airports, and army camps built by the communists (with the help of what eventually became slave labor), had created a transportation-communication infrastructure that now allowed rapid and fairly precise deployment of PLA troops whenever they were needed—a crucial advantage for a totalitarian government intent on ruling vast, inhospitable regions with an iron fist.

Of course, occupying a foreign country was one thing; maintaining control was quite another. By the summer of 1959, Mao had sent in one hundred thousand additional troops. Militarily, he was in control of most of Tibet. Now, short of a full-scale American invasion—something that had never been a possibility—Tibet was doomed to all-embracing colonization.

At the time, however, even after the Han had crushed the Lhasa revolt, the ruin of Tibet was not a foregone conclusion. The rebels saw the situation as a temporary setback. Indeed, seen from a certain angle, it wasn't a setback at all: It marked the spontaneous alliance of all Tibetans against a single enemy. Besides, the turbulence and chaos created by the Lhasan revolt had made possible the Dalai Lama's successful escape—the greatest Tibetan victory imaginable at the time.

Kirti Lhundop remembers: *Our situation was very bad. But no, nobody thought* [the fight for Tibet] *was over. The Dalai Lama was safe in India. That meant everything to us. The Chinese could kill as many of us as they wanted, but if they let the queen bee escape, if you see what I mean, well there's always another day. The Chinese were very angry about it. And stupid. They announced on the loudspeakers that the Dalai Lama had been kidnapped. We laughed out loud. That just showed us how desperate they were. It gave us all the more reason to fight. And then the rumor went around that the Americans were helping Gompo Tashi. And we thought the Americans could do anything. Maybe it would be a while before we got our country back, but, no, we were still optimistic.*[1]

The outside world's interest in the Tibetan situation now reached its zenith. For the first time, the international press covered eyewitness reports of the repression inside the country's borders. Tibet became the newest member of the Cold War, with sympathies falling squarely on either side of Iron Curtain alliances. The news coverage turned the Dalai Lama into an international star. Initially, the foreigners were captivated by the harrowing escape of "the god-king." Then there were accompanying stories sensationalizing the exotic and singularly spiritual culture that fit into an already romanticized notion of the Shangri-la kingdom. A portrait of the Dalai Lama appeared on the cover of the April 20, 1959, issue of *Time* magazine with the needling anti-communist legend: "THE ESCAPE THAT ROCKED THE REDS."

The Dalai Lama was now a *cause célèbre*, a spiritual icon and a political football all wrapped up in one supercharged package. The Chinese propagandists were flummoxed. The now-famous Dalai Lama had slipped through their

---

[1] Kirti Lhundop, interview with the author.

fingers, and there was little they could do other than blame the "reactionaries" and "imperialists"—a stock accusation that had lost its sting. So they added a new name to their stale list of culprits: Jawaharlal Nehru. This caught the Indian Prime Minister off-guard. True, Nehru did not hesitate to grant asylum to the Dalai Lama.[2] But it soon became clear that his assistance would not extend beyond that. He had no intention of allowing the Dalai Lama and his proposed Government-in-Exile to further vex the already infuriated Chinese. In fact, during the

(Time, Inc./Time Life Pictures/Getty Images)

first few weeks of the Dalai Lama's resettlement, the famous exile was forbidden by Nehru to speak to the foreign press. He even managed to prevent the Tibetan issue from being discussed in Parliament until May. Nehru was scrambling for a modicum of calm where there was none.

The Prime Minister lost face with (and garnered severe criticism from) the Indian public. He had no idea how vehement his people were in their sympathy for Tibetans. They were screaming for answers. Why had Nehru lied to them? Why had he downplayed the Tibetan disaster for nearly a decade?

There were demonstrations in all the major cities of India. The Indian press likened China's policy in Tibet to rape, and ascribed Nehru's duplicity to cowardice or gross naïveté. Some of his closest allies in the GOI threatened to resign. The international press went further by suggesting that Nehru was

---

[2]In spite of his favoritism toward China, Nehru never could have withstood the international protest had he turned the Dalai Lama away from the Indian border. It also should be remembered that Nehru saw himself as something of a savior, regardless of political convictions.

keeping the Dalai Lama a prisoner. Nehru had no choice but to allow the Dalai Lama a carefully choreographed press conference. In his first two public appearances, the Dalai Lama dismissed the notion that he had been kidnapped, denounced the communists for their ruthless takeover of Tibet, and rejected the 17-Point Agreement on the grounds that (1) it had been signed under duress, and (2) the Chinese had proceeded to break the agreement many times over.

The Chinese reaction was immediate, belligerent, and, much to the dismay of Nehru, aimed squarely at him. They asserted that Indians, not the Dalai Lama, had written the Dalai Lama's speech—proof that the GOI was meddling with the internal affairs of China. And their resultant moral outrage knew no bounds. A May 1959 issue of *Peking Review* reveals the tone set by the communist ministers of propaganda:

"Imperialist interventions and Indian expansionists, taking advantage of the rebellion in Tibet, have launched an all-out campaign of slander against People's China. Their favorite but long discredited weapons include name-calling, mud-slinging, deliberate distortions and outright lies. All these tricks however will be of no avail once the cold, hard facts become fully known. The motley band of slanderers and liars will stand exposed to the entire world in all their nakedness.... Mr. Nehru has great confidence in himself.... He is inclined to assume that the powerful group in the former local government of Tibet are a flock of milk-white lambs.... No self-respecting independent country, least of all, People's China, will tolerate such outside interference in its domestic politics."[3]

Message to Nehru: Mind your own damn business, little man. The Indian people were outraged by China's haughty tone, even those who most strongly objected to Nehru's leadership. Nehru pleaded for restraint, which only fanned the fire of public outrage.

Restraint? What good had come of restraint? Nehru's policy of appeasement had been precisely what had gotten India into this mess in the first place. Tibet had been, for centuries, India's nonaggressive northern neighbor and, as such, India's greatest ally. Had Nehru not understood what a pro-

[3]*Peking Review,* vol. II, no. 18, May 5, 1959, 3–9.

found asset Tibet had been to Indian national security? Now, a new, openly hostile neighbor patrolled their 2,680-mile northern border. The Chinese were massively armed, unapologetic for their brutal manipulation of the Tibetans, and, most disturbingly, had the effrontery to question the legality of that border, drawn along what was known as the McMahon Line. What was to stop China from "reclaiming" territory along the Himalayan ridge? It most assuredly would *not* be Nehru's policy of appeasement, which had—in part—helped grease the wheels of China's war machine and contributed to the collapse of the Tibetan government.

Assailed from all sides, Nehru's ambition to lead the Asian continent into a new age of brotherhood had never seemed more like a foolish dream.

But this did not stop Nehru's control and manipulation of the Dalai Lama's contact with the outside world. On April 24, he met privately with the Dalai Lama in Mussorrie. The Dalai Lama informed the Prime Minister of his wish to set up a Government-in-Exile and to appeal to the United Nations for aid. Nehru's response was dismissive: He would not, under any circumstances, tolerate Tibetan political activity on Indian soil. And, as for the United Nations, the young Tibetan leader was naïve to think that the international community would do anything to help him. According to the Dalai Lama, *I began to get the impression that Nehru thought of me as a young person who needed to be scolded from time to time.*[4]

Five days later, back in Delhi, Nehru met with the British High Commissioner, Malcolm Macdonald. The Commissioner wanted to be briefed on the Dalai Lama's game plan. Nehru told Macdonald that "the Dalai Lama is not thinking of setting up a Government-in-exile in India . . . nor is the Dalai Lama thinking of appealing to the United Nations."[5]

MEANWHILE, THE CHINESE BORE DOWN HARD ALONG THE INDIAN border. Their official explanation was that, for security reasons based upon internal problems in Tibet, they needed additional troops stationed along the

---

[4]His Holiness the Dalai Lama, *Freedom in Exile*, 146.
[5]FO 371-141593.

General S. S. Uban at home in the Defence Colony, New Delhi, 1998. *(Collection of the author)*

border. In fact, the PLA had already broached Indian soil in some of the higher elevated areas. Nehru's border patrol was minimal to nonexistent, and he knew an increased military presence along the Himalayan frontier was now essential. Perhaps intuiting that the Tibetans still had a part to play with Indian national security, he personally selected a Brigadier General by the name of S. S. Uban to go to Mussorrie to meet with the sequestered Dalai Lama.

S. S. Uban was one of the more colorful personalities in the Indian military. Crowned with a turquoise Sikh turban, and bearing a prodigious mustache that put Gompo Tashi's to shame, this educated and mystically inclined general had built his reputation in World War II by introducing innovative approaches to unconventional warfare. In the interim, however, General Uban had quenched his thirst for spiritual enlightenment by consorting with the top Indian swamis of the day.

When Uban received the order from Nehru, he jumped at the chance to meet with Tibet's spiritual leader:

I first saw the Dalai Lama at Mussorrie, soon after he crossed the border. I arrived at night, around nine o'clock—and an extraordinary thing happened apart from meeting His Holiness—although, perhaps, it was one and the same thing.

Just as I was arriving, on the road, on the left-hand side of my car, there was a rampart. And upon that, a huge male tiger was sitting. I said to myself, "This is strange. I haven't seen tigers so bold around man-made roads!" And I didn't know what he would do. He might jump me, or something like that. But, you see, I didn't care. I passed—slowly, slowly—in front of him, because I wanted to have a good look at him. It was a very ferocious, magnificent beast that simply stared back at me, but didn't move.

I don't know what the tiger was a symbol of, but I just left him there and continued on to where His Holiness was residing. All the time, naturally, the tiger was in the back of my mind.

The Dalai Lama was informed beforehand that I was coming, and so he met me outside and shook my hand. Well, I didn't want to shake his hand, because I respected him: I thought he was an incarnation of Buddha, so I should not shake hands with him but, rather, I should touch his feet—which is precisely what I did. He didn't expect that from a general in the army, I must say. But the point was that my feeling was that I should show respect.

So we sat there, with the tiger somewhere in the darkness.

I found one great thing with the Dalai Lama was that he was constantly smiling—always—whatever he was doing, he always had a broad smile on his face. That appealed to me greatly. He was an unusual being. Not in the least ordinary! Under those circumstances—when he had run like hell from Tibet, and he was being chased all the way along, and he was still smiling—showed me that he was a unique sort of man.

Then the Dalai Lama asked me, "Have you had your food?"

I said, "No, I've not had my food."

He said, "Would you like some food?"

I said, "Yes, I would love to have some food but I must tell you that, because I am busy with some spiritual practices that prohibit meat, I am currently a vegetarian."

He asked, "What do you mean by vegetarian?"

I explained, and he said, "Oh, then there may be nothing here in my house. I'll go inside and find out."

I told him not to bother, but he insisted. He went inside and eventually came up with something for my dinner—I forgot what. And from this beginning—on the evening of the tiger—our relationship grew until the present time. The Dalai Lama loves me, you know. This gold and turquoise ring that I wear, His Holiness gave this to me as a token of our friendship.[6]

---

[6]General S. S. Uban, interview with the author.

. . .

IN THE MEANTIME, FOR THE PAST TWELVE MONTHS, THE CIA'S activities on behalf of Tibet's freedom fighters had geared up significantly. Now more than ever, the Agency could claim to be "in the fight," even if not everyone at the Pentagon was clear where, precisely, that fight was. John Greaney, the agent who had been at the Washington desk receiving radio messages when Athar accompanied the Dalai Lama on his exodus to India, was asked by Allen Dulles (the Director of the CIA at that time) to come up to his office. The Director wanted to be briefed on the Tibetan situation:

Dulles asked me, "Now where is Tibet?" We stand up on the leather couch in his office and he has a National Geographic world map up there, and he's pointing to Hungary, and he says, "Is that Tibet?" And I say, "No, sir, it's over here by the Himalaya."[7]

Prior to 1959, Desmond Fitzgerald, CIA Chief of the Far East Division, had tapped Roger McCarthy to replace Frank Holober as the head of the Tibetan Task Force. (The Agency needed Holober in Japan.)

McCarthy took the position that the Agency had a moral obligation not to leave the Tibetans hanging: The CIA should either support the resistance, as originally intended, or let the Tibetans know support was being withdrawn. Fitzgerald responded by asking McCarthy to put his position in writing and to draw up specific plans. McCarthy's paper strongly recommended the training of additional teams at a suitable location within the United States. The trainees would be provided with the skills and equipment to conduct modern guerilla warfare, and would also learn how to collect intelligence on the plans and intentions of the PLA. Agency approval came through, and the first fifteen-man training group (once again selected by Gyalo Thondup in Darjeeling), arrived at Andrews Air Force Base in late 1958. From there they were flown to CIA's training site in Virginia, Camp Perry (nicknamed "the Farm"), until a permanent camp could be established.

McCarthy's instructor team would include Tony "Po" Poshepny, Tom Fos-

---

[7]John Greaney, author's notes taken during CIA roundtable discussion held in Bethesda, Maryland, 1999.

mire, John Greaney, Harry Archer, Zeke Zilaitis, Bill Smith, Bruce Walker, Ray Starke, and others[8]—all intelligent, hard-working, and hard-playing, a team perfectly suited for the Tibetan rebels' challenges and dispositions.

Meanwhile, the Special Ops office in the Pentagon looked into the matter of selecting a suitable U.S. training site for the Tibetans. McCarthy and John Greaney tentatively chose Camp Hale, a dismantled World War II camp isolated in the Colorado Rockies.[9] McCarthy remembers: *Camp Hale offered everything: mountains, valleys, the Eagle River, remoteness, yet near enough to support facilities to make it ideal. In 1958, there was nothing there. The closest town was Leadville.*[10] *We could shield our effort easily. The entrance was just off a good road, used primarily by tourists.*

The Army enthusiastically supported the Camp Hale project. They put the facilities together and did most of the work during the winter of 1958, which included erecting barracks, classrooms, kitchen facilities, as well as facilities for the instructors. The Army, however, was not given specific details about the purpose of Camp Hale, other than that a foreign national group would use the facilities. To simplify matters, the CIA supplied the Army with a cover story for civilian consumption: the area was off-limits to locals because "atomic-related research" was going on there, a ruse that would cover any noise factors or unusual traffic coming in and going out.[11]

---

[8]Roger E. McCarthy, letter to the author, in which he includes a breakdown of the staff: ". . . staff headed by Tom Fosmire, a first-rate paramilitary officer. Under him were Tony Poshepny, Al (Zeke) Zilaitis, Bill Smith, Bruce Walker, Don Cesare; Marines Sam Poss, Bob Laber, Jack Wall, Ray Starke, Harry Wallace, (medical technician) and Gill Strickler; Army cooks Joe Slavin and Bill Toler on "special assignment." Supplementing the training staff were Harry Archer and Ken Knaus who occasionally traveled to Camp Hale from my Tibetan Task Force at Langley, as did John Greaney (my deputy), Clay Cathey (who would be headed for Calcutta a year hence), and Joe Murphy. Joan Kiernan, the talented and capable TTF intelligence/researcher, was already on the 'Desk,' having worked with Frank Holober from the early days of the project. In addition was the exceptional Mongolian Geshe Wangyel who was primarily responsible for the telecode book as well as translating radio messages as they came in. Bruce Walker was the only Tibetan-speaking case officer in the project, having studied Tibetan at the University of Washington and in Bhutan. He conducted his classes at Camp Hale in Tibetan, and later served in India as the Tibetan referent, working with the Indian intelligence service and the Tibetans in a collaborative cooperative effort in India."

[9]Ibid. John Greaney finalized the Camp Hale package, which was built from scratch—much aided by the Camp Carson engineers.

[10]The highest incorporated town in the United States, elevation 10,430 feet.

[11]Roger E. McCarthy, letter to the author.

Aerial view of Camp Hale training area—east of billet and living area.
(Collection of Bruce Walker)

Two advantages of the Camp Hale site were its terrain and weather conditions, which were not unlike those of Tibet. Tashi Chutter, one of the Tibetan
translators who had studied English in Darjeeling under Gyalo Thondup's
supervision, was now flown to Colorado (along with the Prince of Derge).
When he arrived, he thought that he was actually back in Tibet: *We drove up
to the camp after dark. When I climbed out of the truck, I saw snowy moun-
taintops all around me and I was shocked for a moment. The Americans called
Camp Hale "the Ranch." But we Tibetans came up with our own nickname.
We called it* Dumra, *Tibetan for "flower garden." It really did feel like we were
back home.*

*That's also when I met Mr. Roger McCarthy for the first time. He was very
tall. Very strong. Very big hands. Big voice. Very much the leader but also a gen-
tleman. He believed in our cause and still does. One time he came back from*

Washington with a photograph of President Dwight Eisenhower, and the President had written on the photograph, "To my Tibetan friends: I wish you all the success." It made me very happy and proud. You see, I thought, if the President of the United States were offering us this gift, then the Americans would eventually invade Tibet and fight by our side. The Americans never told us that, but that was what I assumed or hoped.[12]

If Tashi Chutter thought of Camp Hale as a flower garden, the American trainers were inclined to view the facility from a historical context: They put up a nonofficial, roughly painted sign at the front gate of the camp, which read: "Welcome to Camp Mule Shit." In World War II, the legendary Tenth Mountain Division (the ski patrols of the Italian Campaign) had trained at Camp Hale; pack mules were used in mountaintop exercises. After the first Tibetan trainees arrived at Camp Hale, Roger McCarthy revived the tradition: *When you airdrop supplies into denied territory, it is obviously important to clear the DZ [drop zone] as quickly as possible. We had designed the loads so that they could be slung over the backs of ponies or yaks—with bundles resting on either side of the animal's flanks. The pack animals would save both time and manpower. So we rented two enormous mules, fifteen hands high, from a local farmer and introduced them into the airdrop exercises. Except for Tony Po, none of the instructors could handle them. The Tibetans, of course, had no problem whatsoever in communicating, controlling, and making friends with the stubborn beasts.*[13]

As in Saipan, the instructors fell in love with the Tibetans. One of their favorite images of their students was when they made their first parachute jumps. During their first jump, the Tibetans were serious in demeanor. But by their second jump, all that changed. They had steerable chutes, and they screamed "Geronimo" as they jumped, then chased each other down through the sky—yelling, laughing, trying to catch each other—"just having a hell of a time," as Frank Holober put it. The instructors had never seen such high spirits among foreign nationals.[14]

---

[12]Tashi Chutter, interview with the author.
[13]Roger E. McCarthy, telephone conversation with the author.
[14]Frank Holober, interview with the author.

Ray Starke remembers that the Tibetans were fond of intentionally leaving doors open, to get a rise out of him: *I told them that when I visited them in a free Tibet, I was going to rip their tent flaps off. They thought this was hysterical . . . They really enjoyed blowing things up during demolition class, but when they caught a fly in their mess hall, they would hold it in their cupped palms and let it loose outside.*[15]

The Americans brought in Hollywood movies for them. The Tibetans loved westerns and war movies—*Viva Zapata!, Walk East on Beacon, Rogers' Rangers, Merrill's Marauders*—the more action the better they liked it.[16]

It didn't take the instructors long to realize that the Khampas were drawn to anything promising danger. Roger McCarthy remembers driving training at Camp Hale: *Imagine Khampas behind the steering wheel! They found any potential mishap hilarious. There were never any injuries but there were definitely some close calls—let's just say the terrain and vehicles took a beating.*[17]

John Greaney, who was now McCarthy's deputy and made frequent trips to Camp Hale, was particularly struck by their dedication: *I've never seen anything like it. After dinner, they would go back to practice Morse code. Really, we used to comment back and forth that we were grateful that we were working with the Tibetans instead of the Central American problem, which was the Bay of Pigs. We knew we were fortunate to be involved with a good program.*[18]

The instructors also came to realize that the Tibetans had remarkably inquisitive and inventive natures. Within the Agency, the Technical Services Division (now DDS&T) had developed a means for the Tibetans to make homemade rockets. The concept was brought to Camp Hale and, according to McCarthy, the Tibetans were instantly smitten:

With a simple trough—made of wood or metal, around five feet in length— a "rocket" consisting of homemade napalm, with either an explosive or incendiary head, propelled by gunpowder, could be fashioned and launched at a target some distance away. It was far more successful as an area weapon than a preci-

---

[15]Quoted in Kenneth Conboy and James Morrison, *The CIA's Secret War in Tibet*, 108. Starke was the highly esteemed communications instructor.
[16]Roger E. McCarthy, interview with the author.
[17]Ibid.
[18]John Greaney, author's notes taken during CIA roundtable discussion held in Bethesda, Maryland, 1999.

sion weapon, but it also served as a psychological weapon, especially at night. The Tibetans loved it. One evening, the final "launch" went down range, but then veered considerably to the right and disappeared over a distant hill. Suddenly, the faint lights that came from a molybdenum mine, east of Leadville, went out. The Tibetans cheered. (One of our officers went to the mine's office the next morning to assuage plant management and offered to pay for the "interruption." The charge to the project was $25,000 ... but the incident did bolster our cover story that our site was engaged in explosive-related development work.)[19]

Field exercise, Camp Hale.
(Collection of Bruce Walker)

Tibetan and major U.S. holidays were dutifully celebrated at Camp Hale, usually by a day off from training—volleyball and kegs of beer available to all. The training staff put on skits as part of the celebrations, and the Tibetans reciprocated by accurately imitating the instructors.

But no one forgot the reason why they were at *Dumra.* The teams were training for reinfiltration, for on-the-ground surveillance, for setting up airdrop receptions, for radio operation, for sabotaging and interrupting Chinese transportation and, once they had returned home, for training other rebels. They were going to take Tibet away from the Chinese and give it back to His Holiness the Dalai Lama—nothing less.

THERE WERE NO *DUMRAS* AWAITING THEM IN THEIR HOMELAND.

Lhasa was now under martial law and curfew, completely suppressed by the PLA. South of Lhasa, the *Chushi-Gangdruk* continued fighting. When

[19]Roger E. McCarthy, letter to the author.

Camp Hale trainees holding up signal flags.
(Collection of Bruce Walker)

Athar and Lhotse weren't organizing airdrops, they organized impromptu training sessions in which they would impart CIA guerilla techniques to turn small groups into an advantage when engaging the PLA. These trainees were, in turn, to pass the information along to other rebels. But Lhoka was already beginning to look like a battle lost. It was all about manpower. The Chinese continued to bring in additional troops, by the thousands of truckloads, and the numbers simply became overwhelming. With each additional firefight, Gompo Tashi and his men saw their casualties mount—their retreats become more harrowing. And the lack of modern communication continued to plague rebel groups. They rode into battle without any reliable knowledge of the whereabouts of other *Chushi-Gangdruk* units. Thupten Dargyal, a member of the wealthy Demaltengkher merchant clan, who was now captain of a resistance group besieged in the Kongpo region, remembers the situation at the beginning of April 1959:

We had heard that the Dalai Lama had left Lhasa, but we had no idea he was escaping to India. We didn't know anything. We didn't even know that there had been a general uprising in Lhasa. All we knew was that our situation, in Kongpo, was very bad.[20]

Thupten's scouts came riding in one day reporting that a huge group of PLA were heading straight for their *magar* via the new Chinese road. It was a Chinese ploy. The main contingent of the PLA offensive moved farther south, along the Yarlung River, so that they could attack from a surprise position. Thupten didn't discover the ruse until it was almost too late. A sympa-

---

[20]Thupten Dargyal, interview with the author.

thizer came running into camp yelling that the Chinese were surrounding Chamnang Monastery—a mere six miles from the *magar.*

Thupten continues: *We mounted our horses and rode hard to the monastery. When we got to a mountain overlooking the monastery, we pulled up. Below we could see the PLA approaching from three directions. The Chinese spied our position and began shelling the mountainside with heavy artillery. That was around eleven in the morning. We started picking them off with our rifles and we soon had reinforcements from the locals who wanted to protect their monastery and especially their high lama, who they knew was inside. The problem was that for every Chinese we killed there was a hundred to take his place. And because of our limited ammunition, we had to make every single bullet count. All day the fighting was terrible. Wa-di-di-di-di-di-di-di! Wa-di-di-di-di-di-di-di! The whole afternoon was filled with the Chinese automatic weapons.*[21]

By sunset, Thupten still held the mountain, but the monastery had been overrun. Unaware that Lhasa, too, was lost, Thupten decided to lead his men to the capital to see what he could do to help the city.

If only we would have had a wireless back then! Of course the revolt had already come and gone! Looking back, it's a miracle that any of us survived.[22]

After two days riding west, Thupten finally learned of Lhasa's fall and the Dalai Lama's successful exodus to India. He had to make a quick decision. By now, the Chinese had cut off the route southwest of him, preventing him from joining Gompo Tashi. To make matters worse, Chinese planes were making reconnaissance flights—sometimes almost directly overhead. He and his men were spending more time hiding than they were riding. Finally, Thupten led his men southeast—having no idea what awaited them except that the trail would take him over a series of high passes reputed to be the most difficult in Tibet.

It was terrible. We had to leave our horses behind, and many of us were with our families. And there were rivers to cross. We were wet the whole time. Many didn't make it, especially the very young and the old. By the time we got to the Indian border area—the place was called Tsari Kyinghor Ta—I was barefoot and many of my friends were dead.

---

[21]Ibid.
[22]Ibid.

It wasn't just my men. How many families froze to death while climbing the Himalaya? I don't have any idea. But I do know that my health was never the same after that. And then, once you got across, you had to survive the refugee camps. Thousands and thousands died after they made it to India. The refugee camps were full of sick Tibetans and dying Tibetans. It was terrible. Terrible. Even that was better, though—better than what I left behind. That's the terrible truth.[23]

The flow of refugees was never-ending. By mid-April 1959, there were already six thousand Tibetans crowding into Bomdila alone—a hastily constructed camp of bamboo huts steaming from tropical rain and heat.[24] It was from this forlorn refugee camp that Gyalo Thondup selected yet another group of young warriors to be sent to America.

BACK IN LHOKA, BY MID-APRIL 1959, ATHAR AND LHOTSE HAD caught up with Gompo Tashi just south of Lhuntse Dzong. It was only then that Gompo Tashi heard that the Dalai Lama was safely in India and that he had bestowed upon Gompo Tashi the title of "General Dzasak."

Of course Gompo Tashi was very happy about that news, Athar said, *but the situation at Lhuntse Dzong was bad. The PLA were coming in from two directions, hoping to cut us off. Gompo Tashi's men were very discouraged by that time. Provisions were very low—food, ammunition—many of the guys had injuries and they were all worn out. I radioed the Americans. I told them the situation was serious and that we needed an airdrop of provisions immediately.*[25]

The CIA scrambled to load a C-130 with supplies and to get it to the East Pakistani airport. But by the time it was primed to fly over the Himalaya, Athar sent them a devastating message: "Cancel the airdrop—it is too late."

Within a few days, several strategic towns had fallen to the PLA in rapid succession: Tsethang, Yamdrok Dagye Ling, Lhodrak, and the southernmost fortress in Tibet, Tsona. Gompo Tashi found Tsona's loss especially difficult to accept because of its strategic location as an escape route. He called a

[23]Ibid.
[24]Bomdila is located in the northeast state of Arunachal Pradesh.
[25]Athar, interview with the author.

meeting to discuss plans for recapturing Tsona, only to discover the morale of his men had reached rock bottom. They were physically exhausted and psychologically incapable of rallying to yet another offensive, even at the bequest of their beloved leader. They told Gompo Tashi that the truth was staring them in the face and that it was time to admit that the *Chushi-Gangdruk*'s only recourse was to join the growing ranks of refugees in India—if for no other reason than to regroup and rehabilitate for a later incursion into Tibet. The meeting was a jolt and a bitter disappointment for Gompo Tashi. Unwilling to give up the fight, but undecided how best to deal with his troops, Gompo Tashi became uncharacteristically taciturn.[26]

Kirti Lhundop, who, by that time, had joined up with Gompo Tashi's army and traveled south with them, remembers the situation:

The reports coming in made it clear that, if we waited much longer, we might be cut off from the Indian border and lose our chance to escape. We were very low on supplies and many of the guys' families had already gone to India. They were losing their heart to continue but they didn't want to go against Gompo Tashi's wish to take back Tsona. Then some guys rode into camp with a message from the Dalai Lama. He said that the wisest thing to do for the present time would be to retreat into India and make future plans from there. Gompo Tashi couldn't go against His Holiness' wishes, so we packed up and rode for the border.

But there was more bad news, once they arrived at the Indian frontier. The Indian patrol turned them away. Why this occurred can only be surmised: The border patrol may have had orders to allow refugees to enter their country, but this was a huge cavalry of very rough-looking rebels, armed to the teeth, looking for trouble—not at all fitting the description of helpless escapees. Whatever the Indians' reasoning, Gompo Tashi was uncharacteristically compliant. Kirti Lhundop thought he understood why:

If you want to know the truth, I don't think Gompo Tashi really wanted to enter India. He didn't put up much of a fight with the Indians, I can tell you that much, and Gompo Tashi never backed down from anything—anybody will tell you that.

Gompo Tashi held a meeting with us and said, "OK, since we can't ride into India, let's go back and attack Tsona." We were all tired, and many of us were

---

[26]Gompo Tashi Andrugtsang, *Four Rivers, Six Ranges*, 103.

really sick—and that included Gompo Tashi—a lot of guys had already died along the way. Anyway, several thousand of us agreed to go back to Tsona with him the next morning. And then, when the sun rose, most of us had changed our minds again. There really was no chance of us taking back Tsona. Gompo Tashi was very upset. But the truth was, it was over—at least for the time being—and he knew it.

So he led the way back down to the border patrol. This time he went with a khata *and gifts as an offering. And this time, the authorities let us pass. We had to hand over all of our weapons and ammunitions. We could keep money and valuables, but we had to give up our guns. Well, I didn't have any valuables, so that didn't make any difference to me. But I had spent my whole life with a rifle, and it was not an easy thing to give up.*

I think it was the beginning of May when we finally crossed the border. It was sad for me and I really didn't know if I was doing the right thing except that His Holiness said it was the right thing. I just thought, well, I will be back [to Tibet], so it really doesn't matter right now.[27]

JUNE 1959.

Approximately twenty thousand Tibetans had fled to India. And many were not simply fleeing, as was later generalized, to be close to the Dalai Lama—although that was no doubt a spiritual plus. The fact was that the Tibetans were getting the hell out of Dodge. They were retreating from a new wave of Chinese "reform."

Although the *Chushi-Gangdruk*'s main contingent now opted to regroup in India, there were many pockets of resistance throughout the country that were entrenched in the mountains, less informed, and less likely to get out of Tibet alive. The immediate concern for the communists was to effect a "mop-up" operation of these unfortunate rebels. More troops were deployed but, even more important, advances on the *political* influences of resistance were set into motion. Anyone who had helped the rebels came under vicious attack and this meant, first and foremost, the monasteries. If even so much as one monk in a monastery had been identified as a resistance collaborator, the

[27]Kirti Lhundop, interview with the author.

entire monastery was deemed guilty. According to Warren Smith, "Lamas and monks who had sympathized with the revolt were accused, 'struggled' and [were] beaten by other monks. High lamas, especially *tulkus* (reincarnate lamas), and monastic officials were arrested and deported to labor camps. Monastic estates were confiscated, the payment of taxes to monasteries was prohibited and any monks remaining in the monasteries were required to be supported by their own labor."[28]

Of the six thousand monasteries in Tibet prior to 1959, only three hundred seventy remained open by 1960.[29]

In addition to destroying the monastic system—the very lifeblood of Tibetan culture—the communists bore down on the rest of the population. All estates were confiscated and redistributed to the lower echelon of Tibetans who, in the past, had rented land from estate owners. (Although this looked democratic in theory, the lion's share of the harvest of crops was promptly exported to starving Mainland China, leaving the new "landowners" worse off than before the reforms.) The Chinese could honestly claim that they had finally eliminated the inequities of the rich: Now *everyone* in Tibet was starving.

To make matters worse, all Tibetans were forced to exchange Tibetan money they still might have for Chinese yuan, and at a rate half its pre-revolt value. A new antirebellion law was put into effect: anyone assisting the rebels in any way would be publicly executed. Also, an influx of Han settlers began in earnest, with the obvious intention of turning the Tibetans into a minority in their own country. *Thamzing* was introduced to even the remotest villages. The accused was brought forward, a list of "crimes" committed was read, the onlookers were forced to denounce the "reactionary," and then the beating began, often followed by execution. Those thrown into prisons were, as often as not, to die from systematic starvation, exposure, or untreated illnesses. New variations of public torture and murder were introduced. Heads were smashed in with rifle butts. Eyes were gouged out with chopsticks. Monks were wrapped in blankets, doused in kerosene, then set on fire. Pub-

[28]Warren W. Smith Jr., *Tibetan Nation*, 473–74.

[29]Jing Jun, "Socioeconomic Changes and Riots in Lhasa" (unpublished paper), 1990, citing Zhang Yanlu, *Population Change in Tibet*, 28.

lic castration, roasting Tibetans over barbecue pits, stripping nuns and forc-ing them to have intercourse, and gang rape by soldiers were among the more imaginative "cleansing" techniques perpetrated by the new rulers of the new and improved Tibet,[30] or, as the propaganda machine called it, "a heaven on earth."

Part of this heaven on earth, according to the Tibetan traitor Cha Teah,[31] was the imprisonment of ten thousand Lhasans, one-fourth of the capital's population.[32] One of the most famous prisoners that dreadful summer was Lhalu Shape, the ex–Governor General of Kham, who had been replaced—disastrously—by Ngabo in 1950, shortly before the communist invasion. In the intervening years, his opposition to the Chinese had become increasingly pugnacious.

A Lhasan woman remembers the spectacle that was Lhalu's capture: *We saw so many people and friends and family members being beaten up on public platforms. But when I saw Lhalu being paraded down the streets, it was really awful. Lhalu wasn't like many of the aristocrats and government officials. The people respected Lhalu and that's why the communists made a special example of him. They hung a heavy stone around his neck with wire, so that he would keep his head down in a shameful position. He had been badly beaten. Both eyes were very swollen. And they put him up on a platform, and the cadres screamed insults at him, and spat on him, and shoved him so that he would fall over, and then they would kick him so that he would get back up on his knees.*

They said he was guilty of many murders, which no one believed. Then they would drag him away like an animal, only to bring him back the next day. That was the worst of it—seeing him brought back many times, wondering how long he could survive, and, of course, we were not able to do anything about it. The thing about thamzing *was that the more you were loved, the more you had to suf-fer. I think that's why the Chinese were so cruel to us—Tibetans loved Tibetans, and the Chinese couldn't get us to stop that. The Dalai Lama says that we must*

---

[30]International Commission of Jurists, *The Question of Tibet and the Rule of Law.*

[31]Cha Teah was the ex-mayor of Lhasa and brother-in-law of Ngabo. Prior to the uprising, Cha Teah worked closely with Ngabo and the communists at the expense of the civilians he supposedly repre-sented. After the uprising, the communists rewarded his efforts by making him a spokesperson for the "new" Tibet.

[32]Quoted in Michel Peissel, *Cavaliers of Kham,* 159.

1959: *Thamzing* is introduced to Lhasa after the Dalai Lama's escape. The victim is Lhalu Shape, the progressive leader who had been Governor of Kham in 1950, before Ngabo replaced him. *(Office of Information and International Relations, Dharamsala)*

not hate anyone, including the Chinese. I know he's right. I pray, but I still hate them. The Chinese killed my father. They killed my two brothers. They raped and killed one of my sisters for being a nun. I was lucky. I escaped Tibet that winter, but I do not forgive them, the Chinese. I am sorry that I can't, but I just don't.[33]

DRAWUPON, THE IDEALISTIC YOUTH FROM JYEKUNDO, NOW A BATTLE-worn commander of the *Chushi-Gangdruk,* led his wounded and underfed troops across the border in mid-May.

It was a difficult process, especially after what my men had been through already. We weren't allowed to enter India with our weapons. That came as a shock to us, and it was humiliating to do it, but, even after we agreed, the border

---

[33] Tibetan woman, interview with the author. (Name withheld by request.)

officials refused to let us in. I talked to the border police for a while and, well, we just sort of barged our way in. That was somewhere around Metok.

For the first five or six days we were completely on our own—nearly a week without food—and many of my people died of starvation. When we killed wild animals, officials scolded us and told us it was not allowed. Of course, we had nothing to eat, so we killed anyway.

Finally, the Indian government decided they had to help us. Supplies were airdropped into the mountains around Metok and, from there, we actually crossed the border into Assam. By that time, I didn't have the stomach to fight anymore. I'd spent my adult life fighting. What I really wanted was a normal life and to be able to provide for my family.[34]

Whatever personal desires Drawupon may have harbored, in the end, Gompo Tashi prevailed upon him to continue his leadership role in the *Chushi-Gangdruk*. And his leadership was much needed. By that time, there were nearly fifty thousand refugees scattered among the Himalayan foothills of northern India. The only organization extant in the refugee camps was the *Chushi-Gangdruk*. The refugees elected Gompo Tashi, Drawupon, and Andro Choe-drak to go to Mussorrie to present the Dalai Lama with a six-point request:

1. The monks and nuns of the camps wanted a separate place to live.
2. The *Chushi-Gangdruk* wanted permission to continue to wage war against China from inside the Indian border. They also wanted permission to get aid from other foreign countries to help the resistance movement.
3. The refugees wanted the world to know of the atrocities taking place in Tibet under the guise of Chinese "liberation." In order to do that, they suggested that ten representatives be given Indian visas so that they might spread the truth.
4. The Tibetans wanted permission to be relocated to a more suitable climate. (Assam, for instance, where Drawupon was camped, is a sweltering jungle with an average yearly rainfall of 120 inches. Thousands were dying from the climate and the various diseases that went with it.)

---

[34]Drawupon, interview with the author.

1959: Some of the first Tibetan refugees spilling into northern India. *(Collection of Athar Lithang)*

5. All the members of the *Chushi-Gangdruk* wanted an audience with His Holiness.
6. The entire refugee community wanted permission to offer long-life prayers to His Holiness.[35]

A few weeks later, the Dalai Lama met with Drawupon and other *Chushi-Gangdruk* leaders. He commended their resistance and told them that the reason for their success was that, in previous lives, they had shared some karmic experience that ensured the good fortune of their future alliance. One other thing that the Dalai Lama mentioned took Drawupon completely by surprise:

He said that the Chinese invasion could be interpreted as a blessing in disguise— that always before, Tibet had been made up of many tribes who wouldn't co-

---

[35]Ibid.

operate with each other. Now our common enemy—the communists—had
united us into one country as never before. He then assured us that he would live
until he was an old man. We all wept with happiness.[36]

REPRESSION AROUND THE REGION OF JOWO ZEGYAL MOUNTAIN—
the holy peak where Cyclone had spent his idyllic childhood—was not yet as
severe as in Lhasa, but it was only a matter of time. Aba, Cyclone's father,
knew the PLA would show his family no mercy. They had several strikes
against them: Aba was a landowner and the administrative head of the small
Goshen Monastery. His wife's lineage, though not aristocratic, certainly put
her on the endangered list as well. Cyclone was an exemplary student at
Riwoche Monastery, destined for rapid accession in the monastic hierarchy
and, as such, a predictable target. And then there was Aba's youngest son,
Goser. Goser, now ten, was a recognized reincarnate: *Tulkus* were at the top of
the communist hit list.

The situation in Riwoche was more volatile. The Head Abbot of the monastery, as well as many monks, had fled, either to join the *Chushi-Gangdruk*
or find their families. Cyclone was still there. One night, PLA troops stormed
the monastery, rounded up the monks, herded them into the open quadrangle of the monastery, and, for the next two days, interrogated the clergy, one
by one. The monastery was ransacked. Ostensibly, the PLA was looking for
arms and ammunition, but it soon looked more like a case of planned van-
dalism. Riwoche was renowned for having one of the greatest libraries in
Tibet; all the sacred manuscripts were hurled to the ground and defiled in
unspeakable ways. All the statues were broken to bits, and the artwork
destroyed. After they were certain there was nothing left of the ancient monastery worth desecrating, the uniformed hooligans fell in line and marched
south, toward Chamdo. Cyclone headed home.

Goser, the ten-year-old *tulku,* was overjoyed to see his older brother.
Together—while Aba made final arrangements for the family's departure—
the two boys walked to Taka, a nearby monastery nearly as large as the one in
Riwoche. Goser remembers what they found:

---

[36]Ibid.

The place was completely empty. All the statues lay in ruins—decapitated Buddhas, arms broken off; precious one-of-a-kind manuscripts ruined—loose leafs of old parchment with beautiful calligraphy just blowing away in the wind like trash. The buildings themselves had been partially destroyed. The roofs were open to the sky. It was a very melancholy place. Palden Lhamo, Chenrezig, Eka-jati, Amitabha, Guru Rinpoche, Manjushri, Maitreya [the Future Buddha]*— all of our sacred images in ruins—and I remember how the wind was whistling through the main chapel. I felt like I was in a huge empty cave.*[37]

CONTRARY TO WHAT NEHRU HAD TOLD THE DALAI LAMA, PRO-Tibetan sympathies among the international community continued to grow.

In June, the International Commission of Jurists published a report called *The Question of Tibet and the Rule of Law.* The report stated that there was "a prima facie case that on the part of the Chinese, there has been an attempt to destroy the national, ethical, racial and religious group of Tibetans by killing members of the group and causing serious bodily harm to members of the group" and that "these acts constitute the crime of genocide under the Genocide Convention of the United Nations of 1948." Perhaps even more significant, the report concluded that Tibet should be regarded historically as an independent nation, not a subsection of China.[38]

Since the International Commission of Jurists enjoyed consultative status in the United Nations, the report carried considerable weight within diplomatic circles. It now looked probable that although there was fierce opposition by the communist bloc, the United Nations would address the Tibetan problem in the fall.

IN LATE AUGUST, A STRAPPING AMERICAN IN HIS PRIME—ATHAR called him a "Khampa in disguise"[39]—stepped off a plane in monsoon-drenched Calcutta. Roger McCarthy was on his way to Darjeeling to finally

---

[37]Goser, telephone conversation with the author. (Real name withheld by request.)
[38]The report was not published until the following year, but it was widely released to diplomatic sources in 1959.
[39]Athar, interview with the author.

meet and debrief Gompo Tashi, the great warrior he had heard so much about from his trainees.

I remember how it was hotter than hell in Calcutta and, by contrast, how nice it was once I got up in the mountains. I was put up in the old Grand Hotel in Darjeeling. I then went to a safe house nearby, set up by Lhamo Tsering. That was where I met Gompo Tashi.

Gompo Tashi arrived wearing an ill-fitting jacket, slacks, leather shoes, socks, a short-sleeved shirt, and a loosely knotted tie. I'm sure it was Lhamo Tsering who put the general in Western clothes. I presented him with two cartons of Marlboros and a couple of bottles of scotch, which went over well. Within the hour, the coat and shoes and socks were off, as was the tie, as he made himself totally comfortable. We got down to what turned into a two-and-a-half-day debriefing.

He was a powerfully built Khampa, but it was obvious that the war had cost him physically: He showed me his scars from battle and recited where they had occurred, like a road map. One could not help but like him. His extensive travels in eastern Tibet and western China and into India and the border countries gave him far more wisdom than most Tibetans, including the cowards in the Kashag who were interested primarily in preserving their own respective niche. Gompo Tashi Andrugtsang was one of the most impressive individuals I have ever met. He was unpretentious, gregarious, of good humor, direct, bright, insightful, proud—yet humble—and totally dedicated to the Dalai Lama, as well as the resistance that eventually caused his death.[40]

McCarthy's primary objective was to debrief Gompo Tashi. After this was completed, however, Gyalo Thondup and Lhamo Tsering presented McCarthy with a proposal to carry on the resistance from a different loca-

---

[40] Roger E. McCarthy, interviews, correspondence, and telephone discussions with author. McCarthy added: "Gompo Tashi spoke with confidence that had the Khampa and Amdoan Tribals united earlier, and had there been outside support in the early 50s, before the Chinese completed the vital roads, the Tibetans would have defeated the PLA, for they would not have been able to sustain their supply lines." Also, it was clear to McCarthy that, although the general was fiercely loyal to the Dalai Lama, he had little use for Lhasan officials and Lhasan politics: "Had there been such a thing as a registry of voters in Tibet, I'm certain that Gompo Tashi would have been listed as 'Independent.'"

tion: The Tibetans wanted to establish an operational base in the Mustang area of north-central Nepal and they were asking for Agency support.

Strategically, Mustang made some sense to McCarthy—especially since it was out of the question that Nehru would allow the *Chushi-Gangdruk* to conduct cross-border raids from Indian territory. Mustang, on the other hand, was nominally part of Nepal. It jutted up into the plateau of Tibet and was populated by ethnic Tibetans. The Mustang population was Buddhist, spoke Tibetan and—even better—the tiny kingdom's monarch was sympathetic to the Tibetan cause. McCarthy balked, however, at the number of men—one thousand—that Gyalo Thondup and Lhamo Tsering wanted to infiltrate into Mustang.

The large number, in my mind, was excessive, especially for such a new effort that had not been explored in more, if any, depth. After a long discussion . . . I said that we [the CIA] could support an initial group of four hundred, and perhaps more when the four hundred proved to be workable and productive. (I knew, given the Tibetan zeal, that the Tibetans would likely exceed that number, but hoped that before doing so they would provide answers to the questions I had posed.) As to leadership of the Mustang effort, I left that up to the Tibetans. It was obvious that Gompo Tashi was not physically fit for the job. His multiple wounds were by that time giving him serious trouble.[41]

Gyalo Thondup and Lhamo Tsering suggested a man from Bathang, a man whose name McCarthy had not heard of until he came to Darjeeling. His name was Baba Gen Yeshi. This struck McCarthy as curious. During the two-and-a-half-day debriefing of Gompo Tashi, the general mentioned Baba Gen Yeshi only twice. Gompo Tashi had used Baba Gen Yeshi during the golden throne effort as one of the collectors of jewels and money—a job, according to Gompo Tashi, that apparently didn't suit Baba Gen Yeshi's opinion of himself.

I don't know if it was Baba Gen Yeshi's attitude, or if the temptation of handling jewels was just too much for him, but I do know that Gompo Tashi never used him again. Nor, if you'll notice in Gompo Tashi's book—a book filled with the names of all the key figures in the resistance—is the name of Baba Gen Yeshi men-

---

[41]Ibid.

Baba Gen Yeshi in Mustang.
(*Collection of Norbu Dorje*)

tioned but in passing. Baba Gen Yeshi, of course, would later come back to haunt the entire resistance.[42]

The following day McCarthy met with and debriefed Athar and Lhotse. It was a warm reunion. McCarthy was heartened to see that their spirits were as irrepressible as ever. But they were furious with Ngabo. By that time Ngabo had become the official spokesman for the Chinese propaganda released to the press. They told McCarthy that there was a group of Khampas prepared to infiltrate Tibet with the specific goal of assassinating Ngabo, and it was McCarthy's impression that Athar and Lhotse wouldn't have minded volunteering for the assignment themselves. McCarthy changed the subject by offering them a job at Camp Hale as assistant instructors. There was a new group of young Tibetans scheduled to leave soon from India, and he told Athar and Lhotse that they should join the recruits' flight to America. They were thrilled and readily accepted.[43]

McCarthy's last meeting in Darjeeling was with Wangdu. It was an uneasy reunion.[44]

Wangdu—the Saipan trainee whose group had been parachuted into the Lithang, and the nephew of Gompo Tashi—was still feeling the sting of a failed mission. It was only in Darjeeling that McCarthy was finally able to piece together what had happened to the rest of Wangdu's team.

Wangdu, Tsewang, and Dedrup had joined Wangdu's brother's resistance group and had begun to train their compatriots in the techniques and

---

[42]Roger E. McCarthy, interviews, correspondence, and telephone discussions with the author.
[43]Ibid.
[44]Ibid.

maneuvers of their Saipan training. Things were going well until shortly before the Western New Year, when Tsewang was murdered by the PLA in an ambush. That was when the CIA ceased receiving radio messages from the team. A few days later, in another firefight with the PLA, Dedrup was shot between the eyes, leaving Wangdu—the least adept of the trainees in communication—on his own. In the meantime, jump-shy Dreshe had returned to Tibet overland and had headed north in an effort to link up with Wangdu's team. He got as far as the Lithang-Bathang area—perhaps no more than a day's trek from Wangdu—when he was spotted in a clearing and gunned down by the Chinese.

In the ensuing months, Wangdu felt stranded and depressed: his guerilla activities fell short of his expectations. Wangdu did manage to work the radio—at least well enough to request airdrops from the CIA. But he failed to supply the vital information of precise locations for the airdrops. He struggled in Kham for a while, and then headed west, where he finally encountered and joined up with one of Gompo Tashi's guerilla units. The unit, like so many others in April 1959, experienced the heat of the massive PLA offensive and found no option but to exit Tibet. It was a downtrodden Wangdu who met McCarthy at the safe house, and it was obvious that he harbored anger at the Agency's failure to airdrop him supplies.

It was true that Wangdu had radioed us with requests, but his messages contained precious little other information. I reminded him that in his messages he had failed to include any details of even a specific location for the proposed airdrops. He did not seem to understand how important that was to "Headquarters"—that without proper communications, the Agency simply would not risk a flight into the unknown. I also reminded him that his decision not to continue communications training in Saipan (leaving that to Dreshe and the others) had obviously had serious consequences that no one could have foreseen at the time.

We talked a bit more, shedding a tear about Dreshe's, Dedrup's, and Tsewang's deaths.

By the way, Wangdu shared Gompo Tashi's disdain for Baba Gen Yeshi—the proposed leader for the Mustang operation. In the early days of resistance, Gen Yeshi had led a small group from Batang, but afterwards had shown no outstanding signs of leadership. Wangdu left me with the impression that Baba Gen Yeshi was not to be trusted.

I asked Wangdu if he would care to join Athar and Lhotse at Camp Hale. He thanked me, but said he was not interested in working with Tibetans in the United States. He said he hoped to remain with his uncle and continue to fight in Tibet. I did not press the subject, for it was clear that Wangdu was still upset over what he perceived as the Agency not helping him. In his mind, none of the fault was his, and the Agency and I had ultimately let him down.

We hugged and parted as friends, much as we had done prior to his climbing into the B-17 at Kurmitola.

That was the last time I saw him.

Of course, later, in Mustang, Wangdu tried valiantly to salvage what Baba Gen Yeshi had done to ruin the operation. It was there he finally found his chance to prove himself a hero, and he met his death in doing so. The Tibetans could not have asked for a more courageous and dedicated warrior. Even though he was more stubborn than a mule, he was—not unlike his famous uncle— a gifted leader.[45]

SOON AFTER MCCARTHY RETURNED TO WASHINGTON, THE TIBETAN issue was debated on the floor of the U.N. General Assembly. Behind-closed-doors politics—India and Great Britain refusing to come to the aid of the Tibetans—basically followed the earlier U.N. attempts to address the Tibetan issue. This time, however, the resolution to condemn China's gross violations of human rights was approved. The resolution became official on October 21: forty-five countries for, nine against, and twenty-six abstentions.

India and Great Britain—theoretically Tibet's closest allies—abstained.

Although Malaysia and Ireland sponsored the resolution, the United States stepped forward as Tibet's most powerful proponent. America was careful not to cosponsor, lest the debate devolve into standard Iron Curtain hostilities, but once the debate was in progress, the United States lobbied heavily in favor of the Tibetans. Unquestionably, without the U.S. pressure exerted on many of its allies—particularly those allies in South America— the resolution would have failed.

[45]Ibid.

The adoption of the resolution was a huge boost to Tibetan morale if nothing else. It ensured that the topic would not fade from the public forum any time soon.

FIFTEEN THOUSAND MILES AWAY, IN A PASTORAL REGION A WEEK'S ride northeast of Lhasa (where no one had even heard of the United Nations), the baritone vibrations of an airplane interceded the lowing of yaks. The vast expanse was called Pembar—ordinarily the windswept home of a smattering of nomadic herdsmen and their families. That September night, with a full moon rising, the empty plain had become a city: the temporary headquarters of thirty-five thousand rebels with perhaps twice as many attendant animals. The crowd turned their faces upward. Out of the starry sky, eighteen American parachutes magically bloomed. The first Camp Hale graduates were returning home.

They set up their radio and signaled the Americans of their safe arrival and a list of requests. The radio operator also informed the Americans that the two leaders of the massive army had been identified. One was a rugged veteran of the resistance by the name of Jongdung. The other was a young man—the twenty-six-year-old abbot of the local Pembar Monastery. His name was Pembar Tulku Rinpoche. Once again, warriors and lamas had joined forces.

According to Lhamo Tsering, who later wrote a brief on the Pembar Mission, four CIA airdrops were forthcoming. The loads included M-I rifles, mortars, grenades, bazookas, TNT, recoilless rifles, machine guns, more ammunition than any of the natives had ever seen, wireless sets, medicine, food—the thousands of pallets drifting down from the sky made anything look possible to the rebels below.[46]

The idea, of course—at least from the CIA point of view—was for the huge army to be resupplied and trained by the Camp Hale graduates. The most important part of the training would be for the Tibetans to learn how to engage the enemy with flexible, hard-to-target, guerilla warfare tactics. Stressing the value of small group tactics was crucial. The thirty-five thousand Tibetans, slowed down by family members and a host of livestock—no

---

[46]Lhamo Tsering, unpublished mission report given to the author.

matter how well armed—would be a turkey shoot for Chinese artillery or bombings by aircraft. Once the training was completed, the army would immediately split up and engage the PLA, utilizing the advantage of smaller units.

Among the parachutists was the Prince of Derge, who had been singled out at Camp Hale for a leadership role:

Once we landed in Pembar, my main objective was to train the local resistance groups in guerilla warfare. But all the time I was also engaged in firefights with the Chinese, several of which you could consider to be large battles. I also conducted demolition operations. While I was in Pembar, I blew up between fifteen and twenty bridges, which, I later learned, caused the communists a lot of problems. Also, using guerilla tactics, we were successful in killing small squadrons of Chinese who were by themselves. Our method, basically, was to terrorize the Chinese—to make them feel like they would never know where we would strike next. We were quite effective for a few months.[47]

One of the problems with the operation in Pembar was that training had been slowed down by concurrent firefights with the PLA. And as the months went by, there was a steady increase in PLA troops. The last airdrop occurred on January 6, 1960. Because of the PLA buildup, the Camp Hale graduates determined that it would be prudent to move southwest to the Nagchukha area, where PLA presence was less dominant and from which dispersal of units would be less likely to be detected by the Chinese.

Before the army of rebels could retreat to Nagchukha, however, a Chinese plane appeared in the sky. It flew in low over the highlands and dropped leaflets, which warned the rebels not to listen to the imperialist Americans and to surrender immediately.

The multitude refused to do so. According to Lhamo Tsering's report:

On the morning of 11th of January 1960, a large four-engine Chinese airplane, followed by three smaller planes, circled Pembar and bombed the monastery thrice. Casualties were low.

On the 12th, three more planes came and machine-gunned and bombed the guerilla positions. That day, Pembar Monastery was bombed 15 times.

There was bad weather on the 13th so no planes came that day.

---

[47]Donyo Jagotsang, Prince of Derge, interview with the author.

But on the 14th, [the rebels] *realized that Chinese troops had surrounded them. The team members* [from Camp Hale] *went to meet Pembar Tulku Rinpoche and explained to him that the situation was very bad and told him that it would be better to try and escape and organize another resistance elsewhere. But the* [Head Abbot] *told them that he would rather die in the place he belonged to than leave. At this time, Jongdung Bhu Dudul returned to Pembar after having been to another place. They had encountered severe Chinese attacks and only a few of them had managed to return. Jongdung Bhu Dudul asked the team to send a message to the Americans asking them to bomb the entire area so that both the Chinese and themselves would be destroyed, and such a message was sent.*[48]

Obviously, the CIA would not authorize such a request. Dechen, one of the survivors of Pembar, relates what happened next:

Every day, some fifteen jets came. They came in groups of five, in the morning, at midday and at 3 or 4 o'clock in the afternoon. Each jet carried fifteen to twenty bombs. We were in the high plains so there was nowhere to hide. The five jets made quick rounds and killed animals and men.[49]

No one knows the exact death count but, according to Roger McCarthy, thousands upon thousands were slaughtered at Pembar: *At first we didn't believe the reports coming in. We thought it was an exaggeration or an error. But it wasn't.*[50] Aerial bombardment is, by its nature, indiscriminate. In addition, the Chinese came in with long-range artillery. Men, women, and children were blocked off from the escape routes. The combined bombing and strafing created a bloodbath. *It was genocide, plain and simple. And the Tibetans are not to blame for becoming so vulnerable. By then, it was increasingly impossible to escape to India from Central Tibet and families just naturally gravitated to the "safety" of a larger group. It was truly tragic. How many people in the West have even heard of Pembar?*[51]

Of the eighteen Camp Hale graduates who reinfiltrated at Pembar, only five survived to relate the horrors. The Prince of Derge was one of those who made a run for it. It took them six weeks to make it to the Indian border and

---

[48]Lhamo Tsering, unpublished mission report given to the author.
[49]Roger E. McCarthy, conversation with the author and Frank Holober.
[50]Ibid.
[51]Quoted in Joe Bageant, "War at the Top of the World," *Military History,* February 2004.

they were under attack the entire way. The Chinese even began to burn the forests that the Prince of Derge and his team were using to avoid detection from air surveillance. At any minute he thought he would die. He lost count of the number of times he was forced into firefights.

Finally, I managed to get to the mountain passes separating Tibet from India. I had to leave my horse. I put on my American boots and I didn't take them off once, not until I was safely in India—that's how afraid I was of being caught off-guard.[52]

The Prince of Derge escaped into Bhutan, and then met up with the *Chushi-Gangdruk* in Mussorrie. By that time, Lhamo Tsering and Gyalo Thondup had finalized their plans to relocate the main resistance in Mustang and they asked the Prince to go with the recruits as a commander. *I told them no. I'd had enough. I had family to think about—those who made it out of Tibet. After Pembar, I swore to make my family my priority. I never fought again. And I've never regretted that decision.*[53]

Jongdung and the Abbot of Pembar were eventually captured by the PLA. From a propaganda point of view, the two rebel leaders were stellar captives. Shackled, they were flown down to Lhasa, paraded, beaten and finally thrown into the sadistic "care" of a political prison for the next twenty years.[54]

(In Amdo, a similar catastrophe occurred in Nira Tsogo, where a huge encampment of rebels and their families were sitting ducks. Thousands were massacred in air strikes. Those who dodged the slaughter fled west, to the arid plains of Lhadak, where the remaining majority succumbed to fatigue, starvation, and the slow but lethal coup de grace of dehydration.)

BY THE FALL OF 1959, THE CHINESE WERE IN CONTROL OF MOST THE country. But there were significant pockets of resistance still very much alive in Kham. As always, the smaller the size of the unit, the more successful their strike-and-retreat tactics became. The vertiginous mountains and shadowy gorges were still the Khampas' haunts, and they knew how to exploit them

---

[52]Donyo Jagotsang, interview with the author.
[53]Ibid.
[54]Ibid. Also as reported to the author by Tashi Chutter.

against the lumbering masses of PLA. In many cases, being well armed was less vital than being able to disappear into the forests. Khampa warriors interrupted the flow of traffic along the Chinese road and, in general, continued to be the Chinese convoys' nightmare—this at a time when the communists were boasting that the rebellion was completely over. There were no great victories to be recorded, but the disruption the Khampas created allowed untold thousands of Tibetans to make their way safely to the border—a major contribution that has often been overlooked by Western historians.

But not by the Tibetan runaways. Cyclone's family took flight that autumn, and without the resistance effort, they would not have been able to escape Tibet. Goser, Cyclone's younger brother, remembers:

The reason we hadn't left sooner was that my youngest sister, Ting-Ting Karmo, who was only five, had been ill. She was so frail and had a chronic illness— I don't know what American doctors would have called it. "Ting-Ting" was her nickname—like the sound of a bell. "Karmo" means white. Anyway, Ting-Ting got better and we took off. There were six of us: my parents, Cyclone, Ting-Ting, my nine-year-old sister Yangzom, and me.[55]

Since they were traveling by foot and over difficult terrain, they were forced to leave most of their possessions behind. They had to carry everything themselves: extra clothing, dried meat, butter, and *tsampa*. They also carried what little money Aba had scraped together; also dharma books and a few religious objects, including Cyclone's begging bowl.[56] They headed down the upper reaches of the Po Valley. At that time, the Upper Po was swarming with *Chushi-Gangdruk.* It meant that they were safe, but not immune to a certain amount of harassment. *Every time we would encounter the* Chushi-Gangdruk, *they would admonish us: "Why are you leaving? Don't go! Don't you realize that we are going to push the Chinese back to the old border? Don't worry!" Their spirits were really quite high. It felt good to hear their optimism, but Aba was resolved to get out while it was still possible.*[57]

The closer they came to the Lower Po Valley, the more dangerous it became. There was still rebel activity, but the family saw less of the *Chushi-*

---

[55]Goser, interview with the author.
[56]One of the few objects Cyclone still has from his youth in Tibet.
[57]Goser, interview with the author.

Gangdruk, because they were in hiding when they weren't actually engaged in firefights with the Chinese. Lower Po had become a major junction for the PLA. Along the way, someone told them that four famous brothers of the *Chushi-Gangdruk* had just recently captured a huge cache of guns and ammunition from the PLA, and that the Chinese had doubled their effort to find them. (Later, Goser's family heard that the four brothers were captured alive. For many days they were submitted to *thamzing,* beaten mercilessly, and finally murdered in a particularly cruel and drawn-out manner: The brothers were forced to watch each other die, very slowly, so that their mental anguish would be greater than their physical pain.)

Because they had a small child and their loads were heavy, Goser and Cyclone's family's progress was excruciatingly slow. *The fear of being caught never left us.*[58] One night they set up camp in what looked like a secure spot. It was a small valley surrounded by dense forest that rose on all sides of the clearing. Everything seemed quiet and, in any case, they were so exhausted that, after eating *tsampa,* they fell fast asleep.

In the dead of night, we awoke to the sound of shells exploding all around us. The ground shook, and the noise was louder than thunder. The Chinese had spotted us from the jungle and now they were firing mortar shells into our little clearing from the east, the south, and the west. It was very frightening and disorienting. Fortunately, Aba made sure we never bedded down with things unpacked, so it only took us moments to grab our belongings and head north, the only direction from which the Chinese didn't have us surrounded. It was a miracle that we got away, but it was a very dark night—no moon—and I'm sure that must have helped us.[59]

For several days they retraced their footsteps north, not knowing what else to do. Then suddenly Aba stopped and said, "What's the logic in going home where we know we'll be persecuted, unable to practice Buddhism, and perhaps killed? At least we have a chance of survival in India." Other families who were also in retreat tried to convince Aba that it was crazy to head back south. Aba responded that it was crazier *not* to. He turned his family around and moved them south.

---

[58]Ibid.
[59]Ibid.

Two weeks passed. They had managed to regain lost ground and then some; by now they were deep into the Lower Po district. Their food supply was dangerously low. One night they found an abandoned hut in which to bed down. In the middle of the night, the PLA barged in and dragged Aba and Cyclone away, without explanation. Goser, his mother, and his sisters were convinced they would never see Aba and Cyclone again. But the next morning, Aba returned for them. He told his family that he and Cyclone had been interrogated throughout the night but that neither of them had been hurt. Aba had been ordered to bring his family back to the PLA camp. Cyclone was being held hostage to ensure Aba's return. If he didn't come back with the family, Cyclone would be unceremoniously shot in the head.

So that's how we ended up being captured and thrown into a prison camp. The prison was near an old fortress called Dzong-na Thang. Several years before, the Chinese had built a labor prison camp there. The inmates were forced to work on the Chinese road. But about six months before—right about the time the Dalai Lama was making his escape—the Chushi-Gangdruk had ambushed the camp. They killed the Chinese, released the prisoners, and burned the place down. By the time we were captured, the place had been turned into a kind of makeshift outdoor holding pen for Tibetan families caught trying to escape. It was not a big operation, it was poorly organized and, when we arrived, there were probably no more than one hundred prisoners.[60]

It soon became apparent to Aba that the guards were more worried about the constant sound of firefights in the distance than they were about watching their prisoners. Every few nights, another family would manage to escape. The reason Aba didn't attempt to do the same was because Ting-Ting again fell ill—too ill to move on her own, which would be crucial if they were to survive a breakout. Everyone would have to be able to carry his or her own weight.

Sometime in October, in the middle of the night, the prisoners heard a plane fly over. The rumor went around that it must have been an American plane, because the Chinese didn't have the technology to fly at night. The next morning, at the daily indoctrination session, which the prisoners were forced to attend, the cadres made no mention of the plane. In the minds of

---

[60]Ibid.

the prisoners, this was a significant omission. The inevitable theme of the meetings was the greatness of all things Chinese. Had it been a Chinese plane, there would have been no end to communist boasting. A few mornings later, the prisoners' hunch proved correct. Goser recalls:

A "guest speaker" came to the camp and led the indoctrination session. We had heard about this man. His name was Tungtson Druk-druk, a Khampa who worked for the Chinese as a translator. But he wasn't really a collaborator. He pretended to help the communists when, in fact, he worked for the Chushi-Gangdruk *by providing the prisoners with coded messages. That morning he said, "You people are so stupid! Why can't you understand that the imperialists are our enemy—not the Chinese! The imperialists want to take over our country! Why, didn't you hear their plane the other night!"[61] The Chinese cadres just smiled and failed to understand what Tungtson Druk-druk was really saying to us. (In our eyes, Tungtson Druk-druk was a great hero. We heard that he helped many Khampas escape before the Chinese eventually found out. When they did, they tortured him and then killed him.)[62]*

South of the prison camp was an area called Pemako.[63] It was through Pemako that the Tibetans of that area could escape into India. As October turned into November, and November into December, more and more imprisoned families managed to slip away from the camp. The guards were quite aware the escapees all headed to Pemako, but so inundated had the surrounding area become with *Chushi-Gangdruk,* they were too afraid to pursue them more than a mile or so outside of camp.

Finally, in early January, Ting-Ting had recovered from her illness. One morning before sunrise, Aba signaled his family, and they slipped out under cover of darkness. Goser continues:

Escaping the camp was the easy part. Our next challenge was crossing the Pachu River a few hours south of the prison camp. It was daybreak when we got to the bank of the river. Where we came upon it, the river was very wide. My mother just froze with terror. None of us could swim. Mother cried that the

---

[61]Goser, interview with the author. When Roger McCarthy was told this story, he confirmed that it must have been one of the CIA overflights carrying bundles for the resistance below.
[62]Ibid.
[63]Pemako was the southernmost area of Kham. Later it would be incorporated into the Indian state of Assam.

water would take us all down. Fortunately, the current wasn't strong
and the river was pretty shallow, so
Aba and Cyclone linked arms with
me and the three of us forged the
stream with most of the bags. We
deposited the bags on the far bank
and Aba and Cyclone went back to
get the rest of the family. You could
see in Mother's face that she understood the water wouldn't kill her.[64]

Once on the far bank, the family spread out on the smooth
white river stones to dry out. Their
sheepskin *chubas* blended in with
the beach. After a while, they
heard a PLA patrol approaching
the river. They gathered up their
belongings and hid in the dense
forest that rose beyond, trying to

PLA patrol along the Tsangpo (Brahmaputra)
River just north of Pemako. The Himalaya can be
seen in the background. *(Collection of the author)*

see what the PLA had in mind. The troops came by several times but never
tried to ford the river.

That afternoon, the family penetrated the jungle in earnest. Fellow prisoners had told Aba that there was a village, not too far ahead, where the
people would be disposed to help escapees. But as they neared the village,
Aba lost his nerve. There were too many Tibetan collaborators, and his family had come too far and suffered too much to be turned over to the Chinese
yet again. As they approached the village, the local dogs began to bark, no
doubt smelling the would-be intruders. He stopped his family at the edge of
the clearing that gave way to the village.

*What finally gave Aba the courage to enter the clearing were the village
women. At dusk, a group of them came within hearing distance of our hiding
place. "Oh," they were saying, "the gods must be smiling on us! It's been three*

---

[64]Goser, interview with the author.

days since the Chinese have come to bother us." Then they all started chanting the mantra of Guru Rinpoche: "Om Ah Hung Benzra Guru Pedma Siddhi Hung!" The village was Nyingmapa—the same school of Buddhism that my family practiced! We were so happy we just rushed in. The women first moved back, frightened—we could have been anybody. But we had torches. We held them to our faces so that they could see us and, after that, there was no problem.

We stayed a week, getting our strength back, learning many details of our escape route and replenishing our food supply for the difficult trek ahead of us.[65]

The next leg of the journey followed the course of the Pachu River for a while—not too far from a major PLA garrison at Tamo—then veered away from the river due south. From there, the trail descended into a long, lush valley. It seemed like a magical place. Even though it was February, the family was surrounded by a surreal verdancy and an abundance of wildlife that belied the location: Up ahead, just beyond a dormant apple orchard, rose the glittering massif of the Himalaya—the family's last challenge.

In the following days, as they gained altitude, the temperature continued to drop—an unwelcome reminder to the family that this was the dead of winter, the worst possible time to be attempting an escape over the mountains. Little patches of snow began to appear. By the time they passed the tree line, it was very cold. Their path became salted, and then heaped, with snow. The incline of the trail became steeper, then turned into endless series of switchbacks. When the children broke into tears, Aba and Cyclone somehow managed to cajole them into moving on. Aba and Cyclone went first, followed by Goser, and then his mother and sisters, so that the youngest members' snowy path would be, at the least, somewhat tamped down.

About halfway up the mountain, several hours after the sun had set, they reached a snowbound monastery called Gawa-lung. Although tiny, it was quite well known. Tacshan Terchen, a great lama and *terton* (incarnate who discovers lost teachings hidden by Guru Rinpoche), had founded the monastery many centuries before. Aba said that, even though they were half-frozen, it was their great fortune to be at this holy spot.

They went inside the temple. They were totally surprised at what they saw.

---

[65]Ibid.

Over thirty fellow escapees were asleep on the stone floor in front of the main altar. They made prostrations and lay down beside the slumbering mass. They closed their eyes, feeling completely safe.

Sometime in the middle of the night, a monk came running in and yelled, "They're coming! Right now! The moon is up and we can see the Chinese coming up the mountain!"

It was confusing—really horrible—within minutes, our entire group was outside, going around the back of the monastery and heading up the mountain. In the moonlight, we could see the top of the mountain. It seemed very distant to me, but Aba thought it was only a mile or so away. He told us we could do it and not to waste energy looking back. Just keep moving, he said.

At times, the snow was above our knees. At times it was just ice. We used axes, knives—any sharp implement we had to get over the slippery parts. People carrying small children had the worst time of it. Everyone tried to help each other as much as possible, but mostly everyone was on their own. I can remember Cyclone kept encouraging me to keep going.

We reached the crest of the pass at dawn. The summit was colder than any place I have ever been. My hands and feet were numb. And windy! The wind cut through our chubas like a knife. But do you know that none of us cared? It's really true. Below us was freedom. All of us were just weeping with happiness. Then someone said, "Do you realize that this morning is the first day of Losar?"[66] Well, we just stood there for a moment trying to take in this incredible information and then we started jumping and yelling—the coincidence of our freedom happening on Losar really seemed like a miracle.

And then we headed down the slope—each step became easier. I remember how much every part of my body hurt. But it just didn't matter. Below us was Pemako. We sang all the way down to the valley.[67]

Joy was short-lived.

New enemies awaited Goser and his family. Their immune systems suffered a head-on collision with the bacterial diseases thriving in the subcontinent.

---

[66]The Tibetan New Year. Tibetans believe Losar is the most auspicious day of the year—a day of elaborate celebration.
[67]Goser, interview with the author.

One month into their confinement in an overcrowded and squalid refugee camp, Goser and Cyclone's mother came down with a high fever. She died two days later. No one could tell the family what exactly had killed their mother.

Two months later, Yangzom, the oldest daughter, died as well.

Ting-Ting, the youngest and frailest, held on almost until the end of the year.

Only the males survived the journey into exile.

Chitipati: The Master and Mistress of the charnel ground *(Jamyang of Amdo)*

10

LAST STAND

On May 1, 1960, an American U2 spy plane took off from East Pakistan and hauled itself up over the Himalaya en route to the Soviet Union. It was on a routine photographic spy mission. The Soviets shot it down at Sverdlovsk.

A summit meeting between Eisenhower and Soviet Premier Nikita Khrushchev, which was scheduled to convene in Paris just a few days later, was canceled. Eisenhower's dream of conducting an international peace conference was shattered, and East–West diplomatic relations took an ugly, U2-like nose-dive. The Cold War was, in fact, red hot.

This was to have serious ramifications for the Tibetan resistance.

Eisenhower immediately shut down all flights over the communist bloc. The CIA tried to win a waiver for the Tibet operation but was denied, which ended air support for the *Chushi-Gangdruk* for the near future.

The timing could not have been worse. The Tibetan mission was just beginning to hit its stride. Camp Hale was running smoothly. Future airdrops were being lined up. Intercommunication with all concerned parties had never been better. Everything was falling into place.

There were additional political problems. The presidential election was coming up—a tight race, as it turned out—between Richard Nixon and John Kennedy. The Republican administration was still stinging from the U2 incident. President Eisenhower's political gurus advised him against renewing any potentially dangerous covert actions, lest they backfire and affect election results. This was doubly unfortunate since, weather-wise, late fall was one of the better "windows" for parachuting over Tibet. The morale of the trainees was also a consideration. The psychological value of maintaining momentum was not to be overlooked. Keeping a Tibetan warrior in a holding pattern after he had learned how to man a bazooka was like hobbling a stallion two feet away from its feed.

In November, Kennedy was elected the thirty-fifth president of the United States. He walked into the Oval Office with deteriorating situations in Cuba, Laos, and South Vietnam. Tibet was no longer front-page news.

IN THE MEANTIME, BABA GEN YESHI HAD STATIONED HIMSELF IN Mustang as the resistance operation's general. Despite Gompo Tashi's reservations about Baba Gen Yeshi—particularly about his limited military experience—Baba Gen Yeshi did exhibit qualities that, at least in the beginning, seemed to offset his deficiencies. Baba Gen Yeshi's skill as an orator was second to none. He could saber-rattle with the best of them and was said to be able to conjure up tears on cue. His political savvy was also heralded: He gained the reputation of pouncing on trouble before it got out of hand, and, indeed, his nickname was "Cat."[1]

Baba Gen Yeshi was also a monk. He was unencumbered by dependents—an asset for any general involved with a long-term mission in a remote outpost. He dressed simply, practiced his Buddhist devotions daily, had the approval of the Dalai Lama, and used his religious station as a means of persuading others to do his bidding.

---

[1]Tashi Chutter, interview with the author.

His initial task was to gather recruits to go with him to Mustang. Escorted by an ailing Gompo Tashi, he made the circuit of refugee camps in India, gave emotionally pitched speeches, and gained followers wherever he spoke. The previous year, McCarthy had agreed to support three hundred to four hundred volunteers in the operation. Within a year of Baba Gen Yeshi's relocation to Mustang, he had approximately three to four times that number. In addition, many of the rebels had brought their families to the desolate frontier.

Mustang was perched high in the Himalaya. It looked down over the Tibetan plateau along the north boundary of Nepal—a no-man's-land of arid gorges, windblown palisades, and protracted snowbound winters. From the beginning, the remoteness of the operation was troublesome and unwieldy. Nevertheless, in February1961, Kennedy gave permission to continue Eisenhower's covert support for Tibetan resistance. Once the CIA was given the okay, it authorized its first arms drop into Mustang the following month. Initially, the reports coming back to Washington indicated that Baba Gen Yeshi was doing his job: His primary objective was to prepare the trainees to conduct cross-border raids.

But there was a problem—at least from an American viewpoint. The element that most favored the operation—Mustang's isolation—was also a stumbling block in terms of the CIA's need to monitor the operation. Sending American agents to Mustang was out of the question. For all practical purposes, Baba Gen Yeshi was free from scrutiny and, as such, a general who was accountable to no one. The CIA had to muster up trust for a man they didn't know. If that man turned out to be dishonorable, then everyone would suffer, Americans and Tibetans alike.

Whatever the CIA's misgivings may have been, in October 1961, Baba Gen Yeshi's men enjoyed a spectacular success on a routine "strike-and-run" operation into Tibet.

The location was a hard three-day ride north of Mustang. The rebels ambushed a Chinese jeep and truck traveling along the Lhasa-Xinjiang road—the only road connecting PLA garrisons along the southern route. Though new, the quality of the highway's construction was substandard: Laid across vast tracts of sand, the road was partially hidden by shifting dunes. Traffic was forced to proceed at a crawl, and the military vehicles in question slowly made their way toward the ambushers. From a nearby rocky

Troops in Mustang. (*Collection of Norbu Dorje*)

hill, the Tibetans waited until their target was directly below them, then they took deadly aim. One of the rebels, who participated in the raid, recounts what happened next:

Bullets ripped through the windshield, the driver's head snapped back, and the jeep veered to a halt on the shoulder. Two others in the front seat—one male, one female—slumped as their bodies were riddled by gunfire. Leaving the safety of the boulder, Ross[2] exchanged his weapon for the camera. But as he moved forward to take photographs, gunfire began to pour from the rear of the jeep. Ross dove for cover while the three other guerillas resumed their fusillade toward the back of the vehicle. After a minute, they converged on the now-silent target and removed four dead Chinese. . . . The bodies were laid on the ground and stripped of uniforms, shoes, socks, and watches. After setting the jeep on fire, Ross blew a whistle as the signal for the rest of the guerillas strung along the ridgeline to rendezvous near their horses.[3]

Rara and his men didn't know it, but they had uncovered a veritable gold mine of Chinese intelligence. Along with some carbines and one machine gun, they also took back to Mustang headquarters a large, official-looking

---

[2]"Ross" was the *nom de guerre* of Rara, a Camp Hale graduate. Rara subsequently became one of Mustang's commandants.

[3]Quoted in Kenneth Conboy and James Morrison, *The CIA's Secret War in Tibet*, 161–62.

satchel. The satchel was stuffed with documents. It was couriered to a CIA officer stationed in Calcutta, Clay Cathey, who, in turn, personally took it to Washington for a thorough examination.

Especially impressive were the bullet holes through some of the documents as well as the blood smeared on them, McCarthy said.[4]

The CIA was astonished. The custodian of the satchel gunned down by the Mustang rebels had been a regimental commander in the PLA. Among the documents the officer had been carrying were over two dozen issues of a classified PLA journal titled *Bulletin of Activities*. The bulletins detailed the many problems plaguing the PLA in Tibet, including discussions of economic problems, food shortages, lack of combat experience among junior officers, and ongoing armed uprisings in various parts of Tibet. Another document was a frank discussion of the intense discord between Mao and the Soviet government. Still other documents listed top-secret communication codes. Before it was all over, more than one hundred CIA reports would be generated from the contents of the satchel.[5] In one fell swoop, Rara's raiding party had inadvertently supplied the CIA with a "bible" on Chinese army intelligence—the only one it would have for several years to come.

It might be rightly assumed that, had there had been any naysayers on the Tibet question in Foggy Bottom, the satchel's contents would surely put doubt to rest: The Tibetan Task Force now had incontrovertible proof of the Mustang operation's benefits.

But then politics came into play.

John Kenneth Galbraith—the newly appointed Ambassador to India and one of Kennedy's most trusted advisors—openly worked against the Tibetans. Galbraith was overloaded with credentials, and was clearly someone to reckon with: a Harvard professor, a prolific writer of economic treatises, a novelist, a TV commentator, editor of *Fortune* magazine, and social buddy of the Kennedy clan. More important, he echoed Kennedy's own sentiment that the key to Asian politics resided in America's ability to nurture good relations with India[6]—if necessary, at the expense of the pre-

---

[4]Roger E. McCarthy, letter to the author.
[5]Kenneth Conboy and James Morrison, *The CIA's Secret War in Tibet*, 162.
[6]Ibid., 155.

existing friendship with Pakistan that had been carefully cultivated during Eisenhower's administration. (America's good relations with East Pakistan had made it possible for the CIA to smuggle Tibetans to Saipan and beyond.) In addition, Galbraith's dislike for the Tibetan project ventured into personal distaste: Tibetans were repugnant and barbaric—those "deeply unhygienic men,"[7] as he put it.

Ambassador Galbraith lobbied heavily *against* any airdrops to the Tibetans—either in Mustang or Tibet proper. (In his memoirs, Galbraith unabashedly recalls writing a memorandum advising the State Department to immediately terminate CIA aid to the Tibetans. He also asserts that his influence with Kennedy resulted in a change to minimum support of the Tibetan freedom fighters.[8]) The Ambassador may not have been dictating U.S. foreign policy, but he was definitely Kennedy's "eyes and ears" in the subcontinent, and the upshot was that JFK (giving a nod to Galbraith), placed a condition on future CIA airdrops into Mustang: They would be allowed to resume *only* if the operations were first blessed and backed by the Indian government.

This was Galbraith's not-too-subtle way of ensuring that the operation would be scrapped. Given Nehru's sycophantic relationship with China, it was a given that India would never help. Nehru and his influential pro-communist Defense Minister, Krishna Menon—who loathed America anyway—precluded any possibility that the CIA could meet Kennedy's new stipulation. Plans for future airdrops to Mustang were thus put on hold.

Many of the Camp Hale staff were reassigned. Roger McCarthy left his position as head of the Tibetan Task Force for a new assignment in Taiwan. (This left Ken Knaus to assume command over a skeletal version of McCarthy's original program.) The shadow cast by the Kennedy-Galbraith-Nehru fraternity was very long indeed. There was even talk of shutting down the Tibetan task force altogether.[9]

---

[7]John Kenneth Galbraith, *A Life of Our Times: Memoirs*, 395.
[8]Ibid.
[9]Kenneth Conboy and James Morrison, *The CIA's Secret War in Tibet*, 167.

. . .

THE REBELS IN MUSTANG, OF COURSE, KNEW NOTHING OF AMER-
ican politics. Their immediate concerns, in 1962, were reduced to one thing:
surviving the hostile conditions of their surroundings.

Tinzing Jyurme, one of the Khampa commanders serving under Baba
Gen Yeshi, remembers those harsh early days and his utter inability to understand why American assistance suddenly stopped:

*All that time, Tibetan refugees kept coming across the border into Mustang.
We already found it very hard to support ourselves, and with the additional numbers—the population grew to around three thousand people—it just got harder.
We never had adequate supplies. After a couple of airdrops from the Americans,
everything stopped. It was horrible. We knew the Indians would never help us. We
depended on the local Mustang people for clothing and food, and they were
almost as poor as we were. We had to sell everything of value to survive. We even
sold our silver amulet boxes that we always wore around our necks for protection.
(We took out the prayers inside the boxes and kept them, but we sold the silver
guas.) We had to construct our own shelters out of any trees and leaves and stones
that we could gather. Many died, especially during the first two winters.*[10]

Relief for the Mustang refugees was on its way, however. In a bizarre twist
of fate, an event occurred that, although only indirectly related to the Mustang
resistance, sufficiently gagged the anti-Tibetan opinions of Ambassador Galbraith. More important, the event threw Nehru and company into a defensive position. After a bout of soul-searching, Nehru finally reevaluated
the potential worth of his neglected neighbors to the north. Suddenly, the
Tibetans were *fellow* sufferers and promoted to a new category: They were
now Nehru's brothers-in-arms. And whom did the Tibetans have to thank for
this swift shift in sympathy? What event had created such a dramatic U-turn?

On October 22, 1962, China invaded India.

THE NORTHERN BORDER OF INDIA, FOR DECADES CALLED "THE
McMahon line," roughly followed the eastern Himalayan watershed through

---

[10]Tinzing Jyurme, interview with the author.

Assam into Burma. Since 1914, the Chinese had disputed this boundary. In that year, Sir Henry McMahon headed a British conference with the Thirteenth Dalai Lama in Simla, India. It was at the Simla Convention that the two countries negotiated the border between Tibet and India (which was still under British rule). China was not consulted in nor invited to these meetings—an omission, the Tibetans quickly pointed out, which indicated Britain did *not* regard Tibet as a suzerainty of China, but rather as an independent nation that could and did conduct its own international treaties. Not surprisingly, China refused to ratify any agreement that would, in the process, recognize Tibet's sovereignty. The McMahon Line had drawn a path of gnawing contention as well as a geographic boundary.

By 1947, when India gained its independence from Great Britain, the McMahon Line was better known as the Northeast Frontier Agency (NEFA). The names changed, but not the dispute. Mao's new China and Nehru's new India remained at loggerheads about the border but, because of a preponderance of other problems occupying the neonatal nations, the border dispute was relegated to a back burner.

The fire was turned up as early as the mid-50s. The Indians discovered—after the fact—that Mao's southern Tibetan highway, "a feat of modern engineering," had cut through a slice of the NEFA. Nehru voiced concern, and Chou En-lai worked his charm. By 1959, however, after the Dalai Lama escaped to India and the Sino-Indian relationship eroded, the NEFA question became a rallying point for the growing hostilities. Nehru's stance was that the border was "traditional"; that it followed the logical, geographical contours of the Himalaya; and that its legitimacy had been secured at the 1914 Simla Convention. Chou En-lai, in turn, expressed surprise that a country such as India, which had suffered so much under imperial Great Britain, would now base its argument on an imperialist treaty.[11]

The situation went downhill from there. By 1962, diplomatic relations between India and China were at an all-time low. The PLA began a massive buildup along the southern Tibetan-Indian border.

In October, twenty-five thousand PLA troops invaded India over the Thangla Ridge. The PLA pushed all the way to Bomdila in the east, with the

---

[11]Warren W. Smith Jr., *Tibetan Nation*, 490. The dispute continues in the twenty-first century.

Indians fearing that the Chinese would then continue southward into the plains area of India.[12]

General S. S. Uban was one of the first, within the Indian military, to be alerted of the invasion. He held emergency meetings with the field general staff as well as British officials. Then he went with the Chief of the General Staff up to the disputed area in the mountains. There, they found their troops demoralized and in disarray.

The troops had no weapons, no transportation facilities—totally unprepared. Very sad state! It was not the fault of the Indian army. All along, our British advisors had been informing us that the Chinese were "India's brothers" and had advised us that there was no need to adopt a strong defensive position along the border. We had listened to the British, and suddenly we were in a frightful mess!

Of course, not all of us had fallen for that British nonsense. One year before, I had made a tour of the border—almost all of it on foot—and in the process had ruminated on our vulnerability up there. And while on this trek, the thought occurred to me that we should have some Tibetans stationed with our border patrol. There were already thousands of Tibetan exiles inside the Indian border with nothing to do. I thought, "If you leave these warriors alone, they'll probably do some mischief. The best answer is to hire them, get them in shape, and, anyway, the Indo-Tibetan border is the most crucial point of our dispute with China. We must have some people belonging to that area, so that they can inform us and deliver valuable information to us."[13]

This, then, was the beginning of India's Special Frontier Forces (SFF), which would eventually include a small army of Tibetans named Unit 22. S. S. Uban called them Unit 22 because, at one time, he had commanded twenty-two mountain regiments—an artillery group of which he was very fond. With Unit 22, his idea was defensive—to have the Tibetans simply occupy the border and stop the communists should they try to come in. Unfortunately, Unit 22 was still only an idea when the Chinese invaded.[14]

---

[12]Roger E. McCarthy, *Tears of the Lotus,* 238. Also, according to McCarthy, in the west, "a similar-sized Chinese force attacked Indian army forces in Ladakh," seizing "some 14,500 square miles of the Aksai Chin."

[13]General S. S. Uban, interview with the author.

[14]Ibid.

In the meantime, after the invasion, Nehru and Defense Minister Menon took the brunt of the vicious political backlash that followed. In what must have been one of the most humiliating moments in his career, Nehru begged the United States for help, while Menon resigned in shame.

Conversely, Roger McCarthy was suddenly brought back into the picture. He was in Taipei, in October, when he received a cable from Dave Blee, the COS in India. Blee requested that he fly to New Delhi immediately to assist in a special program that the GOI had asked the Americans to support.

The morning after I arrived in India, Blee and I had a meeting with B. N. Mullik, the head of the Indian Intelligence Service (IIS). The gist of the meeting was that the GOI wanted U.S. assistance in providing the Indian Army with weapons, ammunition, and other equipment to be airlifted by clandestine flights into Agra, the main Indian Air Base west of New Delhi. Mullik explained the desperate situation India faced because of the invasion. . . .[15]

Mullik then called T. M. Subranhmanyam (rhymes with "subterranean") into the office to meet McCarthy. Subranhmanyam had just been tapped to serve as the Indian Intelligence Service's first liaison officer to the CIA—there had been no such contact with America prior to Nehru being slapped in the face by the Chinese.

In the days that followed, Subranhmanyam accompanied McCarthy to the Agra Air Base; McCarthy worked out the various problems Subranhmanyam presented. In the course of their time spent together in Agra, the two men had the opportunity to exchange views concerning the threat of China. Subranhmanyam made it clear to McCarthy that he was particularly chagrined with the Indian Army's lack of mountain training, which had allowed the Chinese to simply roll into the subcontinent without a fight. This dissatisfaction echoed McCarthy's feeling on the subject.

I pointed out that the Indians already had a large, ready-made, highly motivated group of men who could handle the border area better than anyone: the Tibetans, who had fought so courageously against the Chinese for years.[16]

Subranhmanyam was all ears; a rapid succession of questions ensued. Did McCarthy think the Tibetans would agree to such a venture? How would Bei-

---

[15]Roger E. McCarthy, letter to the author.
[16]Ibid.

jing react to the enlistment of Tibetans in the Indian Army? Would the Dalai Lama approve? McCarthy suggested that the Indians contact Gyalo Thondup and Gompo Tashi to get more definitive answers. Subranhmanyam said he would talk to Mullik, his boss, as soon as he returned to New Delhi.[17]

Upon completing his assignment in Agra, McCarthy returned to India's capital. He met Mullik at a restaurant in Old Delhi. Over a superb tandoori chicken dinner, the head of the IIS presented McCarthy with a small gift as a token of appreciation for his work. *Then Blee took me to the airport; I headed back to Taipei and thence to South Vietnam, the Delta, Father Hoa, and his Sea Swallows.*[18]

Uban got his go-ahead for Unit 22 from the Indian brass. It was the CIA that supplied Unit 22 with weapons and much of its training in Agra. Uban personally worked with the Tibetans in unconventional warfare.

And then something quite unexpected happened. The Chinese withdrew from India. The reasoning behind this is unclear. No doubt there was an order from Beijing—perhaps the PLA was ordered to concentrate on other priorities, or perhaps the invasion had been merely a probe to determine the strength of Indian border patrol. Whatever the reason, the PLA had killed many Indians, captured many others, only to release them during its retreat. And given India's unprepared state along the NEFA, it was an enormous relief for the Indians to see the Chinese leave, whatever their reasons.

No one in the subcontinent thought the danger was over, of course. Uban's Unit 22 proceeded with its training. Uban was particularly keen on the Khampas being paratroopers. If the necessity again arose, the only way Unit 22 could get to a contested area of the Himalaya quickly would be to jump. Gyalo Thondup, however, had his doubts about Uban being able to handle the unruly Khampas. He took the general to the side and warned him: *"Khampas are like training tigers—it won't be easy."*

---

[17]Roger E. McCarthy, telephone conversation with the author. McCarthy's conversation with Subranhmanyam begs the question: Was Unit 22 created *prior* to McCarthy's trip—as Uban asserts—or *after* McCarthy's brainstorming with Subranhmanyam? McCarthy offers the possible explanation that Mullik "got it from Uban and from me via Subranhmanyam within days or hours of one another."

[18]Roger E. McCarthy, interview with the author and subsequent telephone conversation.

Uban answered: *"Yes, I can see that—from their faces, the looks they give me, the way they behave. But don't bother about me. I think it will work out."*

Initially, it's true, I found some roughness in the Khampas' character. Khampas are a very independent, self-willed people. But somehow they responded to me and came to understand that I gave the orders. In no time I had no doubt that they would fight and die for me. Problems occasionally arose, but I'll tell you how I remedied that. I would say to the miscreant Khampa, "Go inside the corridor and you'll be fasting for three days—no food. And think about this. Why have you done this? You have come here for a sacred *cause. Religion is involved. God is involved.* Buddha *is involved. And you do such a silly thing like this? Just sit there for three days and fast."*[19]

In Uban's mind, training Khampas was child's play compared to certain army regulations, which he now felt obliged to ignore. No one in the Indian Army, who was over the age of thirty-five, was allowed to jump from a plane. *My problem was that nearly all my Tibetans were thirty-five or above. And I was fifty-two.*[20]

Nevertheless, Uban ordered his officers to proceed with the preparatory ground training of the Tibetans. When it came time for a real jump from a plane, Uban's officers, knowing quite well that they were acting in violation of military regulations, approached the general with their concerns.

Uban replied they need not worry: *"It's all a false rumor,"* I told my officers. *"Everybody above thirty-five is allowed to jump.* I am saying that. I am your general. And I am fifty-two! And come tomorrow morning, I will be the first to jump!" *I'd never seen a bloody parachute. Really. I'd never so much as thought of jumping from a plane. And now I had committed myself in front of the whole parade and my only thought was, "What the hell have I done!"*

That night he called an American instructor to his room and ordered him to teach him how to jump. The American was completely taken aback. He asked Uban, "Are you suggesting I show you how to jump from a tea-table?" Uban replied, *"Yes, that's precisely what I want! You stand on this tea-table and tell me how to jump."*

---

[19]General S. S. Uban, interview with the author.
[20]Ibid.

The next morning, Uban boarded the airplane with his Khampa trainees. He was the first to jump and, according to him, took a perfect roll when he hit the ground. Before he could dust himself off, however, an underling ran up saying that Mullik, the head of the IIS, wanted to speak to him immediately. *I took the call right there on the dropping zone while watching the pleasant spectacle of my boys parachuting from the sky. On the other end, Mullik said, "Uban, is that you? Number one: Do not jump!"*

I said, "Well, I've already jumped."

Mullik said, "What are you saying? You know very well about the age limitation! You should have waited for the Prime Minister's permission. I must inform you that the Prime Minister wants to see you. Now. In Delhi."

In the meantime, everybody who was over thirty-five was jumping from the sky. Even the Khampa cooks.

I got into my jeep and drove straight to Delhi to meet the Prime Minister. I thought he would probably sack me. I went in. I saluted.

Nehru asked, "What is your age, Uban?"

"Fifty-two, sir."

"Do you know the rule that states . . . ?"

"Yes, sir, I know the rule."

"Then why did you do that?"

I explained the situation, how some bloody fool comes along saying my Khampas couldn't jump, demoralizing the whole unit.

"Yes, yes, I heard all that," he said. With a broad smile across his face, he shook my hand and said, "The next time you jump, take me with you."

The small incidents in life! But the point is, my Khampas were at last properly trained and now ready to go. And a better group of boys cannot be imagined.[21]

BECAUSE OF THE CHINESE INVASION OF INDIA, THE TIBETAN issue was back in favor—not only in India, but stateside as well. The Agency's Far Eastern Division was now given the green light to plan a long-range resistance movement inside Tibet and further support for Mustang. Camp

---

[21]Ibid.

Hale was reopened with renewed vigor. Furthermore, Camp Hale training was beginning to pay off. With improvements in the telecode book, the groups who reinfiltrated Tibet sent much more detailed information on a variety of subjects: drop zones; locations of the nearest Chinese units; timely local weather information, such as prevailing winds and the amount of cloud coverage within the four-to-six-hour periods immediately preceding the scheduled drop.[22]

The curriculum was expanded to include, among other things, survival courses, extensive field exercises, driver training of tanks, field expedients, multiple ambushes, diversionary tactics, and a variety of psychological warfare techniques.[23]

CIA propaganda booklets illustrating Mao's promises and the grim reality. Camp Hale trainees distributed these booklets once they had been infiltrated into Tibet. (*Collection of Bruce Walker*)

---

[22]Roger E. McCarthy, *Tears of the Lotus,* 242.
[23]Ibid.

1964: Tibetan trainees sent to Cornell University by the CIA. Third from left is Tashi Chutter; fifth from left, Gelek Rinpoche. *(Collection of Bruce Walker)*

For a few select Tibetans, education was even extended to the American university campus.

Tashi Chutter and Tamding Tsephel, a nephew of Gompo Tashi, were sent to Georgetown University in 1963 to study international relations, political science, and U.S. history. The following year, they and five others would be enrolled at Cornell University. Tashi remembers assisting one of his fellow students at Cornell, who also happened to be an incarnate lama:

He was Gelek Rinpoche—a very important Gelupa lama. Gelek Rinpoche's English was quite poor when we arrived at Cornell, so in the beginning I translated for him. He was so gentle with me and so intelligent! After only six months, he was better versed in English than all the rest of us. His skill and determination were very inspiring. Today, of course, he is the head of one of the biggest Buddhist organizations in America: Jewel Heart.[24]

---

[24]Tashi Chutter, interview with the author.

Meanwhile, in Darjeeling, Gompo Tashi, who had for so many years been physically invincible, had now turned sixty and faced serious health issues. Just as a younger generation of Tibetan warriors were acquainting themselves with Ivy League campus life, the many wounds sustained by the aging general began to take their toll. His hips, legs, and feet were in constant, excruciating pain. Finally, he was rushed to Calcutta, where he was admitted into a nursing home. His condition only worsened. By the beginning of 1963, he was paralyzed from the waist down.

The doctors suggested he seek the help of specialists in England. He was subsequently flown to Maudsley Hospital in London, where a surgeon removed ten shards of shrapnel from his wizened body. For a brief period, he seemed to improve.

He was flown back to a nursing home in Darjeeling for supervised rehabilitation. Nevertheless, he knew the end was near. He wrote his will:

Before I depart I must address a few words to leaders of the Chushi Gangdruk. *All of you should unite in thought and action under the leadership of His Holiness the Dalai Lama. Under his guidance all of you must constantly work with inflexible determination for the liberation of Tibet, even at the cost of your lives. The torch of the Tibetan freedom movement must be passed on to the younger generation so that its flame keeps burning and humanity remains conscious of it.*[25]

In Tibetan iconography, the attendants of death are the *Chitipati*; two skeletons—incestuous brother and sister—embraced in a grotesque dance among the corpses of the charnel ground. Their eyes never leave one another's. An arch of blazing wisdom-fire consumes them. The brother wields a club in one hand and a skull brimming with blood in the other. By contrast, his sister holds a container of the elixir of life in one hand, and in the other a peacock feather. Like the peacock (thought to transform poison into iridescent plumage), death is a symbol for transformation—not a dead end. The *Chitipati* are here to remind us of that promise—the potential that only Death can bring. Perhaps Gompo Tashi was thinking of the *Chitipati* when he predicted, in one of his last written statements:

---

[25]Gompo Tashi Andrugtsang, *Four Rivers, Six Ranges,* 115–16.

Gompo Tashi's funeral procession above the foggy tea plantations of Darjeeling. (*Collection of Kalsang Gyatotsang*)

The doctors have doubtless done their best to give me renewed health and strength . . . but the future is in the lap of the Buddha and if destiny has no more useful activity for me in this span of life, I can only rely on his wisdom and the promise of a new life hereafter.[26]

Gompo Tashi died in Darjeeling on September 27, 1964.

His five-mile funeral procession is still talked about among the Tibetan Diaspora. Draped in flowers and *khatas,* his body was placed in the back of an army jeep—appropriate transportation for a general. On a mountain road overlooking tea plantations shrouded in mist, the cortege of Tibetan refugees numbered in the thousands. The cremation was held outside, under a somber Darjeeling sky. And then the icon of the *Chushi-Gangdruk* was gone. His death marked the end of an era. The resistance would never be quite the same.

Metaphorically, the funereal mists of Darjeeling blew across the Himalaya and drifted down into Mustang. Tinzing Jyurme, who had served as one of the commanders in Mustang since the operation's inception, described the degeneration:

---

[26]Ibid.

When we first arrived, Baba Yeshi made a big speech. He said, "I come to Mustang as a simple monk and I will leave Mustang as a simple monk—with no money of my own." We believed him and respected him for his virtue.[27] But after the CIA resumed airdrops of supplies and money, Tinzing became suspicious of Baba Gen Yeshi: Each freedom fighter was supposed to receive fifty rupees per day; they received eight. Baba Yeshi explained that he was keeping the surplus as a kind of savings fund, just in case the CIA airdrops suddenly stopped again. When asked where he was going to keep the extra money, Baba Gen Yeshi said it would be sent on a regular basis to the Government-in-Exile's Defense Department in Dharamsala. *He lied to us. He kept all the money for himself. And all the time he was doing that, we were nearly starving.*[28]

To augment the lack of food, Baba Yeshi sent teams across the Tibetan border to steal and drive yak and sheep herds back into Mustang. But after the ambush in which the rebels captured the famous satchel, the CIA became more convinced that there was value to the Mustang enterprise: It stepped up the airdrops as well as the money within the bundles. That's when the real trouble began. According to Tashi Chutter, the CIA earmarked a significant portion of this money to be used by Baba Yeshi as meat rations, so that the rebels could buy meat from the locals. But Baba Yeshi continued his livestock raids across the border and pocketed the CIA money for himself. *Baba Gen Yeshi was an embezzler—it's as simple as that. The soldiers never saw one rupee from the CIA meat rations.*[29]

Other allegations surfaced: Baba Gen Yeshi began to steal from his own people. Tibetans, who had just escaped the Chinese and crossed the border into Mustang, were stopped by Gen Yeshi's men and charged to enter. The cost of safe passage was whatever valuables the refugees had managed to carry with them—usually jewelry and Buddhist statues.[30]

In 1963, the Mustang general moved his headquarters to the southern edge of Mustang, to a village called Kagbeni,[31] where the winters were less

---

[27]Tinzing Jyurme, interview with the author.
[28]Ibid.
[29]Tashi Chutter, interview with the author.
[30]Kalsang Gyatotsang, interview with the author.
[31]Kagbeni, as Baba Yeshi's headquarters, is disputable. Kenneth Conboy and James Morrison identify the southern village as Kaisang, *The CIA's Secret War in Tibet*, 197–98.

severe. He built a large, well-appointed house for himself and his personal bodyguards. Once ensconced in his comfortable compound, he was seen less and less. If rebels went to Kagbeni to speak to him, more often than not they were turned away because, according to his guards, "The general is meditating and cannot be disturbed."[32]

There were worse allegations to come. Kalsang Gyatotsang, brother of Wangdu and nephew of Gompo Tashi, grew to despise the general:

Baba Yeshi was so sweet talking—always fingering his mala and praying—it was all a lie. He wasn't a good Buddhist. He stole from the refugees who came across the border. He stole from the village people. He even allowed his bodyguards to rape local women. It got terrible up there.

There was one guy I knew in Mustang—his name was Tsewang, from Garba—he was a leader in Mustang and he had trained at Camp Hale. Sometime in 1964 or 1965, Tsewang broke away from Baba Gen Yeshi because he couldn't take the corruption anymore. Tsewang relocated with his wife and family and six other guys, and he set up his own camp. Baba Gen Yeshi was furious. He sent Rara [the same Rara who captured the famous satchel] to find Tsewang and to kill him. Rara found him and shot him down in cold blood. Rara told me that himself. He also said he killed Tsewang's wife, because that was Baba Gen Yeshi's orders.[33]

The complaints of misdeeds mounted and trickled down Nepal's Kali Gandaki Valley and, from there, to Dharamsala (the new seat of the Dalai Lama's Government-in-Exile), to Delhi, and finally to Washington. As for Baba Gen Yeshi, he continued to enjoy the comforts of his aerie-compound, secure in the knowledge that he was on the CIA payroll and that the CIA was very far away.

WITH DISCOURAGING REPORTS COMING IN FROM MUSTANG, THE Agency set about looking for alternatives for their Camp Hale trainees. One idea was to transfer Mustang soldiers to S. S. Uban's Unit 22. The CIA also sent three of the Cornell students to New York City, where they helped to set

---

[32]Tibetan interviewed by the author. (Name withheld by request.)
[33]Kalsang Gyantotsang, interview with the author.

up Office of Tibet, an organization that subsequently thrived and continues to be a major center for winning support for the Tibetan cause. Another CIA creation was Tibet House, a cultural organization located in the heart of New Delhi and still a going concern, as is its sister organization located in New York City.

More pertinent to the resistance, however, was the plan to reinfiltrate groups of radio teams from New Delhi to Tibet. The teams would be flown to the edge of the Himalaya and, from there, cross into Tibet on foot. Their mission was to gather intelligence. In what areas of Tibet were the PLA most concentrated? What activities were the PLA currently involved in? What was the political climate? How were the people being treated by the Chinese? Where were the locations of new bridges and roads? This was the kind of information the CIA wanted to know. The teams would relay this information via wireless, to the CIA through the Special Service Office in Delhi.[34]

Chumi Namgyal Tundupon, originally from Amdo and a 1964 Camp Hale graduate, was a member of one such radioteam. He arrived in Delhi in the late fall of 1965. Chumi's five-man team reinfiltrated through Pemako (Assam). Once inside Tibet, they headed northwest, into the Kongpo region. The terrain they passed through was jungle, the climate subtropical. Half of the water sources were said to be poisonous, as were many of the trees and plants. Bears and big cats were an additional danger. Chumi's team had been outfitted with guns, but they were afraid to use them, lest the Chinese be tipped off of their whereabouts. The locals went barefoot; to avoid leaving telltale tracks for PLA patrol units to discover, the team went without shoes. Building fires was also a problem, for the same reason. Food was scarce. According to Chumi, it was the worst year of his life:

We didn't dare go too far north into Tibet, because the entire area was over-run with Chinese military. I never let my guard down. The Chinese knew me quite well from my fighting days in Amdo and, later, from my association with the Chushi-Gangdruk. We found out that there was a standing five hundred Chinese dollar reward for the capture of spies, so we also had to be very careful which Tibetans we made contact with. I would have felt better if the CIA had given me a cyanide tablet, but only the paratroopers got to have them.

---

[34]Chumi Namgyal Tundupon, interview with the author.

Several months after we arrived in Kongpo, the Chinese captured two of my buddies. They were most certainly interrogated, tortured, and killed. That left three of us. We made a pact: If the Chinese were about to capture us, we would turn on each other and shoot each other at the same time. I think all of us believed that we would die. There was just no room to make a mistake, especially at that time. We got to Tibet right before Mao Tse-tung started the Cultural Revolution.[35]

WHATEVER HAD HAPPENED IN TIBET SO FAR, THE REAL DANCE OF the *Chitipati* was about to begin.

In 1965, Mao Tse-tung looked around his expansive kingdom and decided he didn't like what he saw. The lovely and lean collectivism of the early years had disappeared—gobbled up and transformed by gluttonous bureaucrats and revisionists and other self-proclaimed party bigwigs. This would have to stop. In his infinite wisdom, Mao decided to create a "Cultural Revolution." Rather than working with what he had—which he regarded as indescribably disgusting and not worth salvaging—he decided to start from scratch. He would obliterate the "Four Olds": Old Ideas, Old Culture, Old Traditions, Old Customs. The way he would implement this would be to invite the youth of China to confront party members whose loyalty was in question, as well as civilians who showed attachment to the "Four Olds." Mao would call these young crusaders the "Red Guards."

Mao's "Cultural Revolution" arrived in Tibet in 1966.

Giant posters of Chairman Mao inundated the streets of Lhasa. Every monastery and sacred building that hadn't already been destroyed was ransacked. Scriptures, clay statues, prayer flags, stupas, temple murals, roadside shrines—anything that smacked of "the old religion" had to be systematically destroyed (although the more valuable artifacts such as gold statues were quietly trucked back to Beijing). Even the colorful decorations on the facades of Tibetan houses had to be painted over. The remaining monasteries were emptied of their inhabitants, who were then forced to forsake celibacy.

---

[35]Ibid.

Abbots and high lamas were automatically subjected to *thamzing*, imprisonment, and even execution. Traditional songs and dancing were banned. All Tibetan street signs were banned, replaced by Chinese ones. *Chubas* and traditional Tibetan clothing were banned—from now on, Tibetans would dress like Chinese proletarians. Long hair on men was banned. Tibetan earrings were banned. Prayer flags were banned. All Tibetan holidays were banned, replaced by the Chinese counterparts. All Tibetans were ordered to relinquish even the smallest Buddhist statue to the authorities. Personal altars in the household were banned. Traditional Tibetan weddings were banned.

Being Tibetan was banned.

And what did this brand-new religion—this cult of Mao—cost the Tibetan people?

By the time the Cultural Revolution was over, of the original six-thousand-plus monasteries in Tibet, only fifteen were left standing. No one knows how many people were thrown into prison for political reasons—it certainly numbered in the tens of thousands. According to the Dalai Lama's Government-in-Exile, 1.2 million Tibetans died at the hands of the Chinese—either before or during the Cultural Revolution.

CHUMI AND HIS TWO SURVIVING TEAMMATES FIRST HEARD ABOUT the Cultural Revolution from families escaping through Kongpo on their way to the Indian border. They captured Chinese newspapers, which provided additional information, though facts were difficult to extricate from the gummy rhetoric of party-line propaganda. They passed these details on to the CIA, as well as important data pertaining to the whereabouts and details of military installations and bridges. They also photographed all PLA constructions they encountered, later to be evaluated and assimilated into Washington's intelligence data bank.

They continually relocated camp, covering every track they made. They kept the wireless and other important possessions buried, except when actually using them. They burned all trash and then buried the ashes. They kept their cameras—expensive Canons with zoom lenses—wrapped in *khatas*. In their own minds, they were voluntary fugitives. Not being caught was their overarching objective; in fact, they had already been imprisoned by loneliness.

One morning, Chumi climbed a tree to photograph a military camp three hundred yards away. He stayed there all day. Then, late in the afternoon, just as he was preparing to lower himself down the bole, *three very pretty Kongpo women came walking along the mud path below me. One of them slipped and fell in the mud. They all started laughing. Then suddenly they looked up in my direction with a worried look. I realized that I had laughed with them. Luckily they didn't see me behind the leaves. If they had—well, I don't know what would have happened—they could have reported me, I could have been captured, and that would be the end of it. After they walked on, I climbed down from the tree and moved away as fast as I could.*

My mind was in a bad way. Not too long after that, my buddies and me approached a new PLA bridge that crossed a river. The Chinese had around-the-clock patrol there. There was no way to shoot the patrol without giving away our hiding place, so we decided to go upriver, which made it necessary for us to go through a village. We didn't stop to talk to anyone, although I really wanted to. I just wanted to stop in the village and stay there. When we got back to the river, we tried to make our own bridge. We cut down trees but the trees kept washing away in the strong current. That was the worst day for me—watching the trees wash away, unable to make the bridge, thinking about the people in the village, not being able to talk to them.

At some point, I decided that if I ever got out of there alive, I would never work for the Americans again. I liked the Americans. And I know that the information I got for them helped them and somehow probably helped the Tibetan people. But I had gone to America to learn how to fight. Once I got back to Tibet, I wasn't allowed to use the skills I had learned. I was shooting Chinese with a camera, not a rifle.[36]

Having finished their one-year mission, the surviving three members of the team returned to Delhi where they were debriefed, relieved of their cameras, and—along with twenty other Camp Hale graduates—treated to a beer party by an American agent working in Delhi at Special Operations. Chumi knew the agent as "Mr. Mark."

Mr. Mark told us that night that he was sad about the whole operation. What we had done had helped Indian and American intelligence, but not the Tibetans.

---

[36]Ibid.

He didn't think the Indians would ever really help us to get Tibet back. He said the Americans had camps in Orissa and somewhere in Thailand and that they were ready to go into Tibet any time they got the go-ahead, but he didn't think that would ever happen, either.[37]

Chumi was struck by the agent's remarks. It was the first time he had heard the Americans voice such pessimism. The pessimism echoed Chumi's own thoughts. But until that night, he had never actually admitted to himself how he felt.

From the Special Services office in Delhi, Chumi was invited to join the resistance in Mustang. He turned down the offer. Then they asked him if he would like to join S. S. Uban's Unit 22. He turned that down as well.

I had spent the best years of my life learning how to fight, and then I was turned into a spy who wasn't allowed to fight. Nobody was killing Chinese in Mustang. Nobody was killing Chinese in Unit 22. And during all those years, I had never had the time to pick up a profession, a livelihood, or have a family. All the guys I knew who had died—some of them right before my eyes—what did they die for? That's when I decided to move down to southern India and settle down in a refugee camp. No matter what was going on down there, it had to be better than what I was doing.[38]

THE LAST CIA AIRDROP INTO MUSTANG WAS IN 1965. IN THE early years, the rebels had been able to interrupt communications along the Chinese road. But by the mid-60s, the PLA had constructed a new road further north, which rendered the old route hardly worth traveling—and, for the rebels, hardly worth attacking. With Baba Gen Yeshi instigating very little useful activity, while lining his own pockets with CIA money, Mustang was rapidly beginning to look like a tragic sideshow.

Camp Hale was shut down. But CIA-sponsored activity continued.

In June 1965, Tashi Chutter and the other students from Cornell were brought back to India. Tashi was assigned a desk job at the Special Service Center—a top-secret safe house located in the Haus Kaus district of New

[37]Ibid.
[38]Ibid.

Delhi. The Special Service Center operated as a communal hub for the CIA and IIS support system for Tibetan-related activity. The staff included seven Tibetans and four Indians. All resistance operations were conducted from there: the Mustang operation, the radioteams sent into Tibet, and Unit 22. General S. S. Uban was a frequent visitor. Tashi's superior language skills— Tibetan, English, Hindi—were obviously of value in Haus Kaus.[39]

When Tashi joined the Delhi team, the most formidable challenge of the Special Service Center revolved around Baba Gen Yeshi. What was happening to the money he received from the CIA? Annually, they were sending Baba Yeshi fifty thousand laks, and the Mustang general wasn't accounting for any of it.

In the early months of 1966, the CIA called a debriefing meeting in Darjeeling, in which all the Mustang commanders were summoned. Baba Yeshi was not invited. Tashi Chutter served as translator:

The Mustang commanders confided with the CIA that the big problem was that Baba Gen Yeshi had no system for accounting. And they also voiced a frustration or concern that the Dalai Lama's brother [Gyalo Thondup] had blind faith in Baba Gen Yeshi, which, in turn, made Baba Gen Yeshi arrogant and impossible to reason with.[40]

In the course of the debriefings, it became clear that the commanders were afraid to remove Baba Yeshi by force, because it wasn't a matter of just the one man: Baba Yeshi still had many followers in Mustang, and their power base was substantial. The commanders' recommendation was to send someone to Mustang who would, initially, take over fiscal authority from Baba Yeshi. The question was: who? It would have to be a man with enough moxie to stand up to Gen Yeshi and enough popularity to gain the support of the freedom fighters stationed in Mustang.

Gyalo Thondup suggested Wangdu. He was the nephew of the resistance's patron saint, Gompo Tashi and, as such, revered by the *Chushi-Gangdruk*. He had been in the first group trained by the CIA in Saipan. He had boots-on-the-ground experience. And he was fearless. Wangdu accepted the assignment, but not without misgivings.

---

[39]Tashi Chutter, interview with the author.
[40]Ibid.

Just before leaving for Mustang, Wangdu met with his brother Kalsang. He told Kalsang that he had been promoted to general and that he was honored. But he confided that he didn't really want to go to Mustang—that he would have preferred to fight the communists from a different location along the Tibetan border. *Wangdu told me, "The Dalai Lama has personally ordered me to go to Mustang. How can I disobey his order?" So my brother did what he was told to do.*[41]

Wangdu arrived in Mustang in 1967. Lhamo Tsering, Gyalo Thondup's right-hand man, accompanied him. Lhamo Tsering's presence was to be a temporary and symbolic one: He would serve as a reminder to Baba Gen Yeshi that Wangdu's selection had come from the highest level.

Baba Gen Yeshi was furious.[42]

Of course he was furious, McCarthy agrees. Baba Gen Yeshi had been caught with his hand in the cookie jar. All this time, there may have been an assumption on the CIA's part—particularly the New Delhi guys—that no Tibetan would do that to his own men. When the truth came out, Gyalo Thondup was incredibly shocked, as was Lhamo Tsering. Dharamsala was in deep denial. And as for Wangdu—bless his heart—it was no big surprise that he and Gen Yeshi didn't get along. They were total opposites. Wangdu was the complete patriot while Gen Yeshi was a man without honor. Think about it: Here was a man who was guilty of gross mismanagement of the payroll, of selling ammunition and other supplies to his own troops instead of giving it to them, of taking advantage of refugees as they came across the border, and of causing extensive friction with local civilians in the Mustang area. Frankly, I think Wangdu would have shot Gen Yeshi, if he had been given the chance.[43]

After General Wangdu's arrival, the initial restructuring seemed to go well. Baba Gen Yeshi was playing it cool, remaining for the most part in his comfortable home and working his beads. Wangdu headed north, determined to get the men back in shape so that they could resume collecting intelligence

---

[41]Kalsang Gyatotsang, interview with the author.

[42]Ibid.

[43]Roger E. McCarthy, interview with (and letters to) the author. McCarthy added, "In fact, I'm somewhat surprised Athar and Lhotse didn't pursue killing Baba Gen Yeshi. And certainly, had Gompo Tashi lived into that period—Gen Yeshi would have definitely been gone."

across the Tibetan border. Improvement within the thirteen resistance camps soon became evident.

Tinzing Jyurme, commander of one of the largest *magars*, was overjoyed by Wangdu's arrival. Suddenly, for the first time, his men had enough food. Whatever the Americans sent them, it now actually found its way to the rebels: good wool coats, warm shirts, shoes that fit, good mattresses, and top-quality arms and ammunition. The men's salaries were increased dramatically. Now they had enough money to trade with the locals. A few of the more enterprising men even opened up shops in local villages. Pensions for the oldest soldiers were established. Wangdu stopped the livestock rustling. Womanizing was no longer tolerated under his command, and the military training was professional. *He even built a small hospital for us. Before, if we got wounded, we would have to be taken all the way down the Kali Gandaki Valley to Pokhara, which was a week's ride away.*[44]

In the meantime, the full extent of Baba Gen Yeshi's corruption became evident: The Dalai Lama's Government-in-Exile summoned Baba Gen Yeshi to Dharamsala, where the *Kashag* ordered him to relinquish his command. According to Tashi Chutter, *The Cabinet tried to be nice. They told Gen Yeshi, "You have worked hard for the resistance. But now you are old. You should stay here and become a deputy cabinet member. Otherwise, the suppliers [the CIA] will cut off our resources. They don't want you anymore. Besides, we need someone younger, like Wangdu."*[45]

Gen Yeshi was in no position to reject their offer. He did, however, ask the *Kashag* to grant him one favor: Before he stepped down, he wanted to go to Delhi to take care of some personal affairs, after which he would return to Mustang and officially pass the baton to General Wangdu. The *Kashag* agreed to his plan.

But when he got down to Delhi, the Indians and the Americans immediately intervened. They feared that if he returned to Mustang, he would just stir up trouble again. The Americans could have ordered his arrest, but they just wanted to make sure he kept out of trouble, so they offered to lodge him in the

---

[44]Tinzing Jyurme, interview with the author.
[45]Tashi Chutter, interview with the author.

Mustang leaders under General Wangdu's command. Tinzing Jyurme, center. *(Collection of Norbu Dorje)*

safe house in M4 [Haus Kaus]. They told him he should write a Mustang history and they would help him.

But Baba said, "No, no. I would rather stay with Tashi Chutter in Lajpat Nagar." So that's how he came to live with me.[46]

Tashi Chutter's cohabitation with Baba Gen Yeshi went well for a while. But several months later, the CIA called Tashi to Darjeeling for a week. In the interim, Baba Gen Yeshi disappeared. When Tashi returned, he asked one of Gen Yeshi's servants the whereabouts of his master. The servant answered that Gen Yeshi was temporarily staying with a friend nearby, a man Tashi had met and who hailed back to Gen Yeshi's youth in Bathang. Because Gen Yeshi's personal effects were still in his house, Tashi wasn't unduly worried. Then, three days later, the Special Service Office received a message from Wangdu: Baba Gen Yeshi was back in Mustang.

Gen Yeshi had two loyal groups of soldiers still stationed in Mustang. Kelsang Bhuk commanded one company. Gen Yeshi ordered Bhuk to join forces

---

[46]Ibid.

with the other loyalist group—the Thirteenth Company—located far north, almost on the Tibetan border.

In the meantime, Wangdu and Lhamo Tsering were training new recruits in a different area. When Wangdu heard of Gen Yeshi's return, Wangdu pretended to be happy: He sent a message to Gen Yeshi, welcoming him back. He told him not to worry. But, of course, Wangdu knew trouble was brewing.

Tashi continues:

The real reason Baba Gen Yeshi had disobeyed everyone's orders and returned to Mustang was to retrieve all the money he had embezzled all those years. He had left two huge trunks full of money in a small village called Tserok, where an old loyal attendant of his was watching over it. Those are the only known trunks, but there were probably others I never learned about. What I do know is that Bruce Walker [instructor at Camp Hale who had been reassigned to the Special Services Office in Delhi] *told me that, in all, America had sent 1.5 million dollars to Mustang, and very little of that was ever accounted for. So anyway, once Baba Gen Yeshi had Bhuk's group join with the Thirteenth, he took his retrieved money and fled south to Pokhara, where he felt he would be out of harm's way.*[47]

This did not keep Gen Yeshi from causing Wangdu further trouble, however. General Wangdu had a group of couriers whose job was to carry messages up and down the Kali Gandaki Valley—from Pokhara to Mustang and back again. It was an extremely dangerous job. Even though Baba Gen Yeshi had left Mustang, the couriers still had to stay on the lookout for Gen Yeshi's most loyal men who, it was rumored, had stationed themselves within the Dhaulagiri Gorge. Dhaulagiri was the seventh-highest mountain in the world, and the gorge at its base was the deepest on the planet. The dark shadows cast by Dhaulagiri, and the countless recesses within the gorge, made for ideal ambushes.

One of Wangdu's couriers was a fearless youth by the name of Gyantso Tsering. Gyantso was on horseback working his way to Pokhara with a cloth bag containing a letter Wangdu had written to the *Kashag*. Gyantso had just entered the Dhaulagiri gorge when Baba Yeshi's men rode out from behind a

---

[47]Tashi Chutter, interview with the author.

Mount Dhaulagiri (26,811 feet), seen from the Kali Gandaki Valley, heading south into the gorges. *(Collection of the author)*

wall of boulders. Norbu Dorje, Gyantso's best friend and also a courier, recounts what happened next:

Baba Gen Yeshi's men completely surprised Gyantso. He didn't have a chance. They gunned him down. Then they stripped Gyantso of his mailbag and his valuables and rode away with his horse, leaving him there to rot in the gorge. Gyantso Tsering was the best man I ever knew—completely loyal to the resistance and the best rider we had in Mustang. I never thought he would be the one caught by Baba Gen Yeshi's gang. Just two weeks before he was murdered, I had my picture taken with him and the other couriers at our Nilgiri camp.[48]

Wangdu had had enough: It was time to bear down on the men in Mustang who still felt an allegiance to Baba Gen Yeshi. He combed his companies, culled Baba Gen Yeshi's followers, interrogated them, and either reassimi-

---

[48]Norbu Dorje, interview with the author.

lated them into the companies or imprisoned them until he could decide what to do with them. Unfortunately, one night, many of them escaped. Several skirmishes and incidents of arson followed. Some of the escapees were killed, but the majority joined up with the Thirteenth Company, Baba Gen Yeshi loyalists one and all. The Thirteenth Company was protected from Wangdu's men, because it was situated on the other side of Nadu-La, a very high mountain pass. Wangdu left them alone for the time being.

After Gyantso's murder, Baba Gen Yeshi realized he needed extra protection. Wangdu's capacity for seeking justice—if not revenge—was well known. Gen Yeshi was also aware that the Nepalese government had grown tired of the rebels in Mustang and wanted them out. Gen Yeshi and one hundred fifty of his followers gave themselves up to the Nepalese authorities in Pokhara. This marked the beginning of Gen Yeshi collaboration with the Nepalese Army. *He told the authorities that Wangdu was a very bad character,*

Couriers for General Wangdu's army. Gyantso Tsering, bottom row, middle; Norbu Dorje, top row, second from right. *(Collection of Norbu Dorje)*

Tashi Chutter said, *but that he, Gen Yeshi, would help them get rid of him.*[49] The Nepalese government gave Gen Yeshi a huge sum of money.[50] After this windfall, the monk-turned-general donned yet another hat: He set himself up as a businessman. Gen Yeshi established several carpet factories in Khathmandu. He also purchased a very big house in Bodhinath, just outside Khathmandu, where he and twenty of his lieutenants, attendants, and guards settled down to a life behind high walls.[51]

MUSTANG WAS DOOMED FROM ANOTHER DIRECTION: WASHING- ton, D.C.

Establishing diplomatic relations with China became a major priority for America's next president, Richard Nixon. In 1969, after Henry Kissinger met with Mao Tse-tung in China, the two countries inaugurated a policy of *rapprochement*. In the aftermath, the CIA announced to the Delhi team in Haus Kaus that they were no longer able to continue their support of the Mustang resistance. Why? Because Nixon and Kissinger wanted it that way.[52]

There has been considerable conjecture whether or not Mao actually told Kissinger that the Mustang rebels would have to be eliminated before the *rapprochement* could take effect. Many have argued that it was a foregone conclusion rather than the result of an actual conversation between the two politicos. Gyalo Thondup, however, insists that Mao spelled it out in no uncertain terms:

The CIA told me that the Chinese government had made two conditions in order for the United States to establish diplomatic relations with China: (1) the United States must cut off diplomatic relationship with the Republic of China— Taiwan, and (2) the United States must cut off all connections and all assistance for Tibet, including Mustang.[53]

---

[49]Tashi Chutter, interview with the author.
[50]Some estimates are as high as $500,000, but the amount has never been verified.
[51]Tashi Chutter, interview with the author.
[52]Ibid.
[53]Interview with Gyalo Thundop, *The Shadow Circus*, a documentary by Tenzing Sonam and Ritu Sarin. (Tenzing Sonam is the son of Lhamo Tsering.)

Holober and McCarthy, the two retired CIA agents who, in tandem, had headed the Tibetan Task Force, agreed with Gyalo's assessment. McCarthy says: *The idea that the Tibetan situation was* not *a caveat to rapprochement goes against everything I ever heard. The two clearly stated stipulations were Taiwan and Tibet. If Henry Kissinger now states otherwise, it is not a surprise, but the Chinese made their views crystal clear about our relationship with Taiwan and Tibet.*[54]

Regardless of Washington politics, the Americans who had been working with (and had become friends of) the Tibetans felt terrible about what could only be interpreted as a betrayal on their part. Frank Holober, Bruce Walker, John Greaney, and Ken Knaus all voiced their disheartened reactions, and Roger McCarthy said:

As a United States employee, it still smarts that we pulled out in the manner we did. . . . Granted, in many other operations, we did it even less gracefully and more abruptly.[55]

The intransigence of Nixon's relationship with Mao notwithstanding, the CIA tried to sweeten the pill as much as possible by providing a three-year period in which it would financially support *Chushi-Gangdruk* members, until they were able to support themselves in the civilian world. The nuts and bolts of this transition plan were largely left to Tashi Chutter to work out:

They [the CIA] *told me, "You still have fifteen hundred rebels in Mustang. You must write up a plan: How much money will it require to rehabilitate fifteen hundred people over a three-year period?" Lhamo Tsering and I set to work and we calculated that it would take ten thousand Indian rupees per man. The CIA approved our plan and we proceeded to implement it. We bought land that could be cultivated. We created business ventures for the rebels. We built the Annapurna Hotel, for instance, in Pokhara, Nepal, which is still popular with Western tourists who go to the Himalaya for trekking. Lhamo Tsering and I made many trips—he more than I—to Pokhara and Khathmandu to help get all these*

---

[54]Roger E. McCarthy. (Frank Holober, who was sitting next to him and also taking part in the interview, nodded in agreement.)
[55]Notes taken by the author during roundtable discussion by CIA Tibetan Task Force members in Bethesda, Maryland, 1999, at the home of John Greaney.

business ventures and Tibetan settlements started: carpet factories, tourist guest-houses, rehabilitation centers. Most of these places are still operational.[56]

While these efforts were underway, in 1971, the CIA called a meeting in Delhi and summoned General Wangdu. Coming with Wangdu were the commanders of his main fighting groups: Rara, Pachin, Chamdo Tsering Dorje, Derge Tondu Ponzo, and Tinzing Jyurme. Also in attendance were Tashi Chutter, Lhamo Tsering, and Gyalo Thondup.[57] It was in Delhi that Wangdu and his men learned of the CIA termination of support. Tinzing Jyurme remembers Wangdu's reaction as one of devastation:

Wangdu begged the CIA to continue their support. He was committed to fighting and had no plan to leave. But the CIA said they had no choice, because Mr. Kissinger was negotiating with the Chinese. Their hands were tied, they said. But they offered to help him start a new life in Pokhara. Wangdu tried to negotiate. He wanted to keep at least four hundred guerillas in Mustang to continue the fighting, but the CIA said they absolutely could not help Tibetans any longer.[58]

To make matters worse, the Chinese knew that the CIA was pressuring the freedom fighters to get out of Mustang. This prompted the Chinese to exert pressure on the Nepalese king to kick the resistance out of Mustang once and for all.

Other shifts in the political landscape conspired to work against the Mustang rebels. Nixon was said to have despised Mrs. Gandhi, the Prime Minister of India at the time. Henry Kissinger later said that Nixon's epithets for Mrs. Gandhi "were not always printable."[59] For her part, Mrs. Gandhi distrusted President Nixon because of his policy with Pakistan. Even if Nixon hadn't struck a deal with Chairman Mao, the idea of the CIA working in concert with India on any kind of covert activity became highly improbable, if not pure fantasy.

This included CIA assistance given to S. S. Uban's Special Frontier Force and his Tibetan Unit 22. Uban was in close contact with Mrs. Gandhi, primarily because a civil war in East Pakistan (the future Bangladesh) seemed imminent.

---

[56]Tashi Chutter, interview with the author.
[57]Ibid.
[58]Tinzing Jyurme, interview with the author.
[59]Henry Kissinger, *The White House Years,* 862.

Mrs. Gandhi wanted nothing to do with the Americans, of course. But by 1971, things were heating up in East Pakistan. There was a great upswell of insurgency in East Pakistan—local secessionists who wanted their own country. Civil war was at hand. The West Pakistani army replied by doing all sorts of mischief. A lot of mischief. They were completely and horribly controlling the Bangladeshis— raping their women, doing all kinds of unspeakable things that no real soldier does—but they did that as well as other crimes against humanity.

Mrs. Gandhi called me into her office and told me to report immediately to East Pakistan, carry out reconnaissance, and conduct whatever unconventional warfare I deemed necessary.

I asked her, "Will you allow me to take all my men with me, Tibetans and all?" She said, "Tibetans? Goodness! Will you be able to control them?"

"Yes," I said, "leave that to me. They can do anything I ask of them."[60]

Soon after the monsoon season was over, in the autumn of 1971, the Bangladesh War began. Two thousand Tibetan troops—mostly Khampas— accompanied General Uban to East Pakistan. They were utilized in small groups, ten or twelve soldiers per group. Their tactics were ones of unconventional warfare, and therefore they had no heavy weapons. They were armed with Bulgarian AK-47s and, in Uban's words, *very lethal knives.*[61]

Uban's main fighting force consisted of twenty thousand Bangladeshis. Their point of attack was in and around the Dacca area. The Tibetans were dropped off in different locations. The Tibetans were the first to go in. They charged in surprise attacks and quickly overran and destroyed Uban's designated targets. It was a crucial element of Uban's plan. Had the Tibetans failed in their mission, Uban was prepared to simply blow up Dacca. Fortunately, because of the Tibetans' success, genocide did not become a component of the Bangladesh War.

And do you know why my Unit 22 was so successful? Their reputation preceded them. The very idea of Tibetans struck terror in the hearts of the Pakistanis. They heard "Unit 22" and the whole bloody world was running away! To give you but one example: The first night of the attack, the Tibetans had a surprise attack on the main food source for the Pakistani army—it was about nine

---

[60]General S. S. Uban, interview with the author.
[61]Ibid.

o'clock at night. The Pakistanis left so quickly that they left their food, their weapons—even their shoes! I tell you, my Tibetans were natural guerillas, and their morale—you should have seen—sky-high! They felt they could take back Tibet tomorrow! Today, it's not like that, but back in 1971, there was nothing they couldn't do. They were thrilled that, finally, they had someplace to use their training. You see, the Chinese had not obliged them by invading India again, so, for the last eight years, their work had been limited to border patrol and a few infiltrations into Tibet to wiretap various Chinese army installations—all very well and good from an Indian point of view, but not satisfying for soldiers who wanted to kill Chinese.

But here is the point: The Bangladeshis owe their independence—at least in part—to the Tibetans. You don't hear anyone talking about that, do you?[62]

SOON AFTER THE BANGLADESH WAR, NEPALI–TIBETAN RELATIONS rapidly deteriorated. King Mahendra, who, in the past, had handled the Mustang question by simply looking the other way, died in 1972. The heir apparent, Prince Birendra, was eager to endear himself to China. He had made a trip to Beijing the year before and—now that he had become king—wanted the Tibetans out of Mustang at all costs. By 1973, 20 percent of Nepal's much-needed foreign aid was coming from Beijing. Finally, toward the end of 1973, at the insistence of the Chinese, the young King Birendra publicly demanded that the Mustang guerillas surrender or face the consequences.

Tinzing Jyurme described the reaction in Mustang:

I had been up there since the very beginning. What would you do if you had spent the last twelve or thirteen years freezing your ass off? We were ready to fight. We were willing to fight the whole Nepalese army, if we had to. We weren't afraid of the Nepalese, and they knew it.

It was Wangdu who calmed us down. He reminded us that there were many thousands of Tibetan refugees living in Pokhara and Khathmandu—many were relatives of ours and all of them were guests of the Nepalese government. And

---

[62]Ibid. For a detailed look at the Bangladesh War, see General Uban's *Phantoms of Chittagong: The "Fifth Army" in Bangladesh.*

there were a lot of Nepalese who weren't very happy about our presence anyway.
If we fought the Nepalese Army, we would only create additional hardships for
our families. We knew Wangdu was right, but I also knew that Wangdu would
never just give up.[63]

Whatever the feelings of the rebels, King Birendra's ultimatum was temporarily—quite literally—put on ice. The brutal Mustang winter arrived, and
the accompanying snowfall closed off passage into and out of Mustang.
Nothing could be acted upon until the spring of 1974. But even after the
March and April thaws had cleared the mountain passes, Wangdu refused to
initiate surrender.

It is possible that he was waiting for some cue from the Government-in-
Exile. It is equally possible—during that last, desolate winter—that he made
the decision to go out in glory rather than admit defeat. Over the last fifteen
years, Wangdu had experienced Tibet's organized resistance being squeezed
and shoved around by every conceivable outside force: First they had been
pushed out of their own country by the PLA; then they had been refused
sanction while on Indian soil; then they were abandoned by the Americans
because, apparently, Nixon wanted to make friends with Wangdu's mortal
enemies, the communists; then they had been betrayed by the vampiric Baba
Gen Yeshi—a fellow Tibetan and, even worse, a fellow Khampa; and now,
finally, Wangdu's army was being evicted by the Nepalese. The only political
force that hadn't turned on him was the Dalai Lama's government in
Dharamsala. And who knew how long that would last? What were Wangdu's
options? He could always join Uban's Unit 22, but he had already turned
down that offer years before, because he saw that as an Indian ploy to use
rebels for their own purposes, not the Tibetans'. He was a warrior. He had no
other skills. Wangdu's brother, Kalsang Gyatotsang, said that, during the icy
gloom of that last winter, no one knew what Wangdu was really thinking. But
one thing was certain: To imagine Wangdu simply giving up and settling
down in the pacific squalor of a refugee camp, was unthinkable.[64]

---

[63]Tinzing Jyurme, interview with the author.
[64]Kalsang Gyatotsang, interview with the author.

On April 19, 1974, several Nepalese police paid a visit to Lhamo Tsering, who was staying in Pokhara at the recently opened, resistance-owned Anna-purna Hotel. The Nepalese were quite deferential. They were there to invite Lhamo to a meeting at the local constabulary; his presence would be much appreciated. Lhamo Tsering went with the police. Once he entered the police station, he was surrounded and thrown into jail. Lhamo Tsering's connections in both Mustang and Dharamsala were well known. The Nepalese intended to use him as ransom: his life in exchange for Wangdu's surrender. After Lhamo Tsering's arrest, the word went out: Anyone helping the Mustang rebels would now be treated as an enemy of the Nepalese government.[65]

A few weeks later, in May, Baba Gen Yeshi had a meeting in Khathmandu with the brass of the Nepalese Army. He announced that he was prepared to identify all the Mustang commanders and provide the army with exact locations of the commanders' respective *magars*. (Although the amount is not known, the Nepalese monarchy rewarded him for his services.) A week later, forty-eight of Baba Gen Yeshi's followers, acting as guides, led army officials to Mustang and instructed them where the *magars* could be located.[66]

Wangdu's spies kept him apprised of movement to the south, but, in the meantime, Wangdu's scouts also reported that a small contingent of Chinese troops had crossed into Mustang from the north—dangerously close to where Tinzing Jyurme's group had its headquarters. Wangdu's worst fear had become a reality: The Nepalese Army was now working in concert with the Chinese. And to make matters worse, at Jomsom, the southernmost town in Mustang, the Nepalese Army built a little helicopter port, while ten thousand of their troops marched up the Kali Gandaki Valley. It was a Sino-Nepali trap.

General Wangdu held an emergency meeting. He told his commanders that they had no choice but to strike a deal with the Nepalese before the PLA made their next move from the north. They would surrender half of their weapons and ammunition on the condition that the Nepalese released Lhamo Tsering, who was still in the Pokhara jail. Upon his release, they would surrender the rest of their weapons.[67]

---

[65]Tashi Chutter, interview with the author.
[66]Tinzing Jyurme, interview with the author.
[67]Ibid.

Wangdu sent an underling down to Jomsom to present the plan to the Nepalese general. The general agreed to Wangdu's plan. As promised, two days later, half the rebels surrendered their weapons in Jomsom. Wangdu waited for the news that Lhamo Tsering had been freed. The news never came. The Nepalese Army reneged on their deal.

In the meantime, the GOI was pressuring the Dalai Lama to intervene. If war broke out in Mustang, the Dalai Lama—a guest of India—would be blamed for the conflict, not only by the Indian government but also by the Nepalese government, which was host to many thousands of Tibetan refugees as well. The Dalai Lama was left with no choice. He recorded a message on a tape recorder, gave the tape to P. T. Takla, who then hand-delivered the tape to the Mustang resistance. From *magar* to *magar*, Talka gathered the men and played the tape. In the recording, the Dalai Lama asked the rebels to surrender. He applauded the freedom fighters' motivation but told them that, whatever their personal feelings may have been, the fact was that their continued presence in Mustang was only creating negative results—further resistance was useless. Tinzing Jyurme remembers when the tape was played at his camp:

Many of us cried when we heard his words. In our hearts we couldn't go against the Dalai Lama's wishes, but neither could we surrender after already losing so much. Besides, if we surrendered, what would the Nepalese do to us? They had already betrayed us over the release of Lhamo Tsering. We knew all too well that the Nepalese word meant nothing.

Rather than go against the Dalai Lama, some of the guys committed suicide. Pachin, one of the five commanders, cut his own throat. He did it with so much power that his head fell off. Tsewang Gyapo, my personal secretary, also killed himself. He climbed up to the top of an old rock building that was high above the river and just jumped without saying anything to anyone. There were many who took their own lives. Others just went mad. They wandered around crying, like they didn't even know where they were.[68]

And in the meantime, the PLA moved south while Baba Gen Yeshi's guides led the Nepalese Army north. According to Tinzing Jyurme, Wangdu was more afraid of the Baba Gen Yeshi's men than he was of the Nepalese or the

---

[68]Ibid.

PLA: *Wangdu knew that if he surrendered, the Nepalese would let Baba Gen Yeshi's men have their way with him. But I don't want to give you the wrong impression. At that point, I don't think Wangdu cared if he lived or died. What was really bothering him was that he had certain things he didn't want the Nepalese to get their hands on: an American wireless and important records, including ones that involved the CIA.*[69]

The Dalai Lama's tape had persuaded most of the rebels to surrender. Group by group, they headed south and turned in their arms at Jomsom, leaving only three *magars* left: Wangdu's, Rara's, and Tinzing Jyurme's.

The Nepalese closed in on Tinzing Jyurme's *magar*, which was high in the mountains. A Nepalese messenger arrived at his camp, warning that the Nepalese Army would storm the camp if he didn't surrender. Tinzing Jyurme persuaded the Nepalese to give him three days so that Rara and Wangdu's troops could join him, thus creating a much larger surrender. Wangdu and Rara's groups arrived at Tinzing's *magar*. The people of the local village were brought to the camp and given most of the arms and ammunition. They took the heavy load down the mountain to the Nepalese. *Wangdu also sent along a note for the Nepalese general. It said, "Come up to Tenzing Jyurme's camp with your personal guards—no more than forty soldiers—you and I will have dinner together and discuss my surrender in a civilized manner." But the Nepalese betrayed us again. He came up the hill the next morning with four hundred armed troops.*[70]

Wangdu and thirty of his men bolted from camp. Thirty more troops formed a line with their guns trained on the Nepalese.

And then something very strange happened. The Nepalese general didn't do anything to stop Wangdu. Maybe the general was under orders not to fire the first shot—I don't know. Whatever the reason, Wangdu got away with a well-

---

[69]Ibid. McCarthy agreed with Tinzing Jyurme. In a letter to the author, McCarthy said that Wangdu had key documents with him, "including not only records of the Mustang force, but names of those who had helped the resistance efforts in various ways, plus financial records . . . Wangdu was intent upon reaching India with this valuable cargo. That was his main motivation for making a run for it. He was not the kind of man to concern himself with personal safety. He sure as hell was not afraid to fight the Chinese nor, for that matter, anyone else."
[70]Tinzing Jyurme, interview with the author.

armed group with the Nepalese just looking on. Then the Nepalese retreated back down the slope.[71]

Rara and Tinzing got away, too, along with six of their bodyguards. They caught up with Wangdu that night. They pored over maps. Wangdu calculated that it would take him eighteen days to head west, through the Dolpo region, and, from there, reach the Indian border. But in order to do that, he would need Rara and Tinzing to stall the Nepalese general. They were to go back to him and explain that Wangdu insisted on surrendering in a traditional, Tibetan manner: Wangdu, Rara, and Tinzing would meet the general in Jomsom with a herd of yaks and sheep to be slaughtered; the Tibetans and Nepalese would then sit down to big feast, thereby avoiding dishonor done to anyone. Wangdu's real plan, however, was to flee west with his documents, and, once safely in India, he would negotiate a peaceful settlement for the remaining guerillas in Mustang.

The next morning, Rara and Tinzing said good-bye to Wangdu and rode south, to intercept the Nepalese general. It was the last time they would see Wangdu.

In Jomsom, the Nepalese general fell for the ploy. Herding livestock was a laborious and slow process in the Himalaya. For twelve days, the general awaited Wangdu's arrival without complaint.

But on the thirteenth day, Nepalis spied Wangdu's group in Dolpo—very far to the west. The Nepalese ran to the local authorities, who, in turn, radioed Jomsom. Rara and Tinzing were immediately arrested. The general told them they would not be harmed but, rather, helicoptered to Pokhara, where they could join other Tibetan refugees in the resettlement camp. Rara took Tinzing off to the side and told him, *"This is just another trick. Remember Lhamo Tsering? You know we're going to be put in prison—or worse—don't you? When we get on the helicopter, I'm going to pull my knife on the pilot and make him fly us to India. If he doesn't do what I say, I'll kill him." I begged Rara to calm down, and I reminded him that we had both promised Wangdu that we would not cause trouble until he reached India.*[72]

---

[71]Ibid.
[72]Ibid.

General Wangdu three weeks before his death.
(Collection of Kalsang Gyatotsang)

Reluctantly, Rara promised to be good and boarded the helicopter without incident. The moment the aircraft landed in Pokhara, Rara and Tinzing were surrounded by police and thrown into jail with Lhamo Tsering—just as Rara had predicted.

By late August, Wangdu and his men had reached the Jumla region of Nepal—very mountainous and very near the Indian border. In the interim, flight had been hellish. Their route darted back and forth over the Tibetan border, including several skirmishes with small units of PLA. At one point, Wangdu pulled up short at a spot overlooking a large Chinese encampment: He was forced to backtrack deep into the Nepalese mountains, which cost him time he could ill afford to lose. They had ridden hard the whole way, and his men were near exhaustion.

But in late August, the end was in sight. Wangdu had one last mountain pass to cross—Tinker-La.[73] On the far side was India. What Wangdu didn't know as he made his last push upward was that he was riding into a trap. The spies in Dolpo had tipped off the Nepalese; given his location, his most likely exit would be Tinker-La. Baba Gen Yeshi's men were about a day's march behind Wangdu; the Chinese were just to the north of him; and the Nepalese army had set up a large ambush group toward the summit of Tinker-La.

The sky was cloudless—visibility went on forever. Wangdu and his men rounded a mountain bend and, up ahead, less than a mile away, soared the summit of Tinker-La. The men wanted to stretch their legs before going to the summit. Wangdu allowed most of the men to dismount, but took six others ahead to search for forage and water for the horses. The rebels who had been left behind watched their leader disappear over a small rise. A few seconds later, they heard gunfire—heavy gunfire. Without saying a word, they remounted their horses and galloped toward the firefight. *They got to the crest of the hill just in time to see that all of Wangdu's men were down and that Wangdu—the only one still on horseback—was charging straight into the enemy fire.*[74]

The Tibetans, who had come up from behind, fired on the Nepalese position, but they were heavily outnumbered. Wangdu was shot off his horse. His horse rode off without him. All day the rebels kept up the fight, but—one by one—they were picked off by the Nepalese above them. Finally, the sixteen men who weren't yet wounded abandoned their horses and circled away from the Nepalese. They scaled Tinker-La from a different direction, where a recess in the mountain hid them from view. In that way, on foot, they safely reached India territory. Of the original group, they were the only ones who survived the ambush.

Wangdu was dead, lying in a heap in a gully.[75]

I'm not sure if Baba Gen Yeshi was actually flown in by helicopter to identify Wangdu's body, or if it was just one of his lieutenants. Either way, Wangdu's body was correctly identified and flown down to Khathmandu.

---

[73]Eighteen thousand feet above sea level.
[74]Tinzing Jyurme, interview with the author.
[75]Ibid.

King Birendra made a big show of his big victory. Right in the center of town, he set up a large tent so that the public could see what the Nepalese Army had done. He had all of Wangdu's personal effects spread out on tables: his rings, his wristwatch, his gua, his sword, his rifle, the wireless, some personal photographs he had carried with him—everything.

But the big prize was Wangdu himself. King Birendra put his corpse on display. That's what the Nepalese crowds came to see. Thousands came and filed by his mutilated body—this went on for several days before the stench got so bad that they had to close down the show.[76]

Not many blocks away, Lhamo Tsering, Rara, Tinzing Jyurme, and five other captured guerilla leaders sat in a dark Khathmandu prison. They would remain there for the next seven years.

Just across town, Baba Gen Yeshi settled into a life of urban comfort, surrounded by a score of soldiers who catered to his every need. His business ventures thrived. He even created a little museum open to the public, which housed first-rate Tibetan artifacts. Refugees could go in and revisit possessions that had once been theirs.

The resistance was over.

---

[76]Ibid.

Maitreya: the Future Buddha *(Jamyang of Amdo)*

EPILOGUE

WHERE IS TIBET?

D r. Lobsang Tensing was born in Kham in 1956.
        At the age of three, he was recognized as a *tulku*—a reincarnation of a famous lama. When the Chinese discovered that the locals venerated Lobsang, they carried the child to the town square and, in front of the assembled village, screamed at him: "If you are a *tulku,* then you must be able to tell the future. So predict the future for us!" The three-year-old could say nothing. *I grew up believing I was a bad boy. It was the only logical explanation why my parents didn't protect me from the communists. I couldn't understand that they were helpless. I spent my childhood hiding from adults. I was afraid they might expect me to say something.*[1]

Lobsang was singled out by the Chinese for another reason. Soon after the Dalai Lama escaped in 1959, Lobsang's father joined the resistance alongside a famous incarnate by the name of Pula Lama. The two resistance fighters were captured three months later. They were subjected to *thamzing* and

---

[1]Dr. Lobsang Tensing, interview with the author.

thrown into prison for the next eight years. Sometimes, at night, Lobsang would hear the elders whispering about the "good old days," when people didn't commit suicide. Lobsang found that hard to believe: Suicide seemed like a permanent fixture of Khampa existence.

In 1966, the Cultural Revolution was introduced to Kham. Lobsang's father and his compatriot, Pula Lama, were released from prison that year, but they were still regarded as "enemies of the people." They were dragged to the town square, labeled "Black Hats," and forced to wear black dunce hats at all times. The villagers were afraid to consort with "Black Hats," so the entire family was ostracized.

Then the Red Guards came to Lobsang's district. The local monastery, which had been stripped of its valuables but was still standing, was now razed to the ground—the monks expelled and forced to take wives. *Thamzing,* which had become an intermittent horror, was now utilized with renewed vigor and dreaded regularity. Lobsang, who was now ten, had long since denied that he was a *tulku,* but there was nothing he could do about his family's "reactionary" history.

Dr. Lobsang Tensing
(*Collection of the author*)

The best thing I could do for myself was to just stay out of the way of the Red Guards, who had now taken over the local communist organization. The Red Guards had just introduced something that really shocked us. We Tibetans were now encouraged to criticize the local leaders of the communist party. According to the Red Guards, it was part of Mao's cleansing strategy: Mao wanted to see who was really loyal to him and who wasn't. But, to some extent, the Red Guard's activities backfired on the Chinese. When we heard the Chinese speaking against other Chinese, we became encouraged to rally and criticize the party leaders as well. It was spontaneous and very widespread. Most

*everyone—throughout the twenty-two districts of Kham—was involved. It was the
Red Guards who brought on the new wave of resistance of 1966.*[2]

Khampas stormed the local Chinese garrison. Armed with nothing but
swords, the Tibetans prevailed, killing all the PLA troops and running off
with their rifles and ammunition. Thus armed, they rode into the neighboring district and took over its garrison. Overnight, the revolt spread to every
district in Kham. It lacked the organization of the old *Chushi-Gangdruk*. The
rebels hid in the mountains and attacked small units of PLA whenever the
opportunity arose. But there was neither the time nor a communication network available to put a more encompassing resistance together. In any case,
tens of thousands of PLA were swiftly deployed throughout Kham, and the
rebellion was brutally suppressed.

*The PLA came into the local villages at night and dragged people out into the
streets. "Where is your brother? Where is your son? Where is your uncle?"—that
sort of thing. They handcuffed relatives of the rebels, beat them, dragged them to
the main square, and used them as hostages. Most of the rebels turned themselves in after that. But the Chinese were still not satisfied. In our village, there
were thirteen people not yet accounted for. One of them was Pula Lama, the
"Black Hat" who had been imprisoned with my father. The Chinese really
wanted him. His wife and his four sons were with him.*

*So here's what the Chinese did. They caught two local rebels, stripped them
naked, and hung them by their armpits in the town square. They hung them so
they were facing each other—almost touching each other. They built fires under
their feet. The two friends screamed and cried in agony. I saw their blood dripping
into the fire. The stench was terrible. The smoke rising up choked them. If they
fainted from pain, they were brought down until they regained consciousness.
Then they strung them up again. Finally, the poor guys told the Chinese where
our lama, Pula Lama, and his family were hiding. (Of course, everybody in the
village had known all along where they were hiding, but no one had talked.)*[3]

The next morning, the Chinese strapped them onto the backs of ponies—

---

[2]Ibid.
[3]Ibid.

their hands were broken so they couldn't hold the reins—and made them lead PLA troops to Pula Lama's location in the mountains.

They surrounded Pula Lama's hideout during the night. At daybreak, a fusillade of bullets sprayed Pula Lama's *magar*. The rebels returned fire as best they could but they were soon overwhelmed. One by one, Pula Lama and his family were killed. The last four men to survive finally threw down their weapons and came out with their hands up. The PLA marched them to the nearest cliff and pushed them over the edge.

The PLA triumphantly reentered Lobsang's village. They had Pula Lama's bullet-riddled body with them. They propped the corpse up in the town square and made the entire village witness Pula Lama's *thamzing*, as if he were still alive.

It was truly grotesque. All day long we were forced at gunpoint to yell at Pula Lama's corpse. We had to belittle Pula Lama for all the crimes he had committed against "the people." Since Pula Lama hadn't done any bad things to "the people," we just had to make things up. And then it got more grotesque. We had to ask the corpse if he was sorry for the things he had done. And when the corpse didn't respond, we had to say, "You see how stupid you are? Even now you won't admit to your mistakes! Do you feel happy now?"[4]

It didn't end there. More people were arrested—brought in from all the neighboring villages. Now the inevitable *thamzings* were followed by execution. Lobsang calculated that nearly one-third of the male population of his district died in public executions in 1968–69.

This is how they would do it. There were three Chinese for every "enemy" to be murdered. Two guys would hold the Tibetan's arms on both sides. The third guy was the beater, kicker, and executioner. By the time the Tibetan was ready to be killed, he or she would already be barely conscious because they had been so badly pistol-whipped. They were turned around and shot in the back of the head.

I remember how the Chinese never watched the execution. They watched us. They seemed to savor the reaction of the family members and friends. It was truly sadistic. It was like they wanted to remember every detail of our sadness.[5]

By the early 1970s, the Chinese seemed to have run out of "enemies of the

---

[4]Ibid.
[5]Ibid.

people." In any case, the public executions ended, and the Cultural Revolution was over. In the meantime, those like Lobsang, who survived, had no idea what was happening in the outside world. They knew that the Dalai Lama was safe but, beyond that, their information was reduced to whispered rumors.

But it seemed wiser to never put any trust in these rumors. Our hope rested with the Americans. There was always this general belief that the Americans would one day save us. We never doubted that they would come, but we did wonder what specific problem had occurred that kept them from freeing us.

To show you how prevalent this hope was, whenever an "undesirable" sympathizer was arrested, the first thing the Chinese would ask him was, "Where are your Americans now?"

Maybe we loved the Americans so much because the Chinese hated them so much. But I think part of it had to do with us being Buddhists. We believe in a doctrine that leans toward individuality and democracy, so maybe America just seemed like a natural philosophical ally to us.

I've learned since then that, in the American universities at that time, Mao Tse-tung was very popular among the students. Why was that? Did no one tell them how many millions of people in Tibet and in his own country he killed? Maybe they were just as ignorant of us as we were of them.[6]

In 1979, Lobsang's family moved to Lhasa. Lobsang was twenty-three. He entered the Tibetan medical college to become a traditional Tibetan doctor. He graduated eight years later, in 1985. It seemed to Lobsang that, at long last, the most harrowing events of his life were well behind him and that he could settle down into the respectable vocation of medicine.

But by that time, there was a new wave of resistance surfacing in Lhasa.

On September 27, 1987, a few monks from Drepung Monastery came into Lhasa, performed three *choras* around the perimeter of the old Barkhor District, and shouted two treasonous words: "Free Tibet!"

The city was galvanized.

We Tibetans watched in a kind of astonished fascination—particularly people my age—because we had never envisioned such bravery. We joined in with the monks, and suddenly there was a huge demonstration.

I think the Chinese were just as stunned as we were. They were completely

---

[6]Ibid.

unprepared for that kind of outburst. After we circled Old Town three times, we ended up at the main governmental office, and the Chinese didn't do anything. When evening came, we all went home, very excited and happy—and scared. We didn't know what the Chinese would do next.

Four days later, on October 1, a few hundred monks from Sera Monastery came into Lhasa to have their own demonstration. There had been five days to think about what had happened. To protest openly was such a wonderful new thing. I think we all had it in the back of our minds that now was the time to let the Chinese know what we really thought of them and that maybe, just maybe, they might leave.

This time, however, the Chinese were ready for us.

Lhasa turned into a battlefield. People were murdered. Buildings were burned down, the police fired into the crowds; many monks were arrested, beaten, and thrown in prison. By the time I joined the demonstration, the Chinese had already captured the Sera monks and taken them away to a jail. That's where we all headed. We surrounded the jail. There were thousands of us. We demanded the monks' release, but the Chinese refused, so we set the building on fire. We set military vehicles in front of the jail on fire as well. The military police arrived in full force. They opened fire on us.

Right in front of me, a man had been struck by a bullet and went down. Several of us lifted him up and shouted protests even louder. Two more guys were shot right next to me. Since I was a doctor, I began doing anything I could to help— stanching the bleeding, moving the wounded to the side—anything I could think of. After the shooting stopped, many of us helped the wounded to hospital.[7]

By five o'clock in the afternoon, all the crowds had dispersed. People returned to their homes wondering what would happen next. On October 2, the streets were unusually quiet. No one went out.

On October 3, the Chinese struck back. During the second demonstration, there had been numerous Chinese photographers planted in the crowd. The police were now rounding up all the protesters who had been recognized in photographs. People were being dragged away all over the city, but monks at Sera Monastery were especially hard hit. Every day after that, even more people were thrown into jail.

---

[7]Ibid.

Lhasa riots of October 1987. A monk who suffered serious burns while rescuing prisoners in a burning police station is lifted in victory. *(Jampa Tenzin © John Ackerly/Tibet Images)*

All the news was bad: Yesterday they got so-and-so; today they took away so-and-so. Each additional piece of news made me more afraid. I had no idea if I had been photographed or not. And there was no knowing what the Chinese were doing to my friends. Under torture, anyone would talk. I knew that I might be picked up at any moment.

On the 15th, I heard from an old friend from medical school. Since college, he had joined the city police department, and he left a note at my parents' room. The note said that I was in several of the photos, that I had been identified, that the police were looking for me, and that I should meet him at his place immediately.[8]

Lobsang's friend convinced him that his only option was to flee to India. Hiding out in his friend's room, Lobsang cut off his long hair, dressed in a trader/businessman's disguise, and bought fake identity papers. He didn't

---

[8]Ibid.

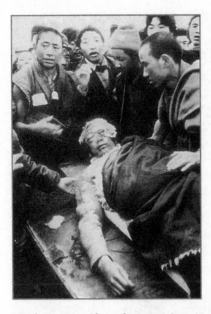

March 5, 1988, Lhasa demonstration: A Tibetan protester shot in the head by a Chinese soldier, from the rooftop of a building. Later the man died. *(Office of Information and International Relations, Dharamsala)*

contact his parents, hoping that their ignorance would protect them. On October 22, he climbed into the back of a truck that took him to the Nepalese border. At the border, he handed his false papers to the PLA cadre and was waved through. Once inside Nepal, he hired a local to guide him over the mountains. Two weeks later, he walked into the city limits of Khathmandu.

Later, I came to India where I live today. I never saw my family again.

I want people to hear my story, because—now that I live in India and have read Western newspapers and learned so many things that I didn't know while I was in Tibet—I want Westerners to understand that the Chinese are still lying to the world. They now say that, yes, bad things happened during the Cultural Revolution, but now everything is fine in Tibet.

Everything is not fine in Tibet. I lived in Tibet after the Cultural Revolution, and I can say that there was no freedom for me or for my family. I can never forget how many Tibetans lost their lives, their families, their property—everything. I can never forget the cruelty of the Chinese. The Chinese always looked down on the Tibetans. This has not changed. And there have been additional waves of resistance since I escaped. The year after I left, there was another uprising in Lhasa and there have been others that were not covered by the Western newspapers.

The Chinese still think Tibetans are barbarians. That has not changed. And so, their treatment of us has not changed. The only thing that has changed is that Tibet has been completely swallowed by the Chinese—like a big fish swallows a small fish. Tibet is inside the belly of China. That's where Tibet is.[9]

---

[9]Ibid.

. . .

DR. TENSING MAY HAVE BEEN SPEAKING METAPHORICALLY, BUT IF
you look at a modern map of Asia, you will see that the fish imagery is literal.
Within China is a section called "T.A.R." (Tibetan Autonomous Region).
T.A.R. is a significantly reduced version of Tibet. Many of the places written
about in this history are not included in T.A.R. Jyekundo, Derge, Kanze,
Lithang, Markham, Bathang, Dartsendo, the entire Golok District, and much
of Amdo—the most populous areas of ethnic Tibet—all have disappeared
into the belly of mainland China.

What this means politically is that even if the Dalai Lama were able to
return to Tibet, most of the aging warriors (and their descendants) would be
left out of the loop. Once again, the Chinese ploy of "divide and conquer" has
worked in their favor.

There are now more Chinese living in Tibet than there are Tibetans, making the indigenous population a minority in their own country. Children
who are sent to Tibetan-speaking schools are automatically excluded from
higher education and meaningful occupations. Killing a language is the best
possible way to kill a culture: Parents must choose between either bequeath-
ing their national heritage to their kids, or providing them with the opportunity to survive in a Chinese-speaking world.

Many of the nearly six thousand monasteries destroyed by the communists
have now been (on a modest scale) rebuilt—not by the Chinese, but by the
Tibetans themselves. This provides the Chinese with an excellent propaganda
tool for Westerners: "See? There is freedom of religion in Tibet. Just look at
those monks!" Bringing tourists into Tibet—a major economic consideration for the Central Government—means creating showcases of religious tol-
erance. But behind the facade, the monks are continuously monitored, and
the populations of monasteries are kept to a fraction of the pre-communist
numbers. Samye Monastery, for instance: In the old days, thousands of
monks practiced and studied there; today, 175 monks are allowed to live on
the premises. The moment a monastery shows signs of *spiritual* success, of
building up a local following, the place is unceremoniously shut down—the
monks and nuns expelled. Monasteries are for tourists. The holiest building
in Tibet—the Jokhang in Lhasa—is the ideal kind of Chinese "Tibetan" mon-

astery. It's a great moneymaker. Westerners pay admission fees, and much higher fees if they want to take pictures inside. The Chinese even have strategically placed vending machines on the rooftop of the Jokhang so that tourists can drink Coca-Cola while enjoying the view: a modern, typically ugly Chinese concrete sprawl replete with smog, karaoke bars, and brothels.

The raping of Tibet's natural resources, the continuation of high numbers of political prisoners, the never-ending state of dread that hangs over the Tibetan people is not going to go away any time soon. Short of a Chinese economic meltdown, or the kind of implosion the USSR suffered in the early 1990s, it seems unlikely Tibet will ever expel itself from the belly of China—particularly when every Western corporation is investing as much money into China as it possibly can, in an effort to cash in on the purchasing power of a billion-plus Chinese. The question is, if the moment ever arrives—if Tibetans once again take control of their country—will there be anything of the old Tibet left to salvage?

Another question is, what will happen to the younger generations of the Diaspora who have grown up *outside* Tibet? Some are highly motivated, retain a strong sense of Tibetan identity, and have organized themselves

May 1990: PLA soldier on the rooftop of a Lhasa building. His machine gun is aimed at the Jokhang Temple, the holiest building in Tibet. *(Office of Information and International Relations, Dharamsala)*

into groups that lead protests—often in front of various Chinese embassies throughout the world. They have found their voice. They seem resolved to fight the good fight while earning college degrees that will afford them the means to financially better themselves and their families. When I interviewed these young people, I always asked what they would do if the Chinese ever allowed the Dalai Lama to return to Tibet. Would they return to Tibet with him? The youth from Central Tibet said, "Absolutely," but the Khampas, Amdoans, and Goloks were doubtful. The T.A.R. boundaries preclude any hope for autonomy in their homeland. Lithang, Derge, and Kumbum, for instance, would remain "Chinese," even if the Dalai Lama did resume authority in Lhasa. Eastern Tibetans are political orphans, and they know it. Like their forefathers, they would not be able to count on a Lhasan government to protect them.

"The Meeting in 1936 Between Zhu De and dGe-stag Tulku," Kanze school, 1980. The Chinese have adopted the traditional religious Tibetan art form of *thankgha* painting for propaganda purposes. Instead of using images of Buddhist iconography, this painting depicts a lama who collaborated with the communists during the Long March and is therefore elevated to godlike status. *(From Robert Barnett and Shirin Akiner,* Resistance and Reform in Tibet, *Indiana University Press)*

There are many other youths, however, who have completely lost their sense of identity. On one of my trips to a refugee camp—this was in India—a teenager in a punk outfit, who was having difficulty standing up and keeping his eyes open, accosted me. Even in his heroin daze, his English was fairly good. He grabbed my elbow and said he was trying to get to Dharamsala. His story was almost convincing: He wanted to see the Dalai Lama and all he needed was eighty-four more rupees for bus fare. Would I help him? I told him that since I knew that the Dalai Lama was currently in Germany, it would be better if he waited until His Holiness returned to India before attempting such a trip. He shrugged and weaved toward three European backpackers who were just then approaching the entrance to the camp.

The next morning, I returned to the camp, and again the same Tibetan addict waylaid me and offered the same story as the day before—only this time he needed 130 rupees for bus fare to Dharamsala. I told him that he should get his story straight, adding, "You told me all this yesterday, don't you remember? It's bad that you are using the Dalai Lama as an excuse to score drugs." He scratched his neck and looked at me for a moment, then said, "Fuck you!" and stormed off.

He, too, is part of Tibet's future.

IN 1999, I INTERVIEWED BABA GEN YESHI IN HIS UPPER-CLASS compound in Khathmandu. I had to work for it. For three days, my buddy Jamyang Lama went to his house and entreated his nephew—who acted as

Chinese tourists in Lhasa, 1993. The plane is a MiG-19 put on display by the communists. *(Nancy Jo Johnson)*

Baba Gen Yeshi's bouncer—to let me speak to him. It was a hard-sell job, because the nephew was wary of Westerners. It was only after he was told that I was a Buddhist that the interview was secured.

I went to Gen Yeshi's house for a precondition meeting with the nephew. Before I would be allowed upstairs, I would (1) promise to limit the visit to twenty minutes—Baba Gen Yeshi meditated around the clock and did not like to be disturbed; and (2) not ask anything that might upset his equanimity.

I agreed to the stipulations without having any intention of sticking to my promises.

With Jamyang acting as my translator, we were led up a torturous, twisting stairwell and ushered into Baba Gen Yeshi's innermost refuge—his altar room. It was quite large. Magnificent *thangkhas* hung on every wall, and glass-enclosed cabinets housed an extraordinary collection of antique statues—many of which I assumed to have been confiscated by him during his "booty" years in Mustang.

The nephew left us for a moment and then returned with his famous uncle.

He was frail and shrunken. He almost disappeared under his monk's robes. He had a *mala* in his arthritic hand, which he never stopped fingering during my interview.

Baba Gen Yeshi had one of the saddest faces I ever saw, and the devastation therein quite disarmed and rather paralyzed my thirst for vilification.

I don't know what I had expected—I suppose I thought I would charge into his house and make him suffer for his transgressions with my penetrating interrogation—but instead, I was completely thrown by the sadness and defeat emanating from his eyes.

I was shocked at myself. The questions that came out of my mouth were lame and became increasingly amateurish as my precious twenty minutes ticked by—the nephew listening very carefully to every question Jamyang posed on my behalf. Finally the nephew tapped the face of his watch and indicated that it was time for me to leave.

I asked one last question: *Baba Gen Yeshi, is there anything you regret in your life?*

Gen Yeshi thought about it for a moment before answering. His lips were trembling:

There are many things that I regret. I practice eighteen hours a day in front of Buddha, but there are not enough days left in this lifetime to make up for my mistakes. I pray. That is all that is left for me to do.

I took a photograph of him in front of his loot, and then Jamyang and I returned to the Shangri-la Hotel, where my friend Roger McCarthy was waiting.

From Nepal, we flew to Delhi, where Roger and I were reunited with Athar at the Imperial Hotel. There were many old stories to be remembered and even more the following day, when we drove to the outskirts of Delhi to the Tibetan refugee center next to Maju Ka Tila. The *Chushi-Gangdruk* has its Indian headquarters there, and I had interviewed twice before the leaders living there. Now that Roger was in town, the aging rebels dressed up a little and had refreshments awaiting his arrival. Athar, Kalsang, Drawupon, the Prince of Derge, Tinzing Jyurme, Roger, and I sat around a large table, with younger family members respectfully listening in the background.

Baba Gen Yeshi in later years.
(Collection of the author)

The conversation was lively, and the old warriors were generally appreciative of Roger's many years of effort on their behalf—though there were a few dissident voices (the Prince of Derge included) of those who still felt betrayed by the CIA.

Nevertheless, to a man, they all harbored hope that eventually America would somehow help them take back Tibet. There was also a general disgruntlement about the Dalai Lama's willingness to accept the Chinese boundaries of the T.A.R..

Roger gently scolded them by saying this was precisely the kind of attitude the Chinese relished:

lack of unity in the Diaspora. Roger urged them to, at least publicly, support the efforts of the Dalai Lama. He was their one great hope—the one Tibetan voice the entire world listened to.

From Delhi, Roger and I took the night train to Dharamsala, where we jointly interviewed His Holiness the Dalai Lama. As a practitioner of Tibetan Buddhism, I had brought a *khata* with me. I was about to make the traditional prostration, when the Dalai Lama grabbed my elbow, took the *khata*, handed it to an attendant, and motioned me to sit down next to him. He is not a man to stand on ceremony when he doesn't have to. He immediately put us at ease and was obviously most interested in Roger, a man he had heard of from his brothers, and with whom he was now face to face. I think the highlight of the forty-five-minute interview occurred after Roger praised the Tibetans he had met and worked with. The Dalai Lama smiled and responded:

Of course I have the opinion—as a U.S. government policy—I do not think that they [the CIA] *came to help the Tibetans out of genuine sympathy or genuine concern. . . . But there was anti-communism in Eastern Tibet at the time so, accordingly, they helped the Tibetan resistance movement. However, it became quite clear—quite convincing—that many American individuals who mixed with Tibetans, who trained Tibetans, who spent extended time with Tibetans— they eventually developed some kind of genuine feeling. That, I appreciate.*

The violence of resistance action, whether we agree with it or not, whether that violent action is right or wrong, the Tibetans carried out that action with sincere motivation and they suffered—these things are true. So it is really worthwhile to remember these things. . . . Fact is fact. Quite a number of Tibetans died—were killed by the Communist Chinese—not for their individual interests or individual gain, but rather for the Tibetan nation and Buddha dharma, so it is really worthwhile to remember them.[10]

A YEAR AFTER I HAD GONE TO CENTRAL ASIA WITH MCCARTHY, I received a letter from him in response to various questions I had posed about

---

[10]His Holiness the Dalai Lama, interview with Roger E. McCarthy and the author.

Camp Hale trainees and the lasting relationship created with their instructors. As an afterthought, Roger wrote something that still strikes me as penetrating: *What is it about the Tibetans? Do we think of them as similar to the "American Indians" our forefathers met? Or do we see in them (the good ones), what we want to see in others, but can't or seldom do find in our fellow Americans? Are we surprised and taken by them because freedom and religion mean so much to them? Americans, who distrust patriotism in other Americans, can admire it in Tibetans. There's a kind of glamour about their patriotism that we don't possess in the United States.*[11]

Most of the old warriors now live in refugee camps in India and Nepal. Many of these places—and the dire poverty therein—bear an eerie resemblance to the dismal reservations allotted to Native Americans.

Other warriors have passed on since I befriended them. Athar is gone, Kirti is gone, as well as others whose sad tales did not make it through the final edit of this book.

Frank Holober is dead. S. S. Uban is dead.

Ngabo lived to a ripe old age as Chairman of the Standing Committee of the People's Congress of the Tibet Autonomous Region, Vice Chairman of the Standing Committee of the Chinese National People's Congress, and who knows what else.

Not so fortunate was the Tenth Panchen Lama, whose free ride, subsidized by the communist party, became a dangerous roller coaster: Mao turned on him. During the Cultural Revolution, he was subjected to *thamzing* and thrown into solitary confinement. Most people thought he was dead. After Mao died, however, he suddenly resurfaced—a "rehabilitated" man. Back in the good graces of the party, he married—something no Panchen Lama had ever done—and settled into the luxurious life of the Beijing privileged. But again, he made the mistake of speaking his mind when, in 1987, he protested the PLA treatment of monks during the Lhasan revolt of that year. He began to criticize other government policies as well, and worked for the release of unjustly imprisoned clergy. He was playing a very dangerous game. In 1989, while in Shigatse, he suddenly collapsed and died. "Heart attack" was the official cause of death, but the rumor spread he had been poisoned.

[11]Roger E. McCarthy, letter to the author.

. . .

THE DALAI LAMA HAS MENTIONED THAT, IN TERMS OF THE
dharma, the tragedy of Tibet has become a blessing in disguise. Today, the
religious leaders of the Diaspora have scattered and taken root all over the
world. Of all the exiles I have encountered, the ones who have met with
the greatest success are the lamas—like Cyclone and Goser—who now share
their ancient teachings with an international multitude, myself included.

Perhaps Maitreya, the future Buddha, will locate Tibet in people's hearts
rather than on a page in an atlas—thus bringing Tibet's mysteries full circle
to a time, before 1950, when it was just a blank space on a classroom globe.

The way to Jowo Zegyal. *(Collection of the author)*

ACKNOWLEDGMENTS

I am indebted to the Tibetans who entrusted me with their stories, as well as the numerous translators in refugee camps who spontaneously donated their skill and time. Their collaborative effort engendered the soul of this book. It is something I can never repay, but would dearly love to.

Roger McCarthy provided the backbone. In terms of content, his enormous contribution will be obvious. But it was his friendship and unassailable sense of honor that instructed less visible aspects of the narrative. He is that rarest of things, a hero, and I count my blessings that he became an integral part of a seven-year undertaking.

Cyclone and Goser smiled and encouraged me to write the truth, whether it was flattering to Tibetans or not, thus eliminating a hesitancy on my part that would have otherwise blocked the project. I would not have written *Buddha's Warriors* without their blessing.

Jeremy Tarcher, Chris Byrne, William Hinman, Pema Wangyal of Dolpo, Jamyang Lama, Ashley Shelby, Tashi Chutter, and Bruce Walker: In various ways, they vitalized and, more important, revitalized the book at precisely the right moments.

Last but not least, Bonnie Solow: She is the agent who writers dream of but never really hope to meet. In Tibetan parlance, she is a literary *dakini*, and nothing less.

All of you share a common characteristic—big hearts—and I salute you from the deepest part of mine.

BIBLIOGRAPHY

Addy, Premen. *Tibet on the Imperial Chessboard.* Calcutta: Academic, 1984.

Ahmad, Zahiruddin. *China and Tibet, 1708–1959: A Resume of Facts.* Oxford: Oxford University Press, 1960.

Amdo, Jamyang. *The Art of Tibetan Painting.* Dharamsala: Sherig Parkhang, 1994.

Andrugtsang, Gompo Tashi. *Four Rivers, Six Ranges: A True Account of Khampa Resistance to Chinese in Tibet.* Dharamsala: Information of the Publicity Office of His Holiness The Dalai Lama, 1973.

Anon. "The Escape that Rocked the Reds." *Time Magazine,* vol. LXXIII, no. 16, April 20, 1959.

Anon. *Tibet: Myth vs. Reality.* Beijing Review Publication, 1988.

Anon. *Tibetans on Tibet.* China Reconstructs Press, 1988.

Antin, Parker, and Phyllis Wachob Weiss. *Himalayan Odyssey: The Perilous Trek to Western Nepal.* New York: Dell, 1990.

Arpi, Claude. *The Fate of Tibet: When Big Insects Eat Small Insects.* New Delhi, Har-Anand, 1999.

Avedon, John F. *In Exile from the Land of Snows.* New York: Vintage Books, 1986.

Bagby, Wesley M. *The Eagle-Dragon Alliance.* Newark: University of Delaware Press, 1992.

Bageant, Joe. "War at the Top of the World." *Military History,* February 2004.

Bailey, F. N. *No Passport to Tibet.* London: Rupert Hart-Davis, 1957.

Baldizzone, Tiziana and Gianni. *Tibet on the Paths of the Gentlemen Brigands: Retracing the Steps of Alexandra David-Neel.* London: Thames and Hudson, 1995.

Barber, Noel. *From the Land of Lost Content: The Dalai Lama's Fight for Tibet.* London: Collins, 1969.

Barnett, Robert, and Shirin Akiner, eds. *Resistance and Reform in Tibet.* Bloomington: Indiana University Press, 1994.

Beckwith, Christopher I. *The Tibetan Empire in Central Asia.* Princeton: Princeton University Press, 1987.

Beer, Robert. *Tibetan Symbols and Motifs.* London: Serindia, 2000.

Bell, Charles. *Tibet Past and Present.* Delhi: Motilal Banarsidass, 1992.

———*The Religion of Tibet.* Oxford: Clarendon, 1931.

———*The People of Tibet.* Oxford: Clarendon, 1928.

———*Portrait of a Dalai Lama.* London: Collins, 1946.

Bernard, Theodore. *Penthouse of the Gods: A Pilgrimage into the Heart of Tibet and the Sacred City of Lhasa.* New York: Charles Scribner's Sons, 1939.

Bernstein, Richard, and Ross H. Munro. *The Coming Conflict with China.* New York, Knopf, 1997.

Bhushan, Bharat. "I'm Not Seeking Independence from China: Dalai Lama." *The Hindustan Times,* November 15, 1997.

Blum, William. *The CIA: A Forgotten History.* London: Zed Books Ltd., 1986.

Boashan, Huang. *Snowy Mountains and Grasslands: Travels in Northwestern Sichuan.* Beijing: Foreign Language Press, 1990.

Bower, Captain Hamilton. *Diary of a Journey Across Tibet.* London: Rivington, Percival & Co., 1894.

Brands, H. W. *Inside the Cold War: Loy Henderson and the Rise of the American Empire, 1918–1961.* New York: Oxford University Press, 1991.

Brauen, Martin. *The Mandala: Sacred Circle in Tibetan Buddhism.* London: Serindia, 1997.

Bull, Geoffrey T. *When Iron Gates Yield.* London: Hodder & Stoughton, 1955.

———*Tibetan Tales.* London: Hodder & Stoughton, 1966.

Carnahan, Sumner, and Lama Kunga Rinpoche, eds. *In the Presence of My Enemies: Memoirs of Tibetan Nobleman Tsipon Shuguba.* Santa Fe: Clear Light, 1995.

Chapman, Spencer. *Lhasa the Holy City.* London: Readers Union Ltd., 1940.

Chang, Kuo-hua. "Tibet Returns to the Bosom of the Motherland: Revolutionary Reminiscences." Beijing: *SCMP,* no. 2854, 1962.

Cheng, James. *The Politics of the Chinese Red Army.* Palo Alto: Stanford University Press, 1966.

Chitkara, M. G. *Toxic Tibet Under Nuclear China.* New Delhi: APH, 1996.

Choedon, Dhondup. *Life in the Red Flag People's Commune.* Dharamsala: Information Office of H. H. the Dalai Lama, 1978.

Chophel, Norbu. *Folk Culture of Tibet.* Dharamsala: Library of Tibetan Works and Archives, 1983.

Chutter, Tashi. *Confidential Study on Deployment of Chinese Occupational Force in Tibet.* Delhi: Self-published, 1998.

Combe, G. A. *A Tibetan on Tibet.* Kathmandu: Ratna Pustak Bhandar, 1975.

Conboy, Kenneth, and James Morrison. *The CIA's Secret War in Tibet.* Lawrence: University Press of Kansas, 2002.

———*Elite Forces of India and Pakistan.* London: Osprey Press, 1992.

"Continued Violations of Human Right in Tibet." Geneva: Bulletin of the International Commission of Jurists No. 21, December 1964.

Craig, Mary. *Tears of Blood: A Cry for Help.* London: HarperCollins, 1992.

———*Kundun.* Washington, D.C.: Counterpoint, 1997.

Crystal Mirror Series, Volume V. *Lineage of Diamond Light.* Berkeley: Dharma, 1991.

Das, Sarat Chandra. *Journey to Lhasa and Central Tibet.* Delhi: Cosmo, 1988.

Dawidoff, Nicholas. "Asia's Last Forbidden Kingdom (Mustang)." *Travel & Leisure,* June 1994.

Deane, Hugh. "The Cold War in Tibet." *Covert Action,* no. 29, Winter 1987.

Defying the Dragon: China and Human Rights in Tibet. London: Law Association for Asia and the Pacific Human Rights Standing Committee and Tibet Information Network, 1991.

De Riencourt, Amaury. *Roof of the World.* New York: Rinehart, 1950.

Development for Whom? A Report on the Chinese Development Strategies in Tibet and Their Impact. Dharamsala: Tibetan Youth Congress, 1955.

Dewatshang, Kunga Samten. *Flight at the Cuckoo's Behest.* New Delhi: Paljor, 1997.

Dhondup, K. *The Water-Horse and Other Years: A History of 17th and 18th Century Tibet.* Dharamsala: Library of Tibetan Works & Archives, 1984.

Duncan, Marion H. *Love Songs and Proverbs of Tibet.* London: Mitre Press, 1961.

Dunham, Carroll, and Ian Baker. *Tibet: Reflections from the Wheel of Life.* New York: Abbeville, 1993.

Dunham, Mikel. *Samye: A Pilgrimage to the Birthplace of Buddhism.* San Diego: Jodere, 2004.

Elchert, Carole, ed. *White Lotus: An Introduction to Tibetan Culture.* Ithaca: Snow Lion, 1990.

Evans-Wentz, W. Y., ed. *Tibetan Yoga and Secret Doctrines.* London: Oxford University Press, 1958.

Faison, Seth. "Uncivil Rights: Are Tibetans 'Citizens' of China?" *The New York Times,* August 31, 1999.

Fearless Voices: Accounts of Tibetan Former Political Prisoners. Dharamsala: Tibetan Centre for Human Rights and Democracy, 1998.

Fisher, Margaret W., Leo E. Rose, and Robert A. Huttebback. *Himalayan Battleground.* London: Pall Mall Press, 1963.

Fleming, Peter. *Bayonets to Lhasa.* New York: Harper Brothers, 1961.

Forbes, Ann Armbrecht. *Settlements of Hope: An Account of Tibetan Refugees in Nepal.* Cambridge: Cultural Survival, Inc., 1989.

Forbes, Ann, and Carole McGranahan. *Developing Tibet? A Survey of International Development Projects.* Washington, D.C.: Cultural Survival and the International Campaign for Tibet, 1992.

Forbidden Freedoms: Beijing's Control of Religion in Tibet. Washington, D.C.: International Campaign for Tibet, 1990.

Ford, Robert. *Captured in Tibet.* Hong Kong: Oxford University Press, 1990.

From Liberation to Liberalization: Views on "Liberalized" Tibet. Dharamsala: Information Office of His Holiness the Dalai Lama, 1982.

From the Roof of the World: Refugees of Tibet. Berkeley: Dharma, 1992.

Galbraith, John Kenneth. *A Life in Our Times.* Boston: Houghton Mifflin, 1981.

Gergan, J. *A Thousand Tibetan Proverbs and Wise Sayings.* Kathmandu: Tiwari's Pilgrim Book House, 1991.

Getty, Alice. *The Gods of Northern Buddhism.* New York: Dover, 1988.

Gilbert, Rodney Yonkers. *Genocide in Tibet: A Study in Communist Aggression.* New York: American-Asian Educational Exchange, 1959.

Ginsburg, George, and Michael Mathos. *Communist China and Tibet: The First Dozen Years.* The Hague: Martinus Nijhoff, 1964.

Goldstein, Melvyn C. *A History of Modern Tibet, 1913–1951.* Berkeley: University of California Press, 1991.

———*The Snow Lion and the Dragon.* Berkeley: University of California Press, 1997.

———"Tibet, China and the United States: Reflections on the Tibet Question." *The Atlantic Council,* April 1995.

Goldstein, Melvyn C., and Matthew T. Kapstein. *Buddhism in Contemporary Tibet: Religious Revival and Cultural Identity.* Delhi: Motilal Banarsidass, 1998.

Goodman, Michael. *The Last Dalai Lama.* London: Goodman, Sidgwick and Jackson, 1986.

Gordon, Antoinette K. *The Iconography of Tibetan Lamaism.* Tokyo: Charles E. Tuttle, 1959.

Gould, B. J. *The Jewel in the Lotus.* London: Chatto and Windus, 1957.

Gregson, Jonathan. *Massacre at the Palace: The Doomed Royal Dynasty of Nepal.* New York: Hyperion, 2002.

Gross, Ernest A. *The United Nations: Structure for Peace.* New York: Harper and Brothers, 1962.

———"Tibetan Plans for Tomorrow." *Foreign Affairs,* October 1961.

Gyatsho, Thubten Legshay. *Gateway to the Temple: Manual of Tibetan Monastic Customs, Art, Building and Celebrations.* Kathmandu: Ratna Pustak Bhandar, 1979.

Gyatso, Palden. *Tire Under the Snow: Testimony of a Tibetan Prisoner.* London: Harvill, 1997.

Gyatso, Tenzin, His Holiness the Dalai Lama. *Freedom in Exile: The Autobiography of the Dalai Lama.* New York: HarperCollins, 1991.

———*My Land and My People.* New York: McGraw-Hill, 1962.

———*The Collected Statements, Interviews and Articles of His Holiness the Dalai Lama.* Dharamsala: Information Office of His Holiness the Dalai Lama, 1982.

Harrer, Heinrich. *Seven Years in Tibet.* New York: E. P. Dutton, 1954.

Hedin, Sven. *A Conquest of Tibet.* New York: E. P. Dutton, 1934.

Hicks, Roger. *Hidden Tibet: The Land and Its People.* Dorset: Element Books Limited, 1988.

Holober, Frank. *Raiders of the China Coast: CIA Covert Operations during the Korean War.* Annapolis: Naval Institute Press, 1999.

Hopkirk, Peter. *Trespassers on the Roof of the World.* Los Angeles: Jeremy P. Tarcher, 1982.

Illion, Theodore. *In Secret Tibet: In Disguise Amongst Lamas, Robbers, and Wise Men.* London: Rider, 1960.

International Commission of Jurists. *The Question of Tibet and the Rule of Law.* Geneva: H. Studer, 1960.

Jackson, David. *A History of Tibetan Painting.* Vienna: Verlag der Österreichischen Akademie der Wissenschaften, 1996.

Jackson, David P. *The Mollas of Mustang: Historical, Religious and Oratorical Traditions of the Nepalese-Tibetan Borderland.* Dharamsala: Library of Tibetan Works & Archives, 1984.

Jacob, Lt. General J. F. R. *Surrender at Dacca: Birth of a Nation.* New Delhi: Manohar, 1997.

Karmay, Samten G. *The Arrow and the Spindle: Studies in History, Myths, Rituals and Beliefs in Tibet.* Kathmandu: Mandala Book Point, 1998.

Kelly, Petra K., Gert Bastian, and Pat Aiello, eds. *The Anguish of Tibet*. Berkeley: Parallax, 1991.

Kirk, Donald. "The Legend of Tony Poe, CIA." *True Magazine*, January 1972.

Kissinger, Henry. *The White House Years*. London: Weidenfeld & Nicolson, and Michael Joseph, 1979.

Knaus, John Kenneth. *Orphans of the Cold War: America and the Tibetan Struggle for Survival*. New York: Public Affairs, 1999.

Kvaerne, Per. *The Bon Religion of Tibet: The Iconography of a Living Tradition*. Boston: Shambhala, 1996.

Laird, Thomas. *Into Tibet: The CIA's First Atomic Spy and His Secret Expedition to Lhasa*. New York: Grove, 2002.

Lamb, Alastair. *The China-India Border: The Origins of the Disputed Boundaries*. London: Oxford University Press, 1964.

Lane, Fred. "The Warrior Tribes of Kham." *Asiaweek*, March 2, 1994.

Lazar, Edward, ed. *Tibet: The Issue Is Independence*. Berkeley: Parallax Press, 1994.

Leary, William M. "Secret Mission to Tibet." *Air & Space*, December 1997–January 1998.

The Legal Status of Tibet: Three Studies by Leading Jurists. Dharamsala: Office of Information and International Relations, 1989.

Lehnert, Tomek. *Rogues in Robes*. Nevada City: Blue Dolphin, 1998.

Leidy, Denise Patry, and Robert A. F. Thurman. *Mandala: The Architecture of Enlightenment*. New York: Asia Society Galleries, 1998.

Leung, John K., and Michael Y. M. Kau. *The Writings of Mao Zedong, 1949–1976. Vol. 2*. Beijing: M. E. Sharpe, 1984.

Lhalungpa, Lobsang P. *Tibet: The Sacred Realm*. Philadelphia: Aperture, 1983.

Li, Zhu. *Tibet: No Longer Mediaeval*. Beijing: China Publications Centre, 1981.

Liu, Melinda. "A Secret War on the Roof of the World." *Newsweek*, August 16, 1999.

Lobsang and Jin Yun. "Tibet: History and Anecdotes." *Beijing Review*, June 13, 1983.

Loftis, Zena Sanford. *A Message from Batang*. New York: Fleming H. Revell, 1911.

Long, Jeff. "Going After Wangdu. The Search for a Tibetan Guerilla Leads to Colorado's Secret CIA Camp." *Rocky Mountain Magazine*, July–August 1981.

MacDonald, Malcolm. *Inside China*. Boston: Little, Brown, 1980.

MacFarquhar, Roderick. *The Origins of the Cultural Revolution, the Coming of the Cataclysm*. Oxford: Oxford University Press, 1997.

McCarthy, Roger E. *Tears of the Lotus: Accounts of Tibetan Resistance to the Chinese Invasion, 1950–1962*. Jefferson: McFarland, 1997.

McNallen, Steve. "Leadville to Lhasa." *Soldier of Fortune*, April 1991.

Mao, Tse-tung. "On the Policies of Our Work in Tibet." *Selected Works*, vol. 5. Beijing: Foreign Languages Press, 1977.

Maraini, Fosco. *Secret Tibet*. London: Harvill, 1998.

Marchetti, Victor, and John D. Marks. *The CIA and Cult of Intelligence*. New York: Knopf, 1974.

Mehra, Parshotam. *Tibetan Polity, 1904–37: The Conflict Between the 13th Dalai Lama and the 9th Panchen*. Wiesbaden: Otto Harrassowitz, 1976.

Menon, V. K. Krishna. *India and the Chinese Invasion*. Bombay, India: Contemporary, 1963.

Meyer, Karl E., and Shareen Blair Brysac. *Tournament of Shadows: The Great Game and the Race for Empire in Central Asia*. New York: Counterpoint, 1999.

Migot, Andre. *Tibetan Marches*. London: Rupert Hart-Davis, 1955.

Miller, Daniel J. *Fields of Grass: Portraits of the Pastoral Landscape and Nomads of the Tibetan Plateau and Himalayas*. Kathmandu: International Centre for Integrated Mountain Development, 1998.

The Mongols and Tibet: A Historical Assessment of Relations Between the Mongol Empire and Tibet. Dharamsala: Department of Information and International Relations Central Tibetan Administration, 1996.

Mullik, B. N. *My Years with Nehru: The Chinese Betrayal*. Bombay: Allied, 1971.

The Myth of Tibetan Autonomy: A Legal Analysis of the Status of Tibet. Washington: International Campaign for Tibet and International Human Rights Law Group, 1994.

New Majority: Chinese Population Transfer into Tibet. London: Tibet Support Group UK, 1995.

The Next Generation: The State of Education in Tibet Today. Dharamsala: Tibetan Centre for Human Rights and Democracy, 1997.

Ngapo, Jigme. "Behind the Unrest in Tibet." *China Spring,* vol. 2, no. 1, January/February 1988.
———*Tibet.* New York: McGraw-Hill, 1981.
Norbu, Dawa. *Red Star over Tibet.* New Delhi: Sterling, 1987.
———*Tibet: The Road Ahead.* New Delhi: HarperCollins, 1997.
Norbu, Jamyang. *Horseman in the Snow: The Story of Aten, an Old Khampa Warrior.* Dharamsala: Information Office, Central Tibetan Secretariat, 1979.
Norbu, Namkhai. *Journey Among the Tibetan Nomads: An Account of a Remote Civilization.* Dharamsala: Library of Tibetan Works & Archives, 1997.
Norbu, Thubten Jigme, and Heinrich Harrer. *This Is My Country.* Boston: Wisdom, 1986.
Olschak, Blanche Christine, and Geshe Thupten Wangyal. *Mystic Art of Ancient Tibet.* Boston: Shambhala, 1987.
Padmasambhava. *The Legend of the Great Stupa: The Life Story of the Lotus Born Guru.* Berkeley: Dharma, 1973.
Paljor, Kunsang. *Tibet: The Undying Flame.* Dharamsala: Information & Publicity of His Holiness The Dalai Lama, 1977.
Paltseg, Lotsawa Kaba. *A Manual of Key Buddhist Terms: A Categorization of Buddhist Terminology with Commentary.* Dharamsala: Library of Tibetan Works and Archives, 1992.
Patt, David. *A Strange Liberation: Tibetan Lives in Chinese Hands.* Ithaca: Snow Lion, 1992.
Patterson, George N. *Requiem for Tibet.* London: Aurum, 1990.
———*Tibetan Journey.* London: Readers Book Club, 1956.
———*Journey with Loshay: An Adventure in Tibet.* New York: Norton, 1954.
———*Tibet in Revolt.* London: Faber and Faber, 1956.
———*Peking Versus Delhi.* New York: Frederick A. Praeger, 1964.
Peissel, Michel. *Cavaliers of Kham: The Secret War in Tibet.* London: Heinemann, 1972.
———*Mustang, The Secret Kingdom.* New York: E.P. Dutton, 1967.
———*The Last Barbarian.* New York: Henry Holt, 1997.
———*The Secret War in Tibet.* Boston: Little, Brown, 1972.
Peking Review. May 5, 1959. Special Tibet Number. Peking, China.
Pemba, Lhamo, ed. *Tibetan Proverbs.* Dharamsala: Library of Tibetan Works & Archives, 1996.
Penick, Douglas J. *The Warrior Song of King Gesar.* Boston: Wisdom, 1996.
Perkins, Jane. *Tibet in Exile.* San Francisco: Chronicle, 1991.
Phala, Lord Chamberlain of His Holiness the Dalai Lama. *The Autobiography of Phala.* Dharamsala: Office of Information of His Holiness the Dalai Lama.
Powell, Andrew. *Heirs to Tibet: Travels Among the Exiles in India.* London: Heinemann, 1992.
Prados, John. *The President's Secret Wars.* New York: Morrow, 1986.
Prouty, L. Fletcher. "Colorado to Koko Nor." *Denver Post Sunday Empire Magazine,* February 6, 1972.
Rawson, Philip. *The Art of Tantra.* London: Thames and Hudson, 1978.
———*Sacred Tibet.* London: Thames and Hudson, 1991.
Richardson, H. E. *Tibet and Its History.* Boston: Shambhala, 1984.
Roberts, John B. II. "The Dalai Lama's Great Escape." *George,* October 1997.
———"The Secret War Over Tibet." *The American Spectator,* December 1997.
Rockhill, William Woodville. *The Land of the Lamas.* London: Longmans, Green, 1997.
Rubin, Alfred P. "The Position of Tibet in International Law." *The Chinese Quarterly,* July/September 1968.
Schell, Orville. *Virtual Tibet: Searching for Shangri-La from the Himalayas to Hollywood.* New York: Holt, 2000.
Schwartz, Ronald D. *Circle of Protest: Political Ritual in the Tibetan Uprising.* Delhi: Motilal Banarsidass, 1996.
Sen, Chanakya, ed. *Tibet Disappears: A Documentary History of Tibet's International Status, the Great Rebellion and Its Aftermath.* New Delhi: Asia Publishing House, 1960.
Shakabpa, Tsepon W. D. *Tibet: A Political History.* New York: Potala, 1984.
Shakya, Tsering. *The Dragon in the Land of Snows: A History of Modern Tibet Since 1947.* London: Pimlico, 1999.
Sinha, Nirmal C. *Tales the Thankas Tell.* Calcutta: Radiant Process, 1989.

Sis, Peter. *Tibet: Through the Red Box.* New York: Farrar, Straus and Giroux, 1998.

Smith, Warren W., Jr. *Tibetan Nation: A History of Tibetan Nationalism and Sino-Tibetan Relations.* Boulder: Westview Press, 1996.

Snellgrove, David L. *Himalayan Pilgrimage.* Oxford: Bruno Cassirer Ltd., 1961.

———*A Cultural History of Tibet.* New York: Frederick A. Praeger, 1968.

———*Indo-Tibetan Buddhism.* Boston: Shambhala, 1987.

Sperling, Elliot. "The Chinese Venture in Kham, 1904–11, and the Role of Chao Erh-feng." *Tibet Journal,* vol. 1, no. 2, 1976.

The Status of Tibet: A Brief Summary & 1959 Tibet Documents. Dharamsala: Information Office, Central Tibetan Secretariat, 1987.

Subba, Tanka B. *Flight and Adaptation: Tibetan Refugees in the Darjeeling-Sikkim Himalaya.* Dharamsala: Library of Tibetan Works and Archives, 1990.

Tales of Terror: Torture in Tibet. New Delhi: Tibetan Centre for Human Rights and Democracy, January 1999.

Taring, Rinchen Dolma. *Daughter of Tibet.* London: Wisdom, 1986.

Teichman, Eric. *Travels of a Consular Officer in Eastern Tibet.* Cambridge: Cambridge University Press, 1922.

Thomas, Lowell, Jr. *The Silent War in Tibet.* Garden City: Doubleday, 1959.

———*Out of This World.* New York: Greystone, 1950.

Thondup, Tulku. *Buddhist Civilization in Tibet.* New York: Routledge and Kegan Paul, 1987.

Thurman, Robert A. F. *Essential Tibetan Buddhism.* New York: HarperCollins, 1995.

Tibet and Peace in South Asia. New Delhi: National Committee for Tibet & Peace in South Asia, 1991.

Tibet and the United States of America: An Annotated Chronology of Relations in the 20th Century. Second Edition, February 1994. International Committee of Lawyers for Tibet.

Tibet in the United Nations. New Delhi: Bureau of His Holiness the Dalai Lama, 1988.

Tibetan People's Right of Self-Determination: Report of the Workshop on Self-Determination of the Tibetan People: Legitimacy of Tibet's Case 1994/1996, India. New Delhi: Tibetan Parliamentary and Policy Research Centre, 1996.

Tibet: The Facts. A Report Prepared by the Scientific Buddhist Association for the United Nations Commission on Human Rights. Dharamsala: Tibetan Young Buddhist Association, 1990.

Tibet Under Chinese Communist Rule: A Compilation of Refugee Statements: 1958–1975. Dharamsala: Information and Publicity Office of His Holiness the Dalai Lama, 1976.

The Trek to Freedom: Tibetan Women and the Refugee Experience. Dharamsala: The Tibetan Women's Association, 1995.

Trest, Warren A. *Air Commando One: Heinie Aderholt and America's Secret Air Wars.* Washington, D.C.: Smithsonian Institution Press, 2000.

Trungpa, Chögyam. *Born in Tibet.* Boston: Shambhala, 1995.

Tsering, Tashi. "Nag-ron mGon-po rNam-gyal: A 19th Century Kham-pa Warrior." *Soundings in Tibetan Civilization.* New Delhi: Manohar, 1985.

Tsomo, Tsering, ed. *The Road to Beijing: The Tibetan Women's Association Campaign Strategies for the United Nations Fourth World Conference on Women, Beijing 1995.* Dharamsala: Tibetan Women's Association Central Executive Committee, 1995.

Tucci, Giuseppe. *To Lhasa and Beyond.* Ithaca, NY: Snow Lion, 1983.

———*The Religions of Tibet.* Berkeley: University of California Press, 1980.

Tulku Thondup Rinpoche. *Hidden Teachings of Tibet: An Explanation of the Terma Tradition of the Nyingma School of Buddhism.* Boston: Wisdom, 1986.

Uban, Major General Sujan Singh. *Phantoms of Chittagong.* New Delhi: Allied, 1985.

———*The Gurus of India.* New Delhi: Vaikunth, 1988.

Vitali, Roberto. *Early Temples of Central Tibet.* London: Serindia, 1989.

Von Erffa, Wolfgang. *Uncompromising Tibet: Tradition, Religion, Politics.* New Delhi: Paljor, 1996.

Waddell, Austine L. *Lhasa and Its Mysteries: With a Record of the British Tibetan Expedition of 1903–1904.* New York: Dover, 1988.

———*Tibetan Buddhism: With Its Mystic Cults, Symbolism and Mythology.* New York: Dover, 1972.

Willis, Michael. *Tibet: Life, Myth, and Art.* New York: Stewart, Tabori & Chang, 1999.

Wise, David. *The Politics of Lying.* New York: Random House, 1973.

World Press on Panchen Lama. New Delhi: Tibetan Parliamentary and Policy Research Centre, 1996.

Yeshe De Project Staff, ed. *Ancient Tibet: Research Materials from the Yeshe De Project.* New York: Dharma, 1986.

Younghusband, Sir Francis. *India and Tibet.* London: J. Murray, 1910.

———*India and Tibet: A History of the Relations Which Have Subsisted Between the Two Countries from the Time of Warren Hastings to 1910; with a Particular Account of the Mission to Lhasa of 1904.* Hong Kong: Oxford University Press, 1985.

INDEX

Page numbers in italics indicate illustrations.

Aba (father of Cyclone), 31–32, 254, 330
   escape from Tibet, 341–48
Agriculture, Lithang District, 34n
Airdrops, 224, 254, 263, 337, 338
Airplane, Tibetan's first ride, 199–200
Alo Chonzed (*Mimang* leader), 153–54
Altar rooms, 14n
Ambush exercises, 205
Amdo province, 7–8, 20–28
   communist occupation, 140–42, 148, 167
      resistance to, 169, 219, 234
Americans, Tibetans and, 401
   first contact, 199–200
   See also CIA; United States
Ampas, 21–22
Amyemachin (mountain deity, Kham), 32
Andro Choedrak, 328
Appeasement, by Nehru, 310–311
Archer, Harry, 315, 315n
Aristocracy, Tibetan, communists and,
   120–21
Army, modern, Thirteenth Dalai Lama and, 48
Army, U.S., and Tibetan training site, 315
Assistance programs for refugees, 252
Aten (opium trader), 56–57, 259
Athar Norbu, 10, *35*, 35–37, 40, 62–64, 79,
   118–19, 129–30, 150, 218, 221, 334,
   410, 412
   CIA and, 197–200, 241–42, 301
   and Dalai Lama, 144–45, 185, 300, 302–5
   India trip, 174, 176, 179–80, 186–87
   and Lhasa uprising, 279
   and Lithang uprising, 160–62, 163–64
   resistance activities, 173–74, 207–8, 245–46,
      254–55, 263–64
      letters to Lhasa from Eastern Tibet, 170–71
      reinfiltration, 221–22, 225, 227–30, 235–38
      training of rebels, 320

Atrocities by Chinese, 39–40, 258–60, 325–26,
   342, 398
   Eastern Tibet, 166–68, 208–9
   Amdo province, 234–35
   Kham province, 156–57, 158, 188–89, 260,
      399–400
   See also Massacres; *Thamzings*
Aufshnaiter, Peter, 51
Autonomy of Tibet, 2, 7
   China and, 6, 104
Avedon, John, 74

Baba Gen Yeshi, 333–34, *334*, 335,
   352–53, 378–82, 394, 408–10,
   410
   betrayal by, 388, 389–90, 393
   CIA and, 375–76
   corrupt practices, 368–69, 377–78
Bajpai, G. S., 110
Bangladesh War, 385
Barber, Noel, 268, 272, 287
Bardo, 136
Bathang Regiment, *Chushi-Gangdruk*, flag, *237*
Beijing
   Dalai Lama's visit, 137–40
   Tibetan negotiations, 98–99, 102–5
Bell, Charles, 48
Bessac, Frank, 51, 51n
Bhugan Gyatotsang, 182, 233
Birendra, King of Nepal, 386–87, 394
Black-necked cranes, 64
Blee, Dave, 360, 361
Blinding, as official punishment, 66
Bodhgaya, pilgrimage to, 180–82, *181*
Bodhi tree (*Ficus religiosa*), 181
Bomdila, refugee camp, 322
Bon (early Tibetan religion), 213–14
Books, Tibetan, 36

Border
  China–Tibet, 47
  India–Tibet, 358
Buddha, *xiv*
  Enlightenment of, *151*, 180–81
  statue of, in Tibet, 36
Buddhism, Tibetan, 8, 16, 23, 59, 213–15
  communist Chinese and, 27
  death as viewed by, 118
  of Khampa warriors, 17, 215
  Buddhist hierarchy, 48–49, 114–15
  Buddhist treasures, destruction of, 167
  Buddhist warriors, 7–8, 9, 24
  See also Khampa rebels; Monks, Tibetan
Bull, Geoffrey, 51
Bumthang (*Mimang* leader), 153
Butsa Pugen, 38

Calendar, Tibetan, 13
Camp Hale, Colorado, Tibetan training site,
  315–19, *316, 319, 320*, 363–64
  closing of, 374
Camp Perry, Virginia, 314
Captured in Tibet (Ford), 69–72
Cathey, Clay, 315n, 355
Census, communist, 236–37
Central Government, Tibetan, 7, 17, 64–68
  and Chinese invasion, 71–72, 93, 182
Central Tibet, rebel control, 230
Central Tibetan Army, 68
Cesare, Don, 315n
Cha Teah, 326n
Chakpori (Iron Hill), 276, *276*
Chamdo, Kham province, 64–68
  Chinese invasion of, 68–79, 91, 95–96, 98
Chamdo Tsering Dorje, 384
Chamnang Monastery, battle of, 321
Chang Chin-Wu (Chinese general), 182
Chang Guohua (Chinese general), 110, 111,
  112–13, 124, 139–40, 175–76
Changtreng, resistance to Chinese, 155–58
Chenrezig (Avelokiteshvara), 26n, 29, *80*, 81
Chiang Kai-shek, 2–3, 5, 39, 47, 137–38
Chieftains of tribes, 15, 36
Children, Tibetan, 16, 29, 31–32
  communist education, 147–48
Chimphu (holy hill), 229–30
China, 19, 38, 50, 404–5
  control of Tibet, 2–6, 103–8, 166, 340–41
  first international recognition, 129
  negotiations, 94–96, 98–99, 102–5
  foreign relations with, 4
  invasion of India, 357, 358–61
  invasion of Tibet, 5–6, 51, 54–68, *55*, 68–79,
    73, 84–86

Khampas and, 17
and Nehru, 309–11
occupation of Tibet, xii, *306*, 307–8
  roads and, 130–33, *131*
and Tibetan history, 46
and Tibet's appeal to U.N., 87–88
U.S. and, 382–83
See also Communists, Chinese; PLA
Chinese Buddhist Association, 120
Chinese people, in Tibet, 6, 19, 56, 154
Chinese quarter, Derge, 18
Chitipati, 350, 366
Chongye Riwodechen (monastery), 300
Chora, 229, 229n
Chou En-lai, 52, *178*, 179–80, 182, 358
Chubas, 21–22
Chumi Namgyal Tundupon, 370–71, 372–74
Chushi-Gangdruk, 196–97, 203, 209–10,
  237–41, *239, 240*, 250, 255–65, 279, 319,
  320
  Cold War and, 351–52
  and Dalai Lama, 285, 289, 303
  flag, *190*, 197, *237*
  in India, 328–30, 410
    retreat to, 324
  and Lhoka area, 230, 300
  Mustang base, 333
  Phala and, 262
  and refugees, 341–42
CIA (Central Intelligence Agency, U.S.), 10, 201,
  351, 355
  and Baba Gen Yeshi, 353, 377–78
  and Dalai Lama's escape, 289, 300–302,
    303–4
  and Lhasa situations, 263–64, 279, 282
  and Tibetan rebels, 182–83, 186, 187, 194–95,
    195n, 199, 314, 322, 335–36, 363–65,
    369–70
  airdrops of weapons, 263
  candidates, 252–53
  Chushi-Gangdruk base in Mustang, 333
  end of support for, 383–84
  information from radio teams, 372
  Pembar Mission, 337–39
  propaganda booklets, *364*
  Tibetan Task Force, 192, 200–208, 215–34,
    251, 252
  and Unit 22 (Indian Army), 361
Clothing, Tibetan, 21–22, 59
Code of Conduct, Gompo Tashi, 241
Cold War, 351
Collaborators, Tibetan, in Lhasa, 270–71
  aristocrats, 261
Colonialism, views of, 129
Comet, Rahula, 45–47

Communications
  CIA training, 206–7
  resistance forces, 168–69, 201, 202
    with CIA, 364, 370, 372
    reinfiltration team, 233–34
  within Tibet, 68, 69
  lack of, 60, 155, 251–52, 320, 321
Communism, 27–28, 39, 115, 133–34
  introduction of, 57–58, 58, 63–64
Communist soldiers, views of, 59–60
Communists, Chinese, 47, 50–51, 239–40, 310
  atrocities. *See* Atrocities by Chinese
  and Dalai Lama, 175–76
  indoctrination of prisoners, 341–42
  Ngabo and, 91–94
  and Tibet, 51–52, 104, 141–42, 236, 266,
    324–27
    Lhasa, 113, 119–22, 145, 299
    Lithang, 150
  and Taktser Rinpoche, 85–86
  See also China; PLA
Conboy, Kenneth, 226
Cornell University, Tibetan trainees, 365
Corrupt practices, 49, 368–69, 377–78
Crafts, Tibetan, 54–55
Cultural Revolution, China
  and Panchen Lama, 412
  and Tibet, 5–6, 371–72, 398–401
Culture, Tibetan, destruction of, 405
Curzon, Lord (Viceroy of India), 3
Cyclone (Gudu Lungstub), 29–33, 46, 62, 72–73,
    79, 253–54, 330, 341–48, 413
  tale of King Gesar, 64

Dalai Lama, 16, 26n, 49
Dalai Lama, Thirteenth, 48, 52, 137, 358
  prophesy of, 40, 42, 48
Dalai Lama, Fourteenth, 10, 81–84, 82, 96–98,
    122, 181–82, 244–45, 266
  Chinese communists and, 85–86, 134, 179, 182
  CIA and, 194, 216–17
  escape from Tibet, 5, 264, 281–85, 286–92
    Lhuntse Dzong headquarters, 299–300
  exile considerations, 111–12
  family members, 126
  and General Chang, 112–13
  General Uban and, 312–13
  and international politics, 95, 100–102
  interview with, 11, 411
  negotiations with China, 98–99
    "17-Point Agreement," 103–5, 108, 111, 115
    repudiation of, 301–2, 310
  news media and, 308–10
  Palden Lhamo and, 249–50
  and Panchen Lama, 138

Phala and, 193, 262, 264
  control of information to, 172, 193, 194, 253
  protection from kidnapping, 268–71
  and resistance to Chinese occupation, 143
  Chushi-Gangdruk and, 238–39, 322, 328–30
  "Freedom Committee," 275
  Khampa rebels, 8, 179–80
  Lhasa uprising, 278–79, 283
  Mustang base, 389
  as temporal head, 90–91, 174–75
  trip to China, 134–43, 139
  and U.S., 97–98
  visit to India, 177–87, 178
    return from, 183–84, 187–88
Darchu River, 54
Dartsendo, Kham province, 54–56, 55
  Dalai Lama's visit, 144
Death, Buddhist views of, 118
Deaths, labor-related, 133
Dechen (survivor of Pembar), 339
Dedrup (servant of Wangdu), 207, 187, 197–200,
    217, 231–34, 334–35
  See also CIA; Tibetan Task Force
Demolition training, 205, 206
Dengko (military outpost), 60, 68–69
Derge, Prince of. *See* Donyo Jagotsang
Derge Tondu Ponzo, 384
Derge kingdom, 13–19, 68, 159–60, 407
Destruction of Tibet, prophecy of, 40, 42, 48
Dharma, 32n
Dhaulagiri Gorge, 379, 380
Dhoshul District, 28–31
Diaspora, Tibetan, 406–11
  See also Refugees
Diet (nutrition), Tibetan, 33
Disarmament of Tibetans, 148, 191
Diseases, 127–28
Dob-dobs (warrior monks), 146, 146
Documents, Chinese, capture of, 355
Doi (Amdo village), atrocities, 167
Donovan, William J., 3–4
Donyo Jagotsang (Prince of Derge), 15–16, 46,
    79, 256, 264, 410
  Pembar mission, 338–40
Dorje Jagotsang, 15, 18–19
Dorje Sherap, and Lithang uprising, 162–63
Dorjee Yudon, 158–59
Drawupon, 21–28, 57–60, 79, 410, 327–28
  resistance activities, 196–97, 256–59
Drepung Monastery, 48
Dreshe, 87, 197–200, 217, 231, 232, 233, 234, 335
  parachute jump, 221
  See also CIA; Tibetan Task Force
Drichu (Yangtze) River, 14, 47
Drop zones for infiltration, 224

Dulles, Allen, 314
Dumra. See Camp Hale
Dungkar Monastery, 97, 108
Dzachu River, 64
Dzo, 34, 34n
Dzogchen Monastery, 259–60
Dzogchen Rinpoche, 260

Earthquake, Lithang District, 47
Eastern Tibet, 7, 20–21
  Army Headquarters, 64–65
  Central Government and, 17, 38
  Chinese atrocities, 166–68, 208–9
  communists in, 147–50, 191
  Dalai Lama and, 142
Economy, Tibetan, 14, 20–21, 34n, 35
  China's pact with India and, 128–29
  Chinese communists and, 104, 120–23
  roads built by Chinese and, 132–33
Education, in Tibet, 16, 31–32, 121
  China and, 104, 147–48
Education Committee, Chinese, 121
Eisenhower, Dwight D., 351–52, 193–94, 201, 317
El Salvador, and Tibet's appeal to U.N., 87
Epidemic, syphilis, 127–28
Events, ominous (natural disasters), 47
Exfiltration of Tibetan rebels, 194, 197–200
Exile, for Dalai Lama, 110–11, 183–84
Expatriates, Tibetan, 406–11

Famine, Tibet, 5, 122–23, 127
Far Eastern Institute, Seattle, 252
Fitzgerald, Desmond, 314
Forced labor, 133, 235
Ford, Robert, 51, 59, 67–68, 79
  and Ngabo, 69–70, 71–75
Fosmire, Tom, 314–15
Fourteenth Dalai Lama. See Dalai Lama, Fourteenth
Fox, Reginald, 51
"Freedom Committee," Lhasa, 274–79
Funding of Tibetan rebels, 195–96, 216–17
Funeral procession of Gompo Tashi, 367

Ga-lag (Chinese general), 164
Galbraith, John Kenneth, and Tibet, 355–56
Ganden Monastery, 48
Gandhi, Indira, 178, 384–85
Gawa-lung (monastery), 346–47
Gelek Rinpoche, 365, 365
Gelung (servant of Gyalo), 198–99
Gelupa sect, 84, 84n
Genghis Khan, 8
Genocide, Tibet, 5–6, 331
Georgetown University, Tibetans at, 365

Gesar, King of Ling, 12, 22–23, 30–31, 148, 214
  tale of, 64
  The Warrior Song of King Gesar, 22–23, 28
Geshe Wangyel, 315n
Glerum, James, 226
Gnomchu River, 64
Gochen village, Dhoshul District, 29
GOI (Government of India)
  and Tibet, 110, 243–44, 309–10, 356
    Chinese atrocities, 165–66
    Chinese invasion, 88–90
    invitation to Dalai Lama, 174–75
    Mustang base, 389
  and U.S. assistance against China, 360
Gold, Tibetan, 26
Golden throne, gift for Dalai Lama, 195–96, 209
Goldstein, Melvyn, 52
Golok people, 7–8, 141–43, 142
  resistance to PLA, 154–55, 219
Golok province, 7–8
Gompo Tashi Andrugtsang, 10, 37, 38, 39, 40, 41,
    46, 79, 147, 173–74, 328, 331–32
  in battle, 255–56
  battle wounds, 264–65
  and China's invasion of India, 361
  and Chinese communism, 166
  Dalai Lama and, 302–3
  and Dalai Lama's trip to China, 135
  defeat of, 322–24
  illness and death, 366–67, 367
  and Phala, 262
  resistance activities, 191–93, 209–10, 236–38,
    256, 264–65, 290, 320
  resistance forces, 183, 250–51, 353
    Chushi-Gangdruk, 238, 240–41
    CIA trainees, 235
    funds for, 195–96
    letter from, 171
  and resistance movement, 153, 196–97
  U.S. contacts, 182, 195
  See also Chushi-Gangdruk
Goser (brother of Cyclone), 330, 341–48, 413
Goshen Monastery, 330
Goshun District, massacre, 256–58
Government, Tibetan, communists and, 121
Grain Procurement Board, 127
Greaney, John, 301, 314, 315, 315n, 383
  and Dalai Lama's escape, 302
  and Tibetan trainees, 318
Great Britain, and Tibet, 2–3, 336
  Chinese invasion, 52–53, 88–90, 94–95
  Tibet's appeal to U.N., 87
Gudu Lungstub. See Cyclone
Guerilla warfare, Tibet, xii, 5, 8, 168, 218
  CIA training, 320, 337–38

Guru Rinpoche (Padmasambhava), 23, 28, 29, 212, 214, 230
Gyalo Thondup (brother of Dalai Lama), 126, 129, 177, 180, 182, 192, 216–17, 242–43, 332–33, 361, 384
and Baba Gen Yeshi, 375–76
and CIA program, 194–95, 197–98, 252–53, 314
and Khampa rebels, 176, 185, 186–87
and Mao, 382
and Uban, 361–62
Gyantso Tsering, 379–80, 381
Gyurme (tribal chief), 158

Han self-image, communists and, 51–52
Harrer, Heinrich, 51, 100
Seven Years in Tibet, 201
Haus Kaus (Special Service Center), 374–75
Health concerns, 127–28
Henderson, Loy, 53, 90, 100–102
Hierarchy, social, in Tibet, 16
History of Tibet, Chinese rewriting of, 6–7
Holober, Frank, 215–17, 216, 242–43, 314, 317, 383, 412
Homes, Derge, 14–15
Horses, 22
Human rights, economics and, 4
Humor, among Khampa warriors, 204–5
Hungry ghosts, 136
Hydroelectric plants, 127

Iconography, Buddhist, 148–49
Identity, Tibetan, China and, 104–5
Independence of Tibet, 52, 53, 115, 143
India
Athar's trips to, 242
CIA overflight, 226
independence of, 53
and Tibet, 252
China's invasion of, 52–53, 71, 88–90, 94–95
Dalai Lama's escape, 302
Tibet's appeal to U.N., 87
trade with, Mao and, 127–28
U.N. debate, 336
Tibetan refugees in, 329, 324
U.S. relations, 198n
See also GOI; Nehru, Jawaharlal
Indian army, and Chinese invasion, 359
Indian public, and Tibet, 309–11
Infant mortality, 128
Information to Dalai Lama, control of, 172, 193, 194, 253
International Commission of Jurists, 5, 235, 331

International community, and Tibet, 128–29, 165, 277, 308–10, 331
International politics, Dalai Lama and, 95, 100–102, 174–75
Isolation of Tibet, 13–14, 46–47, 166, 251–52
Thirteenth Dalai Lama and, 48

Jagotsang, Donyo, 19
Jagotsang family, 15
Jamyang Lama, 408–10
Jamyang Norbu, 158–59
Jentzen Dhondrup, 198–99, 201, 203
Jeuba village, atrocities in, 167–68
Jewel Heart (American Buddhist organization), 365
Jhang Yangpa Ching Battle, 255–56
Jigme Tsering, 24
Jokhang (cathedral), 265–66, 297–98, 405–6
Jongdung Bhu Dudul, 337, 339, 340
Jowo Rinpoche, 265
Jowo Zegyal mountain, 28–30, 330, 413
Jyantsa Khenchen, 186
Jyekundo, Amdo province, 20–28
Chinese occupation, 57, 68, 196–97, 256

Kagbeni village, 368–69
Kalimpong, India, Tibetan community, 126, 129–30, 142, 165–66, 261
appeal to U.N., 243–44
Dalai Lama's visit, 184–87
Khampa rebels in, 174, 176, 197–98
Kalsang Gyatotsang, 10, 37, 40, 46, 79, 125, 133–34, 147, 225, 410
and Baba Gen Yeshi, 369
and CIA, 182–83, 252
and Mustang base, 387
and Wangdu, 376
Kanze, Chinese invasion of, 56–57, 68
Karma, 34n
Kashag (Tibetan cabinet), 3, 46, 50–51, 96, 122, 194
and attack on Chamdo, 70–72
and Baba Gen Yeshi, 377
and Chinese invasion, 86–87, 92–93, 97–98, 126
and escape of Dalai Lama, 282, 284–85
and Lhasa uprising, 271–75, 277–78
Mimang and, 123
Phala and, 262
and progressive reforms, 65–66, 68
and protest leaders, 153–54
resistance forces and, 170
Kelsang Bhuk, 378–79
Kennedy, John F., and Tibet, 353, 356
Kham province, 8, 9, 17, 47, 64–68
Chinese invasion, 54–68, 55, 188–89

ithang District, 33–42
esistance to Chinese occupation, 155–58,
169–71, 219, 232–33, 340–41, 399
ee also Khampa rebels; Khampas
mpa rebels, *171*
merican university education, 365, *365*
IA training, 201–7, 314–19, *320*
selection for, 187, 195
)alai Lama and, 288–89
escape of, 288–89
nd *Kuomintang*, 36
nd refugees, 341
nd U.S. assistance, 357
mpas, 7–9, 17–18, 148
'entral Government and, 38
ommunist indoctrination, *58*
arriors, 8, 9, 24
ee also Khampa rebels
ngsar Rinpoche, 160
·nchung Thupten Legmom, 95–96
rnan, Joan, 315n
:i Lhundop, 123–25, 136, 154, 308, 412
nd defeat of Gompo Tashi, 323–24
nd Lhasa uprising, 290–91, 292–96
,inger, Henry, 382–83, 384
us, Ken, 315n, 356, 383
gpo district, 256
attle of, 264–65
czowski, "Big Mac," 231
ean War, 60
)alani, Acharya, 129
nbum Monastery, 84–86, 407
ga Samten Dewatshang, 47
·mintang (Nationalist China), 54
nd Tibet, 18–19, 25–26, 27, 36, 39,
137–38
mitola, Pakistan, 225, 231
ung Depon, 268, 286

tablets, 223–24
er, Bob, 315n
rang, 49n
ias, Tibetan, 413
d reform, Chinese, in Tibet, 5
guage, Tibetan, banning of, 6, 405
34n
bchug (*Mimang* leader), 153–54
lu Shape, 65–67, 326
mo Tsering, 242, 253, 332–33, 383, 384,
388–89, 394
nd Baba Gen Yeshi, 376
nd Pembar Mission, 337, 338–39
sa, Tibet, 26–27, 48, 49–50, 265–66
'hinese occupation, 113–15, *114*, 118–19,
172–73, 188, 319

destruction of, 299–300
popular uprising, 268–82, *280*, 290–99
refugees in, 172–73, 235–36
resistance movement, 173–74, 183, 209, 236,
261–64, 401–4, *403*, *404*
Lhodrak, fall of, 322
Lhoka area, 230, 320
Chushi-Gangdruk forces, 237–41, *240*, 300
Lhotse, 187, 197–200, 205, 218, 246, 279, 301, 334
and Dalai Lama, 300
resistance activities, 254–55, 263–64
infiltration, 221–22, 227–30, 235–38
training of rebels, 320
See also CIA; Tibetan Task Force
Lhuntse Dzong fort, 299–300, 301, 322
Lingtsong village, 23
Lithang District, 33–42, 46, 47
Chinese occupation, 62–64, 68, 407
resistance to, 160–65
and Dalai Lamas, 144
Khampa warriors from, *171*
Lithang Monastery, 34–36, 150, 161–62
atrocities, 41, 167
destruction of, 163–65
Lithang River, 34
Lobsang Tensing, 397–404, *398*
Longhis, 197
Lotus, 214n
Lungshar (Governor of Kham), 65–66

McAllister, Edward, 199
McCarthy, Roger E., 10–11, 109, 192–94, 209,
316–17, 356, 410, 412, 416
and Baba Gen Yeshi, 376
and Chinese invasion of India, 360–61
and CIA project, 201–7, *202*, 314
airdrops, 263
parachute training, 219–21
trainees, 317
and Dalai Lama, 289, 300–302
and destruction of Lhasa, 298–99
and Khampa rebels, 169, 215, 216, 218, 225,
227, 231–32, 236, 331, 334–36
and maps of Tibet, 224
and PCART, 139
and U.S. abandonment of Tibet, 383
Macdonald, Malcolm, 311
McElroy, Jim, 219–20
McMahon, Henry, 358
McMahon Line, 357–58
Magars (resistance camps), 219
Mahabodhi Temple, 181, *181*
Mahendra, King of Nepal, 386
Maitreya (future Buddha), *396*, 413
Manjushri, Bodhisattva of Wisdom, 118, 148, 197

Mao Tse-tung, 47, 50–52, 382
  Cultural Revolution, 371–72
  and Dalai Lama, 137–40, *139,* 184, 188
  Ngabo and, 105–6, *107*
  and Nehru, 53, 88
  and Tibet, 5–6, 8, 27, 54, 60–61, 107–8, 115,
    120–22, 124–25, 154, 166, 307
    political control, 134, 139–40
    trade relations with India, 128–29
Maps of Tibet, 224
Mara, Lord of Illusion, 181
Marksmanship of Khampa rebels, 206
Massacres, 41, 155, 256–58, 260, 339, 340
  See also Atrocities
Meat, in Buddhist diet, 33
Medical treatment, 64, 127–28
Mekong River, 64
Menon, Krishna, 356, 360
Merchant-traders, Tibetan, communists and,
  121
Midsummer Festival, Lithang, 62–63
Military organization, Tibetan, 122
Mimang, 123–25, 127, 168, 169, 173, 239, 290
  and Dalai Lama's trip to China, 135
  leaders in Lhasa, 153–54
  monasteries and, 145
Mining, in Tibet, 26
Minyag Gangkhar, Dalai Lama in, 144
Modernization, 127
  Thirteenth Dalai Lama and, 48–49
Molha Khashar village, 224
Monasteries, Tibetan, 14, 16, 27–28, 168, 214
  communists and, 145–47
  destruction of, 5–6, 85, 142, 155, 163–65, 230,
    259–60, 330–31, 372, 398, 405–6
    Amdo province, 234
    Samphe-Ling, 156
  Jyekundo, 20, 21
  Kham province, 8, 54, 56, 61–62
  Lhasa, 48–50
  Lithang, 34–36
  resistance forces and, 170
Monastery system, destruction of, 324–25
Monastic hierarchy, communists and, 120
Monks, Tibetan, 146, *146,* 148–50, 214
  renunciation of vows, 147, 148
Monlam, 267n
Moral code, Khampa, 8
Morrison, James, 226
Mother of Dalai Lama, *126,* 282, 286
Muja Dapon, 60, 69, 77
Mules, used at Camp Hale, 317
Mullik, B. N., 130, 243–44, 360–61, 363
Murphy, Joe, 315n
Mustakos, Harry, 205

Mustang, *Chushi-Gangdruk* base, 330, 333,
    352–55, *354,* 357, 384, 386–93
  leaders, *378*
  Wangdu's reorganization, 376–77
My Land and My People (Dalai Lama), 83–84

Nationalist China. *See Kuomintang*
Natural resources, Tibet, China and, 5, 406
Nawang Chenmo, 168–69
Nechung Oracle, *112*
Nedbailof (White Russian), 51
NEFA (Northeast Frontier Agency), 358
Negotiations with China, 94–96, 98–99, 102–3
  "17-Point Agreement," 103–5
Nehru, Jawaharlal, 53, 128–29, *178,* 358, 360
  and Dalai Lama, 90, 174–75, 177, 178, 184,
    302, 303, 309–11
  and parachute jumps, 363
  and Tibet, 97, 178–79, 356, 357
    appeal to U.N., 243–44
    Chinese invasion of, 88
    Chinese atrocities, 166
    Khampa rebels, 176–77
    Lhasa uprising, 277, 285–86
Nepal, and Mustang base, 386–93
Nepalese Army, Baba Gen Yeshi and, 381–82
News media, and Tibet, 251–52, 308–10
  Chinese atrocities, 165
  Dalai Lama's escape, 303
  Lhasa uprising, 277, 279, 286
Newspapers, Tibetan, 127, 251
New Year's celebration, Lhasa, 153
New York City, Tibetans in, 369–70
Ngabo Ngawang Jigme, *67,* 67–68, 122, 176, 2[?],
    273, 412
  collaboration with communists, 91–94
  and Dalai Lama, 185, 283, 301–2
  and defense of Chamdo, 69–79
  "Freedom Committee" and, 274
  Khampa rebels and, 334
  Mimang and, 124
  as negotiator with communists, 95–96, 98–9[?],
    105–8, *106, 107*
  and Panchen Lama, 138, 140
  and "17-Point Agreement," 114
Ngari Rinpoche (brother of Dalai Lama), 282,
    286
Nira Tsogo, massacre, 340
Nirvana, 34n
Nixon, Richard, 382, 384
Norbu Dorje, 380, *381*
Norbulingka (Summer Palace), 267, 274,
    275
  destruction of, 292, 299–300
  popular uprising, 278–79, 281

gchuka village, resistance forces, 170
rong District, 56–57, 158–59
mo River Battle, 255

ce of Tibet, 370
nawa, parachute training, 219–20
um trade, 56
cles, Tibetan, 111, *112*, 186, 254

hin, 384, 389
masambhava. *See* Guru Rinpoche
tings, Buddhist, 148–49
istan, 198n, 385
len Lhamo (Protectress of Tibet), *248*,
    249–50, 255, 265, 279, 287
chen Lama, 137–40, *139*, 175, 412
Dalai Lama and, 301–2
17-Point Agreement" terms, 103–4
isit to India, 177–78, *178*
chshila Agreement, 128–29
achute jumps, 195n, 219–21, 317, 362–63
thasarathi, H. G., 179
terson, George, 127–28, 165, 277
ung Ahnga village, atrocities, 167
ART (Preparatory Committee for the eventual
    establishment of the Autonomous Region
    of Tibet), 138–40, 145, 174
cocks, 250
santry, Tibetan, and communism, 133–34
ssel, Michel, 208–9, 263
ing Review, 310
nako area, 344
nbar region, Tibetan rebels, 337–40
nbar Tulku Rinpoche, 337, 339, 340
kpala (Tibetan official), 270–71
la Thupten Woden, Lord Chamberlain, 111,
    172, *172*, 192, 193
nd CIA programs, 194, 235, 253
nd Dalai Lama, 264
    control of information, 262
    escape of, 281–85, 286, 289, 299, 300, 302
nd Lhasa uprising, 271–74, 277
rogs, 32
A (People's Liberation Army), 234, 322–24,
    340–41
CIA and, 222
nd Dalai Lama's escape, 301
nd India, 311–12, 358–61
    Indian Consulate in Lhasa, 286
nvasion of Tibet, 5–6, 51, *55*, 55–64, 68–79, *73*
Ngabo and, 91–94
occupation of Tibet, 87–88, 307–8, 320–21,
    324–27
    destruction of monasteries, 84–86, 330–31
    Golok people, 141–43, 154–55

Lhasa, 113–15, *114*, 119–20, 261–62, 264,
    406
    murder of *Rinpoches,* 266
    Pembar region, 338–39
    Tsangpo River patrol, *345*
    resistance to, 124, 155–58, 168–70
        Chushi-Gangdruk and, 237, 240–41, 255–61,
            264–65
        Kham uprising, 399–400
        Lhasa uprising, 274, 279, 280–83, 292–99,
            298
        Lithang, 144–45, 160–65
Political leaders, Tibetan, 125–26
Political structure, communists and, 121
Politics, Dalai Lama and, 187
Polyandry, 59
Polygamy, 59, 127
"Population transfer," 154
Poshepny, Tony "Po," 314–15
Poss, Sam, 315n
Potala Palace, 82
Prayers, Buddhist, 24, 69–70
Press, international. *See* News media
Prime Ministers, 122
    removal of, 125–26
Prison camp, Cyclone's family in, 343–44
Propaganda, communist, 310
Propaganda booklets, CIA, *364*
Pula Lama, 397–400

Radio communications, 68, 69
Radio teams, reinfiltration of, 370–71
Ragyaba, 271
Rahula (Jamyang of Amdo), *44*, 45–47, 50
Rara (Camp Hale graduate), 354–55, 369, 384,
    390–92, 394
Reagan, John, 194, 215
Red Guards, 398–99
Refugees, 322, 341, 357, 412
    in India, 252, 254, 324, *329*
    in Lhasa, 172–73, 235–36, 261–62
Regents, government by, 49, 83–84
Reincarnation, 250
Reinfiltration teams, 219, 221–34, 227–30,
    370
Religion, Tibetan, pre-Buddhist, 213
    See also Buddhism
Religious leaders, Tibetan, 413
Resistance to Chinese occupation, xii, 5, 153–72,
    166, 218–19, 250–55, 265
    Chushi-Gangdruk, 255–65
    Dalai Lama's views, 411
    Eastern Tibet, 168–73, 233
    Goloks and, 142–43
    Gompo Tashi and, 173–74, 191–93

Resistance to Chinese occupation (*cont.*)
    Lhasa, 145–47
    monasteries and, 147–50
    See also CIA; Khampa rebels
Reting Rinpoche, 49–50
Richardson, H. E., 49n, 51
Rinpoches, PLA and, 266
Rivers, 131
Riwoche, Kham province, 61–62, 68, 79
Riwoche Monastery, 72–73, 330
Roads built by Chinese, 55–56, 130–33, *131,* 144,
    353
Rockets, homemade, 318–19
Rooftops, Tibet, 15
Roosevelt, Franklin Delano, 3–4
Ropka, Lawrence, 226–27

Saipan, training of Khampas, 200–208, 215
Samphe-Ling monastery, PLA and, 155–58
Sampho Tenzin Dhondup, 95–96, 270
Samsara, 34n
Samye Monastery, 214–15, 227–30, *228,* 405
Schools, Chinese occupation and, 121
Secrecy of Tibetan politics, 194, 262
Self-interest, 250
    of Tibetan hierarchy, 49, 114–15
Sera Monastery, 48
Servants, Tibetan, 16
"17-Point Agreement," 103–5
    repudiation of, 274, 301–2, 310
Seven Years in Tibet (Harrer), 201
Shakabpa, 87, 93, 97, 111
Shak Gyatso, 39–40
Shang of U Tsang, arms depot raid, 262–63
Shusor, 118–19
Simla Convention, 358
Sinha, S., 120, 122–23
Skywalkers (*Loung-gompas*), 33–34
Slavin, Joe, 315n
Smith, Bill, 315
Smith, Warren, Jr., 104
Snakes, worship of, 213n
Social elite, and Chinese occupation, 125–26
Social hierarchy, Derge, 16
Special Frontier Forces (SFF), India, 359
Special Service Center, New Delhi, 374–75
Spies, Chinese, Gompo Tashi and, 241
Starke, Ray, 315, 315n, 318
State Department, U.S., 61
    and Dalai Lama, 100–102
    and Tibet, 53, 94–95, 97–98, 109–11
STBARNUM/STCIRCUS (CIA cryptonyms), 224
Strickler, Gill, 315n
Students, Tibetan, in England, 48
Subranhmanyam, T. M., 360–61

Suicides, 208, 389, 398
Suicide tablets, 223–24
Summer Palace. *See* Norbulingka
Surkhang (*Kashag* member), 271
Syphilis, 127–28

T.A.R. (Tibetan Autonomous Region), 5–6, 40
    414–15
Tacshan Terchen, 346
Taka (monastery), 330–31
Takla, P. T., 389
Takla, T. N., 102
Taktra Rinpoche, 49
Taktser Rinpoche (brother of Dalai Lama),
    84–86, 91, 111, *126,* 177, 201, 252
    and CIA project, 200, 203, 226
    and Dalai Lama's return to Lhasa, 185–86
    Gompo Tashi and, 192
    and Khampa rebels, 180, 215
    and U.S., 109
Tamding Tsephel, 365
Tan Kuan-sen (Chinese general), 245, 267–68,
    272–74
    and Dalai Lama, 283–84, 291
    and Lhasa uprising, 277, 292
Tashi Chutter, 253, *365,* 365, 374–75, 383,
    384
    and Baba Gen Yeshi, 368, 377, 382
    and CIA project, 316–17
Tea, Tibetans and, 25–26
Technical Services Division, CIA, 318
Technological development, Chinese and, 127
Telecodes, Tibetan, 202
Tenshuk Shapten ceremony, 195, 209
Thamzings, 157–58, *157,* 188–89, 259–60,
    325–27, *327,* 372, 397–98
Thankgha painting, Chinese and, *407*
Thirteenth Dalai Lama, 48, 52, 137, 358
    prophesy of, 40, 42, 48
    See also Dalai Lama
Thomas, Lowell, Jr., 55, 96–97, 133, 135–36, 13
    149
Thorsrud, Gar, 224, 226
Thubten Jigme Norbu. *See* Taktser Rinpoche
Thupten Dargyal, 196, 320–22
Tibet
    appeals to United Nations by, 87–90, 93–95,
        243–44
    Central Government, 17, 38–39
    Chinese invasion, 54–68, *55*
    history of, Chinese rewriting, 6–7
    ruling classes, 125–26
    "17-Point Agreement," 103–5
    unity of populace, 269–71, 274–79, 290–91,
        329–30

orld War II and, 1–4
e also Lhasa; Resistance to Chinese occu-
    pation
an Army, 122–23, 275–76
an Autonomous Region (T.A.R.), 5–6, 405,
    414–15
an independence, 115, 143
ina and, 52
dia and, 53
an Military District Headquarters, 122
an people
 Bangladesh War, 385–86
d Dalai Lama's trip to China, 135–36
patriate generation, 406–11
 Indian SFF, 359
e also Khampa rebels; Resistance to Chinese
    occupation
an rebels. *See* Khampa rebels; Resistance to
    Chinese occupation
an Task Force, politics and, 355
t House, New Delhi, 370
' magazine, and Dalai Lama, 308, *309*
ing Jyurme, 156–58, 357, 367–68, 377, *378,*
    384, 386, 389–91, 394, 410
, Bill, 315n
ism, Tibet, 406, *408*
e
ina–India agreement, 128–29
stern Tibet, 20–21, 35, 54–55, 56
ors, Gompo Tashi and, 241
ong Detsen, King of Tibet, 46, 213–14
gpo (Brahmaputra) River, PLA patrol, *345*
ng Shakya, 267
ang, fall of, 322
ang, 369
ang (Tibetan Task Force member), 187,
    197–200, 204, 217, 334–35
cident, 222–23
infiltration, 231–34
e also CIA; Tibetan Task Force
ang Dorje, 174
ang Gyapo (secretary to Tinzing Jyurme), 389
a, fall of, 322–24
gdu (National Assembly), 82n
d Chinese invasion, 86–87, 97–98
d negotiations with China, 94
d "17-Point Agreement," 113–14
gkapa, 84
us, 330, 397
ans (Muslims in Kumbum), 84
tson Druk-druk, 344

, S. S. (Indian general), 10, 359, 375,
    384–86, 412

and Dalai Lama, *312,* 312–13
and Khampas, 361–63
Underground army, Tibet, 183
United Nations, 95, 331, 336–37
    Tibetan appeals to, 87–90, 93–95, 243–44
    Nehru and, 311
United States, and Tibet, 1–4, 53, 97–98, 182–83,
        192, 363–65, 401, 411
    Chinese invasion of, 52–53, 88–89,
        94–95
    U.N. debate, 336
    See also CIA
Unit 22, Indian SFF, 359, 361
    Bangladesh War, 385–86
    CIA and, 369

Vajrapani, Bodhisattva, 149
Violence, Buddhist views on, 148–49

Walker, Bruce, 315, 315n, 379, 383
Wall, Jack, 315n
Wallace, Harry, 315n
Wangdu, 40–41, *41,* 46, 79, 187, 197–200, 205,
        207, 217, 384, 386–93, *392*
    and Baba Gen Yeshi, 375–82
    death of, 393–94
    guerilla activities, 231–34, 334–36
    See also CIA; Tibetan Task Force
The Warrior Song of King Gesar, 22–23, 28
Warriors, Buddhist, 7–8, 24
    monks as, 149
    See also Khampa rebels
Weapons
    CIA airdrops, 254, 263
    confiscation of, 191
    Khampas and, 17
    World War II and, 39
Women, Tibetan, 58–59
    and Lhasa uprising, 280
    and resistance movement, 168–69
World Church Services, 252
World War II
    and Khampas, 39
    Saipan battle, 208n

Yama, Lord of Death, *116,* 117–18, 250
Yamantaka (Killer of Death), 118, 148
Yamdrok Dagye Ling, fall of, 322
Yatung, Dalai Lama in, 93, 97–98, 108, 113
    Chinese delegation to, 110
Yunri Ponpo, 161–64, *162*
Yutok, theatrical performance, 272

Zilaitis, Al, 315, 315n

ABOUT THE AUTHOR

India: The author (right) with one of his translators,
a Khampa warrior's son. *(Jampa Dorje)*

Author, artist, and photographer Mikel Dunham grew up on an Ozark cattle ra
and has lived in Paris, Munich, Crete, and New York. In the 1980s, the Alexande
Milliken Gallery in SoHo represented his sculptures. In the 1990s, he authored
Rhea Buerklin series of murder mysteries, published by St. Martin's Press. In the
fifteen years, he has spent much of his time on extended trips to Central Asia. After
apprenticeship with Pema Wangyal of Dolpo, the late *thangkha* master, Dunham
made art director for the murals of two major Nyingma Buddhist temples—
located in Sarnath, India, and the other in upstate New York. His most recent boo
a photographic history of the oldest monastery in Tibet, *Samye: A Pilgrimage to
Birthplace of Tibetan Buddhism*. Dunham has two sons, Adrian and Zachary, and l
in Santa Monica, California, with his wife, Margaret.